POLITICAL ISLAM

SOAS MIDDLE EAST ISSUES

Political Islam

Context versus Ideology

Edited by

Khaled Hroub

SAQI

in association with

LONDON
MIDDLE EAST
INSTITUTE
SOAS

ISBN: 978-0-86356-659-2

A full CIP record for this book is available from the British Library.

A full CIP record for this book is available from the Library of Congress.

Printed and bound by CPI Mackays, Chatham, ME5 8TD

SAQI
26 Westbourne Grove, London W2 5RH, UK
www.saqibooks.com

in association with

The London Middle East Institute
School of Oriental and African Studies, Russell Square, London WC1H 0XG
www.lmei.soas.ac.uk

Contents

Acknowledgements

The idea for this collection came about after the success of short courses on political Islam that were organised by the London Middle East Institute (LMEI) of the School of Oriental and African Studies in London. Thanks go out first and foremost to the contributors of this volume who welcomed enthusiastically the idea of such a publication, and submitted their material against racing deadlines.

A number of wonderful people and friends have helped make the publication of this book possible. Robert Springborg, a friend and former Director of the Institute was always very encouraging and supportive of the initial proposal to run courses on contemporary Islamism at the LMEI. Bob suggested the idea of soliciting chapters from the distinguished contributors that we had invited to lecture at the courses, and bringing those chapters together in a volume. Hassan Hakimian, a colleague and current Director of the Institute, has injected new energy into the place and shown great support for the short courses and this publication.

The friendly staff at the Institute and the SOAS Interface have provided – and in fact are still providing – every possible support to make the courses and the publication a success: my sincere thanks go to Sarah Stewart, Deputy Director of the Institute and co-convenor of the political Islam courses; Sossie Kasbarian and David Harris who helped greatly in setting up the courses and both of whom have now left to assume other posts; Susan Yeats who has recently retired; and to Tony Doherty, Louise Roberts and Tin Ming Kaw from SOAS's new Research and Enterprise Office. Thanks are also due to LMEI's Vincenzo Paci-Delton, Anabel Inge and Arwad Khalifeh, and to the interns who helped in the organisation of the courses at different stages; Elisa Moscolin, Engy Mansy and Giovanni Bressan; and to Cody Phillips who helped to compile the bibliography. And finally, my warmest and special thanks go to Louise Hosking, the LMEI Executive Officer, who has been a great friend and super professional throughout the process of producing this volume, and during the organisation of every round of the political Islam course.

My friends at Saqi Books in London have been wonderful as usual in their follow up, commitment and proficiency. I am grateful to all the staff and editors. I am also very thankful to Charles Peyton for his skilful editing and to John Skermer for his meticulous proofreading..

ONE

Introduction

Khaled Hroub

In understanding and explaining Islamist movements, are we better served by relying on an understanding of their context or an analysis of their ideology? The easy answer, of course is 'both', because these two undertakings should not be mutually exclusive. This is true, yet it leaves much to be answered. Few would deny that historical and contextual socio-political and economic conditions have been heavily detrimental to the shaping and evolution of political Islam. But the religious and ideological fundamentals of these movements have also been greatly significant in the development and expanding appeal of these groups. The persistent question here remains whether, in dealing with the world around them, Islamist movements are led by their context or their ideology. If the easy and immediate answer is opted for – that is, 'by both' – then a number of questions follow. The first question would be: What parts do both the context or ideology occupy in the body politic and practical conduct of a certain movement? Secondly: Which conditions would make the driving force of one – context or ideology – override the other? A third question relates to the status of a given movement, and whether it is a mainstream movement or a small fringe group. Here, size does matter. The unavoidable influence of context and the luxury of adhering to uncompromising ideology are very much functions of the size of each movement. A pragmatic concluding question would perhaps enquire as to what favourable circumstances might lead these movements to become more consistently shaped by context than by rigid ideology.

Facing endless specific and pragmatic situations, a process of immediate and ongoing negotiation continues to take place between the contextual pressures and the underpinning ideology, producing particular responses. My argument here is that what appear to be similar movements often show different responses to the immediate, and sometimes similar, practical pressures surrounding them. These responses are shaped mostly, if not completely, by the nature of these pressures, not by a supposedly common ideology. The ideology of these movements remains significant, but mainly at a rhetorical level, thinly concealing politics and responses that are formed by the contextual reality. The responses that a certain movement would show towards such pressures are particular to the given set of conditions (responses to elections, to poverty, to oppression and so on). It is thanks to this multiplicity of contexts and responses that the spectrum of Islamism has become truly broad, comprised of a wide range of movements and groups that would make any single definition lumping them together unattainable. In his in-depth survey of *Global Political Islam*, Peter Mandaville engages closely with numerous Islamist experiences, analysing them against the local context of each movement and its understanding and internalisation of 'Islamic politics'. In concluding his volume, he notes that it is unrealistic to draw final observations that could connect diverse and sometimes divergent experiences: 'Islam and politics commingle in almost infinite variety across a vast range of settings, issues, actors, and levels of analysis'.[1]

Obituaries have often been written announcing the death of political Islam. These have, perhaps ironically, become an integral part of the seemingly never-ending debate on the subject of Islamism. In 1992 Olivier Roy published his challenging book *The Failure of Political Islam* (which appeared first in French).[2] As bluntly as was suggested in the title of the book, Roy argued that political Islam had failed to realise the goals it had set for itself: reviving the Muslim *umma*; establishing Islamic states; and remoulding Muslim societies to fit a new, Islamised vision. Since then, many scholars and experts, in various ways and to different degrees, have subscribed to this 'failure' thesis.

But political Islam has proved more resilient that previously thought. Reproducing itself in novel, expansive forms, and reaching out to new geographical areas, political Islam has confounded the expectations of many, and disappointed the hopes of many more. Developments have seemed to point in the opposite direction from the thesis of failure: Islamism has kept expanding and occupying new spheres, running boldly against the 'failure' argument. The contention between the arguments in favour of 'success' and

---

1. Peter Mandaville, *Global Political Islam*, London and New York: Routledge, 2007, p. 332.
2-. Olivier Roy, *The Failure of Political Islam*, Cambridge, Mass: Harvard University Press, 1994.

'failure' is highly charged in the field of social movement activism, not least because of the problematic definition of these two terms. First of all, there is the difficulty of judging 'success' or 'failure', for each depends on a set of criteria that are largely subjective, giving rise to different conclusions from different observers and actors. But what should be underlined here is that an assessment of the success or failure of Islamist movements from the perspective of power alone would certainly overlook changing realities. Aspects of sociality, patterns of daily life and effects on local politics and value systems evolve in directions that point to the heavy influence of these Islamist movements. In short, if the success of political Islam is in doubt, its failure is, if anything, in even more doubt.

In fact, the 'project' of Islamism is still unfolding at various levels, in various forms, and in diverse countries and societies. Hasty attempts to apply any success/failure label are premature, to say the least. But the mere expansion of political Islam is no indicator of its eventual success. In this regard, Roy's suggested criteria against which any claimed achievements of political Islam might be measured – namely, the acquisition of power and the bringing about of 'new' societies – continue to retain strong merits. But the picture as far as Islamism's achievements are concerned is mixed, with a success/failure balance sheet that continues to fluctuate. One could make the claim that Islamism has manifested aspects of success and failure simultaneously, and when combined they make the ground under either side of the argument – in favour of success or failure – very unstable indeed.[3]

But the failure or success of political Islam is not the question that this collection of essays attempts to address. Rather, their focus is on what lies in the background of any assessment of success or failure: context. Not only does context influence the outcome of any given experience of an Islamist movement; it also makes it difficult to settle on a definition of either success or failure. In fact, contextual considerations always provide the broad and case-specific criteria through which any movement can be considered a success or a failure. For example, if the Islamist movement in Tunisia had allowed the *hijab* in state institutions, against the will of a secular government, this would be considered a great success for them. This would be less true in

---

3. I have discussed the argument on the success or failure of political Islam elsewhere. See Khaled Hroub, 'Whether "National" or "Global" Political Islam is Doomed to Failure', *New Global Studies* vol. 3, no. 1, 2009, available at www.bepress.com.

Jordan, Egypt and Morocco where women already wear the *hijab* freely in governmental institutions. Whereas a criterion of success in Tunisia could be based on state and public recognition of the Islamists, criteria of success in the other three countries would go beyond that to include the degree of power-sharing or power-controlling of government.

In April 2009 several voices within the Egyptian Muslim Brotherhood (MB) strongly criticised Hizbullah for threatening 'Egyptian national security'. This criticism came about in the midst of a political and media debacle that broke out between Egypt and Hizbullah because Egyptian security had arrested a military cell that Hizbullah had dispatched to Egypt to smuggle weapons and channel support to Hamas in the Gaza Strip. Kamal Nour al-Din, a leading MB member in the Egyptian parliament, had been the most vocal in attacking Hizbullah – on 'nationalist Egyptian' grounds that have little, if anything, to do with the notions of a 'pan-Islamic *umma*'. Other leading MB members, including the prominent Isam al-Aryan, expressed the same sentiment, stating that 'the national security of Egypt is a red line'.[4] Mahdi Akif, the head of the MB, attempted to formulate a middle-ground position, issued a statement supportive of Hizbullah as a resistance movement, but at the same time expressed reservations against its use of Egypt for its operations. Taken together, these statements are indicative of the nature of an internal transformation that has been taking place within the MB. The statements reveal how the mother organisation of all MB branches has in fact been moulded, more than anything else, within its particular territorial context.

Why would leaders of an Islamist party as old and powerful as the MB in Egypt exhibit what seem to be contradictory positions on ideological principles in supporting *jihad* in Palestine? According to the literature and public pronouncements of the MB, sending weapons to Hamas in Gaza, as Hizbullah was trying to do, should not only be welcomed – constituting as it does support for the resistance of 'our brothers' in Palestine – but encouraged. But the MB position reflected great ambivalence between its deeply rooted 'Egyptianism' and its determination to adhere to its 'Islamism' and its ideology. In fact, the politics of the Egyptian MB can be seen as substantively more nationalist than 'Islamic'. The tension between

---

4. 'Parliamentarian members of the Muslim Brotherhood: Hizbullah crossed the red line and damaged Egypt's security', available at http://www.alarabiya.net/articles/2009/04/14/70652.html.

Islamist and nationalist tendencies, and between ideological and pragmatic components, is a deep-seated dilemma facing groups throughout political Islam. But this tension is essentially a response to context, to which Islamist movements seem to respond and correspond more clearly than to their underpinning ideologies.

It is helpful to clear up from the outset any potential misunderstandings resulting from the fact that the arguments in this volume tend to juxtapose sharply the socio-political context and ideological foundations of the emerging movements of political Islam. These two approaches to understanding Islamism are certainly not mutually exclusive, but rather complementary. Although most of the literature on Islamism since at least the late 1970s has been attentive to historical and societal settings, renewed and expanded interest in political Islam since 9/11 has tilted the debate in the direction of ideology as the main shaper of Islamist currents.[5] Islamist groups have been depicted in the latter corpus of literature as mostly if not exclusively driven by rigid and 'out of context' ideological ideals. The ideology of these movements, as the argument runs, is characteristically orthodox, allowing little room for negotiation with the surrounding and changing contextual conditions. The assumed inflexibility of these movements, combined with ideological detachment of reality, produces, in this vein of analysis, unattainable agendas that end up in mutual destruction. This understanding leads to policy propositions advocating stricter security measures and the use of force to defeat these movements or at least weaken them – the 'securitisation paradigm'.

The dominant influence of context is perhaps most visible in the case of the Egyptian Muslim Brotherhood, which is rightly considered to be the mother of most, if not all, movements of political Islam. At the time of its

---

5. The post-9/11 interest in political Islam has seen the emergence of the paradigm of 'securitising Islamism' as intellectual support and justification for the George W. Bush administration's 'war on terror'. The diverse phenomenon has been reduced to a 'global security threat' conflating 'moderate' with 'radical', and 'violent' with 'non-violent' groups. A plethora of publications within this paradigm could be cited, but examples include Bernard Lewis, *What Went Wrong? Western Impact and Middle Eastern Responses*, Oxford: Oxford University Press, 2002; Daniel Pipes, *Militant Islam Reaches America*, New York and London: W.W. Norton & Company, 2002; Melanie Philips, *Londonistan: How Britain is Creating a Terror State Within*, London: Gibson Square, 2006; Bruce Bawer, *Why Europe Slept: How Radical Islam Is Destroying the West from Within*, New York: Broadway Books, 2006.

emergence in the late 1920s, there were many other Islamic organisations striving to promote an understanding of Islam that was not dissimilar to what the MB would later advocate. But the rise of the MB resulted from its peculiar connection with its societal setting rather than from its ideology alone, which was shared by other groups. Examining the formative years of the MB in Egypt, Brynjar Lia argues: 'While not denying the importance of ideology, it seems appropriate to look for characteristics and qualities other than just ideological particularities when searching for the reasons behind the Society's remarkable expansion in the 1930s.'[6] Over the decades that followed its emergence, as outlined in Kamal Helbawy's chapter in this volume, the MB continued to evolve in ways that were very much reflective of its changing context.

Any broader perspective that would include the rise of different waves of Islamist radicalism should take into account the 'radicalising' reality of the Middle East, largely influenced by foreign hegemonic interventions. Such a reality is captured well by David Gardner's book *Last Chance: The Middle East in the Balance*, in which Gardner gives a thorough explanation of the adverse impact of intrusive Western policies in the region: 'There is no other part of the world – not even China – where the West operates with such lethal condescension and so little regard for the human and political rights of local citizens.'[7] Gardner identifies five areas of political despair that have created the frustrating atmosphere that has allowed, and in fact forced, Islamism to emerge and become dominant. These areas are: how Islam lost to the West; Europe's colonial legacy, with its fragmentation of the Arabs and the creation of Israel; the failure of pan-Arab nationalism; US and Western support for tyrannical Arab rulers; and the double standard of Washington's seemingly indiscriminate, and invariably unconditional, support for Israel.[8]

Many scholars have laboured to contextualise the rise of Islamism in the twentieth century, producing an enormous corpus of scholarly literature. The lines of enquiry into Islamism that have given priority to historical and contextual factors can be summarised by three approaches. The key argument in all of these approaches is that Islamism is highly responsive to contextual

---

6. Brynjar Lia, *The Society of the Muslim Brothers in Egypt: The Rise of an Islamic Mass Movement 1928–1942*, London: Ithaca Press, 1998, p. 2.

7. David Gardner, *Last Chance: The Middle East in the Balance*, London: I.B. Tauris, 2009, p. xv.

8. Ibid., p. 28.

conditions. Or, as Gilles Kepel argues, 'Modern Islamist ideology did not materialise in a vacuum. It emerged within a tradition from which it borrowed and exaggerated certain elements while downplaying others.'[9]

The first line of inquiry explains Islamism as a response to colonial and imperial hegemonies. Islamist movements are best understood, according to this approach, when situated within the period of colonial power politics that the Muslim and Arab world experienced prior to the emergence of Islamism as a political force. Like nationalism, Islamism is an expression of liberation against direct Western military control, and later against indirect control over Muslims. Even in the postcolonial era, the various faces of Western domination – mostly seen in the backing of authoritarian regimes and support for Israel – provide the root causes of anti-Western sentiment, and continue to feed waves of Islamism.[10]

The second approach understands Islamism as a response to a multiplicity of sudden ruptures which took place in the twentieth century: the collapse in 1924 of the Ottoman empire, the pan-Islamic caliphate system that for centuries had given Muslims a sense of unity and belonging; the pressures of modernity and Westernisation; and the emergence in the Arab and Muslim world of the nation-state system, which was seen as a fragmentary system imposed by the West. The shattering of the Muslim *umma* left deep collective wounds and disorientation. Islamism offered a comfort zone – a hope that the glory of the past could be restored. Using the appeal of Islam as a unifying force against destructive fragmentation, and as an intellectual and overarching system that could preserve group identity, Islamism emerged as a timely and powerful agency of mobilisation.[11]

A third tendency approaches movements of political Islam from the perspective of social movement theory. Islamist movements fall within the

9. Gilles Kepel, *Jihad: The Trail of Political Islam*, London: I.B. Tauris, 2002, p. 24.
10. See, for example, François Burgat, *L'Islamisme au Maghreb: La voix du sud*, Paris: Editions Karthala, 1988 and *Face to Face with Political Islam*, London: I.B. Tauris, 2003; Ali Mazrui, *Islam Between Globalization and Counter-Terrorism*, Oxford: James Currey Ltd, 2006; Alastair Crooke, *Resistance: The Essence of the Islamist Revolution*, London: Pluto Press, 2009.
11. The writings of James Piscatori and John L. Esposito, among others, represent this approach. See, for example, Piscatori's *Islam in a World of Nation-States*, London: Royal Institute of International Affairs, 1986 and Esposito's *The Islamic Threat*, Oxford: Oxford University Press, 1992.

broader category of social formations that result from a response to a multiplicity of societal strains, unleashing local forces that seek to change the status quo. The failure of postcolonial states in most of the Arab and Muslim world, the unjust and worsening distribution of wealth, the remoteness of ruling elites and concomitant marginalisation of the masses, the failure to forge notions of citizenship and higher levels of loyalty than those to ethnicity and sect – all of these take place within failing economic structures and authoritarian political regimes. In settings marred by these frustrating conditions, movements adhering to appealing ideologies prove to be more successful in mobilising support and challenging the dominant systems. The appeal of Islamist movements has been enhanced by their exploitation of the failure of two other ideologies: socialism and nationalism; and they have exploited an indigenous culture and value-system that is deeply rooted in the collective identity and history of the people: Islam. In this regard, Islamist movements are now among the most active: 'Given the variety of collective actors that operate in the name of "Islam" ... one might even make a strong claim that Islamic activism is one of the most common examples of activism in the world.'[12]

If 'contextualisation' offers flexible approaches to the understanding of Islamism where the specificities of each context and case are given primacy, 'ideologisation' offers an opposite approach heavily reliant on 'textual' rather than 'contextual' interpretation of the phenomenon. 'Ideologisation' acknowledges few differences across the extremely diverse spectrum of Islamist movements. The common ground among all these movements is a rigid religiosity that is disconnected from the present, lives in the past, and nurtures an apocalyptic view of the future. To ideologise Islamism is to claim that there are no true differences between violent and non-violent movements; between democratic and non-democratic tendencies; between moderates and radicals. Apparent diversity only expresses various shades of what is fundamentally a monochrome movement. The literature on 'ideologisation' focuses on the sacred Islamic scriptures and adopts a culturalist approach. Here, the body of religious knowledge and culture is seen to be radical by definition, rigid by nature, and moulded only in the past.

---

12. Quintan Wiktorowicz, ed., *Islamic Activism: A Social Movement Theory Approach*, Indiana: Indiana University Press, 2004, pp. 4–5. See also Wiktorowicz, *The Management of Islamic Activism: Salafis, the Muslim Brotherhood, and State Power in Jordan*, New York: State University of New York Press, 2001.

An underpinning culturalist argument of the 'ideologisation' approach is that Muslims have been unable to develop in modern times; it asks why the Muslim world has stood still when it comes to development (or progress). The answer lies in the nature of Islam and Islamic culture. The best exponent of this argument is Bernard Lewis, whose post-9/11 publications revolve around it; but it is also pursued by others, including Dan Diner, in his recent book *Lost in the Sacred: Why the Muslim World Stood Still*. While almost absolving any external contextual actors from responsibility, the book asks: 'Does the phenomenon of decelerated time express material circumstances or perhaps a cultural anthropology particular to the Middle East? Or does the key lie in Islam as a religion?'[13] The culturalist approach places the responsibility for Muslim backwardness on the nature of Islam as a religious body of knowledge, but does not explain to us why Muslims experienced long centuries of success despite that supposed nature. Martin Kramer writes:

> In the year 1000, the Middle East was the crucible of world civilization. One could not lay a claim to true learning if one did not know Arabic ... an Islamic empire, established by conquest four centuries earlier, had spawned an Islamic civilization, maintained by the free will of the world's most creative and enterprising spirits ... [T]here could be no doubt that the dynasties of Islam represented the political, military, and economic superpowers of the day ... This supremely urbane civilization cultivated genius. Had there been Nobel prizes in 1000, they could have gone almost exclusively to Moslems.[14]

Not surprisingly, perhaps, a variant of the culturalist approach can be found in writings that are supportive of Islamism. A recent example is Alastair Crooke's book *Resistance: The Essence of the Islamist Revolution*. Crooke stretches the debate beyond politics, context and foreign policy to the realm of philosophy and the 'essence of man'. His argument is that 'the conflict between Islam and the West is at core a religious one – even if the policies pursued by the West are avowedly secular'. Although taking a position supportive of the Islamists, Crooke finds himself – even if unintentionally – on the same neo-orientalist ground on which many anti-Islamist writers labour. Whereas the proponents of the context thesis continue to insist on the overriding

---

13. Dan Diner, *Lost in the Sacred: Why the Muslim World Stood Still*, Princeton: Princeton University Press, 2009, p. 8.
14. Quoted in Graham E. Fuller, *The Future of Political Islam*, New York: Palgrave Macmillan, 2003, p. 1.

importance of changing socio-political factors as the main drive behind the rise of Islamism, neo-orientalists argue that it is in the nature of Islam, not in the particularities of the context, that the root of political Islamism should be sought. In an argument which is related, but which evaluates the question from an opposing perspective, Crooke argues that the West 'keeps misreading events in the region because the West interprets Islamism as a simple struggle over power and sovereignty. It is not. It is a distinctive view of human behaviour that posits an alternative method of thinking about the human being.'[15] In fact this argument is not only highly contentious epistemologically, but would in fact meet with the disapproval of many Islamists. Much of the intellectual production of many Islamist writers over the past two decades has been striding in the opposite direction from what is implied by Crooke's argument. In the literature of mainstream Islamism, in relation to Crooke's thesis, one could identify two major themes: that the conflict with the West stems from Western foreign policies, and not from any contradiction between Western and Muslim value-systems; and that there are more aspects of Islam that are compatible with Western modernity than there are that conflict with it.[16]

It could also be argued that the contextualising of Islamism represents the middle ground between the demonisation and glorification of political Islam. Retaining context as a benchmark frees the debate both from the existential and the apocalyptic associations of a demonising approach, and from the utopian and the salvational elements of the tendency towards glorification. This collection belongs to, and advocates, this very middle ground, which gives primacy to sociological, historical and conjunctural factors over nihilistic or ideologically fixated perspectives. A contextualising approach is thus

---

15. Alastair Crooke, *Resistance: The Essence of the Islamist Revolution*, London: Pluto Press, 2009, pp. 4–29.
16. Examples of a dense literature on this topic include the writings of Rachid Ghannouchi, the leader of the Al-Nahda Islamist party, and in particular his book *Al-Hurriyyat al-'Amma fi al-Dawla al-Islamiyya* [Public Liberties in the Islamic State], Beirut: Centre for Arab Unity Studies, 1993; the writings of Hassan Turabi, leader of the Sudanese Islamist movement, and in particular his book *Al-Siyasa wa'l-Hukum* [Politics and Governance], London: Saqi Books, 2003; as well as Tariq Ramadan, *Western Muslims and the Future of Islam*, Oxford: Oxford University Press, 2004; Asef Bayat, *Making Islam Democratic: Social Movements and the Post-Islamist Turn*, Stanford: Stanford University Press, 2007.

neither apologetic nor pejorative: it offers no defensive thesis of the agendas of the Islamists, and presupposes no anti-Islamist position. A normative judgement of the conduct and achievements of the Islamists (or the lack of them), though necessary, is not the focus of the following essays.

Perhaps it is a good idea to conclude this Introduction, and to start delving into the case studies by borrowing Graham Fuller's description of Islamism, which states that 'Islamism is ... not an ideology, but a religious–cultural– political framework for engagement on issues that most concern politically engaged Muslims.'[17]

---

17. Fuller, *Future of Political Islam*, p. 193.

TWO

Umma, State and Movement:
Events that Shaped the Modern Debate

Abdelwahab El-Affendi[1]

The modern debate on Islam and the state was shaped by two seminal events, both revolutionary in the full sense of the word: the Constitutional Revolution in Iran (1905–11) and the Kemalist Revolution in Turkey (1919–24). In both these cases, newly emerging forces and ideas produced by Islam's encounter with modernity came into conflict with the embattled traditional Islamic monarchies struggling with the challenges of a new era. And in the background (and sometimes in the foreground) was the ever-present allure and threat of the imperial West.

The Iranian Constitutional Revolution erupted in late 1905 in the form of protests by merchants and the clergy over specific policies, but snowballed to become a fully fledged constitutional revolution which, by the end of 1906, forced the shah to sign a new constitution modelled on the Belgian one. Like most attempts at reform, the revolution grappled with two key challenges. At one level, there was the need to reform the state and make it more just and more responsive to the wishes and needs of the people; at another, there was the concern with making the state stronger and more stable, so as to provide security and protect against foreign encroachment.[2] However, the revolution remained unique at that stage of development in the Muslim world, in that it was a genuine popular uprising led by a coalition of merchants, *'ulama* and intellectuals. This coalition came together around the objective of curbing the autocratic power of the shah and the influence of foreign economic interests.[3]

---

1. The author is currently an ESRC/AHRC Fellow in the Global Uncertainties Programme. He would like to express his gratitude to the two centres for their support for his research.
2. Said Amir Arjomand, *The Turban for the Crown: The Islamic Revolution in Iran,* New York: Oxford University Press, 1989, p. 35.
3. Nikki R. Keddie, *Modern Iran: Roots and Results of Revolution,* New Haven:

The revolution was also unique in having achieved a quick and decisive success against the Qajar dynasty, with the establishment of a parliament and the passing of a new constitution, which was also unique, in having combined democratic ideals with provisions of conformity to *shari'a*. The latter objective was achieved through the institution of a committee of *'ulama* within the Majlis (parliament) to vet legislation for conformity with *shari'a*. However, the dominance of secular intellectuals, and the orientations of the Majlis and government, led to a rift with conservative *'ulama*, some of whom sided with the shah, helping him to regain autocratic power in 1908. The constitutionalists succeeded in recapturing power the following year, only to be thwarted by Russian intervention, which (with British complicity) brought Iran's constitutional experiment to an abrupt end in 1911.[4]

The Kemalist Revolution was different in origin and motivation, but its impact was equally decisive. It was the result of upheavals that destabilised the Ottoman Empire, Islam's premier sovereign power at the dawn of modernity, subjecting it to a humiliating defeat and foreign occupation. The Kemalist movement thus started in 1919 as a national liberation movement against foreign occupation (by Britain, which occupied Istanbul and imposed surrender terms on the Sultan, and Greece, which invaded the mainland). Mustafa Kemal was sent by the Sultan to Anatolia to demobilise the remaining forces there, arriving at his post a few days after Greek forces had occupied Izmir with support from Allied ships. He decided instead to lead resistance to the humiliating terms imposed on Turkey by the Allies. After achieving victory against the invading Greeks (and the Sultan's army which fought the nationalists as rebels), Mustafa Kemal was able to negotiate a new treaty that restored Turkish sovereignty, becoming a hero to Turks, and to Muslims more widely.[5] He then used his newfound power and prestige to mould the country and the state into a new shape, starting by abolishing the sultanate and establishing a republic in 1923, redefining the caliphate as a separate non-executive post, which was in turn abolished in 1924.[6]

Yale University Press, 2006, p. 180.

4. Arjomand, *Turban for the Crown*, pp. 35–46; Keddie, *Modern Iran*, pp. 67–71.
5. Bernard Lewis, *The Emergence of Modern Turkey*, Oxford: Oxford University Press, 1961, pp. 243–9.
6. Lewis, *The Emergence of Modern Turkey*, pp. 250–9.

The collapse of traditional monarchies

In both revolutions, what was at issue was the traditional legitimacy of what were seen as outdated absolutist monarchies versus that of modern, effective forms of rule, whether by army officers or technocrats. In both cases, the monarchy had deep historical roots and was both inextricably linked to the identity of the nation and legitimised by religious beliefs. The Qajar dynasty of Iran (established in 1781) may not have been as ancient as the Ottoman sultanate, but it was a successor to the Safavid dynasty, which created Shi'i Iran back in the sixteenth century. The Ottoman sultans also doubled as caliphs for the whole of Sunni Islam. However, both monarchies undermined their own legitimacy by failing to protect the country from foreign political and economic domination. This delinquency reached absurd proportions in the case of the Ottoman sultanate in the post-war era, when it signed the ignominious treaty of Sèvres (in August 1920),[7] but declared the nationalist resistance to foreign occupation under Mustafa Kemal as a renegade rebellion against the caliph, which could and should be crushed with impunity. The shahs of Iran were also accused of selling Iran's vital assets to the highest bidder to keep their finances afloat.

In both cases, fundamental issues of religious doctrine were raised in the contests that ensued. In the Iranian experience, the seductive idea of combining democracy with some form of religious oversight became a template for Islamic models of governance – whether those that remained in the realm of theory, such as the models proposed by Rashid Rida (1865–1935) and Abu al-A'la al-Maududi (1903–79), or those that found their way to implementation, like the *wilayat al-faqih* model of Ayatollah Khomeini (1902–89). Of great interest in this regard was the initial convergence between the stance of Shi'i and Sunni thinkers in spite of the deep schism – precisely on the issue of governance – that had divided these schools for centuries. The Shi'i believe that only 'infallible', divinely designated imams who are descendants of the Prophet are entitled to govern, while Sunnis argue that any competent and devout individual chosen by the community can rule.

---

7. The Treaty of Sèvres was signed on 10 August 1920 between the Allied powers and the Ottoman state, forcing the latter to renounce its Arab possessions, recognise the independence of Armenia, and give Kurdistan autonomy. It also legitimised Greek control over the Aegean islands and eastern Thrace, and Greece's invasion of the Anatolian west coast.

However, as secularisation threatened both communities, *'ulama* from both sides began to close ranks with one another. This rapprochement is underlined by the fact that the genesis of modern Sunni Islamic activism is usually traced back to the influence of Sayyid Jamal al-Din al-Afghani (1838–97), a charismatic activist of Iranian origin who succeeded in influencing a whole generation of intellectuals and activists in both the Shi'i and Sunni worlds. His disciples included Muhammad 'Abduh (1849–1905), the father of modern Islamic reformism in Egypt and the Arab world, Saad Zaghloul (1859–1927), the leading figure in Egyptian nationalism, and Rashid Rida (1865–1935), 'Abduh's leading disciple.

The secular/Islamic polarisation manifested itself during Iran's brief interlude of constitutional rule in the form of a precipitate collapse of the initial alliance between the traditionalists (*'ulama*, merchants, notables) and the liberal/secularist intellectuals and politicians, and was repeated in the Kemalist revolution, which initially enjoyed overwhelming *'ulama* support. As the secularists and liberals proceeded to implement measures that the traditionalists found unacceptable (such as weakening the role of the *'ulama* in society, and education and equal rights for women in Iran, and the abolition of the caliphate in Turkey) some of the *'ulama* rebelled against the government.[8] The pattern repeated itself incessantly thereafter, as national liberation coalitions fractured when the more secular-minded practical leaders lost patience with intransigent dogmatism and took matters into their own hands.

The Shi'i–Sunni convergence also revealed itself in the *khilafa* debate, provoked by the threat posed to the caliphate by Turkey's defeat in World War I. A main influence in the debate was the *Khilafat* movement (1924) which evolved in India in the immediate post-war period to agitate for the preservation of the caliphate, and in the process became a catalyst for the rise of the national independence movement in India.[9] However, the Shi'i *'ulama* in Iraq and elsewhere also joined calls for the preservation of the caliphate, siding with Turkey against the Allies. In a supreme irony, the appeal by two key leaders of the movement – the Agha Khan (leader of the Ismaili Shi'i) and

---

8. Stephen C. Poulson, *Social Movements in Twentieth-Century Iran: Culture, Ideology, and Mobilizing Frameworks*, New York: Lexington Books, 2006, pp. 118–22.

9. Naeem Qureshi, *Pan-Islam in British Indian Politics: A Study of the Khilafat Movement 1918–1924*, Leiden: Brill, 1999.

Ameer Ali (himself a Shi'i) – to the Kemalist leaders to preserve the caliphate was denounced by the latter as the act of 'heretics' belonging to sects that did not believe in the Sunni caliphate anyway.[10] However, the *khilafa* agitation marked an unprecedented (and, some might add, unrepeated) example of very close Sunni–Shi'i cooperation on a common cause.[11]

The Kemalists initially entered the ideological battle with a tract entitled *The Caliphate and the Authority of the Community*, published by the Grand National Assembly in 1922. It rejected the claim that the *khilafa* was a religiously sanctioned institution, arguing that, in any case, no genuine caliphate had existed since the Righteous Caliphate.[12] A revival of the institution would face many obstacles, for Muslim unity was currently unattainable, while trying to find a caliph who satisfied the traditional qualifications (such as being from the tribe of Quraysh) would be impractical.[13] In any case, power and sovereignty should be vested in the people, not in the caliph, which means that their representatives (in this case the Grand National Assembly) are fully authorised to institute the system of government that they believe is best suited to them.[14]

The Kemalists initially received some support for their stance; even Rashid Rida backed their uprising against the supine sultan and his coterie of subservient *'ulama*. But as the Kemalists took a more secular turn, support for them dwindled. Exceptions included the renowned philosopher and poet, Muhammad Iqbal (d. 1937), who described the Kemalist move to vest authority in an elected assembly rather than in an individual sultan

10. Qureshi, *Pan-lslam in British Indian Politics*, pp. 368–9; see also Hamid Enayat, *Modern Islamic Political Thought: The Response of the Shi'i and Sunni Muslims to the Twentieth Century*, London: I.B. Tauris, 2005, pp. 43–4, 54–5.

11. Enayat, *Modern Islamic Political Thought*, p. 54.

12. The term Righteous Caliphate (*al-Khilafa al-Rashida*) is used to describe the period from the death of the Prophet in 10/632 to the murder of the fourth Caliph 'Ali in 40/661. It is regarded by the majority of Muslims as the Golden Age of post-Prophetic Islam, with the conduct of rulers seen as exemplary and normatively relevant for future generations of Muslims.

13. Enayat, *Modern Islamic Political Thought*, pp. 55–7; Albert Hourani, *Arabic Thought in the Liberal Age: 1789–1939*, Cambridge: Cambridge University Press, 1989, pp. 183–4; Abdelwahab El-Affendi, *Who Needs an Islamic State?* London: Malaysia Think Tank in London, 2008.

14. Enayat, *Modern Islamic Political Thought*, pp. 55–66; Majid Khadduri, *War and Peace in the Law of Islam*, Baltimore: Johns Hopkins Press, 1955, pp. 289–90.

or caliph as a 'perfectly sound' *ijtihad*.[15] Iqbal did express misgivings about
Western democracy and its suitability for Muslims, and for multicultural
societies in general, but he argued that the 'republican form of government
was not only thoroughly consistent with the spirit of Islam, but has also
become a necessity in view of the new forces that are set free in the world
of Islam'.[16] The restoration of the *khilafa* and the unity of the *umma* must
come at the end of a quest for national independence and identity, and must
take the form of a 'league of nations' – a commonwealth of autonomous
national entities.[17]

More enthusiastic support for the Kemalist position came from the
Azharite Shaykh 'Ali 'Abd al-Raziq (1887–1966), who echoed the views of the
Grand National Assembly in his 1925 book *al-Islam wa Usul al-Hukm* ('Islam
and the Principles of Governance'), arguing that the caliphate was a despotic
and repressive institution for most of its history, and could not be justified
by reference to basic Islamic teachings or texts.[18] However, 'Abd al-Raziq's
clumsy defence of the secularist cause was disastrous for both him personally (he was condemned by al-Azhar and stripped of his degree), and for the
cause, which was set back by his intervention.[19] His claim that the Prophet's
mission was a purely spiritual one with no political content overstated his
case. Most commentators agree that his claim that the Prophet did not have
any political role in the community was 'hardly acceptable from the historical
as well as the traditional point of view'.[20] These inflated claims damaged his
otherwise more defensible argument (at least from the Sunni perspective)
that Muslims should be free to adopt whatever system of governance reason
and human experience suggested was the most suitable.[21]

---

15. Muhammad Iqbal, *Six Lectures on the Reconstruction of Religious Thought in
    Islam*, Lahore: Ashraf Publishers, 1930, p. 220.

16. Ibid., p. 220.

17. Ibid., pp. 222–3.

18. 'Ali 'Abd al-Raziq, *al-Islam wa Usul al-Hukm*, Cairo, 1925, pp. 13–33.

19. For a detailed account of the controversy, see Muhammad 'Imara, *Ma'rakat
    al-Islam wa Usul al-Hukm*, Cairo: Shorouk, 1989; Diya' al-Din al-Rayyis, *al-
    Islam wa'l-Khilfah fi'l-'Asr al-Hadith*, Beirut: Al-'Asr al-Hadith li'l-Nashr, 1973;
    and Hourani, *Arabic Thought*, pp. 182–92. See also Leonard Binder, *Islamic
    Liberalism: A Critique of Development Ideologies*, Chicago: The University of
    Chicago Press, 1988, pp. 128–69.

20. Binder, *Islamic Liberalism*, pp. 131–2.

21. 'Abd al-Raziq, *al-Islam wa Usul al-Hukm*, pp. 102–3.

The majority of Muslim opinion, however, was opposed to the Kemalists and their stance – and this included, as we have seen, Shi'i and Ismaili *'ulama* and intellectuals who did not even believe in the legitimacy of the caliphate in the first place. A leading voice in the pro-*khilafa* campaign was that of Rashid Rida, who reaffirmed the orthodox view that the establishment and maintenance of the *khilafa* was a religious obligation on all Muslims, and not merely a rational and utilitarian expedient, as the Mu'tazilites and others had earlier argued.[22] Rida agreed with the Kemalists that the genuine *khilafa* had existed only for a very brief period, giving way to the '*khilafa* of necessity', or of 'coercion', but insisted that this did not justify the scrapping of the institution altogether. The caliphate system incorporated a corrective mechanism in the shape of the institutions of *ahl al-hall wa'l-'aqd* (community leaders – those who 'loosen and bind' or 'unite and tie'), which comprised the electors of the caliph, the guarantors of people's freedoms and rights, and the guardians of the implementation of *shari'a*.[23]

The positing of *ahl al-hall wa'l-'aqd* (rather than the nation or *umma*, as in the Grand National Assembly's document) as the locus of authority has raised some important questions about whether the concept could have practical relevance for modern political practice – especially given that it appears to suffer from a circularity, as Malcolm Kerr and others have noted. For it seems to refer to people who are actually in authority (military commanders, tribal chiefs, prominent *'ulama*, and other individuals occupying prominent social roles) regardless of how that authority has been obtained, which makes it almost meaningless as a marker of legitimacy.[24] Rida tried to skirt around this problem by giving the competent *'ulama* a key role within this group. However, given that the *'ulama* have historically often been subservient to incumbent rulers, and given that classical theory of the caliphate makes it a condition for the *khalifa* to be the most learned person of his time, there are both practical and theoretical impediments to the *'ulama*'s assumption

22. *Al-Manar* 23 (1922), pp. 775–6; and M. Rashid Rida, *al-Khilafa aw al-Imama al-'Uzma*, Cairo: Dar al-Manar, 1925.

23. Abdal-Ilah Balqaziz, *al-Dawla fi'l-Fikr al-Islami al-Mu'asir*, Beirut: Centre for Arab Unity Studies, pp. 95–7.

24. Malcolm H. Kerr, *Islamic Reform: The Political and Legal Theories of Muhammad 'Abduh and Rashid Rida*, Los Angeles: University of California Press, 1966.

of this key role of oversight over the ruler.[25] Later theoreticians, like Hassan al-Banna, attempted to deal with this problem by reverting to the Grand National Assembly's view that the elected representatives of the *umma* were indeed the people who should be designated as *ahl al-hall wa'l-ʿaqd*.[26]

However, in spite of hostility to the Kemalists, most of their opponents ended up agreeing with them on many issues, including the difficulty of reviving the caliphate in its traditional form, and on the need to build new institutions that would respond better to modern realities (including that of a disunited *umma*), and to give greater scope to popular oversight over rulers.[27] This position was confirmed when a number of conferences called to revive the caliphate in some form (Bombay in 1919 and 1920, Cairo in 1926, Makkah in 1926, and Jerusalem in 1931) failed to reach consensus on any practical steps towards doing so.[28]

The 'Islamic State'

As a result of the Constitutional Revolution in Iran (and other revolutions and upheavals in the region) and the *khilafa* debate, a consensus began to emerge around the idea of the 'Islamic State' as a new slogan to replace that of the caliphate. The idea of constitutional rule, which was first officially accepted with the promulgation of the 1876 Constitution of the Ottoman state (which was suspended the following year by Sultan Abdulhamid, before being revived again after the 1908 coup) and later implemented in Iran in 1907, gained almost universal acceptance. This consensus expressed the rejection of all forms of despotic rule, a theme which informed the writings of leading

---

25. Enayat, *Modern Islamic Political Thought*, pp. 72–3; see also El-Affendi, *Who Needs an Islamic State?*, pp. 60–80.

26. Al-Banna expressed support for constitutional government and the parliamentary system as the closest available model to the Islamic ideal, although he suggested some reforms to the system, including the abolition of the party system, which he deemed divisive and corrupt. Hassan al-Banna, *Majmuʿat Rasail al-Imam al-Shahid Hassan al-Banna*, Beirut: al-Muassasa al-Islamiyya li'l-Tibaʿa wa'l-Nashr, 1974, pp. 162ff, 357ff. See also Balqaziz, *al-Dawla*, pp. 138–9.

27. Enayat, *Modern Islamic Political Thought*, pp. 74–82.

28. Majid Khadduri, *War and Peace in the Law of Islam*, Baltimore: Johns Hopkins Press reprinted Clark, New Jersey, Lawbook Exchange, 2006, pp. 290–91; Qureshi, *Pan-lslam in British Indian Politics*, pp. 120–22.

reformers at the turn of the century, the most prominent among whom was 'Abd al-Rahman al-Kawakibi (1855–1902), whose book *Taba'i al-Istibdad wa Masari al-Isti'bad* [The Nature of Despotism and the Harm of Enslavement], published in 1905, was among the most eloquent statements of the thesis.[29] Even prominent proponents of the caliphate like Rida accepted the dependence of caliphal authority on popular legitimation – even though, as we shall see, some theoreticians would qualify popular authority by stipulating conformity to *shari'a*.

In the process, however, the debate raised a number of fundamental questions not only about the nature of political institutions within Muslim communities, but also about deep issues of identity. It has often been argued (by leading Islamic scholars, Orientalists and others) that, for Muslims, the defining identity is that of belonging to the *umma* (the Muslim community), 'a people who follow the Imam, and the Imam is the guide of the Muslims, be that the ideal book-guide: the Qur'an, or their ideal human guide: the Prophet'.[30] According to this view, the community is a non-territorial entity defined in terms of symbols and texts, and the ideals these texts prescribe. By contrast, this same author denies the prevalent view that the *dawla*, in Muslim terminology, is synonymous with the modern term 'state', since the Islamic *dawla* is not a sovereign entity. In Islamic thought, sovereignty resided in the *umma*, while the *dawla* 'refers to any authoritative political arrangement. It is temporary, not territorially fixed, and usually associated with the ruling elite.'[31] More important, a *dawla* is accountable to the whole *umma*, even if it only rules over a fraction of it. That explains why current Muslim regimes need to explain their policies not merely in terms of national interest, but also in terms of the wider interests of the *umma*. Thus, the Egyptian regime feels compelled to explain its peace with Israel in terms of serving the interests of the Palestinians, other Arabs and all Muslims; and Pakistan explains its collaboration with the US in the war on terror along similar lines. Another important corollary is that major non-state actors such as al-Qaeda, Hizbullah and the PLO (Palestine Liberation Organisation) fit the definition of *dawla* in every sense.

---

29. Ryuichi Funatsu, 'Al-Kawakibi's Thesis and its Echoes in the Arab World Today', *Harvard Middle Eastern and Islamic Review* 7 (2006), pp. 1–40.
30. Tamim al-Barghouti, *The Umma and the Dawla: The Nation State and the Arab Middle East*, London: Pluto Press, 2008, p. 38.
31. Ibid., p. 57.

There are several problems with this analysis. For one thing, there has always been a territorial dimension to the self-perception of the *umma*, since its existence is inextricably linked to the sovereign existence of *dar al-islam* ('Islamic territory'). In this regard, it might be appropriate to reiterate a necessary correction of another common misperception regarding the term *dar al-harb*, the counterpart of *dar al-islam* that is usually translated as 'abode of war' and used by both Orientalists and Islamic radicals to promote a theory that Islam advocates perpetual war outside its territories. However, the term should more accurately be translated as 'hostile territory', which is a common-sense factual description of relations between entities. It is not a legal prescription, but a determination of current status. A territory is defined as hostile when it has initiated a state of war with the neighbouring Muslim entity, and has not concluded a treaty to earn the designation *dar al-'ahd* ('treaty-bound territory') or *dar al-aman* ('territory of peace and security'), where Muslims can enjoy peaceful existence as a matter of course. The former included Nubia (today's northern Sudan), and the latter Abyssinia.[32]

The *umma* is thus inseparable from the existence of sovereign territory, even though in its wider, more abstract sense, the term *umma* can incorporate all believers, including those from earlier monotheistic communities. But as a juridico-political concept, the *umma* has to have a territory, and also a government. The equation of the term *dawla* with 'regime' rather than a state may have a justification; but this goes for all pre-modern polities, where Louis XIV's famous remark *'L'état c'est moi'* held for all monarchs and dynasties. Similarly, the accountability of states to broader constituencies than their own citizens is not restricted to Islamic states. Even before the modern international community took its current forms, states felt responsible for events outside their borders, and were also held morally responsible by others (states and individuals) for their actions.

Moreover, the modern debate on the caliphate and actual developments on the ground have given new meanings to these terms and many others. The de facto existence of separate Muslim 'nations' (where the term *umma* came to be used in this sense), and the rise of nationalist ideologies – including some, like pan-Arab nationalism, which were informed by Islam – all led to

---

32. El-Affendi, *Who Needs an Islamic State?*

the term *umma* being used in a number of novel senses: to refer to all Arabs, or the Egyptian, or Iraqi or Indonesian 'nation', and so on.

One of the most decisive and traumatic developments of the modern Muslim experience – one which destabilised many traditional ideas and perceptions – was the actual and sudden 'disappearance' of *dar al-islam* in many areas, as most parts of the Muslim world came under foreign (non-Muslim) colonial domination. This situation had only occurred before in Spain, Sicily and (temporarily) parts of Palestine and Syria during the Crusades. The traditional response in such cases was to declare *jihad* to restore Muslim control, and in the meantime for Muslims to emigrate to nearby safe areas. In most cases, the invaders left the people no option: they were massacred or forced to flee. However, the colonial experience appeared to be different. Muslims in Algeria and India, for example, contemplated emigration, and many undertook it – especially following the failure of *jihad* campaigns. Colonial authorities in both countries, alarmed by this prospect, sought *fatwas* from leading *'ulama* in Mecca and Egypt, confirming that colonial territories were indeed Islamic territories, and not part of *dar al-harb*, from which emigration was obligatory. The French, in particular, sought to stem the alarming mass exodus from Algeria in the 1890s, and argued that, given that religious freedoms were guaranteed in Algeria, and the injunctions of *shari'a* were provided for (in private matters), the country should be regarded as *dar al-islam*. The Meccan and Cairene muftis consulted were happy to concur.[33]

For many Muslims who fell under the colonial yoke, the symbolic existence of the caliphate played a reassuring role. That is why Indian Muslims were at the forefront of the campaign to safeguard the caliphate. For them, it offered the ultimate guarantee of their Islamic identity in a similar way that gold reserves guaranteed paper currencies. Once the caliphate campaign had failed, the movement in India became the nucleus of the nationalist independence movement, and later the movement for establishing Pakistan as an Islamic 'homeland'. In a similar fashion, the debate on the caliphate shifted in the Arab world towards setting up an Arab kingdom (which would have become the locus of a new Arab caliphate). When this failed, activists began once again to move in different directions.

33. Rudolph Peters, *Islam and Colonialism: The Doctrine of Jihad in Modern History*, The Hague: Mouton Publishers, 1979, pp. 61–2.

After the caliphate

With the violent split between traditionalists and modernists during both the Kemalist and Iranian revolutions, and the subsequent failure of attempts to resurrect the caliphate, a new trend of thinking emerged which began to see the problem in a new light. The instinctive reaction of the traditionalists was to mobilise the masses to challenge the secular trends and policies and their bid for hegemony, as had happened in Iran, and to a lesser extent in Turkey. But as time went on, this was becoming more difficult. In places like Egypt, the masses themselves began to drift in the direction of Westernisation, especially the educated and urbanised population. Suddenly it was not possible to count on the masses to support the conservative point of view automatically. More importantly, neither the religious nor political authorities appeared willing or able to stem this tide of Westernisation.

As is customary in such cases, complaints about this 'moral decline' abounded: in the media, in mosque sermons, and in general conversation. The next development saw the emergence of men like Hassan al-Banna (1907–49), a charismatic young schoolteacher, and Sayyid Abu al-A'la al-Maududi (1903–79), a campaigning Indian journalist and intellectual, neither of whom were satisfied with preaching against decadence and lack of direction in the community. Rather, they took steps to create modern, organised movements to work more systematically to promote and defend religious values. Al-Banna established the Muslim Brotherhood (*al-Ikhwan al-Muslimun*) in Egypt in 1928, while Jamaat Islami was created by Maududi in Pakistan in 1941. Combining the organisational structure of modern elite parties with the mass appeal of the mainstream parties, these movements worked on the assumption that the Muslim community needed to be reconstructed anew.

For these groups, the nominal Muslim communities, which had regressed dismally and 'reached the lowest point of moral decline',[34] were themselves in need of education and transformation; so it was not only necessary to reorganise the affairs of the Muslim community and convince the people that the reforms were necessary and did not contradict Islamic teachings. What was also needed was a thorough re-Islamisation of these communities

---

34. Abu al-A'la Maududi, *Minhaj al-Inqilab al-Islami*, Cairo: Dar al-Ansar, 1977, pp. 21–3.

which, as Maududi argued, had reverted to *jahiliyya* (pre-Islamic barbarism). Only when a group committed itself to the principles and values of Islam, and Islam alone, would a genuine Muslim community emerge that could lead the revolution necessary to establish a state in its own image.[35] Al-Banna was less extreme in his judgement, believing that the task was much easier. But even he called for a bottom-up approach, starting with the creation of the Muslim individual, then the Muslim family, and finally the Muslim society.

This view naturally affected the attitude towards the role of existing 'Muslim' communities. Expressing support for constitutional government and the parliamentary system as the closest available model to the Islamic ideal – as did al-Banna, though he suggested some reforms to the system, including the abolition of the party system, which he judged to be divisive and corrupt – would imply an acceptance that these communities were in fact fully Muslim.[36] This was also the view of those *'ulama* who supported the constitutional movement in Iran. But, as we have seen with that movement, the more conservative *'ulama* in fact supported the monarchy against the democratic forces.

Departing from a negative view of the Islamic credentials of existing Muslim societies, Maududi was naturally more suspicious of both the 'Muslim nationalism' of his compatriots and of democracy – which, without the attainment by the public of an adequate Islamic awareness and commitment, would not create an Islamic system.[37] Maududi's suspicion of democracy, which he at first condemned unequivocally, was conditioned in part by the fear that, in a Hindu-majority country like India, democracy was being used to promote Hindu supremacy.[38] But he later sought to accommodate democracy in his model of the Islamic state by proposing a 'democratic caliphate' or 'theo-democracy' (a democracy governed by divine law). In this state, the leader would be elected and held accountable to popular representatives, but ultimate authority would rest with Islamic law (*shari'a*). But since the leader would be the ultimate interpreter of the law, he would have absolute power during his reign, and could disregard

---

35. Ibid., p. 28ff.
36. al-Banna, *Majmu'at Rasail*, pp. 162ff, 357ff. See also Balqaziz, *al-Dawla*, pp. 136–44.
37. Balqaziz, pp. 20–28.
38. Seyyed Vali Reza Nasr, *Mawdudi and the Making of Islamic Revivalism*, New York: Oxford University Press, 1996, pp. 83–9.

the wishes of the elected assembly, and everyone else for that matter.[39] Maududi's radical views were also espoused by Sayyid Qutb (1906–66), who argued that political debate about democracy and political reform was redundant, and that believers must concentrate on creating the new Muslim society and not be sidelined into debating the politics of *jahili* societies.[40]

Umma, state and movement

The models proposed by advocates of the Islamic revival appeared to converge towards some form of limited democracy under the watchful guardianship of the *'ulama* (along the lines established by the Constitutional Revolution in Iran). However, apart from the Iranian Revolution, these proposals remained largely utopian prescriptions. The debate has thus progressed from discussion of actual reforms, like those that comprised the nineteenth-century Tanzimat reforms in the Ottoman Empire, and the similar reforms advocated by Khayr al-Tunisi and Afghani, to reflections on how the caliphate could be restored. And while authors like Rida drew inspiration from historical experience, like that of Iran and later Saudi Arabia, others were critical of the Islamic polities that actually existed, such as the Saudi or Yemeni monarchies.[41]

The 1979 Islamic Revolution in Iran seemed to offer a giant leap forward, by putting some of these ideas into practice. The model proposed by Ayatollah Khomeini was based on the principle of *wilayat al-faqih* ('the mandate of the jurist'). As spelled out in Article 5 of the Iranian Constitution of 1979, it stipulated that, in the time of the absence of the twelfth imam, 'in the Islamic Republic of Iran the mandate to rule and leadership of the people are the responsibility of a just, pious jurist aware of the time, brave and with drive and initiative, whom the majority of the people know and accept as their leader'. The Iranian Constitution still accepted the principle of popular sovereignty and the role of elected institutions (parliament, presidency, and so on) – but the role of the leader remained dominant, and was even reinforced by the 'absolute mandate of the jurists', which meant that the leader–jurist could

---

39. Abu al-A'la Mawdudi, *Islamic Law and Constitution*, Lahore: Islamic Publications, 1967, pp. 147–9; and *Tadwin al-Dustur al-Islami*, Cairo: Dar al-Ansar, 1991, pp. 25–50. See also Nasr, *Mawdudi*, pp. 85–95.

40. Sayyid Qutb, *Ma'alim fi'l-Tariq*, Beirut: International Islamic Federation of Student Organizations (IIFSO), 1978, pp. 34–7.

41. Enayat, *Modern Islamic Political Thought*, pp. 89–91.

overrule explicit Islamic legal provisions in the interest of the Islamic state. A special council, the Expediency Discernment Council of the System, was set up to undertake the task of determining when provisions of Islamic law could be disregarded (Articles 111 and 112 of the amended 1989 Constitution). This development was extremely significant, since it impinged on Khomeini's characterisation of the Islamic state as one in which the law is supreme, coupled with his affirmation that the divine law had already been laid down and did not need to be elaborated anew, but only interpreted and obeyed. These provisions indicate that the divine law was not as clear cut as the theory of *wilayat al-faqih* suggested and, more significantly, that it could be overruled by appeal to considerations of (secular) interest.

This brings us to the heart of the question of the character of the Islamic state and the way in which the debate has shifted. The modern debate started during the rule of traditional monarchies claiming Islamic legitimacy. The claim of the Ottoman sultans to the caliphate was also a claim to being the supreme authority on both temporal and religious matters in Islam. In this respect, the leader not only leads the *umma*, but must also speak for it; the *umma* was supposed simply to follow the commands of its leader, and to ask no questions. However, as the countries involved collapsed, sank deeply into dispute and lost their independence, this argument began to crumble, so the *umma* could no longer afford to be absent and 'represented' by the caliph or sultan. So new 'representatives' emerged in the shape of activists and community leaders making specific demands in the name of the *umma*, and claiming the right to speak in its name. For this group, the state is no longer identified with the sultan or caliph, but a set of autonomous institutions accountable to the *umma* as a whole.

The representatives were not initially elected by the people, but they emerged either out of street battles, as in the popular struggles in Iran and elsewhere – including the nationalist agitation in Egypt – or from actual wars, as was the case in Turkey and parts of the Arab world. But these new leaders were in turn challenged by others – in particular those claiming to be the voice of religion. In a sense, the contest was between those who had argued that the claim of caliphs and other earlier leaders to an authoritative religious voice was invalid and had to be abandoned altogether, and those who argued that the claim would be valid in principle if it was made by the right claimants. The first argued that the institution of the caliphate had to be scrapped in favour of a modern, secular and democratic state, while the latter argued that the institution of the caliphate had to be preserved and reformed.

The dilemma was that proponents of the caliphate, though they opposed democracy, appeared to enjoy the support of the masses, while the presumed proponents of democracy lacked mass support and had to resort to repression. So the democrats could not afford to be democrats, while the champions of the caliphate admitted that it could not be restored in its original form, leaving much room for innovation and change that brought them closer to their opponents. All now agree that government should be representative of the *umma* and accountable to it, even though the more religiously inclined argue that Islamic law and doctrine must limit the sovereignty of the *umma*. The majority now agree that it is not possible to reunite the *umma* in the short term, and many argue that even in the long term Muslim unity does not have to mean joining a unitary state, but could be achieved through a confederacy or commonwealth.

In this process, the concept of the *umma* passed through many redefinitions, and is used to refer to the nation-state as well as to the imagined pan-Arab entity and to the Muslim community as a whole. It is very important that emerging Islamic groups press their claim to represent the *umma* – or even *to be* the *umma*. For the more moderate voices who acknowledge the continuing existence of the *umma*, the claim is that the Islamic movements are the real representative of the *umma* – its vanguard, so to speak. For more radical factions that do not recognise the Islamic credentials of the majority, their own Islamic movement *is* the *umma*. Its leadership is therefore the only authoritative voice, as the existing state has no claim to legitimate authority.

For all Islamic groups, the circle will be closed when the movement is broadened to incorporate the majority of the people, or succeeds in taking over the state to become the legitimate authority, or both. Only then can Islamic legitimacy pass from the movement back to the state, which now submits to Islamic law. But this position is somewhat circular, since, as was shown in the Iranian experience, the claim to supreme authority in the name of religion can generate outcomes that may themselves be challenged in the name of religion. When the Ottoman sultan–caliph declared Mustafa Kemal a renegade apostate for rebelling against the caliph, it was the caliph who was regarded by the majority of Muslims as the renegade, since he had agreed to submit to foreign occupation and permit the dismemberment of the state. Also, Ayatollah Khomeini's modification of the principle of *wilayat al-faqih* to give absolute powers to the leader – even in defiance of Islamic law itself, in the name of 'state interest' – appears to turn the principle on its head. For the very justification of *wilayat al-faqih* rests on the necessity to determine and obey Islamic law, not to follow other principles, such as regime interests. It should be recalled that earlier leaders from the Umayyad period onwards made claims to supreme religious authority, not always with success. So, unless claims for authority are arbitrated by mechanisms which take into account the popular will, the questions of who can speak for the *umma* and who can run the state will remain unresolved.

THREE

Salafism: Doctrine, Diversity and Practice[1]

Roel Meijer

Salafism is often associated in the public mind with the intolerance and violence that are usually ascribed to Wahhabism, the dominant form of Islam in Saudi Arabia. Moreover, it is often regarded as rigid, and its rapid spread around the world is ascribed to the de-contextualised, scripturalist character of its doctrine, which emphasises a return to the pristine form of Islam and the sources of Islam, the Qur'an and the *hadiths*. This chapter shows that Salafism has a longer history than Wahhabism, and that its doctrine, although highly formalised and de-culturalised, is adaptable to the political context in which its followers find themselves, and has evolved over time. This is the result of a fundamental ambiguity within Salafism between a quietist and an activist form, manifesting themselves in two principles that are closely associated with Salafism – namely, the duty to command good and forbid wrong (*hisba*), and the principle of loyalty to Muslims and disavowal of non-Muslims (*al-wala wa'l-bara*). This chapter traces the history of the quietist and activist sides of Salafism by means of these two principles of its doctrinal implementation, which can adopt a peaceful and political as well as a violent form, depending on the local circumstances.

Doctrine

Salafism is usually seen as a modern phenomenon that has emerged since Saudi Arabia has become a power that has been able to promote its form of

1. I am hugely indebted for my knowledge on Salafism to the contributors to the anthology *Global Salafism: Islam's New Religious Movement*, Hurst/Columbia University Press, 2009, which I had the privilege of editing. I am especially indebted to Harald Motzki, Joas Wagemakers and Martijn de Koning for their comments on an earlier draft. Needless to say, all the mistakes in this chapter are my own.

Wahhabism – a reformist, purist movement founded by Muhammad ibn 'Abd al-Wahhab (1703–92) – under the more abstract, less sectarian term of Salafism. In fact, as Bernard Haykel has pointed out, the phenomenon has a long ancestry, and the concept has been current since the Abbasid Caliphate (750–1258).[2] The term Salafism derives from the Arabic *al-salaf al-salih*, the 'pious forefathers', considered to be the first three generations of Muslims who were either close to the Prophet Muhammad, or had first-hand knowledge of Islam in its pristine form, or had contact with those who had.[3] The golden age of Islam, during which the purity of the Muslims is linked to their impressive military conquests, is usually limited to the period of the four rightly guided caliphs, between 632 and 661.[4] Salafis have a deeply pessimistic view of history, which for them represents only a decline after this golden age.[5]

The whole idea of Salafism is that the only way to lead a pure Muslim life is to return to this period and emulate the life of the Prophet Muhammad and his companions. Only then can one attain paradise. The emphasis is therefore on the sources of Islam – the Qur'an and the *hadiths*. As the *hadiths* are the traditions about the sayings and deeds of Muhammad – on his *sunna* ('mode of life') – it is especially the *hadiths* that have attracted the attention of the Salafis.[6] Due to the extreme importance of these texts, Salafis are scripturalists. Moreover, they are literalists: all human actions have to be covered by the sources of Islam to be legitimate; otherwise they are condemned, and in some cases their perpetrator even loses the right to be called a Muslim. As Muhammad is regarded as an exemplary, perfect model,

---

2. Bernard Haykel, 'On the Nature of Salafi Thought and Action', in *Global Salafism*, pp. 33–57.

3. Most of the companions of the Prophet, who obtained first-hand knowledge of the rise of Islam, had died by 690 CE; most of the second generation, the followers (*tabi'un*), who had obtained their knowledge directly from the first generation around 750 CE; and the third generation, the followers of the followers (*atba' al-tabi'in*), around 810 CE. Personal communication with Professor Harald Motzki.

4. The four rightly guided caliphs are Abu Bakr (632–34), 'Umar (634–44), 'Uthman (644–56) and 'Ali (656–61).

5. For a excellent general introductions to Salafism, see Bernard Haykel's chapter mentioned in note 2, and Quintan Wiktorowicz, 'Anatomy of the Salafi Movement', *Studies in Conflict and Terrorism* 29 (2006), pp. 207–39.

6. For the best analysis of the issue of *hadith*, see Harald Motzki, 'Introduction', in *Hadith: Origins and Developments*, Harald Motzki, ed., Aldershot: Ashgate/ Vararium, 2004, pp. xii–lxiii.

a close reading of the Qur'an and *hadiths* is essential for leading a correct life and walking the straight path. This applies to thought and behaviour, as well as to codes of dress.

The attraction of Salafism lies in the rigorous logic of its central concepts, which together form its *'aqida* ('creed'). Although Salafism has been associated with Hanbalism and its jurisprudence (*fiqh*), the emphasis of Salafism, especially in its modern form, is on creed and religious practice based on the Qur'an and *hadiths*. The central concept around which Salafi doctrine revolves is *tawhid*, or the Oneness of God, captured for the Muslim in the first part of the pillar of the faith termed the *shahada*, 'There is no God but God'.[7] More than other Islamic currents, Salafism stresses the strict monotheism of Islam reflected in the term *tawhid*. According to the Salafis, *tawhid* is divided into three different forms that reinforce each other: *tawhid al-rububiyya* – the Oneness of Lordship – denotes the all-powerful character of God the Creator of the universe; *tawhid al-uluhiyya* – the Oneness of divinity – implies that all forms of worship must be devoted to God alone, and deals with religious practice; *tawhid al-asma wa'l-sifat* – the Oneness of Names and Attributes of God– means accepting the revelation about God's names and attributes literally, without inquiring into its meaning. Rationalism and *qiyas*, or analogous reasoning, are rejected as being based on fallible human reason. All that contradicts *tawhid* and all that is not covered by the Qur'an and *hadiths* are rejected as innovation (*bid'a*) and considered unbelief (*kufr*). Innovators are regarded as sinners who must be fought. Not surprisingly, Salafism can therefore be aggressive towards other Muslims if they are lax according to Salafi standards, for only a total submission to God and complete compliance with Islamic law – the *shari'a* – makes one a Muslim. The Shi'is are by definition considered members of a heretical sect, or rejectionists (*rawafid*), as they do not recognise the first three caliphs and those of the companions of the Prophet, whom they regard as usurpers of the right of 'Ali, the son-in-law of Muhammad, to succeed Muhammad.[8]

---

7. The complete *shahada* is 'There is no God but God [there is only one God] and Muhammad is his Prophet'. The other four pillars are: *salat* – performing prayers; *zakat* – giving alms to the poor; *sawm* – fasting during the month of Ramadan; the *hajj* – performing the pilgrimage to Mecca.
8. For more on the condemnation of Shi'ism especially by Wahhabism, see Guido Steinberg, 'Jihadi-Salafism and Shi'as: Remarks about the Intellectual Roots of Anti-Shi'ism', in *Global Salafism*, pp. 107–25.

The ultimate punishment for not adhering to the right creed and practice and, consequently becoming an apostate, or *murtadd*, is excommunication (*takfir*), and ultimately death.

Salafism is known not only for its emphasis on creed and its strict upholding of *tawhid*, but also for its strict practice, called *manhaj*. The concept of *tawhid al-uluhiyya* forbids all forms of intercession with God, which is called *shirk* ('idolatry'), or giving God associates or partners. Associatism can take the form of venerating trees or the tombs of saints, seeking holy men or soothsayers as intermediaries with God, or putting one's faith in astrology. Other distractions from God, such as music, or in the modern era television, are also condemned. *Shirk* is divided into greater sin, or *al-shirk al-akbar*, such as religious innovation, and lesser sin, *al-shirk al-asghar*, such as listening to music, or wearing Western clothes; the first is punishable by death, the second is considered a misdemeanour.[9]

Due to its strong association of creed with practice, Salafism can be compared with Christian Puritanism (or in some ways with left-wing activist movements and their concept of praxis).[10] Like its European counterparts, it is a reformist and revivalist movement, directed to the purification (*tazkiyya*) of the faith by returning to the sources or fundaments of its religion, and attacking the accretions that have tarnished the original doctrine over the centuries. The revivalist movement rejected the practice of religious students studying only the commentaries of the four law schools,[11] instead

9. For the most detailed, but sometimes biased analysis of Ibn 'Abd al-Wahhab's theology, see Natana J. Delong-Bas, *Wahhabi Islam: From Revival and Reform to Global Jihad*, Oxford: Oxford University Press, 2004, pp. 41–91.

10. See my analysis of the ideologue of al-Qaeda on the Arabian Peninsula, Yusuf al-'Uyairi (also known as Yusuf al-Ayiri), 'Yusuf al-'Uyairi and the Making of a Revolutionary Salafi Praxis', *Die Welt des Islams* vol. 47, nos 3–4 (2007), pp. 422–59.

11. The four law schools (sing. *madhhab*, pl. *madhahib*) are: the Maliki school, founded by Malik ibn Anas (d. 796), followed in Muslim Africa, except Lower Egypt and the east coast of Africa; the Shafi'i school, founded by Muhammad ibn Idris al-Shafi'i (767–820), followed in Lower Egypt, East Turkey, in Muslim countries along the Indian Ocean, especially East Africa, the southern shore of the Arabian Peninsula, and Indonesia; the Hanafi school, founded by Abu Hanifa (d. 767), and followed by countries belonging to the former Ottoman Empire in the Balkans and the Arab world, Pakistan and India; and the Hanbali school, the latest and smallest law school, founded by Ahmad ibn Hanbal (d. 855), followed especially in Saudi Arabia. The derivation of

of the Qur'an and *hadiths* directly. Like Protestants, Salafis reject the 'blind' authority (*taqlid*) of religious teachers of the law schools (*madhhab/madhahib*) and urge the individual to study the sources as a means of discovering the Truth. Except in Saudi Arabia, where since 1971 a Council of Senior *'Ulama* has tried to control doctrine, Salafism is therefore mostly characterised by informal study circles, or *halaqat* (sing. *halqa*), in which teacher–student relations form a network which resembles the medieval system of teaching.[12] Like Protestants, Salafis also consider themselves the victorious group (*al-taifa al-mansura*), or the saved sect (*al-firqa al-najiya*);[13] but, in contrast to Protestants, they already know they will be saved. Nevertheless, despite their claim that the text is transparent and that Truth can be obtained as long as one studies the *hadiths* long enough, their internal debates are ferocious. Due to the tremendous differences that have emerged – especially in the modern era, as a result of external Islamic influences – Salafis can differ in both their *'aqida* ('creed') and their *manhaj* ('practice').[14] An understanding of the context of Salafism is therefore crucial for understanding its different manifestations.

---

principles of law is called *fiqh*, and the sources on which it rests (*usul al-fiqh*) are the Qur'an and the *hadiths*, the consensus of the scholars (*ijma'*) and analogy (*qiyas*). Before the fourth-century Hijra it was common to use individual interpretation (*ijtihad*), but after that period it was discouraged, and the 'gate of *ijtihad*' was closed.

As a result, religious scholars have tended to restrict their study of Islam and the *shari'a* to the commentaries of the law schools, and for centuries have hardly studied the sources of Islam, the Qur'an and the *hadith*. Salafism has criticised the 'blind' following (*taqlid*) of the law schools. It regards the neglect of the Qur'an and *hadiths* as the reason for the decline of Islam, and argues that a revival of Islam is only possible by a return to the study of these sources by means of individual reasoning – *ijtihad*. To what degree the law schools have to be abandoned, however, is a matter of dispute; Hanbalism is the official law school of Saudi Arabia and the Hanafi law school is practised in Pakistan and India.

12. See Quintan Wiktorowicz, *The Management of Islamic Activism: Salafis, the Muslim Brotherhood, and State Power in Jordan*, Albany: SUNY Press, 2001, pp. 128–43.

13. Salafis believe they belong to the saved sect, a belief that is based on the *hadith* that states '[T]his *umma* will be divided into seventy-three sects all of which except one will go to Hell and they are those who are upon what I and my Companions are upon.'

14. Most scholars argue that Salafis share a common *'aqida*, but differ in their

Doctrinal rigour, political ambiguity

One would expect, on the basis of the close relation between creed and practice and its puritan rigour, literal exegesis and mental urgency, that Salafism would give rise to a highly activist movement, demonstrating a missionary zeal in converting Muslims whose lives have not become fully submitted to the rules and behaviour of Salafi *'aqida* and *manhaj*. Moreover, the 'de-territorialised' abstractness of Salafism, condemning all local traditions as deviations from a universal creed, would lead one to believe that Salafism would be a strong transnational movement, sweeping away the obstacles to conversion of the masses to becoming members of the 'saved sect'.[15] Historical and contemporary evidence does not confirm this expectation. In fact, one of the most fascinating aspects of Salafism is its political ambiguity, oscillating between quietism and activism.

Part of the explanation of Salafism's ambiguity lies in the complex relationship between Salafism and political authority. Perhaps due to its strict nature and emphasis on doctrinal purity, Salafism demonstrates a larger degree of internal tension in its relations with political authority and political involvement than is normally the case in movements that have embraced political Islam, such as, in modern times, the Muslim Brotherhood.[16] The ambiguity in Salafism's political behaviour must be ascribed to its basic predicament: on the one hand, as in many revivalist movements, politics and contact with authorities are regarded as corrupting, leading to a compromising of religious belief. On the other hand, these movements inevitably seek power – although they might not acknowledge it – and act politically in the pursuit of their reform programme.

This tension is reflected in the oscillation between different strategies or practices (*manahij*) that Salafism uses to achieve its ends. As a rule of thumb,

---

manhaj, or practice (see, for instance, Wiktorowicz, 'Anatomy', p. 213); but there is cause to doubt that one can have the same *'aqida* if practices differ so much. Although Salafis share the same principles, such as *tawhid*, and use the same terms, such as *bid'a* and *shirk*, activists will provide a different interpretation of the *'aqida* and derive different strategies from it than quietists. Moreover, almost all Salafi groups start by publishing an *'aqida*, in order to distinguish themselves from other Salafi groups and Islamic currents.

15. See especially Olivier Roy for the concept of de-territorialisation, in his *Globalised Islam: The Search for a New Ummah*, London: Hurst, 2002.

16. For more on the ambiguity of 'political Islam', see my 'Towards a Political Islam', *Clingendael Diplomacy Papers*, 22, (2009).

one can state that Salafism usually distrusts politics, and that Salafis keep a distance from the authorities, regarding them as a source of moral corruption. In that case, Salafism adopts what has been called an apolitical or quietist attitude, based on piety, and concentrates on learning and acquiring religious knowledge (*'ilm*). It accepts authority according to the principle of obedience to the ruler (*wali al-amr*) and is willing to cooperate with political power, but mostly at a distance, and its practice is limited to education (*tarbiya*) and spreading the word (*da'wa*). However, it can become activist when political power supports the spread of Salafism, by supporting its *da'wa* as a means either to legitimise itself, or, in extreme cases, to harness its religious zeal for political goals, such as the accumulation of power, territorial expansion and plunder. In that case, the Salafi *manhaj* can be transformed into a *jihad* against deviants and unbelievers (*kuffar*), even if they are normally considered to be Muslims. This cooperation between secular and religious forces is usually limited to a 'moment of enthusiasm',[17] as politics will come into conflict with religious revolutionary zeal as soon as it has achieved its goals, or when it runs into problems.

It is only in the modern era that Salafism has adopted a more directly oppositional attitude towards political authority, as a result of the influence of Islamism, or what is normally called (overt) political Islam, which was developed by the Muslim Brotherhood in the Middle East by Sayyid Qutb (1906–66), and by Sayyid Abu al-A'la al-Maududi (1903–79) in Pakistan. Under the influence of Islamism, the Sahwa ('revival') movement in Saudi Arabia has emerged, which embraces politics and actively criticises the state for its foreign and internal policies, demanding reform.[18]

Next to the quietist, apolitical current and the political current, a third current has emerged that upholds the original concept that politics corrupts, but that, in contrast to the quietist current, advocates an active resistance against the state or a foreign threat by means of *jihad*. However, both the

---

17. The term 'in a moment of enthusiasm' derives from Marx. See Leonard Binder, *In a Moment of Enthusiasm: Political Power and the Second Stratum in Egypt*, Chicago: Chicago University Press, 1978.

18. For more on the Sahwa movement, see Mamoun Fandi, *Saudi Arabia and the Politics of Dissent*, New York: Palgrave, 2001. For the way Saudi Arabia became caught up in problems of its own making, see Gilles Kepel, *The War for the Muslim Mind: Islam and the West*, Cambridge, MA: Harvard University Press, 2004, pp. 152–96.

political and *jihadi* currents can revert to a more quietist form, as has happened with the Sahwa movement.[19] From these examples, it is clear that Salafism is a slippery phenomenon that combines a rigorous doctrine with flexible strategy and therefore can move from quietist to a political and *jihadi* movement and back. How this is achieved depends on context but it appears that its flexibility is not unlimited. Some circumstances are not favourable for the expansion of Salafism. For instance, Salafism is weak in establishing local roots when a strong religious–nationalist movement for national liberation exists, such as Hamas,[20] or when strong local customs resist the de-culturalised, de-contextualised character of Salafism.[21] In regions where its violent, *jihadi* form has gained ground, such as Chechnya[22] and Afghanistan,[23] this occurred after these countries were devastated, and all alternatives had been destroyed or discredited. In Europe its quietist form made headway because it empowered second-generation immigrants who rejected both the more traditional folk Islam of their parents and the nation-state's demands of assimilation.

Flexible principles

As we have explained, Salafism is usually divided into three currents. The quietist current is associated with *da'wa*, or the spread of the doctrine; the political current is associated with groups that take part in the political process and press their reform agenda by overtly political means such as demonstrations and petitions and is associated with the Saudi Sahwa movement; and the third current, associated with violence, regards the waging of *jihad* as

19. For an analysis of the original reform programme of the Sahwa and its cooptation by the state, see Madawi al-Rasheed, *Contesting the Saudi State: Islamic Voices from a New Generation*, Cambridge: Cambridge University Press, 2007, pp. 59–101.
20. For the limited inroads Salafism has made in Palestine, see Khaled Hroub, 'Salafi Formations in Palestine: The Limits of a De-Palestinised Milieu', in *Global Salafism*, pp. 221–43.
21. Terje Østebø, 'Growth and Fragmentation: The Salafi Movement in Bale, Ethiopia', in *Global Salafism*, pp. 342–63.
22. James Hughes, *Chechnya: From Nationalism to Jihad*, Philadelphia: University of Pennsylvania Press, 2007.
23. Ahmed Rashid, *Taliban: The Story of the Afghan Warlords*, I.B. Tauris, 2000, pp. 82–94.

the primary means of achieving its goal of a purified Islam.[24] The problem with this division, however, is that it is too rigid. Three remarks are in order here: first, this division concentrates too much on end results, and disregards the internal processes and dynamics of the movement which can bring out one tendency at a certain time and downplay the other; second, it leans too much on the division between peaceful, political and violent practices of the movements and does not allow for transitions from one to the other; third, it does not capture the ambiguity, flexibility and even contradictory nature of Salafism. The following analysis will question the consistency of the threefold rigid division and show, for instance, that a quietist *da'wa* movement can be political, as well as potentially *jihadist*. In my view, there are two principles that capture the multi-faceted, ambivalent and contradictory nature of the movement and demonstrate how it changes depending on the historical, political and social context.

The first principle is that of 'commanding right and forbidding wrong' (*al-amr bi'l-ma'ruf wa'l-nahy 'an al-munkar*), which is referred to several times in the Qur'an,[25] but especially in the famous *hadiths*: 'Whoever sees wrong (*munkar*) and is able to put it right with his hand (*bi'l-yad*), let him do so; if he can't, then by his tongue (*bi'l-lisanihi*); if he can't, then by [or in] his heart (*bi'l-qalbihi*), which is the bare minimum of faith.'[26] *Hisba* is an institution that aims at implementing this concept. It is a principle directed against its own community, and is meant as a means of purification. The first form allows for the use of violence, while the second upbraids the wrongdoer verbally, and the third is confined to an inward, mental condemnation of wrong.

According to the quietist version of *hisba*, the believer is urged to perform his duty civilly and discreetly (one is not allowed to barge into a house or spy on a neighbour). It is not used against authorities unless it is confined to discreet advice. If violence is used, it is only permitted against inanimate objects, such as in smashing wine glasses or musical instruments. The activist

---

24. Wiktorowicz, 'Anatomy'.

25. The conjunction of 'commanding right' and 'forbidding wrong' is found in the Qur'an at 3: 104, and seven other verses (Q3: 110, Q3: 114, Q7: 157, Q9: 71; Q9: 112; Q22: 41, Q31: 17). See Michael Cook's seminal monograph on the subject, *Commanding Right and Forbidding Wrong in Islamic Thought*, Cambridge: Cambridge University Press, 2000, p.13. *Ma'ruf* (what is known) refers to what is known in the *shari'a*. The terms *ma'ruf* is also translated as 'good', and *munkar* as 'vice' or 'abomination'.

26. Cook, *Commanding Right*, p. 33.

interpretation, on the contrary, allows zealots to perform their duty at all times, regardless of the consequences, and people are allowed to take the authorities to task publicly, reminding them of their responsibilities in upholding the *shari'a*. As *hisba* in principle leaves room for interpretation, which of these inclinations is followed depends on circumstances. As we shall see the principle of *hisba* is in all cases ambiguous and flexible, having multiple political implications, allowing for peaceful moral righteousness as well as the pursuit of political goals, even by violent means.

The second principle that is closely associated with Salafism is that of *al-wala wa'l-bara*, which is translated as expressing loyalty (to Muslims and God) and disavowal (of unbelievers) or dissociation (from them). This principle was directed towards unbelievers and was meant to maintain a distance from them with the intention of preventing the contamination and corruption of the purity of one's faith (*'aqida*) and practice (*manhaj*). There is a need of consistency of what to put between practice, the Salafi terms or their meanings.[27] This principle, like that of *hisba*, has both a quietist and an activist aspect: the first stressing loyalty to the community of Muslims and dissociation from non-Muslims to enhance that loyalty, and the second, activist form, focusing more on dissociation from unbelievers and actively pursuing that goal by demonstratively hating them or, at its most extreme, waging *jihad* against them, as well as all those who do not dissociate themselves from the unbelievers (*kuffar*), thus becoming unbelievers themselves and liable to excommunication (*takfir*).

Before giving historical examples, a remark must be made on a Salafi movement I do not intend to analyse, but which must be addressed as it puts the movement into perspective. At the end of the nineteenth and the beginning of the twentieth century, a Salafi movement emerged in Egypt, led by Jamal al-Din al-Afghani (1837–97) and Muhammad 'Abduh (1849–1905). Although this movement also intended a return to pristine Islam and rejected *taqlid*, it was a rationalist current that promoted individual reasoning. It was less concerned with *bid'a*, and attempted to produce a synthesis with Western thought, reading Western political and social philosophers like François Guizot, Auguste Comte and Herbert Spencer, mingling and debating with Westerners, and accepting Western political institutions such as parliamentary rule. This modernist Salafi current never wielded the two principles mentioned

---

27. For the history of the concept, see Joas Wagemakers, 'The Transformation of a Radical Concept: al-Wala' wa'l-Bara' in the Ideology of Abu Muhammad al-Maqdisi', in *Global Salafism*, pp. 81–106.

above,[28] with the exception of Rashid Rida (1865–1935), who supported Wahhabism and, on occasion, advocated *hisba* against Sufism (mystical Islam),[29] in addition to contributing to the anti-Western turn of *al-wala wa'l-bara'* in his condemnation of Western imperialism working with Arab rulers to promote Western interests while undermining the pillars of Islam.[30]

The importance of historical context

Historically, Salafism has been closely associated with Hanbalism, the juris-prudential school in Islam most focused on the study of *hadith*. During the Abbasid Caliphate (750–1258) the Hanbalis became known as the *ahl al-hadith* for their focus on *hadith* study. Their opponents were the *ahl al-ray*, or the 'people of opinion', who upheld a rationalist tendency. Ahmad ibn Hanbal (780–855) supported the idea that it was everyone's duty to perform *hisba*, whether one belonged to the elite or the common people.[31] But he refrained from involving the state in punishing the perpetrators, let alone criticising the rulers themselves. According to the prominent researcher on *hisba*, Michael Cook, 'Ibn Hanbal's doctrine is a deeply apolitical one.'[32] The duty of a Muslim was to obey the caliph, because *fitna* ('civil strife') was worse than a tyrannical ruler; or, in Ibn Hanbal's own words: 'If the ruler orders something which implies sin against God (*ma'siya*), you should neither obey nor rebel. Do not support the *fitna* (strife), neither by your hand nor by your tongue.'[33] The concept of *al-wala wa'l-bara* does not occur in his works.[34]

---

28. For an analysis of the modernist Salafi thinkers Jamal al-Din al-Afghani and Muhammad 'Abduh, see Albert Hourani, *Arabic Thought in a Liberal Age, 1798–1939*, Oxford: Oxford University Press, 1970, pp. 103–60.
29. Ibid., pp. 225.
30. Although David Commins does not call it *al-wala wa'l-bara*, it is part of the same theme. See David Commins, *The Wahhabi Mission and Saudi Arabia*, London: I.B. Tauris, 2006, p. 140.
31. Cook, *Commanding Right*, p. 132.
32. Ibid., p. 106.
33. Ibn Hanbal, *Kitab al-Sunna*, Cairo, n.d., p. 35, quoted in Emmanuel Sivan, *Radical Islam: Medieval Theology and Modern Politics*, New Haven: Yale University Press, 1985, p. 91.
34. Joas Wagemakers, 'The Transformation of a Radical Concept,' in *Global Salafism*.

This changed under his followers. In the tenth century, Hanbalites became notorious for attacks against 'innovators', plundering shops, raiding homes for liquor and musical instruments, assaulting men and women walking together, and attacking members of the other three schools of law. They also harassed Shi'i pilgrims.[35] This activist trend was probably reversed at the end of Seljuk rule in the eleventh century. As one scholar put it, it was exactly 'the ability of the Hanbali *ulama* to present themselves as the defenders of "true" religion, as well as the distance many kept from the government, which enabled their movement to cultivate a large following'.[36]

Taqi al-Din ibn Taymiyya (1263–1328), who in modern times is considered one of the towering figures in Islam who helped formulate Salafism, took these concepts a step further. Living in a period of major turbulence, following the Mongol invasion and the destruction of the Abbasid empire in 1258, he was the first to connect *hisba* with *takfir* and formulate the right to revolt and wage *jihad* against rulers who claimed to be Muslims but did not abide by the *shari'a*.[37] For him, the connection was logical, 'since *jihad* is part of the perfection of enjoining right and prohibiting wrong'.[38] He also gave a new spin to the concept of *al-wala wa'l-bara*, using it as a tool against *bid'a*, urging Muslims to keep away from Jews and Christians and not to befriend them, for fear of polluting the purity of their faith and practices.[39]

Muhammad ibn 'Abd al-Wahhab (1703–92), in what would become Saudi Arabia, was to combine all three principles in his highly activist variant of Hanbalism in the eighteenth century.[40] His movement was based on the reassertion of the *tawhid* and the purification of Islam from all forms of *bid'a* and *shirk*. He believed that the people in Najd, the region in the heart of the Arabian Peninsula and the hinterland of the Wahhabi movement, lived in the same degree of ignorance (*jahiliyya*) as before Islam. He himself actively fulfilled the activist obligations of *hisba* early in his career by cutting down

---

35. Cook, *Commanding Right*, p. 117–22.
36. Daphne Ephrat, *A Learned Society in a Period of Transition*, New York: SUNY Press, 2000, p. 141.
37. Cook, *Commanding Right*, p. 152.
38. Ibn Taymiyya, cited in Richard Bonney, *Jihad: From Qur'an to bin Laden*, New York: Palgrave Macmillan, 2004, p. 117. For more on the relation between *jihad* and *hisba*, see 'Ibn Taymiyah and the Defensive Jihad: A Response to the Crusades and Mongol Invasions', in the same volume.
39. Joas Wagemakers, 'Transformation'.
40. The best account of the rise of Wahhabism is Commins, *Wahhabi Mission*.

trees that were believed to be holy, demolishing the tomb of a Companion of the Prophet that was venerated, and stoning to death a woman accused of adultery.[41] The Wahhabi fear of contamination and corruption was also translated into a revival of the principle of *al-wala wa'l-bara*, which was used especially against the Ottoman empire – Western colonialism not yet having reached the interior of the Arabian Peninsula. Repeatedly, he and his followers warned against contact with the 'unbelievers', and believers were urged to dissociate themselves from their influence out of the fear of corruption of the right *'aqida*. Open enmity against them was incited.[42] Finally, the principle of *jihad* was revived and used against people who would normally consider themselves to be Muslims, but who now were asked to 'convert'.

The importance of context in Wahhabism is attested by the fact that the movement would probably have died out as a sect if it had not been supported by Muhammad ibn Sa'ud (d. 1765), a tribal *shaykh*. It is only thanks to the alliance between Muhammad ibn 'Abd al-Wahhab and his descendants – known as the Al al-Shaykh – and the Sa'ud dynasty, during the first (1744–1818), second (1823–87) and third state (founded in 1902, which became Saudi Arabia), and the willingness of the Sa'uds to subsume politics into religion – that the energies of the Salafi/Wahhabi revivalist movement acquired a political dimension, and the former three principles of *hisba, al-wala wa'l-bara* and *jihad* transcended the level of individual and group activism to become state sponsored. This also contained the seeds of the collapse of the activist movement and the subservience of the Wahhabi *'ulama*, once the 'moment of enthusiasm' had passed and ran against the interests of the state after the *ikhwan* revolt in 1927, which was directed against the pragmatism of 'Abd al-'Aziz ibn al-Sa'ud as ruler. From that moment onwards, the principles of the activist movement were taken out of its hands, reappropriated by the state, and included in the dual process of social control and a return to an apolitical, quietist Salafism that would accept the new division of power between the state and the *'ulama*.[43] In this new arrangement, *hisba* became the monopoly of a state-run institution, the Committee for Commanding Right and Forbidding Wrong, which became known as the 'moral police',

---

41. Ibid.
42. Ibid., pp. 33–6.
43. al-Rasheed, *Contesting the Saudi State*, p. 25.

or *mutawwa'*, who were allowed to exercise physical punishment against transgressors.[44] As for the principle of *al-wala wa'l-bara*,

> official Wahhabi scholars retained the social aspect of *al-bara'* ('dissociation from infidels'), which relates to personal relations between Muslims and non-Muslims represented in nourishing hatred and rejecting friendship, but they endorsed and even legitimised political *wala'* ('subservience') to so-called infidels, exemplified by their total silence over Saudi foreign policy, foreign military bases in the country and other manifestations of Saudi alliances with the West.[45]

However, despite the Saudi attempt to spread Wahhabism as a neutral, quietist Salafism through international organisations, it would prove difficult to contain the tensions in Salafism as represented in the ambivalence of the principles once it expanded and amalgamated with political trends that would play on their more activist interpretation. Inside Saudi Arabia, for instance, the more political Sahwa movement revived the activist notion of *hisba* in the 1980s and 1990s by demanding the right to 'disavow the wrong in public' (*inkar al-munkar 'alanan*), thereby contesting the Saudi establishment's belief that Islam is only a set of repetitive rituals, or that politics is limited to discrete advice (*nasiha*) to the ruler.[46] The movement also tried to give the principle of *al-wala wa'l-bara* a more political dimension by turning it against the (Saudi) state.[47] In the end, international circumstance – the stationing of American troops during the Gulf War of 1990–91 on 'holy' soil in Saudi Arabia – was the catalyst that brought the internal tensions between the quietist and activist forms to the surface. By sanctioning the American presence in a *fatwa*, the quietist mufti 'Abd al-'Aziz ibn Baz blatantly demonstrated the ambiguity of the 'apolitical', quietist 'establishment *'ulama*'. Having by that time become internationalised, the split within Salafism reverberated throughout the world. However, all three currents felt themselves vindicated on the basis of the interpretation they upheld of the two principles we have

44. Cook, *Commanding Right*, pp. 180–92; Madawi al-Rasheed, *A History of Saudi Arabia*, Cambridge: Cambridge University Press, 2002, pp. 52–4.

45. al-Rasheed, *Contesting the Saudi State*, pp. 36–7.

46. Ibid., p. 67.

47. See especially Mamoun Fandi, *Saudi Arabia and the Politics of Dissent*, particularly pp. 61–113. Although Fandi does not mention the term *wala wa'l-bara* explicitly, it is clear that the two Sahwists not only used an activist form of *hisba*, but also an activist form of *wala wa'l-bara*.

analysed: the *da'wa* current because the incident proved that staying away from politics was imperative and that a quietist *al-wala wa'l-bara* should be implemented in full; the politicos because it justified their critique of the regime based on *hisba*; and the *jihadi* trend because it demonstrated that quietism and political Salafism were ineffective, and that the only way towards a pure Islam was by means of *jihad* as a cleansing process based on both *hisba* and *al-wala wa'l-bara*. If the 'hypocrisy' of the Saudi regime was perhaps exposed, Salafism was not, because the doctrine of *tawhid*, as well as the ambivalent and multi-faceted principles of *al-wala wa'l-bara* and hisba, emerged vindicated, but now became all the more intractable as they drifted beyond the control of the state.

Hisba as a principle of social action: the case of al-Jama'a al-Islamiyya (Egypt)

It had already become clear, in Egypt, that *hisba* could be turned into a critical and even semi-revolutionary principle of contestation. Not particular to Salafism per se – the Muslim Brotherhood would also use it[48] – it was the main principle of action of Salafi groups in the 1920s,[49] but functioned as an apolitical *da'wa* instrument to purify Egyptian society. In the 1970s it was revived, and became typical for Jama'at al-Islamiyya ('the Islamic Groups'), which were active in the universities.[50] Although they started out as pious study groups (*halaqat*), they were gradually politicised during the second half of the 1970s, as a result of two developments. The first

---

48. In his youth Hassan al-Banna founded, with some friends, the Society for the Prevention of the Forbidden. See Richard Mitchell, *The Society of the Muslim Brothers*, Oxford: Oxford University Press, 1969, p. 2. The Brotherhood also used *hisba* to condemn Western corruption of Islamic morals. Western imperialism brought to Egypt its 'wine, women and sin' (ibid., p. 223). The Brotherhood was, however, different from Salafism, because it was less interested in the purification of doctrine and more in political unity, summed up in Hassan al-Banna's plea: 'Let us cooperate in those things on which we agree and be lenient in those on which we cannot' – exactly the reverse of the Salafi mission (ibid., p. 217).

49. Brynjar Lia, *The Society of the Muslim Brothers in Egypt*, Reading: Ithaca Press, 1998, pp. 59–60.

50. See my 'Commanding Right and Forbidding Wrong as a Principle of Social Action: The Case of the Egyptian Jama'a al-Islamiyya,' in *Global Salafism*, pp. 189–220.

was the policy of President Sadat, who called himself the 'pious president' and became ensnared in contradictions of his own making by promoting religiosity while becoming dependent on the United States – befriending American politicians such as the (Jewish) Henry Kissinger and signing a peace treaty with Israel, which was considered to be the centre of evil. The second development was an ideological one based on the popularity of Sayyid Qutb as a radical Islamic thinker,[51] who brought out the activist dimension in Salafism in his *Milestones*, and inspired a renewed interest in Ibn Taymiyya. Although Qutb has been criticised by apolitical Salafis for his non-Qur'anic terminology and his lack of religious knowledge,[52] his revolutionary concept of *hakimiyya* ('sovereignty of God') and rejection of *jahiliyya* ('pre-Islamic ignorance') coincided with the concept of *tawhid* in Salafism, as well as that of a complete submission to God and the rejection of politics as an infringement on the sovereignty of God.

The result was a broad student movement that not only was increasingly critical of Sadat, but also had the ideological instruments to attack him. After 1978 the movement split into the Muslim Brotherhood, which dominated Lower Egypt and Cairo, and the Jama'a al-Islamiyya (now singular), which dominated Upper Egypt,[53] and which adhered, probably for cultural reasons,

51. Sayyid Qutb (1906–66) is regarded as the most important radical Islamic thinker who is known for his justification of the right to revolt against a ruler who does not implement the *shari'a*. His radical ideas were developed in prison after Nasser had arrested the members of the Muslim Brotherhood and banned the organisation in the 1950s. Terms introduced by Sayyid Qutb were *hakimiyya* ('sovereignty of God') and *jahiliyya* ('pre-Islamic era'). He believed that Egypt under Nasser lived in an era of *jahiliyya*, because Egyptian society was not based on sacred law, the *shari'a*, but on secular law, and the ruler was venerated as an idol (*taghut*). On Sayyid Qutb, see Gilles Kepel, *The Prophet and the Pharaoh: Muslim Extremism in Egypt*, London: Saqi Books, 1983; Leonard Binder, 'The Religious Aesthetics of Sayyid Qutb: A Non-Scriptural Fundamentalism', in his *Islamic Liberalism: A Critique of Development Ideologies*, Chicago: University of Chicago Press, 1988, pp. 170–205; and Roxanne L. Euben, *Enemy in the Mirror: Islamic Fundamentalism and the Limit of Modern Rationalism: A Work of Comparative Political Theory*, Princeton: Princeton University Press, 1999.

52. See Stéphane Lacroix, 'Between Revolution and Apoliticism: Nasir al-Din al-Albani and his Impact on the Shaping of Contemporary Salafism', in *Global Salafism*.

53. Since Pharaonic times, Egypt has been divided into Lower Egypt – essentially the Nile delta, stretching from present-day Cairo to the Mediterranean Sea – and Upper Egypt, comprising the narrow Nile valley, extending south of Cairo

to a conservative Salafism rather than the more sophisticated and politically open Brotherhood.[54] During the end of the 1970s and the 1980s, *hisba* was the main instrument of Jama'a in furthering its influence and spreading its conservative Salafism. In its hands, *hisba* acquired an activist form. In the universities, Jama'a attacked mixed couples seen in public, and at parties and music festivals. Outside the universities, the movement took over mosques, Salafised them, and challenged the authority of the state and the police. Increasingly the movement used violence and intimidation to achieve its ends. Liquor stores, run by Christians, were smashed, and video shops set on fire. In 1992 the openly anti-Islamist publicist Faraj Fawda was assassinated in Cairo. Meanwhile an activist interpretation of *al-wala wa'l-bara* sanctioned attacks on non-Muslims, and armed robberies of Coptic goldsmiths and – increasingly – of Western tourists. In the end, Jama'a al-Islamiyya used Ibn Taymiyya's argument in favour of *jihad* as the ultimate form of *hisba* to attack the state.

By 1997, Jama'a al-Islamiyya and the infrastructure it had built since 1983 was not only smashed by the state – it was also discredited in the eyes of the public. As a solution its leaders returned to a more quietist form of *hisba* and *al-wala wa'l-bara*. Violence was rejected, and *jihad* could now only be declared by the state and used against non-Muslims. They called for a more civil form of *hisba* – namely, handing the perpetrators of wrongdoing over to the authorities, whose legitimacy was now recognised. In addition, *al-wala wa'l-bara* was toned down to a minimal level, accepting contacts with the West 'if they are beneficial'. The movement had returned, in a sense, to what it had been in the 1970s – an apolitical, pious movement.

The politicisation of *hisba* has not been limited to Jama'a al-Islamiyya in Egypt, but has expanded globally. In Sudan, a quietist movement like Ansar al-Sunna al-Muhammadiyya has recently moved to a more politically activist stance, and regards *hisba* as its main tool of action – although it also has the purpose of purification of the faith (*tazkiyya al-'aqida*).[55] In 1979, in Saudi Arabia, Juhayman al-'Utaybi and his group, moving from a quietist to

to the Sudan. Besides a geographical divide, there has also been a cultural, and for a long time political, divide between the two regions.

54. Mamoun Fandy, 'Egypt's Islamic Group: Regional Revenge?' *Middle East Journal* vol. 48, no. 4 (1994), pp. 607–25.

55. Noah Salomon, 'The Salafi Critique of Islamism: Doctrine, Difference and the Problem of Islamic Political Action in Contemporary Sudan', in *Global Salafism*.

an activist form of *hisba*, had occupied the Grand Mosque.[56] Although he refrained from excommunicating the Saudi state, others did, and attacked the state in 1995 during the Riyadh bombing.[57] In the case of the Algerian GIA, the extreme form of *hisba* – *takfir* – was not only directed against the state, but also against society as a whole, with the result that whole villages that did not cooperate were deemed unbelievers, and accordingly massacred.[58] These examples show that *hisba* can assume different forms – quietist or activist, peaceful or violent – and that much depends on the circumstances a movement finds itself in at a particular time.

Al-wala wa'l-bara *and* jihad *against the external enemy*

Ideologically, the term '*jihadi* Salafism' is often regarded as the result of a merging of the rigour and literalism of Wahhabi Salafism and its tradition of pan-Islamist participation in *jihad*[59] with the political activism of the Muslim Brotherhood, especially in its radical version represented by Sayyid Qutb, who also drew on Ibn Taymiyya. The reason why this merging produced such a combustible mixture must also be ascribed to the particular circumstances in which it occurred. Afghanistan and western Pakistan were in the 1980s and 1990s – like Upper Egypt, Yemen, and Iraq after 2003, and certain districts of large cities like Cairo – regions where the state hardly existed, or had collapsed.

56. For a detailed analysis of Juhayman al-'Utayba, see Thomas Hegghammer and Stéphane Lacroix, 'Rejectionist Islamism in Saudi Arabia: The Story of Juhayman al-Utaybi Revisited,' *International Journal of Middle East Studies* vol. 39, no. 1 (2007), pp. 103–22.

57. Thomas Hegghammer, *Violent Islamism in Saudi Arabia, 1979–2006: The Power and Perils of Pan-Islamic Nationalism*, Paris, 2007, p. 85. See Hegghammer for the background to the Riyadh bombing in 1995 as the radicalisation of a *hisba*/ vigilante group, stemming from Juhayman al-'Utaybi (pp. 87–99).

58. On the transformation of Algeria into 'a land of the infidels' and the sanction of large-scale massacres among the population based on a utopian, non-political terminology derived from Salafism, see Luis Martinez, 'The Distinctive Development of Islamist Violence in Algeria', in Amélie Blom and Laetitia Bucaille, eds, *The Enigma of Islamist Violence*, London: Hurst, 2007, pp. 121–35; and Muhammad Hafez, 'From Marginalization to Massacres: A Political Process Explanation of GIA Violence in Algeria', in Quintan Wiktorowicz, ed., *Islamic Activism: A Social Movement Theory Approach*, Bloomington: Indiana University Press, 2004, pp. 37–60.

59. Hegghammer, *Violent Islamism*.

Moreover, the devastation of the Afghan people after the Soviet invasion led to radicalisation; the 'Arab-Afghans', having fled their own countries, were completely isolated from their own people – as well as from the locals, who mostly did not abide by their rigorous form of Islam.

This explains why the principle of *al-wala wa'l-bara* played a more important role than *hisba*. For instance, although Jama'a al-Islamiyya was also present in Afghanistan, as a social movement that upheld *hisba*, it remained focused on Egypt, and did not join Bin Laden's International Front Against Crusaders and Zionists – whereas the Jihad Group, led by Ayman al-Zawahiri, which had always been a conspiratorial organisation that had no interest in the mobilisation of the people, and rejected *hisba* as too dangerous because it attracted the attention of the police, did join. It is interesting to note that Ayman al-Zawahiri wrote a book on *al-wala wa'l-bara*, and not on *hisba*.[60]

The main exponent of *jihadi* Salafism is the ideologue Abu Muhammad al-Maqdisi. If the route of Ayman al-Zawahiri to *jihadi* Salafism was by way of Sayyid Qutb, and his contacts with Salafi thinkers and Bin Laden, al-Maqdisi's route was via the activist Salafist tradition of Saudi Arabia that had been suppressed by the Saudi state in the 1930s, and was later represented by Juhayman al-'Utaybi, who led the occupation of the Grand Mosque in Mecca in 1979.[61] *Al-wala wa'l-bara* stands at the heart of his version of *jihadi* Salafism, and made a priority of waging *jihad* against foreigners, as well as against the rulers who collaborated with and 'befriended' them; it was understood as a personal duty (*fard 'ayn*).[62]

Another example of the violent activist turn Salafism can make is illustrated by Yusuf al-'Uyairi (or Ayiri), the leader of al-Qaeda on the Arabian Peninsula, who was killed in June 2003 after the first explosions occurred in the Muhayya compound in Riyadh.[63] Although Uyairi was known as a strategist, he was also one of the most important ideologues, buttressing the ideological tools of *al-wala wa'l-bara* and *hisba* by means of a detailed political analysis of each particular country that supported a civilisational war with the West. His

60. Ayman al-Zawahiri, *al-Wala wa'l-Bara': 'Aqida Manqula wa Waqi' Mafqud*, accessed at http://www.tawhed.ws, May 2006.
61. Hegghammer and Lacroix, 'Rejectionist Islamism in Saudi Arabia'.
62. Wagemakers, 'The Transformation of a Radical Concept'.
63. See my analysis of his work, 'Yusuf al-Uyairi and the Transnationalisation of Saudi Jihadism', in Madawi Al-Rasheed, ed., *Kingdom without Borders*, London: Hurst, 2008, pp. 221–43.

work should be read as a manual for action to create a revolutionary praxis of interaction of faith/theory (*'aqida*) and practice (*manhaj*) for a generation of fighters who were involved in a transnational life-and-death struggle with the West. In the hands of Uyairi, *jihad* has become so important that one can only become a true Muslim if one is involved in this eternal struggle and is willing to sacrifice oneself in an act of self-cleansing and purification for the sake of God and the preservation of the community. Self-sacrifice has become the ultimate embodiment of the original Wahhabi/Salafi purity, in an activist Salafi mission of the vanguard as the 'victorious sect'.[64]

However, the route to *jihad* can also combine the two principles. It is interesting that Abu Hamza, the notorious imam of Finsbury Park mosque in London, usually known as a (Salafi) *jihadi*, spent much of his time expounding on the character of *hisba* and *al-wala wa'l-bara*.[65] In fact, the feeling of righteousness and being a member of the vanguard is all the stronger for someone living in the environment of moral degeneration described by Abu Hamza as 'a toilet' – namely, Great Britain.[66] The same goes for the youthful assassin of Theo van Gogh in the Netherlands. Bouyeri came to *jihad* through *al-wala wa'l-bara*, while another member of the Hofstad group, Samir Azzouz, wrote pamphlets against Moroccan-Dutch cashiers at supermarkets handling forbidden products such as pork and alcohol. Their alienation and isolation from Dutch society was reinforced by these two principles, which emphasised internal purity and dissociation from unbelievers.[67] A similar development occurred in Indonesia, where a quietist form of *al-wala wa'l-bara* was transformed into an activist form, and provided the arguments for launching a *jihad* against the Christians in the Moluccas.[68]

---

64. Meijer, 'Yusuf al-'Uyairi'. See also Muhammad M. Hafez, *Suicide Bombers in Iraq: The Strategy and Ideology of Martyrdom*, Washington DC: United States Institute for Peace, 2007.

65. Sean O'Neill and Daniel McGrory, *The Suicide Factory: Abu Hamza and the Finsbury Park Mosque*, London: Harper Perennial, 2006, pp. 56, 61–2.

66. Typical of *hisba* is Abu Hamza's diatribe against Western decadence: 'Every place of iniquity, every brothel, every video shop which is selling naked [*sic.*] is a target. If anybody protect these *kuffar* places and these *fisq* [sinful] places is a target. Anybody who propagate these kinds of things amongst Muslims is a target.' Ibid., p. 62.

67. See the collection of pamphlets of the Hofstad Group collected at the International Institute of Social History, Amsterdam.

68. Noorhaidi, 'Laskar Jihad: Islam, Militancy and the Quest for Identity in Post–

As in the case of *hisba*, these examples of *al-wala wa'l-bara* demonstrate that the routes to *jihad* are more complex than the simple and rigid division between *da'wa*, politicos and *jihadis* suggests. Although many have pointed out that many *jihadis* have their origin in quietist Salafism (some of the radical leaders, like Abu Qutada, were students of Nasir al-Din al-Albani),[69] the two principles described here – *hisba* and *al-wala wa'l-bara* – provide the keys to trace the routes they took, and make it possible to analyse this process more thoroughly in their specific political contexts.

Al-wala wa'l-bara, hisba *and internal withdrawal*

Despite the attention that the highly activist form of Salafism has attracted, it is its quietist and apolitical versions that constitute the most important form of Salafism. In Europe, Salafism with *al-wala wa'l-bara* and *hisba* provided the ideal weapon that cuts both ways. In a generational conflict, *hisba* could be used by better-educated and more integrated youth against parents who were adherents of a more traditional form of Islam, or belonged to other East Asian reformist currents such as the Barelwis or Deobandis, which were not as strict and scripturalist as Salafism. On the other hand, *al-wala wa'l-bara* was an ideal means of empowerment for alienated youth against the European nation-state and its policy of assimilation. The paradox was that, in an environment in which the citizen is required to follow the rules of the state, to participate actively in society and adhere to its norms, joining quietist Salafism was in itself a political act. By rejecting all non-Muslim values and laws as *shirk*, apolitical Salafism rejected democracy and identification with the nation-state. Instead, in line with the concept of *al-wala wa'l-bara*, it refuses negotiations with the state and completely withdraws – the ideal objective of its adherents being migration (*hijra*) back to the *dar al-Islam*, in order that their religious purity is not contaminated.[70]

New Order Indonesia', PhD, University of Utrecht, 2005, pp. 140–43, esp. p. 157.

69. See 'Anatomy', p. 213.

70. For an excellent analysis of Salafism in Europe, see Samir Amghar, 'Salafism and Radicalisation of Young European Muslims', in Samir Amghar, Amel Boubekeur and Michael Emerson, eds, *European Islam: Challenges for Public Policy and Society*, Brussels: Centre for European Policy Studies, 2007, pp. 38–51.

A crucial influence on modern quietist Salafism was Nasir al-Din al-Albani (d. 1999). Although he never visited Europe or Asia but remained in the Middle East, he was to have a pronounced influence on the global quietist movement, making it more independent from Saudi domination. First of all, there is a sense in which he radicalised quietist Salafism by calling for immediate *ijtihad*, thereby breaking the link with law schools and the hierarchy associated with them, and prioritising the power of the individual in interpreting the sources of Islam. He called first for a new form of *da'wa* ('preaching'), called *al-tasfiya wa'l-tarbiya*, which was directed at the purification of Islam, and, secondly, for 'instilling into our youth this authentic Islamic creed [*'aqida*] drawn from the Qur'an and the Sunna'. In this way al-Albani placed *'aqida* before politics, and the individual before the state.[71] Although they varied slightly in their approach, and were more supportive of the Saudi regime, this trend was expounded by a generation of influential figures such as the mufti of Saudi Arabia, 'Abd al-'Aziz ibn Baz (d. 1999), Ibn Uthaymin (d. 2001), Salih al-Fawzan, Rabi' al-Madkhali and the Yemeni, Muqbil ibn Hadi al-Wadi' (d. 2001). This current spread its ideas to the West through the Islamic University of Medina, 85 per cent of whose students were recruited outside Saudi Arabia, and were supported by Saudi institutions such as the Dar al-Ifta and charities. Generations of students from Europe and elsewhere visited the religious universities in Medina and Riyadh.[72] But this group did not hold a monopoly over the views of the new generation of international Salafis. Other trends, including the *jihadis* and the Sahwa movement, acquired a following in countries as diverse as Ethiopia, Great Britain and Indonesia.

The impact of quietist Salafism since the beginning of the 1990s has been considerable. On the whole, 'Wahhabi provocation'[73] has pushed existing religious groups onto the defensive, forcing them to legitimise themselves by becoming more scripturalist. As a result of the shift away from practice, rituals and legal matters to belief (*'aqida*), and thus to a greater abstractness, Muslims have become more self-conscious.[74] Sufism has been heavily criticised, and

---

71. Stéphane Lacroix, 'Between Revolution and Apoliticism'.
72. Jonathan Birt, 'Wahhabism in the United Kingdom: Manifestations and Reactions', in M. al-Rasheed, ed., *Transnational Connections and the Arab Gulf*, London: Hurst, 2005, p. 170.
73. Ibid., p. 175.
74. Ibid., pp. 174–6.

movements such as that of the Deobandis have become more self-critical, leading to a greater degree of autodidactic scriptural study. On the other hand, the spread of Salafism has led to new forms of social contact. As faith has become the main criterion for acceptance, and as Salafism is neither ethnically bound nor kinship-related, it has opened up channels for inter-ethnic mixing. In Birt's words, 'it is a young Muslim's social experiment where new social rules are being worked out in a rereading of Islamic tradition'.[75] This seems to be a general phenomenon. In the Netherlands, Salafism has led to the rise of a whole new subculture of Moroccan-Dutch youth who have devised their own social codes on the basis of Salafism – including marriage without parental consent.[76]

The internationalisation of Salafism has, however, also led to globalisation of the tensions within it. In Great Britain, the split between Salafis following the Gulf War has led to profound cleavages between political and non-political Salafis, who have accused each other of heresy. Deviant political Salafis were accused of being *harakiyyun* ('involved in political action'), adepts of *hizbiyya* ('taking part in party politics') or members of the deviant Sururi sect.[77] In retaliation, purists were designated as 'super-Salafis' for their self-righteous haughtiness.[78] Since then, local Salafis have started to adapt to local circumstances. In the Netherlands, different mosques have opted for different means of circumventing the politics ban, finding creative ways of making quietist Salafism political without actually becoming political themselves.[79]

---

75. Ibid., p. 178.
76. See Janny Groen and Annieke Kranenburg, *Strijdsters van Allah: Radicale moslima's en het Hofstadnetwerk*, Amsterdam: Meulenhoff, 2006, and Martijn de Koning, 'Changing Worldviews and Friendship: An Exploration of the Life Stories of Two Female Salafis in the Netherlands', in *Global Salafism*, pp. 404–23.
77. Muhammad Surur Zayn al-Abidin was a former Syrian member of the Muslim Brotherhood, who left it on the grounds that it was not radical enough, did not include Sayyid Qutb's ideas, tolerated Sufism, and did not adhere sufficiently to Salafism.
78. For an analysis of these internal disputes, see Sadek Hamid, 'The Attraction of "Authentic" Islam: Salafism and British Muslim Youth', in *Global Salafism*, pp. 384–403.
79. Martijn de Koning, 'Understanding the "Others": Salafi Politics in the Netherlands', manuscript.

The relationship between politics and religion in Islamic civilisation has been far more complicated than Muslim activists claim, with their statement that Islam encompasses both 'religion and state' (*din wa'l-dawla*). Salafism, with its highly rigorous belief system and quest for purity, is perhaps one of the most interesting illustrations of the way in which the tensions of this relationship have worked themselves out. Throughout the ages, the common trend was to mistrust politics as corrupting and leave it to one side. This attitude proved difficult to maintain in times of crisis, as Ibn Taymiyya makes clear in his work – while in the modern era it has become untenable. With the increasing demands on citizens, it has become extremely difficult to withdraw and isolate oneself from state interference, and this is complicated further by a potentially activist creed such as Salafism, which has both quietist and activist principles: *al-wala wa'l-bara* and *hisba*. The result has been that Salafism has become political whether it recognises it or not. For, while *jihadi* Salafis shun the corruption of politics in a self-sacrificial purity, every act of violence is a political statement. The same goes for the quietists, who are political by virtue of the simple act of accepting the state in Saudi Arabia or rejecting it in Europe. This ambiguity will continue as long as religious tools of purification, with their quietist and activist sides, remain at the heart of the movement. These principles are rich and multifaceted, allowing even an overt political movement like the Sahwa movement to retreat to a quietist position under state duress. Which tendencies in the ambivalent and multifaceted principles of *hisba* and *al-wala wa'l-bara* emerge will depend on circumstances.

FOUR

The Muslim Brotherhood in Egypt: Historical Evolution and Future Prospects

Kamal Helbawy

As a member and ex-leader of the Muslim Brotherhood (MB) in Egypt,[1] I will discuss and analyse the historical evolution, intellectual outlook and future prospects of the movement. Writings by or attributed to leading MB figures are available, but mostly in the form of interviews and short accounts, as well as a few books, mainly in Arabic. In what follows I will discuss an eighty-year-old movement whose ideas and influence have resulted in the emergence of like-minded organisations in many countries around the world. Branches of the MB have been established in more than seventy countries, and individuals in most of the countries of the world have become involved. The culture and approach of the MB have been adopted completely or partly by these individuals and institutions. Representing mainstream Islamism, the movement has been extensively and closely studied by governments, intelligence services, think-tanks, academics and individual researchers. Debate within the MB abounds, spanning at one end those who advocate isolationist and exclusionary policies and, at the other, those who support the movement's participation in and contribution to politics and society. In general, external research on the MB has always faced great difficulties in properly assessing the MB's internal workings, positions and decision-making processes. Some of these difficulties pertain to problems with documentation, or the difficulty in communicating with the right representatives or senior members of the movement, since many of the founding members have passed away, as have many of their family members who were involved in the movement. Other difficulties are linked to the fact that the huge and rich archive of its

---

1. I have been a member of the Muslim Brotherhood since 1952. From the early 1970s I have held various leadership positions, only resigning from the highest executive leadership Guidance Bureau in 1997.

history is still in need of extensive work to collect and classify information from the organisation's files and members. Adverse influential propaganda employed against the MB by governments and the movement's adversaries has certainly distorted perceptions of the MB in many circles, and has created considerable prejudices.

This chapter is divided into three parts, discussing the historical evolution of the Muslim Brotherhood in Egypt over three periods of time: the first begins with the emergence of the MB in 1928 and ends with assassination of the its founder, Hassan al-Banna in 1949; the second begins immediately after that in 1949, and ends in 1975 when many MB leaders and members were released from Egyptian prisons; and the third opens in 1975 and runs to 2008..

The first stage (1928–1949)

The Muslim Brotherhood evolved between 1928 and 1933 in Ismailya, Egypt. The family of Imam al-Banna came from a village called Shamshera, in the Fowah region,[2] not in al-Mahmoudiah, as many accounts claim. He was born in 1906. The family moved to al-Mahmoudiah when al-Banna was still very young. His father worked in his own shop, and was called al-Sa'ati (the watch repairer). Al-Banna studied in the primary school in al-Mahmoudiah, continued his education at the Teacher Training Institute in Damanhour, then attended the Dar al-'Ulum (School of Knowledge and Sciences) in Cairo, where he studied Arabic language and literature, and Islamic studies. He graduated in 1927, aged twenty-one, first in his class. By the time of his graduation, he had memorised the entire Qur'an, the six authentic books of the *hadith* – the Prophet's sayings – and 19,000 lines of poetry. When asked in his graduation interview which was the best line of poetry he had come across. He said

تُنَى عُنِيتَ فَلم أَقْعُد و لم تَبلُد

إنا القوم قَلوا من قَى خَلتَ

---

2. Mahmud 'Abd al-Halim, *Al-Ikhwan al-Muslimun – Ahdath Sana'at al-Tarikh* [Events that Made History], vols 1–3, Alexandria: Dar al-Daw'a, 1978–1983, vol. 1, p. 57.

which translates as: 'If the people are looking for someone to face the challenge, I believe that they are looking to me and I shall not sit behind or be lazy.'[3]

Not only was al-Banna well educated, informed and knowledgeable about the Qur'an, the *hadiths*, and Arabic language and literature, he was also aware of the challenges facing his society. Al-Banna was also very ambitious. Of his time studying in the Dar al-'Ulum, he said, 'My heart was burning with pain [because of Egyptian and general Muslim affairs] exactly like others around me. I thought deeply and I found that there was no meaning for the pain we felt if it did not spur us into action.'[4]

Egypt at the time was under British colonial rule, with all its implications and impositions. The democratic system was corrupt, with political parties all eager to please the palace and King Faruq. Egyptian society was becoming increasingly Westernised in values, characters, morals and behaviour, but not in administration, science or technology. There was an invitation by liberal and Westernised intellectuals towards the liberation of women in the Western style, as a part of the de-Islamisation of the society and its British-isation, and Sufi groups were encouraged to divert people's attention from the proper understanding and practice of Islam. The *khilafa* had disintegrated by 1923, following the Sykes–Picot Agreement and the Balfour Declaration of 1917 – the first of which divided Arab lands between the colonial powers, while the second gave Palestine to the world's Jews as their national homeland.

Imam al-Banna stayed in Ismailya, in northern Egypt, for just five years (1928–33), teaching in a primary school, before he moved to Cairo to continue his work as a teacher. Ismailya at that time was very European in character, ruled as it was by the British army. Close to Ismailya, the Suez Canal was run by both the French and the British. Egyptians workers were largely confined to the service sector, though some were small contractors. Young men spent their leisure hours sitting aimlessly in coffee shops. Hassan al-Banna visited these coffee shops and talked with young men about Islam, the occupation and their duties, and managed to move them from these places to the mosques, where they would get more induction and education. Through their new understanding of the *da'wa*,[5] there was a change in their personal dealings

---

3. Ibid., p. 58.
4. Ibid., p. 60.
5. Editor's note: Da'wa is one the most misconceived terms in relation to Western understanding of the workings of Islamist groups. Da'wa is used in various ways denoting different conceptions and functions. It could help in comprehending

and relations, and even inside their places of work. Young men began to pray, to ask their foreign managers for their rights, to feel the need to free their country, to understand the value of time, and to behave in an Islamic fashion. This attracted the attention of the Suez Canal managers, and of foreign troops. The young men became very brave, discussing the occupation forces and different problems with their foreign managers. However, during this period the *da'wa* had spread only in a limited neighbourhood – namely, Suez, Port Said, and a few places in the Sharqia and Dakahlia governorates, all of which are very close to Ismailya.

Imam al-Banna married at this time into the al-Suli family from Ismailya. The criteria for selecting the wife were knowledge of the Qur'an and its proper recitation, as well as being a member of a committed family. His mother had recommended such a wife for him and she – Latifa al-Suli – proved to be an excellent choice. She gave him five daughters and one son. She was also very patient and steadfast during al-Banna's busy life, supporting him through the many hardships he faced. The movement held many conferences, meetings and seminars in different areas and cities of this region, where al-Banna and other scholars expounded Islam in a lively and comprehensive way that

---

the multiple meanings of this term if an analogy is drawn between the 'state' and the 'Islamist movement'. If we think of the state, its ideology and its government as an interrelated construct that could be equivalent to an Islamist movement, the term da'wa could refer to all three components separately or collectively. Thus, within the self-generated jargon, da'wa could refer to a given Islamist movement, or its ideology or its political and social agenda. Literally and linguistically speaking da'wa means the propagation of Islam or preaching to the world about Allah, according to the perception and interpretation of the group engaged in da'wa. This could be seen as the overarching ideological goal, the Islamisation of societies. Da'wa could also be used as an internal 'misnomer' or 'nickname' of 'the movement' itself, mostly employed for security reasons. For instance, members of an MB organisation or any other Islamist group would use the term da'wa to refer to their group indirectly to avoid spelling out its actual name, thereby averting and misleading surveillance. Also, da'wa could be used to refer to the general effort of the group as a whole denoting political and social agendas that are implemented or pursued; when applied to the state it means the government. This multiple and overlapping use of the term da'wa has rendered it a much misunderstood notion, where in many cases people would read a different meaning from that which was originally intended. In Helbawy's article, da'wa is used in all these three ways depending on the context; throughout the text the editor attempts to clarify the specific use of the term so that readers are able to infer the immediate meaning intended.

appealed to young men. The first six members of the emerging group named the new movement the Muslim Brotherhood. The movement diverted the attention of the youths towards reading Islamic books and meeting together weekly in small circles, to study Islamic literature and to pray together. One of the main books that they read, after the Qur'an and the books of the *hadith*, was *Ihya 'Ulum al-Din* ('Reviving the Knowledge of Religion') by Imam al-Ghazali, and *The Attack on the Muslim World*, by Shaykh Muhib al-Din al-Khatib, who was a well-known Islamic scholar and editor of the *Al-Manar* magazine and who, though originally from Syria, lived in Egypt. He was a student of Muhammad 'Abduh and Jamal al-Din al-Afghani – the early-twentieth-century pioneers who advocated reform in Islam in order to advance the status of Muslim countries.

The new understanding of Islam

What evolved out of this process became quite clear from the manifesto that was published in *Al-Ikhwan al-Muslimun*, a magazine published by the Muslim Brotherhood after it had moved to Cairo. The *Ikhwan* manifesto set out seven main tenets of belief: that complete trust be placed in Allah and the Qur'an, and in the *sunna* (sayings and deeds of Prophet Mohammad); that straightforwardness, virtue and knowledge are the pillars of Islam; that it is the responsibility of every Muslim to earn his living, be charitable to the poor, and support fellow Muslims financially in all possible ways that conform to Islam; that responsibility to one's family extends to their health, creed and character, and that every opportunity must be taken to spread Islamic teachings at all times; that the revival of Islam is the responsibility of all Muslims; that all Muslims are but one *umma* (nation), and any conflicts between groups or sects must be resolved, and that Muslims were only held back because they had distanced themselves from their religion; and, finally, that the basis of all reform is in a return to the teachings and laws of Islam.

The banner of the Muslim Brotherhood movement carried the well-known Qur'anic slogan, 'Believers are but Brothers'. However, this slogan gradually expanded into a more pointed five-part mantra: 'Allah is our objective; the Qur'an is our Constitution; the Prophet is our leader; *jihad* is our way; death for the sake of Allah is our greatest wish.' This new Islamic *da'wa* projected a new understanding and practice of Islam, which embraced the comprehensiveness of Islam and centred on divine worship, focusing especially on spiritual concentration and purification. It dealt with all things from an Islamic stand-point, preaching avoidance of all that is *haram* (forbidden) such as *riba* (usury), cheating and adultery, as well as the minor sins, such as using bad language.

Before al-Banna, only very old people went to pray in the mosque, per-formed the *umra* or *hajj* pilgrimages or thought of such things as Islamic banking. In Cairo, after 1933, the same initial steps taken in Ismailya to spread this *da'wa* were necessary, in addition to maintaining contact with the regions in which *da'wa* had already spread, or become known. After the initial period in Ismailya, al-Banna sought to introduce the *da'wa* in its new form to Egyp-tians, especially in Cairo. At first he focused his energies on Cairo University, where he attracted many students by addressing issues in their curricula as they related to the Prophet, writing in *Al-Ikhwan al-Muslimun*, the MB magazine. These students soon became voluntary distributors of the magazine. Al-Banna entered into dialogues with existing political parties, however corrupt he felt them to be. The Cairo University students provided a wealth of contacts and connections, and through them al-Banna found himself travelling in summer to different cities, regions and villages, depending on and guided by students from these areas. Introduced to new areas in this way, al-Banna visited mosques, delivered short sermons and held conferences, seminars, meetings and weekly lessons. He contacted the elementary schoolteachers' syndicate, and extended his support to them in their field of work since he was an excellent practitioner, with very good experience and wide knowledge.

During this period *da'wa* emphasised the importance of steering clear of differences in *fiqh* ('jurisprudence'), and keeping a distance from powerful and wealthy hegemonies and secular parties and institutions – particularly out of concern for the effect they would have on new members during their preparatory period. It concentrated on practical aspects and programmes, and on the gradual steps necessary to affect reform, rather than on publicity. Al-Banna capitalised on the *da'wa's* appeal to the spirit of youth, and it quickly spread among them, and through them, to their villages and cities.

The Fifth Conference of 1938

The movement began to attract the attention of others, as well as to sort out its philosophy and define its stance on many issues, including its approach to power, good governance, nationalism, Arab nationalism, Islamic unity and international relations. The Muslim Brotherhood's Fifth Conference enjoyed special significance, as it aimed to focus on broader topics than just the training and the development of Muslim individuals and communities. The *tarbiya* programme (the internal training and education of members of the MB) concentrated on preparing the individual to practise deep faith, correct worship, good character, good health and intellectuality, and to be well organised and punctual, to fight negative impulses, to earn his living, and to be useful to others.[6] In addition to caring for and bringing up a family committed to Islam, individuals were exhorted to spread the *da'wa* in society, build an Islamic government, and believe in and love their own countries and help them work for the evolution of the *umma* for the benefit of humanity.

To achieve these goals, a certain environment and means were required and encouraged. These included weekly lessons in the *usra*, the smallest cellular unit in the party at the grassroots level,[7] and many other activities such as visits to other MB members, training courses held in different Islamic societies and at nearby religious landmarks as well as collective night prayers. Seminars and conferences were to be organised, as well as picnics and day-trips, including outdoor activities, and trips to the seaside and into the desert (especially at night). Such activities were, of course, in addition to daily prayers and worship at night.

In his treatise *Risalat Ta'alim* ('A Treatise on Teachings')[8] al-Banna mentioned thirty-eight duties which MB members should perform, duties concentrated on things such as the proper form of prayers and the prohibition of things such as usury, smoking and drinking alcohol. In these early stages of the *da'wa*, al-Banna hoped to effect changes in Egyptian social life.

---

6. Hassan al-Banna, *Rasail Hassan al-Banna* [Messages of Hassan al-Banna], Beirut: The Islamic Foundation for Printing and Publishing, no date.

7. Literally, *usra* (pl. *usar*) means family. The networks of *usar* are in fact the backbone of any MB organisation in any country, where they comprise and connect the low- and middle-ranking membership with the higher echelons of the organisation – editor's note.

8. Robert Jackson, *Hassan Al Banna – the Qur'anic Man*, translated into Arabic by Anwar al-Jundi, *Al-Rajul al-Qur'ani Hassan al-Banna*, Cairo: Al-Mukhtar al-Islami, 1977.

The MB and the changing political context

Following the Sixth General Conference of the MB movement, which was held in Cairo in January 1941, al-Banna decided to run in the parliamentary elections. He enjoyed great popular support from people who were frustrated with corrupt parties and politics in Egypt, and were enthused by the new understanding of Islam offered by the MB. In 1942 the MB nominated al-Banna to run for the seat in Ismailya, the cradle of the MB movement. However, the prime minister at the time, al-Nahas Pasha of the Wafd party, invited al-Banna to meet with him and informed al-Banna that the MB would be banned and its leaders exiled if he insisted on running in the parliamentary elections. Al-Nahas Pasha informed al-Banna clearly that these decisions had been relayed to him by the British, who were in control of Egypt. Al-Banna met al-Nahas Pasha a second time, and was again warned not to run in the elections. After consulting with the members of the MB *shura* (consultative body),[9] al-Banna decided to withdraw from the elections. The MB membership at large was unhappy with his decision, but al-Banna explained to them the rights that they would be allowed to continue to enjoy: guaranteeing them freedom of movement and the right to continue their activities.

Al-Banna's second foray into parliamentary elections came in 1944. The MB not only decided to nominate al-Banna to run in Ismailya again, but also fielded senior MB candidates in other constituencies. The British Embassy sent a letter to Ahmad Mahar Pasha, who had succeeded al-Nahas as prime minister, asking him to prevent not only al-Banna from running, but also Ali al-Burair – a Sudanese MB member living in Egypt who was a champion of the reunification of Egypt and the Sudan in a unified Nile Valley. The nomination of al-Banna was warmly welcomed in Ismailya, where the townspeople even paid the fees for his nomination. The new government did not openly prevent him from running, but instead rigged the elections and intimidated al-Banna's supporters. This was easily accomplished, as the Chief of National Security of the Canal Governorate was a British officer, the Suez Canal was under foreign administration, and the British army headquarters was based in Ismailya. However, Prime Minister Maher, as a result of his corruption and collaboration with the British, was assassinated by young men affiliated to the National Front of Egypt on 24 February 1945. The National Front,

---

9. *Shura* is the term used for the Consultative Body of the MB. It can apply on many levels: a nation, governorate or city.

which enjoyed the support of the MB, had emerged in the late 1930s as a loose umbrella organisation that strove to bring together several Egyptian parties to fight against the British.

The spread of the MB into other countries

During this period the MB *da'wa* gradually spread into most other Arab countries, mainly as a result of foreign students coming from Iraq, Syria, Jordan, Palestine, Sudan, Algeria, other north African countries and Yemen to study at the al-Azhar institutes, schools and colleges, as well as at Cairo University. The MB disseminated information and organised conferences, which also brought delegates to Egypt. Many were particularly attracted to the MB's stand against British occupation, and its support for the liberation of Palestine. The establishment of the Arab League in 1945 brought about more exchanges between members from Yemen and other Arab countries.[10]

The MB in Yemen

The first proper contact between the MB and Yemen took place in 1938, during the International Parliamentary Conference for Palestine, which decided to send an Arab delegation to the London Conference in February 1939.[11] Yemen delegated two sons of Imam Yahya Hamid al-Din, and the MB delegated Dr Mahmud Abu al-Suwud to assist and translate for them. More contact took place during the preparatory talks for the establishment of the

---

10. At the time, some Western writers who visited the Arab world observed that, while Egypt was 100 years behind Europe, and Saudi Arabia was 300 years behind Europe, Yemen still lived in the age of the Old Testament. This rather simplistic perspective did reflect something of the social situation in the Arab world in the 1940s. But the American writer Robert Jackson, upon meeting al-Banna in 1946, said that if this man lived long he would change the whole region. See al-Banna's speech to leaders of the MB on 8 September 1945 in Cairo, *The Messages of Hassan al-Banna*, p. 263.

11. The London (Roundtable) Conference was convened at St James's Palace to consider the future of Palestine. Representatives of Egypt, Iraq, Saudi Arabia, Transjordan, Yemen and the Palestinians met with British officials, who held parallel discussions with Jewish delegates. When the conference ended after five weeks with no agreement between the Arab states and Jewish delegates, the UK Colonial Secretary, Malcolm MacDonald, proposed that a Palestinian state be created after ten years, possibly a federation with Arab and Jewish cantons. The suggestion was subsequently rejected by the Zionists.

Arab League, and there were additional exchanges that occurred through Yemeni al-Azhar students. A revolution broke out in Yemen in January 1948, which was supported by the MB. Two senior MB leaders travelled to Yemen to lend help and support: 'Abd al-Hakim Abadin and al-Fudail al-Wartalani. The latter was a revolutionary Algerian living in Egypt who had started a business in Yemen before the revolution, and had solid links with 'Abdullah ibn Ahmad al-Wazir, who presided over the first revolutionary government in Yemen after the 1948 Revolution.

The role of the MB in Palestine

The MB showed a great interest in Palestine as early as the mid-1930s while the Egyptian government at the time was reluctant to be drawn into what it saw as a foreign issue. The MB was far less circumspect in its involvement with the Palestine issue, and established a committee to visit Palestine in 1935 to support the Palestinians against the British. The MB received Palestinian leaders in its headquarters in Cairo, arranged meetings and provided a platform for Hajj Amin al-Hussaini – the Mufti of Palestine. The MB formed committees in Egypt to raise awareness of the issue of Palestine among Egyptian people and collect contributions for the Palestinian cause. Al-Banna contended that the MB's fight with Israel was not religious in nature, because the Qur'an urged respectful dialogue between 'people of the Book'; but that MB opposition to Jewish immigration into Palestine was based upon the political and economic threat it posed to the Palestinians. He also said, 'We sympathise with the Jews and feel sorry for the injustices they have suffered, but those injustices should not be addressed by creating injustices to Arabs.'[12]

MB involvement on behalf of Palestine became more focused when it demanded the release of Palestinian prisoners and detainees in occupied Palestine and other countries. After the UN resolution on the partition of Palestine, in November 1947, the MB held demonstrations in Egypt, with the most famous demonstration taking place on 15 December 1947. The MB equipped and trained 10,000 *mujahid* to fight for Palestine and defend the rights of Palestinians. Al-Banna wanted to prepare 70,000 *mujahid* for Palestine, including himself. Great efforts were made to unite the two

12. *Al-Masri* newspaper, 1 January 1948 to end of February 1949; Mahmud 'Abd al-Halim, *Al-Ikhwan al-Muslimun*, vol. 2, pp. 70–72.

well-known Palestinian organisations al-Najada and al-Futuwah, and to train their members for military action. MB volunteers fought bravely in the war of 1948 that broke out in Palestine between Palestinians and Zionist groups.

Aware of the truce of June 1948, in the aftermath of the establishment of the state of Israel, the MB asked the Arabs not to accept the UN proposal; but the first and second truces afforded the Jewish military organisations time to rearm, and ultimately win the war. MB fighters protected the Egyptian army during its withdrawal, and helped the army to regain some of the sites lost before and during the war. Zionist, British and American writers began to attack the MB for its non-acceptance of the UN Resolution dividing Palestine.

As a result of its involvement in Palestine, Jewish organisations, the British, and to a lesser extent the Americans, began to monitor the MB movement and its leaders through the Egyptian monarchy, the corrupt political parties in power, and the police – all of whom preferred to answer to the British Embassy rather than the Egyptian people. The Egyptian authorities, pressurised by the British, took more and more measures against the MB. They prevented or disrupted MB lectures and meetings, and prohibited any Egyptian individual or company from advertising in the MB's daily newspaper *Al-Ikhwan al-Muslimun*, from 5 May 1946 until its licence was cancelled by military order. Its last issue was dated 3 December 1948. They attempted to destabilise the internal structure of the MB by seducing senior members, such as Ahmad al-Sukkary, the MB deputy, with offers of professional promotion. Sukkary accepted the preferment, despite the advice of al-Banna and other senior members. There was a concerted daily press campaign against the MB, while King Faruq and corrupt politicians parroted the British hatred of the MB.

The contest over Egyptian youth

The British established the Society of Freedom Brothers (*Jami'a Ikhwan al-Huriah*)[13] with the aim of attracting young men to Western free-thinking, hoping that this body would affect the activities and affiliation of the MB. Earlier, in 1940, the National Reform Society had been established by Jamal al-Din Hurath Den, a British Muslim. These societies had established educational institutions, sports club and lecture groups, and promoted Western

---

13. Mahmud 'Abd al-Halim, *Ahdath Sana'at al-Tarikh*, vol. 1, pp. 438–9.

freedom between the sexes and attempted to validate the role of the British in Palestine. All efforts were exerted by the British to de-Islamise Egyptian youth. The MB did as much as possible to counter the efforts and influences of these British-proxy societies in a peaceful fashion.

The MB decided to take matters further against the occupation troops and their collaborators in Egypt. Some MB members began to face these challenges and pressures using force. On 22 February 1948, angry members of the MB, who were already affiliated to a secret military organisation that was known as al-Jihaz al-Khas (the Special Apparatus),[14] assassinated the prominent judge al-Khazinder, and burned down the courthouse that held the files of members on trial. The MB leadership declared without hesitation that such actions were wrong and would not be tolerated, al-Banna declaring that 'those killers are neither brothers nor even Muslims'.

Military Order No. 63 of 1948

On 8 December 1948, the Egyptian Interior Ministry issued Military Order No. 63 dissolving the MB society and all its branches. It prohibited all MB activities and dealings and seized all MB belongings, properties and documents. All contracts between MB companies and any third parties were cancelled. MB members were fired from all employment, services and educational institutions. Members were arrested – often taken forcibly from their homes – and their families intimidated. In a conspicuous bid to separate al-Banna from his MB following, he was not arrested. The harshness of these measures was unprecedented, and many thought they might lead to chaos in the country. Mustafa Amin, a prominent writer and journalist, had advised Nuqrashi Pasha, the then prime minister, not to take measures to dissolve the MB, fearing that he – Nuqrashi Pasha – would be assassinated. But Nuqrashi Pasha, like King Faruq, tended to play the hand of the British, and when the American, British and French ambassadors met in the Fayed Military Zone they advised Nuqrashi Pasha to take the measures specified in Military

---

14. Editor's note: The 'Special Apparatus' is a military wing of the MB that was founded in 1940, principally to fight against the British and defend the organisation. The structure, membership and the extent to which the official leadership of the MB had approved its activities all remain uncertain. For further discussion on this wing see Brynjar Lia, *The Society of the Muslim Brothers in Egypt*, London: Ithaca Press, 1998, pp. 177–81.

Order No. 63. Mustafa Amin's advice had been more astute: Nuqrashi Pasha was assassinated on 28 December 1948. Both before and after the dissolution of MB, many MB members were taken into detention, often without charge or trial. All senior members had been detained except al-Banna. Left virtually on his own, he petitioned the government to release the twelve MB Guidance Bureau members to help him to calm the situation. Young men were furious to see their headquarters and MB institutions confiscated and their senior members detained. Al-Banna proposed that the government should release senior MB members, offering to leave Cairo, retire to the countryside or travel abroad. In the end, sensing that he was being set up to look bad by virtue of his own freedom, al-Banna pleaded that he should at least to be detained along with other MB leaders.

The government agreed to release the Guidance Bureau, but stalled in delivering on their promise. They asked al-Banna to submit a public state-ment to calm the situation, which he did. But the government amended the statement without his consent, publishing it under the title 'A Statement for the People'. The police took al-Banna's licensed pistol and impounded his private car; while they did not detain him they did not allow him to leave Cairo. Nor did they release the members of the Guidance Bureau, as they had promised. Al-Banna, his family, and even some of his non-MB friends and other politicians, felt that he was being set up for assassination.

The MB in 1948, at its dissolution

In addition to its headquarters in Cairo, in 1948 the Muslim Brotherhood had more than 2,000 branches all over the country and 2,000 societies for charity and social services.

The MB had 10,000 *mujahid* who were well trained and already fighting in Palestine, or ready to do so. It owned many companies across all economic sectors, including the media, printing, publishing, Islamic commercial transactions, mining, hospitals, clinics, weaving, publicity and advertising, trading and land reclamation.

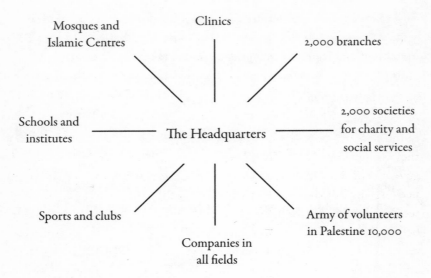

Fig 4.1: The Muslim Brotherhood's network of activities in 1930–1950

The assassination of Imam Hassan al-Banna

On the day he was assassinated – 12 February 1949 – Imam al-Banna had
been invited to meet some government representatives in the evening at
the Society of Young Muslims.[15] He was accompanied by his brother-in-law
Dr 'Abd al-Karim Mansur and after the meeting, as they were getting into
a taxi to go home, they were both shot. Al-Banna was taken to hospital,
but was left untreated and died. His brother-in-law was eventually treated,
and subsequently recovered. Al-Banna was buried quietly; only his family
knew where he was, and only they were allowed to attend his funeral.
Another statement that the government had taken from al-Banna on 12
January 1949 – one month before his assassination – was published after
his death, the 'Neither brothers nor Muslims' condemnation of the killers
of Naqarshi and the bombing of the Appeal Court, which was described
above. Al-Banna had been the main target, and with his death came an
end to the first stage of the Muslim Brotherhood. The second stage was to
prove as gloomy as the end of the first.

---

15. The Society of Young Muslims, *Jami'a al-Shubban al-Muslimin*, had been
    established in 1927 with the aims of addressing social problems and spreading
    da'wa. Hassan al-Banna cooperated with the society as it had similar aims to
    those of the MB.

The second stage (1949–1975)

The struggle for independence and the Suez Canal

After the assassination of al-Banna, it took the MB two years, eight months and seven days to elect a new general *murshid* ('leader'); they did so on 19 October 1951. A less corrupt Wafd government had come to power, aided in the elections by the MB, who had cooperated with the aim of ejecting the existing very corrupt government. On 10 October 1951 the new Wafd government abrogated the Anglo-Egyptian Treaty of 1936, which had codified ongoing British control – particularly of the Suez Canal, after failing to secure independence through talks with the British. It had not been possible before this to elect a new *murshid* to replace al-Banna. The newly elected *murshid*, Hassan al-Hudaiby, made great efforts with the Wafd government and the palace to obtain the release of MB detainees and prisoners who had been imprisoned mainly to satisfy the demands of the king and the British. Al-Hudaiby also worked to calm his members.

Throughout 1951 and 1952 the Ikhwan fought against British troops in the Suez Canal Zone with other Egyptians who had volunteered to liberate their country from foreign occupation. This author still remembers how, in secondary school, he sang songs in praise of the martyrs of Ikhwan, and others killed in the Suez Canal War in 1951 and 1952 and the guerrilla activities of January 1952, among them the well-known students al-Menacy, Shaheen and Ghanem.[16]

The main challenge for al-Hudaiby, as newly elected *murshid*, had been to effect the release of MB detainees and prisoners. But he also needed to bring into line the 'Special Apparatus' wing, which had been a real problem inside the MB organisation since the last days of al-Banna, who had been unable to bring it under control before he was killed.[17] With the new regime, the MB needed to deal with other political parties to coordinate efforts towards the independence of the country.

The king and his court were still riddled with corruption and connections with the occupation forces. The MB sought to work with all interested

---

16. These students fought and died in the Suez Canal War. As committed Islamists fighting to liberate their country from foreign occupation they were venerated as martyrs.

17. Members of the Special Apparatus wing acted independently of the MB leadership, refusing to acknowledge its authority over them.

parties to end colonisation, particularly with those anti-monarchist officers in both the army and the police who were known as the Free Officers and who were to play a particularly important role in the secret preparations before the revolution. Nasser was one of the Free Officers, and since 1941 had been a member of the MB, in common with other Free Officers.

The *coup d'état* took place on 23 July 1952, having been delayed one or two nights in order to gain the approval of the *murshid*, who was in Alexandria at the time. The July Revolution was a success, but soon afterwards differences became apparent in the Revolutionary Council under Nasser. Cracks appeared between Nasser and the MB, amid widening policy disagreements. Nasser started to sack the members of the Free Officers who disagreed with him, beginning with Usuf Siddiq, and later even moving on to the president, General Mohamad Najib.

MB confrontation with Nasser

Early in 1953 – almost a year after the revolution – President Nasser was planning to disrupt the MB and halt its activities. On 12 February 1953 Nasser and other Free Officers visited the grave of al-Banna to show sympathy and loyalty, and to attract some MB leaders to their side. Nasser cultivated a close relationship with the Special Apparatus and some leading members in the MB, establishing two new institutions – the Islamic Conference and the Liberation Authority – in December 1953. Nasser intended to use the Liberation Authority as his new political base and foundation, rather than the Ikhwan. As the year progressed, Nasser dissolved the MB, detained the *murshid* and other leaders of the Ikhwan, and sent them to military prisons. He also made a statement accusing the MB of treachery, contacting the British occupation forces, and forming secret bodies within the army and the police. He accused them of attempting their own *coup d'état*, using religion for their own personal purposes. The situation was exacerbated by internal problems in the MB – especially as a result of the behaviour of the Special Apparatus whose leaders had involved it in extremist activities which had not been sanctioned by the MB leadership. The MB therefore expelled former Special Apparatus leaders 'Abd al-Rahman al-Sanady, Ahmad Adil Kamal, Mahmud al-Sabbagh and Ahmad Zaky from the organisation. These four joined with other disaffected members to occupy the MB headquarters in Cairo on 27 November 1953, demanding that al-Hudaiby resign and a new *murshid* be elected. The MB constitutional bodies convened and expelled three more senior members of the MB – Salih Ashmawy, Muhammad al-Ghazali and Ahmad 'Abd al-'Aziz Jalal – for their involvement in the failed revolt. It was later proved that Nasser had been behind these internal disagreements in the Muslim Brotherhood.

The March 1954 demonstration

On 1 March 1954 the MB organised an enormous demonstration near the palace of Abadin, where Nasser was present with some other Free Officers. It was an intimidating crowd, and Nasser agreed to meet with Ikhwan leaders – particularly 'Abd al-Qadir Uda, with whom he had good relations. Nasser agreed to reinstate President Najib and to accept a constitutional system of rule. He also agreed to release all MB detainees.

As a result of public pressure led by the MB, the Revolutionary Council issued major resolutions on 25 March 1954 allowing the establishment of political parties, while restricting the Revolutionary Council from establishing one of its own; there would be no banning of any parties or suppression of political rights. A General Assembly was to be elected by direct public vote, and the General Assembly would elect a president at its first meeting. The Revolutionary Council would dissolve itself on 24 July 1954.

On 29 March 1954, workers all over Egypt went on strike, commandeering government vehicles and shouting in the streets: 'No parties! No multiparty system! No constitution! No General Assembly!' They did a lot of damage, even attacking the Supreme Council and injuring its president, the well-known and highly respected lawyer al-Sanhuri, and pelting him with shoes.

Friction escalated between Nasser and the MB. In spite of this the *murshid*, al-Hudaiby, sent a letter to Nasser on 4 May 1954:

> It is our belief that – in spite of the challenges facing the MB and your non-compliance with agreements made between us – it is still our duty to give our advice. Stability can be achieved only through justice, reform and mercy. It cannot be achieved through the use of power alone. I put forward to you these means of restoring stability: the resumption of Parliament, the cancellation of Martial Law and the spreading of freedom. Reform – in our opinion – is a vast field. Reformation of the spirit is the foundation of every reform.

Once the strike was over, and Nasser was in control of the Ministry of Interior, and of the army through his friend 'Abd al-Hakim Amir, he set out to disrupt all MB activity, including closing down their magazine. In July 1954 al-Hudaiby criticised the new protocol signed by Nasser between Egypt and Britain, and demanded that such protocols should be agreed only through an elected parliament. This criticism incensed Nasser, who began a virulent media campaign against the MB, which culminated in the events of the evening of 26 October 1954, when the media announced that Nasser had been saved from an assassination attempt while delivering a speech in Alexandria. Some say the incident was staged, but Nasser pointed the finger at the MB. The People's Court sentenced six well-known MB leaders to death. Others were condemned to life imprisonment. Tens of thousands of MB members were detained in military prisons, including formerly close Nasser associates; the majority were young men, but women and men in their seventies were also imprisoned. There followed a series of public trials, which the MB condemned as merely theatrical. But Nasser held fast, and during the next ten years large numbers of the MB remained in prison for crimes against the state. From time to time new sweeps for MB members would take place, followed by more public trials, as, for example, happened again in 1965. During the 1967 War, patriotic MB members in prison asked Nasser to release them to help face the Israelis on the frontlines; but even then Nasser refused and MB members continued to languish in Egyptian prisons.

It was not until after the death of Nasser, on 28 September 1970, that the repression of the MB would start to ease. When Anwar Sadat came to power, political life and governance began to change drastically in Egypt; Sadat's approach was everything that Nasser's had not been. Initially encountering opposition from Nasserites, Sadat had learned from Nasser's mistakes. He hoped to liberate himself and the people from the impact of the defeat of 1967 by giving them more freedoms and a more Western style of politics. Sadat released all MB members still in prison (the last five were released in 1974). Sadat had not forgotten that the MB had provided financial aid to him and his family during the hardships he had faced before the revolution. He extended freedom to students, who started to regain their natural rights and resumed various activities, including Islamic-oriented ones and the study of the *da'wa*, inside higher education institutes and universities. Consequently MB information was available to students as well as information relating to their curricula. Moreover, the MB magazine attempted to help students by printing explanations of university subjects.

The third stage (1975 to the present)

Re-emergence into the community and the Islamic Jamate of Egypt

The Ikhwan gradually began to regain their power. Newly released senior members began to become socially active and talk freely. They began once again to publish their magazine, and ran offices in Cairo and other cities, as well as printing and publishing houses. They benefited greatly from the new freedom under President Sadat.

They found in the university a good place for the *da'wa*, just as al-Banna had taught them. During the first five years of Sadat's rule, the students worked very hard to combat communism and spread Islamism. They established the Islamic Community (Islamic Jamate of Egypt) in all universities as a single, overarching Islamic youth organisation which, by popular vote, soon controlled the student unions after the long period of Nasserism, socialism, liberalism and secularism.

Towards the mid-1970s, the Islamic Jamate divided into two groups. The major part officially joined the MB. The other group continued to call itself al-Jam'a al-Islamiyya, and was later involved in violence, before separating into two groups towards the end of the 1970s. In addition to other traditional Islamic organisations, there were now three Islamic groups operating in the universities and in Egyptian public life: the Muslim Brotherhood, which still believed in peaceful reform through the Islamisation of the individual, the family and society before the establishment of the Islamic state; the Islamic Jamate of Egypt, which had turned to violence; and the Jamate-offshoot, al-Jihad, which also condoned the use of force.

The assassination of Sadat

In 1981 Sadat was assassinated by members of the Islamic Jamate and al-Jihad after visiting Israel and signing the Camp David peace treaty with Israel in 1979. Shortly before his death, Sadat had detained intellectuals who opposed the Camp David Accords, or the political trend adopted by Sadat to detach Egypt from Arab nationalism and Arab unity. These intellectuals were from all walks of life in Egypt. The Egyptian government believed that one of the many barriers to the normalisation of relations with Israel lay in opposition from Islamic groups.

The main force leading this opposition was the MB, and many members were imprisoned, including the new *murshid*, 'Umar al-Tilmisani. Kamal al-Sannaniri, a senior leader of the MB, died – perhaps violently – in prison in 1981, for his part in advocating and coordinating assistance for and unity with the Afghan *mujahidin*, though the Egyptian government claimed that al-Sannaniri had committed suicide.

Following the assassination of Sadat, members of Islamic Jamate and al-Jihad were imprisoned, including al-Zawahari, the future would-be second man in al-Qaeda. Those who were not detained, and those who were released or escaped, managed to flee to Yemen or Saudi Arabia, or to Afghanistan via Pakistan, where the leadership of the Afghani Jihad was very active. In Pakistan and Afghanistan, the Jihadi and Islamic Jamate groups began to reorganise their efforts and structures. The free atmosphere in Pakistan, especially in Peshawar, gave them the time and means to implement their project – especially its violent aspects. These would become the roots of al-Qaeda and other movements that would exploit the name of Islamic *jihad*, and lead to the well-known events that played out in New York, Nairobi, Madrid and elsewhere.

The MB in Afghanistan

The Ikhwan participated in *jihad* in Afghanistan. I myself was in charge of MB activities in Afghanistan for six years, from 1988 to 1994. MB members came from all over the Arab world, the wider Muslim world, and beyond. Social workers and research workers came from outside Egypt, but most of the doctors, teachers and some of its engineers were Egyptians. The Egyptian Medical Syndicate organised and/or funded 95 per cent of the doctors working in Afghanistan, in relief agencies both controlled by the MB and independent of the Brotherhood. There was a coordination centre for the MB in Peshawar. The Institute of Policy Studies (IPS) was established by Professor Khurshid Ahmad in 1979 in Islamabad. The Arabic department of the IPS – that I established in the 1980s – was a joint project between the Ikhwan and Professor Ahmad, the deputy *amir* ('leader') of the Islamic Jamate in Pakistan. The MB started doing some research on Afghanistan in Arabic and published a weekly magazine, *Qadaya Dawaliyya* (International Issues), using the IPS library and training facilities. The author was an advisor of IPS and editor of *Qadaya Dawaliyya* from 1988 to 1994. The Islamic Jamate of Pakistan differs utterly from Egypt's Islamic Jamate in its views, methods of achievement of its aims, political participation and other matters.

But it has been broadly similar to the MB in its manner of reform. Moreover, the Ikhwan managed to establish and run hospitals and schools in cooperation with other groups across Afghanistan, especially along the length of the border with Pakistan. The MB also managed schools, hospitals, clinics and other development projects inside Afghanistan, in places such as Jalalabad, Kandahar, Khost, Helmand and Herat.

One of the major responsibilities of the Ikhwan was to coordinate the efforts of the *mujahidin* leaders, encouraging them to cooperate among themselves, training new individuals who were not exclusively affiliated to their tribes or political parties, and developing strong loyalty to Afghanistan as a nation and to the Muslim *umma* as a whole. Many of the young men trained by the MB during those years have come of age, and are now working for the development of Afghanistan in different fields of activity. They represent the Islamic movement's long-term investment in Afghanistan. During this author's leadership of MB activities in Afghanistan, no distinction was made between the different Islamic groups and their leaders – all of them were considered *mujahidin*. But the majority of Arabs involved in Afghanistan were closer to particular Afghan leaders: 'Abd al-Rabb Rasul Sayyaf and Burhanuddin Rabbani, both members of the MB of Afghanistan (*Akhwan-ul-Muslimen*), were particularly popular leaders. The Pakistanis and some of the Arabs had a preference for Hekmatyar, who, with Rabbani, was among the founders of the Afghan Islamic movement known as the Islamic Society of Afghanistan al-Jamah al-Islamiah, and were hopeful of Afghan leadership potential. However, the MB, and the moderate Wasati Islamic movement[18] in general, did not make these distinctions.

The MB in Egypt under Mubarak (1981–2008)

The International Organisation of Muslim Brotherhoods

As we have seen, before President Sadat was assassinated in 1981 by military jihadists, mainly as revenge for the Camp David treaty and bad governance

---

18. This term refers to a mainstream, moderate movement which aims to emulate the understanding and religious practice of the Prophet Muhammad and his companions. It shuns extreme and radical behaviour.

of Egypt, most leading Egyptian intellectuals had been detained and imprisoned. Mustafa Mashhur – who succeeded 'Umar Tilmisani and became the fifth *murshid* of the MB – was abroad at that time. He began, together with other senior brothers, to think about the future, about spreading the MB's *da'wa* to other countries, protecting their achievements and releasing themselves from the siege imposed on the MB, especially in Egypt. As the mother organisation to so many national Muslim Brotherhoods, Mashhur and the others felt it was in everyone's interest to establish, in early 1982, the International Organisation of Muslim Brotherhoods. It was actually an international or global-coordination body of the MB. This body – meeting mainly outside Egypt – managed to harmonise efforts among MB branches, issue statements on serious matters, support those under siege or in danger and, in general, discuss issues facing the *umma*, such as Palestine, the Gulf crisis, the Iraqi invasion of Kuwait and the American invasions of Iraq and Afghanistan. It managed to discuss other major issues as well, including internal, organisational, cultural, educational and political issues relating to the future of the movement, addressing secularist governance in the Muslim world and discussing how change could best be effected.

Political coalitions

The MB entered political coalitions for the elections of 1984 and 1987 and in the 1990s, with the officially acknowledged Egyptian political parties: al-Wafd, al-'Amal and others. They then began to run in elections as independents in the 1990s and in 2005. In the 1987 elections, the MB achieved around 17 per cent of the vote, against the ruling National Party's 69 per cent, the new Wafd party's almost 11 per cent, the al-Tajamu' 'leftists' more than 2 per cent, and the al-Umma party's 0.19 per cent. This showed clearly that, politically, the MB was becoming the dominant political opposition, even though they had no legal (licensed) political party, since they remained, unjustifiably, banned.

In the most recent elections in 2005, MB candidates were elected in 88 out of 444 seats. Ten additional seats are always appointed by the president; but it is unlikely that any of these would ever be given to the MB. In spite of the MB's political achievements, it continues to be a banned organisation, based on the presumption that it is a violent organisation. It is therefore not allowed any air time in the state-controlled media.

Spreading out into Egyptian society

During the 1980s and early 1990s, the MB managed to control the majority of professional, medical, engineering, science, education, law and journalism unions, in which they made great efforts to stop corruption. Unfortunately, the government saw this as a future political threat. There was a formal government crackdown on the MB in these professional syndicates to prevent the MB in Egypt from accessing these platforms. In spite of this, the MB used what narrow freedom was available to it to spread as much into Egyptian society as it could, providing vital services to needy, neglected and frustrated people. It was especially active in the fields of education, health and social services; through formal parliamentary channels, it tried to Islamise the behaviour of those participating in the political process, and also to Islamise public policies. How far it has succeeded will remain for future researchers to decide.

MB statements on major world events

No major event or issue in the world – whether national, regional or global – fails to merit an official statement from the MB expressing its point of view. Statements are also issued on Egyptian national concerns: on corruption, electoral fraud, the misuse of military courts, police violence, the proper role of Egypt, the building of Egyptian society, the succession of power after Mubarak, relationships with other Islamic groups, women in politics and so on. Statements issued on regional matters have concerned Arab unity, the Arab League, Arab summits, the Palestinian issue, the invasion of Kuwait, the invitation of American troops to the Gulf, Iraq and Afghanistan, the India–Pakistan conflict, the crises in Sudan and Somalia, the Iran–Iraq War, the Lebanon crisis, and many others. On global issues, the MB has issued statements on the Cold War, American hegemony, the economic crisis, and Westernisation, as well as making general pronouncements condemning violence, extremism and terrorism. It has also issued statements on human rights, non-Muslim minorities under Muslim governance and many other matters.

A clear stand on the Arab–Israeli conflict

As we have seen, Hassan al-Banna was actively involved in the Palestine issue as early as 1935, launching supportive media campaigns, relief support, the formation of committees to explain the Palestinian issue to Egyptians, sending delegations to visit Palestine and discussing duties and responsibilities with the Palestinian revolutionary leadership.

This support continued until the main resistance in Palestine had itself become largely Islamic, when part of that resistance, namely the Hamas movement, became associated with the MB in 1987. There are many statements, articles and books that deal with this matter elsewhere. The Islamisation processes of the MB continue to act both horizontally and vertically all over the Arab and Muslim world.

The Military Courts in Egypt (1995 and 2007)

The Military Courts in Egypt represent an extremely black mark in the so-called democratic Egyptian regime that is so admired by the West, and a cause of very deep concern. As the main political opposition in Egypt, the MB as a whole was put on trial in 1948, 1953, 1954, 1965, 1981, 1995 and 2007, and other small factions at dates in between. The current regime has not allowed anyone to run in the most recent presidential elections against the veteran Mubarak. Even the secularist liberal, Dr Ayman Nur – of the Hizb al-Ghad ('Future Party') – is in prison for daring to run in presidential elections against Mubarak. Senior MB leaders in London tried to help Ayman Nur, despite his liberalism and secularism, in an effort to get rid of what has essentially become an unopposed dictatorship by Mubarak.

The MB political programme and the democratisation process in Egypt

Hassan al-Banna understood Islam to be a comprehensive way of life, with politics and governance being parts of Islam. Politics in Islam might operate through a multi-party system, but only if it were without any spirit of partisanship or national division caused by corrupting party influences. For al-Banna, a Muslim is not a full Muslim unless he is interested in politics and does his part to care for his country, his *umma* and the whole of humanity. MB members must always be politicians, but never partisans. Twice before becoming *murshid* of the Muslim Brotherhood, Mamun al-Hudaiby ran in parliamentary elections and in his political programme articulated his clear principles about the place of Islam in the democratisation process. By 2007 the MB had refined these principles into a coherent set of core political beliefs.[19]

The MB bases its political activities on the concept that the people are the source of all power, and that the transfer of power must occur through free, clear elections. It believes that all people should have freedom of belief and worship and that there should also be freedoms of expression, access to the media, forming associations and holding meetings and peaceful demonstrations. There should be freedom to form political parties, or indeed to act independently. The people should be fairly represented through parliamentary elections, and no citizen – male or female – should be excluded from participation, in relation either to being represented or to being an elected member of parliament and its councils, according to properly and legally defined general conditions. The judicial system should be independent at all times, and military courts should have jurisdiction over military personnel only. A distinction should remain between investigative authority and judgment: the attorney bureau should be independent, not affiliated to the Ministry of Justice, and the right of appeal should be guaranteed. The army should be kept away from politics and confined to its own functions. The police and security forces should be civil servants concentrating on the sole purpose of preserving the internal peace of the society.

The Muslim Brotherhood has come to the same conclusion as that expressed by the Middle East Director of Human Rights Watch, Sarah Leah Whitson, who said on 4 January 2007:

> The government [of Egypt] has for decades used the political parties law to fix elections before they begin. Egypt needs a new political parties law that respects Egyptians' rights to form political parties and to vote for whoever they choose.

Today's Muslim Brotherhood could not agree more. This short article has only touched upon many aspects, both positive and negative, of the Muslim Brotherhood's rich and very long history. There is much room for more scholarly research, and access to the many living senior members who have lived through the historical events of the movement described in this chapter.

---

19. The MB prepared a draft of their political agenda for limited circulation to selected intellectuals and politicians. After their advice was incorporated the final agenda was published.

FIVE

Political Islam in North Africa

Youcef Bouandel

North Africa, or the Maghreb, comprises the countries of Algeria, Morocco, Tunisia, Libya and Mauritania. Covering the socio-political developments of Islamism within this vast geographical area in the limited space available here would do no justice to the subject matter. Thus, the following discussion will focus only on the first three countries. The population of these countries is about 78 million, more than 95 per cent of whom are Sunnis, who are also characterised by a wide spectrum of beliefs and practices. Linguistically, even though Arabic is the official language in these countries, French is widely used and there are a number of dialects spoken throughout the region, the most important of which is Berber, or Tamazight. Furthermore, these countries share the same colonial past – they were all colonised by France, and were politically integrated into it.

The impact of France's presence in these countries is most clearly visible in Algeria – which remained under French domination for 132 years (1830–1962) compared with shorter periods in neighbouring countries. Consequently, during this period, France managed to dismantle all the existing social institutions, and replaced them with its own structures. Therefore, by comparison to other countries in North Africa, Algeria was the country least equipped to deal with the new challenges it faced after gaining independence in 1962. What these countries have in common, however, is that after gaining independence, they did not, on the whole, tolerate the expansion of political Islam; on the contrary, they tried to contain and control it. Hence, the state appointment of imams and control over what was preached in the mosques became the norm. The success of these policies varied between the countries. Morocco has allowed the greatest role of Islam in politics, as a consequence of the type of political system operating in the country. The king, in whose hands all powers are concentrated, claims to be a direct descendant of the Prophet Muhammad and holds the title of Commander of the Faithful. He thereby has religious legitimacy, and is perceived to be the guardian of religious values. Consequently, his position and claim to legitimacy are less likely to be challenged by Islamists than in neighbouring republican countries. Tunisia is at the other end of the political spectrum. It is the country that has gone furthest in limiting the role of Islam – not only in politics, but in the average Tunisian's daily life. Former president Habib Bourguiba (1965–87) encouraged Tunisians to adopt Western lifestyles by not observing the holy month of Ramadan, and discouraged women from wearing the *hijab*. Algeria's experience has fallen somewhere in between. The Islamic movement there has been closely invigilated and repressed at times. When it suited the interests of the regime, it was not only tolerated but even encouraged.

Until recently, Islamic political movements in the three countries were not allowed to operate, and were consequently driven underground. Over the last two decades, however, these countries have experienced the growth of political Islam, which represented not only a challenge but also a threat to the stability of incumbent regimes. The threat, it must be stressed, was greater in Algeria than it was in Morocco or Tunisia. In any event, the governments of the three countries did indeed, at least at certain times, encourage the activities of the Islamists to counter the growth of other ideological currents, such as the Berberist movement in Algeria in the early 1980s; they also encouraged the more moderate elements of the Islamist movement in order to weaken the more extremist and radical wing. This, as will be demonstrated later, was the case in Algeria with the creation of Hamas[1] – later the Movement for Society and Peace – which was created to reduce the appeal of the Islamic Salvation Front, and with the Moroccan Party for Peace and Development, which was created in order to counter the popularity of the Jami'a al-'Adl wa'l-Ihsan (Justice and Charity Organisation).

The growth of Islamist political movements in the countries of North Africa followed the same pattern – the political systems allowed them to emerge, to give the appearance of tolerance and reduce the threats of the more radical groups. While there has not been any obvious cooperation between the Islamist groups in the three countries, they seem to have followed the same pattern of action in their three North Africa countries. On the one hand, there are those groups that opted to play the political game and restrain their activities to what was permissible by law. Examples of this include Hamas (the Movement for Society

---

1. It is worth mentioning that there is no official link between this Algerian group and the well-known Palestinian Hamas movement established in the Gaza Strip and the West Bank in December 1987.

and Peace) in Algeria, the Party for Peace and Development in Morocco and al-Nahda in Tunisia. On the other hand, there are groups that opted for violence as a means of changing the regimes in place. They believed that only through sustained violent attacks on the regime and its symbols would they eventually overthrow the government. They adopted a Salafist approach to the idea of *takfir* – the ability to declare someone an apostate – the punishment for which, under Islamic law, is death. Hence these groups called anybody working for the government, whether military or civilian, a *kafir*, with the implication that killing him would not be punishable by God. On the contrary, such an action would be perceived not only as just, but as earning a reward in the afterlife. Hence, terms such as *taghut* ('tyrant') freely entered the Algerian political lexicon to describe members of the Algerian security services. Resisting tyrants by whatever means, including violence, was not only the duty of every Muslim – liberal philosophy and the principles of human rights have even allowed for it.[2]

In this chapter I am going to examine the growth of political Islam in North Africa. I will look at the tactics used by the different groups, as well as the responses of the respective governments in the region. I will begin with a discussion of Algeria, and then move on to Morocco, and finally Tunisia. The chapter concludes with a summary of the similarities and differences between the experiences of the three countries, and makes a number of recommendations of what needs to be done to accommodate the growth of political Islam in the region.

Algeria

While Algeria is a Muslim country and Islam has always played an important part in the daily life of ordinary Algerians, political Islam did not manifest itself fully until the mid-1980s. When the French occupied Algeria in 1830,

2. According to Weston, man entered into a social contract with the state: 'Human-kind surrendered to the state only the right to enforce these natural rights, not the rights themselves [and that] the state's failure to secure these reserved rights (the state itself being under social contract to safeguard the interests of its members) gives rise to a right and responsible popular revolution.' From Burns Weston, 'Human Rights', *Human Rights Quarterly* vol. 6, no. 2, 1984, p. 258. Furthermore, the Preamble of the Universal Declaration of Human Rights, adopted on 10 December 1948, provides that 'it is essential, if man is not to be compelled to have recourse, as a last resort, to rebellion against tyranny and oppression, that human rights should be protected by the rule of law'.

they embarked on a process of dismantling the existing institutions and began to integrate Algeria into the French state. In order to resist such integration, Algerian reformers from the early 1930s organised themselves, under the leadership of Shaykh Abdelhamid Ben Badis, in a group they called Association of Algerian Muslim 'Ulama (AUMA). They started to establish schools to spread their teaching throughout the country, and to raise people's awareness about the Algerian Arabo-Islamic identity. A few members of this organisation, such as Shaykh Ahmed Sahnoun and Shaykh Abdellatif Soltani, would play a significant role in the Islamist movement in Algeria in the 1960s, 1970s and 1980s.

The reformers had exercised strong influence on the nationalist party of Messali El Haj – the Parti du Peuple Algerien (PPA). This influence persisted with the creation of the National Liberation Front (FLN), the nationalist movement that led the armed struggle against France in 1954; after all, the leaders of the FLN were former members of the PPA. The proclamation of 1 November 1954, which declared war against the French occupation, made reference to Islam. Indeed, when the FLN began to attack French interests in Algeria, they found support from the *'ulama* – the FLN's action came under the banner of *jihad*, which was a duty for every Muslim under occupation. According to Hugh Roberts, following 'the allying of the Association with the FLN in 1956, its senior members were permanently represented within the FLN leadership'.[3]

Hence, the nationalist fight for independence that the FLN led was given an element of religious legitimacy. Algerian fighters who took up arms against French occupation were known as *mujahidin* – a clear indication of the influence of religion on the armed struggle. Despite this influence, however, Islam quickly lost its dominant position after the country achieved independence. Successive Algerian governments from 1962 until at least the late 1970s adopted socialism as the state ideology, made Islam the country's official religion and managed to consolidate their grip on the religious sphere – though Boumedienne, the longest-serving Algerian president before the 1991 elections (1965–78), was more successful in this than his predecessor Ben Bella (1963–5).

3. Hugh Roberts, 'From Radical Mission to Equivocal Ambition: The Expansion and Manipulation of the Algerian Islamism, 1979–1992', in Martin Marty and Scott Appelby, eds, *Accounting for Fundamentalists: The Dynamic Character of Movements*, Chicago: The University of Chicago Press, 1994, p. 433.

Nevertheless, the Islamist movement in Algeria remained active without representing a real threat to the regime in place. It was very peaceful, and its challenge to the system did not go beyond criticism of government policies and what it perceived to be a diversion from the true path of Islam. In January 1964, for instance, the al-Qiyam (Values) association was created, which included several former members of the AUMA.[4] It was independent of the state, and Malek Bennabi (1905–73), a well-known independent Islamist Algerian thinker, provided the intellectual leadership for it. It called for the reduction of the continuous influence of French culture, and called upon the government to take positive steps towards promoting the use of the Arabic language and Islamic values in society. The association's president, Hachemi Tijani, clearly identified with Muslim thinkers such as Hassan al-Banna, who founded the Muslim Brotherhood in Egypt in 1928, and Sayyid Qutb, who espoused radical views, such as considering contemporary Muslim societies living in total ignorance of Islam *jahiliyya*.[5] These developments resulted in greater pressure being placed on the regime of Ben Bella, who moved on to dismiss Tijani from his post at the University of Algiers. According to Roberts, the creation of this association led, in the mid-1960s, to a loss of control by the regime over a significant aspect of Algerian life – the 'religious sphere' – when President Ben Bella found himself unable to enlist the support of any respectable Muslim figure to attack al-Qiyam from a religious perspective.[6] The association became a source of embarrassment to the regime in Algiers as Boumedienne, who had toppled President Ben Bella in a bloodless *coup d'état* on 19 June 1965, tried to strengthen his grip on power by presenting his regime as Islamic, and by taking steps towards silencing the organisation.

---

4. It should be pointed out that Abbasi Madani was a member of this association. He played a pivotal role in the Islamist movement in Algeria in the 1970s, and especially in the 1980s, when he became the leader of the Islamic Salvation Front.

5. Willis stated that, despite explicitly claiming to be the inheritors of the legacy and ideals of Ben Badis's AUMA, al-Qiyam was clearly a more radical organisation. The association's hostility towards non-Islamic ideas and organisations, illustrated above, displayed, as Jean-Claude Vatin and Jean Leca rightly argue, 'a fanatical fundamentalism, quite foreign to the thought of the founder of the Association of Ulama'. Michael Willis, *The Islamist Challenge in Algeria: A Political History*, Berkshire: Ithaca Press, 1996, p. 64.

6. Hugh Roberts, 'Radical Islamism and the Dilemma of Algerian Nationalism: The Embattled Arians of Algiers', *Third World Quarterly*, vol. 10, no. 2 (1988), p. 564.

Hence Willis reports that a 'prefectural decree in September 1966 ordered the dissolution of Al-Qiyam in the [region] of Algiers and three and a half years later a ministerial decree banned the association throughout Algeria'.[7]

None the less, despite the dissolution of the association, it had left its mark on the Algerian Islamist movement. The Arabisation programme that the Algerian authorities introduced after independence to make Arabic the official language resulted in an influx of thousands of visiting teachers from the Middle East, especially Egypt. These teachers played a very significant role in spreading the ideas of the Muslim Brotherhood and raising people's awareness of the Algerian Muslim identity, which had been almost erased by the French. The Islamists started to become more visible and active at universities. The opening of mosques at universities and university halls of residence, which began in the early 1970s, played an important role in organising the Islamist movement.

It should be stressed that it was only after the death of President Houari Boumedienne in December 1978 that the Islamist movement in Algerian started to become stronger and more vocal. The regime of Chadli Bendjedid, who assumed power after Boumedienne and remained in power until the era of elections, encouraged the growth of the Islamist movement in order to counteract the growing Berberist and leftist movements, especially within university campuses and halls of residence. Furthermore, the Islamist movement in Algeria has also benefited from international events such as the Iranian Revolution of 1979 and the invasion of Afghanistan by the former Soviet Union. The success of Ayatollah Khomeini in ending the Shah's rule and establishing a Muslim government in Iran gave hope to the Algerian Islamists that such as scenario was plausible for their country too. Moreover, the invasion of Afghanistan galvanised Muslims throughout the world, and volunteers from the Muslim world went to fight alongside their 'brothers' against the communist invasion. Algerians were no exception, and thousands went to Afghanistan. It was in Afghanistan that they were exposed to a more radical brand of Islam, and when the war was over, in the late 1980s – coinciding with the legalisation of Islamist political parties – these fighters, known as Algerian Afghans, returned to Algeria and played an important role in the radicalisation of the movement.

The election of committees at halls of residence in universities and colleges saw a struggle between the communists and Islamists in particular, which

---

7. Willis, *Islamist Challenge*, p. 46.

resulted in violence and even the loss of life. The killing in early November 1982, in Ben Aknoun hall of residence, of the student Kamal Amzal, by Islamists provides a good example.[8] Furthermore, in the early 1980s Islamists had become more visible in the country, and more vocal in their opposition to the regime. They engaged in a number of activities to show their strength and organisation. For example, several mass prayers were conducted in the centre of Algiers; the blockage of main city-centre avenues was common at the time. When Shaykh Soltani, who had been under house arrest, died in April 1984, his funeral was attended by over 20,000 mourners (according to a conservative estimate) despite the media blackout.[9] This showed not only the esteem in which Shaykh Soltani was held, but also the strength of the Islamist movement.

Until that point, the Islamist movement in Algeria had been largely peaceful, despite a few violent incidents.[10] But this was all changed from the early 1980s by Mustapha Bouyali. Bouyali, who remained on the run until his death, led the al-Haraka al-Islamiyya al-Jazairiyya al-Musallaha – the Armed Algerian Islamic Movement (MIAA) – a small and ruthless Islamic armed movement; he was finally killed by the Algerian security service on 3 January 1987.[11] The MIAA was responsible for a number of setbacks for the Algerian security services, the details of which remained unknown because of media censorship and the non-existence of privately owned media in Algeria at the time. The death of Bouyali marked the end, at least temporarily, of the most serious threat to the Algerian regime from Islamist violence.

In the face of the burgeoning radicalisation of the Islamist movement in Algeria, the authorities not only tried to portray themselves as defenders of Islam, but also to promote a peaceful brand of the religion. Hence,

---

8. The beginning of the clash between the two rival groups, which resulted in the death of a student, was witnessed by the author, who was a student at the University of Algiers and resident in the above hall of residence.

9. This is based on a discussion in London on 2 December 1998 with Professor Abdelhamid Brahimi, Algeria's prime minister from 1984 to 1988.

10. In 1979, Mustapha Bouyali, a former veteran of the Algerian war of independence, deeply disillusioned with the regime in Algeria, formed the Group for the Defence Against the Illicit. In April 1982, his brother Mokhtar was killed by the Algerian security services. He went on the run and turned his organisation into a violent one, named the Armed Algerian Islamic Movement (MIAA).

11. For more details, see François Bougat, *L'Islamisme au Maghre: la voix du sud*, Paris: Editions Karthala, 1988, pp. 164–8.

the Algerian government opened the Emir Abd-el-Kader University for Islamic Sciences in the city of Constantine in 1984, and brought in the eminent Egyptian scholar Shaykh Muhammad al-Ghazali to head the university. Al-Ghazali was a member of the Egyptian Muslim Brotherhood, and promoted a brand of tolerant and peaceful Islam. In order to combat the spread of a more radical interpretation of Islam, the Algerian authorities spared no effort in publicising al-Ghazali's ideas and teachings with extensive media coverage. He even had his own weekly television programme, shown every Monday at about 7.30 p.m. – just before the main evening news.

It was not until the late 1980s and 1990s that the Islamist movement in Algeria started to play an increasing role in the political life of the country. The failings of the successive regimes in Algeria led to the opening up of political space to previously excluded groups. The provision of economic and social needs, which had previously provided the basis for the regime's legitimacy, was no longer relevant. With the sharp fall in world oil prices, Algeria's revenues were halved, and the government was no longer able to cater for these economic and social needs to the extent they had been able to in the past. The regime thus sought other sources of legitimacy, one of which was the opening up of political space. Islamic political parties took advantage of these new freedoms and applied for recognition. A number of Islamic parties, such as the Islamic Salvation Front (FIS), Hamas later known as the Movement for Soiety and Peace (MSP), al-Nahda and al-Islah began their legal political activity.[12]

The strengthening of Islamist movements in Algeria was the result of the state's disengagement from traditional sectors, such as the provision of welfare. During the earthquake in Algiers in 1989, for instance, the authorities were late in taking care of the victims and the Islamists were able to capitalise on their mistakes. They provided necessary help and support, according to their means, and comforted the victims of the earthquake. Secondly, the popularity of the Islamists may have been magnified by the level of distrust that ordinary Algerians had for the incumbent regime. In other words, those

---

12. According to some close observers of Algerian affairs, the Algerian Securité Militaire (secret service) was behind the creation of Hamas, whose aim was to split the FIS's support. For further details, see Mohand Salah Tahi, 'Algeria's Democratisation Process: A Frustrated Hope', *Third World Quarterly*, vol. 16, no. 2 (1994), pp. 209–24, and Willis, *Islamist Challenge*.

who opted for the Islamists – the only credible opposition able to put an end to the one-party rule – did so not because they were Islamists themselves, but because they wanted to end the FLN's rule.

Local and regional elections were held in December 1990, and the Islamic Salvation Front won a convincing majority of 57.4 per cent.[13] The results stunned the authorities in Algiers, and for the first time they realised the strength of the Islamist movement in the country. In an attempt to ensure the FIS's defeat, the Algerian authorities had changed the electoral law before the elections, redesigning the electoral boundaries. The FIS's leadership responded by calling a general strike in early June 1991, and clashes with the police ensued. The prime minister, Mouloud Hamrouche, was relieved of his office, and another government, whose main task was to prepare for a clean and transparent legislative election, was installed under the stewardship of Sid Ahmed Ghozali.[14]

When the first round of the legislative election was held on 26 December 1991, the FIS won 188 of the 232 seats declared, and needed only 28 more seats to win a majority in parliament – and thus to form a government – in the second round, scheduled for 16 January 1992.[15] The military responded by nullifying the results of the first round, cancelling the second round and forcing President Chadli Bendjedid to resign. The High Council of State (HCE), a five-man body under the leadership of Mohammed Boudiaf, was entrusted with running the country. Three decisions that the HCE took would have disastrous effects on the future development of the Islamist movement in particular, and the situation in the country in general. The decisions were: the declaration of a state of emergency in February 1992; the banning of the FIS a month later; and the subsequent internment of many Islamist activists in the south of the country.

These actions had a domino effect, turning neutrals into sympathisers, sympathisers into activists, and the activists into radicals. The country experienced a level of violence reminiscent of the Algerian war of independence

13. Belkacem Iratni and Mohand Salah Tahi, 'The Aftermath of Algeria's First Free Local Elections', *Government and Opposition* vol. 26, no. 4 (1992), pp 466–79.
14. Youcef Bouandel, 'Reforming the Algerian Electoral System', *Journal of Modern African Studies*, vol. 43, no. 3 (2005), pp. 393–415.
15. Youcef Bouandel, 'Algerian National Popular Assembly Election of December 1991', *Representation*, vol. 32, no. 117 (Winter/Spring 1993/4), pp. 10–14.

(1954–62). Several terrorist organisations came into being, as the Islamists resorted to violence in order to discredit the regime. Perhaps the most infamous of these organisations were the Islamic Armed Group (GIA), the Salafist Group for Preaching and Combat (GSPC) and, to a lesser extent, the Islamic Salvation Army (AIS). Different groups used different tactics, ranging from the indiscriminate massacre of innocent civilians in remote areas to the targeting of high-profile individuals such as artists and journalists. Government officials, especially those working for the security services, were the particular target of such terrorist attacks. Security personnel were commonly referred to by the Islamists as *taghut* ('tyrant') and *kafir* ('infidel'), providing the moral justification for their killing. In other words, the killing of those that could be termed *kafir* or *taghut* was an action bringing rewards in the afterlife. Other spectacular actions included the targeting of foreign nationals operating in Algeria, the hijacking of a French commercial airline in December 1994, as well as involvement in terrorist activities outside Algeria – particularly in France.

As we have seen, the GIA and GSPC were at the forefront of a campaign of terrorism, leading to the deaths of between 100,000 and 250,000 people.[16] None the less, the violence in the country seems to have declined as a result of both the government and terrorist organisations realising that violence could not resolve the outstanding issues. Consequently, negotiations between the terrorist groups and the Algerian authorities resulted in the adoption of the Law on Civil Harmony in 1999 and the Charter for National Reconciliation in 2005. These measures provided the terrorists with amnesties and lenient treatment in exchange for their abandonment of the armed rebellion, thereby restoring their place in society.[17]

Despite these improvements, however, it should be pointed out that Islamist terrorism was not completely eradicated. As a matter of fact, in an ominous development in 2006, the notorious terrorist group, the GSPC,

---

16. It is very difficult to come to an exact figure of the number of those killed during the Algerian tragedy since 1991. In the late 1990s, Ahmed Ouyahia, then prime minister, put the death toll at about 26,000 people, while President Bouteflika spoke of 100,000 deaths. Opposition figures put the number of deaths closer to a quarter of a million.

17. For further details, see Youcef Bouandel, 'Algeria's Arduous Search for Peace' in David Neville-Wright and Anna Halafoff, eds, *Managing Cultural Conflict in Diverse Societies*, Edward Elgar, (forthcoming).

formally merged with other North African groups and al-Qaeda to form a new organisation, called the al-Qaeda Organisation for the Islamic Maghreb. Terrorist tactics in Algeria seemed to have changed, as innocent civilians were spared and efforts were concentrated against symbols of the Algerian regime. Hence, this newly formed group claimed responsibility for the spectacular and extremely well-coordinated attacks in Algiers in March 2007, which targeted the offices of the prime minister and several police stations. Following the increase in the scale of the group's attacks, the US embassy in Algiers issued a warning that terrorist groups in Algeria were planning a terrorist attack on a commercial flight between Algiers and a European destination. More worrying were the attacks on the offices of the Constitutional Council and of the United Nations in December 2007, in one of the most exclusive and well-protected areas of Algiers. Furthermore, the more recent attacks, in the summer of 2008, in the provinces of Jijel, Skikda and Boumerdes, in which members of the security forces and recruits to the Gendarmerie Nationale were targeted, are proof of the continued determination of these terrorist groups to wage war against the Algerian regime.

Morocco

Like Algeria, and to a lesser extent Tunisia, the independence movement in Morocco was rooted, among other things, in religion. Charitable organisations were set up in the 1920s and 1930s whose aim was to establish free schools to enable young Moroccans to study Arabic and religion, and many leaders of the independence movement were associated with these schools. Consequently, the role that Islam played in the achievement of independence established it as an important feature in the political landscape of independent Morocco. Furthermore, a monarchy was established after independence under King Mohammed V – whose ancestors, it is alleged, go back to the Prophet of Islam. He held the title of Commander of the Faithful, and was both the religious and political leader of his country. The same title and position were assumed by his son Hassan II in 1961, and in 2000 by his grandson, the current king, Mohammed VI. As Commander of the Faithful, and with his alleged descent from the Prophet, the Moroccan king enjoys the religious legitimacy that the leaders of neighbouring Algeria and Tunisia clearly lack.

Islam remains an important component of Moroccan daily life, especially in the countryside. This tradition is supported by the fact that the king enjoys the political and religious authority in the country, as Moroccans hold the 'holy trinity' of God, country and king to be sacred. In other words, according to this trinity, any criticism of the king is perceived as treason. Under these circumstances, it seems that opposition to the regime from the Islamists is most unlikely. After all, how can an opposition in the name of Islam emerge against the symbol and protector of Islam in Morocco, the 'Commander of the Faithful'? None the less, such opposition, both peaceful and violent, challenging the authority of the king, has become increasingly vocal. The strength of this opposition has been on the increase over the last three decades, and has benefited from concurrent developments in neighbouring Algeria, as well as the rest of the world.

The Moroccan Islamist movement shares a number of characteristics with that of Algeria. There are those who are openly critical of the system, and those who have been co-opted by the authorities. Unlike in Algeria, the biggest Islamic group in Morocco chooses not to be involved in the political process, and remains outside the political arena. As in the Algerian experience, however, another group of Islamists chose violence and terrorist activities not only inside Morocco, but also outside it – particularly in Europe. Thus, the Moroccan Islamist movement can be broadly divided into three main camps: the first is the peaceful, non-political anti-monarchy wing, represented by Jami'a al-'Adl wa'l-Ihsan (the Justice and Charity Organisation); the second is the political, pro-monarchy wing, represented by Hizb al-'Adl wa'l-Tanmiyya (the Justice and Development Party); and the third is the violent terrorist wing, represented, among other groups, by the Moroccan Islamic Combatant Group (GICM).[18]

Islamic opposition to the king dates back to the 1970s, but intensified during the 1980s because of the tensions and animosities that existed between the late King Hassan II and Shaykh Yassine, who, in the 1970s, established the Justice and Charity Organisation. The latter is an anti-monarchical group that has found unexpected – and indeed unprecedented – popularity among average Moroccan citizens. Given the popularity of

18. Samir Amghar divides the Moroccan Islamist movement into two main groups – the Justice and Charity Organisation and the Justice and Development Party. See Samir Amghar, *Political Islam in Morocco*, Centre for European Policy Studies, CEPS Working Document 269 (June 2007), p. 1.

this organisation and the unprecedented rise of the Islamists in neighbouring Algeria, in 1990 the Moroccan authorities took the decision to outlaw this organisation, and Shaykh Yassine was placed under surveillance. After King Hassan II died in 2000, his successor, Mohammed VI, ended the surveillance of Yassine and adopted a more flexible approach. The movement is still officially outlawed but has continued to demand recognition by the authorities.

One of the most significant criticisms that the organisation levels against the Moroccan regime is that the monarchy uses Islam for its own benefit. While Islam is used as the basis for conferring legitimacy on the monarchy, the monarch does not necessarily follow the teachings and rules of Islam. Furthermore, the organisation disputes the king's position as Commander of the Faithful, and argues that Islam is against inherited power and that political leadership should be determined through the ballot box. According to Nadia Yassine, the daughter of the Justice and Charity Organisation's founder, 'the monarchy is not made for Morocco ... the Constitution deserves to be thrown upon the garbage heap of history, [and] all signs indicate that the monarchy will soon collapse'.[19] Hence, the organisation calls for the adoption of a republican model of government, and has been at loggerheads with the new king despite his relaxation of the government's position on the organisation and its leadership. None the less, repressive measures have been used to silence the organisation and harass its leadership.

This organisation shares significant political and ideological terrain with the majority of other Islamist movements, in North Africa and elsewhere, which prioritise the creation of a system of government based on the principle of *khilafa*, following the teachings of the Prophet. None the less, in order to achieve its objectives, this organisation, unlike others, not only does not use violence, but has been very vocal in condemning violence and assassinations. On the contrary, it wants to establish an Islamist society through education, and other peaceful and legal means.

In light of the strength of the Justice and Charity Organisation, the Moroccan authorities allowed, and indeed encouraged, the emergence of an Islamic political party to draw support away from Shaykh Yassine and his organisation. The party brought together a number of small, moderate Islamist organisations. When it came into being it was known as the Constitutional

19. Quoted in Amghar, *Political Islam in Morocco*, p. 2.

and Democratic Popular Movement, before changing its name in 1998 to the Party of Justice and Development (PJD).

Given that the PJD has been legalised by the authorities, that it is moderate in its political discourse, which even resembles that of the state; that it does not question the king's authority or legitimacy – indeed, that it is pro-monarchist, working peacefully within the existing system and stressing that Morocco is already a Muslim country – its critics believe that it is no more that a mouthpiece for the Moroccan authorities, designed to encourage a more peaceful, conformist Islamism in the country.[20]

Unlike Yassine's organisation, the Party for Justice and Development has engaged in politics and presented candidates in successive general elections. Over the last decade the party has made significant advances in Moroccan politics and has been improving its showing in general elections. Following the January 2009 general elections, the Party for Justice and Development became the second-largest party in the Moroccan parliament. The strength of Yassine's organisation, together with the impressive recent showing of the Party for Justice and Development, demonstrates the strong appeal of Islamist discourse in Morocco. This is further demonstrated by the fact that Islamic symbols such as the wearing of the veil by Moroccan women have become more popular.

The third camp in the Islamist movement in Morocco is the most extreme and violent one. Like its counterparts in Algeria, it comprises combatants who were trained, and indeed fought, in Afghanistan against the Soviet occupation during the 1980s. The Moroccan Islamic Combatant Group (GICM), a Salafist organisation, was behind the 23 May 2003 bombing in the city of Casablanca, in which over forty people were killed. As in Algeria, attacks of this kind send strong signals to the state authorities, as well as to more moderate Islamists, that their hold on political and religious discourse is by no means complete, and that another 'voice' is challenging them. Their followers, as we have seen in the Algerian case, were behind a number of the terrorist attacks in Europe, in particular the Madrid bombing of March 2004.

---

20. For further details, see Amghar, *Political Islam in Morocco*, p. 2, and Rollie Lal, 'The Maghreb' in Angel M. Rabasa et al., *The Muslim World After 9/11*, Santa Monica CA: RAND, 2004, pp. 161–2.

Tunisia

Tunisia is commonly referred to as the most Westernised country in the Arab world. The Tunisian government, especially under the leadership of Habib Bourguiba (1956–87), was very secular, limiting the role of Islam in public life, reducing the influence of the *shari'a* courts and that of the famous religious institution, Zaitouna University.[21] Other religious activities and symbols – such as fasting for the holy month of Ramadan, pilgrimage, the wearing of the veil for women and the growing of beards by men – were greatly discouraged. [22] When Zine El Abidine Ben Ali removed Bourguiba in a bloodless coup in November 1987, there were signs that the new leadership would loosen its grip on political power and would seek new government partners. Political prisoners were released, including members of the Islamic Tendency Movement (MTI), which subsequently changed its name to al-Nahda. The president committed himself to negotiating with all political currents including the Islamist, to develop a 'national pact' that would define Tunisia's future direction. Rashid Al Ghannouchi, leader of al-Nahda, delegated a member of his party to take part in the consultation process.[23] The honeymoon lasted for three years; in 1990, undoubtedly after establishing his power base and with an eye on developments in neighbouring Algeria, Ben Ali reverted to his predecessor's policy of repressing the Islamists.

Despite his firm grip on power, Bourguiba faced opposition from several quarters, especially the Islamists. Initially, he encouraged the Islamists to counter the growth of the leftists, especially in university campuses. This action helped the Islamists to grow stronger and started to pressure the Tunisian authorities to give Islam a central role in the politics of the country. Bourguiba's declaration making Islam the state religion showed the extent

---

21. Nazih Ayubi, *Political Islam: Religion and Politics in the Arab World,* London: Routledge, p. 113.

22. Jean-Claude Vatin, 'Revival in the Maghreb' in Ali Desouki ed., *Islamic Resurgence in the Arab World,* New York: Praeger, 1982, pp. 238–9; Georges Anawati and Maurice Borrmans, *Tendances et courants de l'islame arabe contemporain, vol. 1: Egypte et Afrique du Nord,* München and Mainz: Kaiser-Grunewald, 1982, p. 216–17.

23. For further details, see Youcef Bouandel, 'Human Rights in the Maghreb' in Yahia H. Zoubir ed., *North Africa in Transition: State, Society and Economic Transformation in the 1990s,* Gainesville: University of Florida Press, 1998, p. 135.

of the growth of the Islamist movement, but even this announcement did not appease the Islamic opposition. The Islamists took advantage of the obvious unpopularity of Bourguiba's regime and pressed more demands. The bread riots that took place in January 1978 marked the end of the traditional alliance between the official Tunisian trade union (Union Generale des Travailleurs Tunisiens – UGTT) and Bourguiba's regime. Hence, in the late 1970s, the Mouvement de Tendance Islamique (MTI) became more vocal in its criticism of the government. It advised Bourguiba that the only way to solve the country's problems was through the application of Islam and urged him to introduce a multi-party system and parliamentary elections – but he proved unwilling to listen to such demands. He allowed other secular groups to form political parties and refused to grant the same privilege to the Islamists. They violently protested against what they perceived to be an unfair decision. Al-Nahda's actions gave Bourguiba the necessary justification to crack down on its activists. His security forces arrested hundreds of its members and the organisation was accused of being a terrorist group manipulated by Iran.[24]

It was not until the mid-1980s that the leadership of the Islamic movement was released from jail. For almost three years, its members kept a low profile and were not involved in any confrontation with the Tunisian authorities. The situation changed in the summer of 1987, when a number of hotels were bombed and the Islamists were blamed. Several members of the movement were arrested and demonstrations were held against the government during their trials. The sentences handed down to those convicted – which included the death penalty and life imprisonment – did not please Bourguiba. He ordered a retrial in October 1987 and demanded harsher sentences. Because of fear that violence might escalate between the government and members of the Islamist group as a result of Bourguiba's instructions, among other reasons, plans were drawn up to remove the ailing president.[25] On 7 November 1987, Bourguiba was removed from office in a bloodless coup by Zine El Abidine Ben Ali.

---

24. Many Islamic movements sought inspiration from the success of the Iranian Revolution of 1979. Several leaders in the Islamic world were quick to point to the Iranians' involvement in supporting the Islamic movements in their countries.

25. On these points, I am grateful to Brahim Toumi, a former secondary school teacher in Tunisia.

Soon after assuming power, Ben Ali made gestures towards the Islamists, and others, seeking to strengthen his grip on political power. Hundreds of political prisoners – most of them members of the Islamist movement – were released, and the death sentence of one of its leaders, Ali Laaridh, was commuted, while charges were dropped against sixty others. In May of the following year, Ben Ali pardoned its most prominent leader, Rachid Al Ghannouchi, two months later he freed all members who had been charged with 'crimes against public rights' and in September he allowed the group's secretary-general, Abd al-Fattah Mourou, to return home from exile.[26]

None the less, despite making these overtures towards the Islamists and including them in the discussion for the 'national pact', like his predecessor, Ben Ali still refused to recognise officially the newly renamed Haraka al-Nahda (Renaissance Movement). Islamists, were, however, allowed to run as independents for the legislative elections in April 1989. Though they gained no seats in parliament, their popularity and appeal were clear. They won 14.5 per cent of the national vote, and almost one-third of the vote in some of the country's major cities.[27]

The Islamists' showing in the legislative election did not go unnoticed and the Tunisian authorities followed these developments very closely. As events in Algeria started to unfold in the late 1980s, Ben Ali stressed that no political party should monopolise religion, as it did in Algeria, and continued in his refusal to recognise al-Nahda as a political party; he prevented the Islamists and other opposition groups from taking part in the June 1990 local elections. Consequently his honeymoon with the Islamists came to an end, relations between the two started to deteriorate and signs emerged of the possibility of a head-on confrontation between the regime and opposition groups – especially the Islamists. Rachid Al Ghannouchi had always called for the government of Tunisia to open up political space to all the excluded

---

26. M. J. Deeb, 'Militant Islam and the Politics of Redemption', testimony in a hearing on Islamic fundamentalism in Africa and its implications for US policy before the House Subcommittee on Africa, Committee on Foreign Affairs, House of Representatives, 102nd Congress, 2nd session, 20 May 1992, pp. 100–101.

27. For further details, see John L. Esposito, 'Islamic Movements in North Africa', testimony in a hearing on Islamic fundamentalism in Africa and its implications for US policy before the House Subcommittee on Africa, Committee on Foreign Affairs, House of Representatives, 102nd Congress, 2nd session, 20 May 1992, p. 34.

groups, including the Islamists, who had a part to play in the future of Tunisia: government exclusion would undoubtedly lead to bloodshed; Islamists were not necessarily anti-democratic, because 'participation by the Islamists in ... elections is a testimony to their willingness to abide by the rules of the democratic process'.[28]

Events that followed placed the two parties at loggerheads. In 1991, the Islamists organised several demonstrations in support of the three-year-old Palestinian *intifada*, and against the imminent war against Iraq. It was during these demonstrations that the headquarters of the ruling party, the Constitutional Democratic Rally, was burnt, allegedly by the Islamists, causing the loss of one life. The leadership of the Islamist party was accused of plotting to overthrow the government and a campaign of intimidation, harassment and arrest began in earnest. Despite the denials of al-Nahda's leaders, fearing arrest Al Ghannouchi chose exile in Europe with several of the movement's senior members. This further strengthened Ben Ali's grip on power and the appeal of Islamism, at least superficially, seems to have declined.

In addition to the peaceful path followed by the Islamists in Tunisia, as in neighbouring Algeria and Morocco, small groups of Tunisian Islamists, not affiliated to al-Nahda, seem to have engaged in several terrorist activities, though not as spectacular as those in the two other countries. These groups have been more willing than al-Nahda to use violence in order to achieve their goals. One tactic that has been used is the killing of a number of foreign tourists in order to damage the country's economy. Perhaps the most spectacular terrorist action was in 2002, when

> a Tunisian suicide bomber, Nizar Nawar, assisted by relatives, orchestrated a dramatic attack on a historic synagogue on 11 April in Djerba that killed 21 people, mainly German tourists. A group called the 'Islamic Army to Liberate the Holy Places' claimed responsibility in a statement after the attack.[29]

The development of political Islam in North African countries has displayed similar characteristics, with small variations. Islam played an important role in

---

28. Rashid Al Ghannouchi, 'Towards Inclusive Strategies for Human Rights Enforcement in the Arab World – A Response', *Encounters* vol. 2, (1996), p. 191.
29. Lal, 'The Maghreb', p. 157.

their nationalist movements for independence. The authorities in both Algeria and Tunisia, though not in Morocco, encouraged the Islamist movement to counteract the emergence of other opposition groups, particularly those of the left. These actions tended to serve the regimes' immediate interests but contributed to the strength of Islamism. Both Morocco and Algeria, but not Tunisia, legalised Islamist political parties that took part in elections. Indeed, the authorities in both countries, aware of the strength of al-'Adl wa'l-Ihsan in Morocco and of the FIS in Algeria, encouraged the creation of other Islamic organisations, such Hamas and the PJD, in order to counterbalance the more radical organisations. The Islamic movements in the three countries had the same objective: the creation of a Muslim state based on the teachings of the Qur'an and the Prophet. The methods they adopted in pursuit of this objective differed between the various groups in each country: in all three countries there were those that followed the peaceful path by educating the population and taking part in the democratic process and those that opted for violence as a means of expressing their views.

Governments in North Africa cannot continue to ignore the Islamists and they should not see them as inherently anti-democratic. The political discourse they engage in – such as in calling for the opening up of political space and the loosening of the authoritarian nature of the regimes in Algiers, Rabat and Tunis – is shared with even the most secular parties in North Africa. It is only by opening up the political systems and inviting the Islamists to participate in the political life of their respective countries through legal and constitutional means that these governments can succeed in alienating the extremists, and eventually reduce violence.

SIX

The Islamists of Iraq and the Sectarian Factor: The Case of Al-Qaeda in Mesopotamia

Murad Batal al-Shishani

Since its occupation and the toppling of Saddam Hussein's regime in 2003, Iraq has emerged as a fertile ground of different types of Islamist movement: Shi'i and Sunni; groups that believe in political participation or so-called 'peaceful change', and groups that believe in armed *jihad* as the only way to achieve their political goals.

Significantly, these Islamist groups and networks emerged in Iraq as manifestations of the new era in Iraq. Shi'i groups looked to the political change in Iraq as a golden opportunity to rule Iraq, just as they viewed the fall of Saddam Hussein's regime as 'a turning point for a group that had suffered many hundreds of years as a marginalized political entity'.[1] The Shi'is of Iraq lost no time in seizing power at this turning-point.

By contrast, Sunni Arab Iraqis found themselves, for the first time since the early attempts to create an Iraqi state under the British Mandate in the early 1920s, out of power and marginalised. This situation has led to the emergence of many groups – either as outright insurgent groups or, in the case of those groups that have chosen to involve themselves in the new political process in Iraq, as movements of political opposition. Furthermore, the Kurdish Islamist movements consider themselves part of a Kurdish national project, and some of these groups have connected themselves to Iraqi insurgent groups, al-Qaeda in particular.

Most Islamist groups in post-invasion Iraq have turned out to represent sectarian interests rather than any nationwide project aiming to create a democratic secular Iraq in the wake of decades of a despotic regime, and the more than ten years of economic sanctions that badly affected the country.

---

1. Graham E. Fuller, *Islamist Politics in Iraq after Saddam Hussein*, United States Institute of Peace (www.usip.org), 2003.

Describing the division between Sunnis and Shi'is on a sectarian basis, and how it has affected Islamists in Iraq, Graham Fuller argues that 'as a result of years of brutal sectarianism and political violence in Iraq, the Islamist movements of the two communities each operate as independent and separate vehicles for the interests of each community – and are to some extent political rivals.'[2]

Within the context of post-war Iraq, this chapter focuses on the rising importance of religious sects and/or local communities as the background to the emergence of Islamist groups in Iraq today. The discussion will also examine al-Qaeda (and its manifestations) in Iraq as an example of the role of the local community either in directing the political behaviour of Islamist movements, or in legitimising their existence among them.

Al-Qaeda in Iraq (which has since renamed itself the 'Islamic State of Iraq') represents a radical foreign force that has brought to Iraq a 'model of an Islamist group' that had never existed in the country before. Initially, it had been accommodated in Sunni Arab areas of Iraq, but this community subsequently rejected it, as we shall see below. What will follow is first a mapping of Iraqi Islamists and the contexts of their emergence, and then an examination of Iraq from the Salafi-Jihadist perspective, the structure of Salafi-Jihadist groups in Iraq, and finally an assessment of Salafi-Jihadist relations with the Sunni Arab community.

Shi'i Islamists

Three factors have played a major role in shaping political Shi'i Islamism in Iraq. The first of these is the difference in vision of 'Iraqi Shi'i theorists of the Islamic state ... from that of Ayatollah Khomeini'.[3] The second is the conflicting perceptions of religious authority and its role in society. As

---

2. Ibid.
3. Juan I. Cole, 'The Ayatollahs and Democracy in Iraq', ISIM paper 7, Amsterdam: ISIM/Leiden-Amsterdam University Press, 2006, pp. 6–7. This difference appeared in the writings of the main Shi'i ideologues, such as Ayatollah Muhammad Baqir al-Sadr (b. 1933 and executed by Saddam Hussein in 1980), who envisaged an Islamic republic, but not one necessarily ruled by clerics; and Ayatollah Ali Sistani (b. 1930), who has had a major impact on Shi'i Islamist politicians recently in Iraq, and whose political views, according to Cole, are inspired 'by the ideals of the Constitutional Revolution in early twentieth-century Iran (1905–1911). In post-Saddam Iraq, Sistani referred proudly to the

Hanna Batatu notes, Iraqi Shi'is are divided on the ethnicity of *marji'iyya* (religious authority), which historically included class-based differences. The Iraqi Shi'is recognise seven *marji'iyya*, all but one of which is of non-Arab origin, the exception being al-Sadr (Baqir and later Sadiq), whose followers came mostly from poor backgrounds.[4] The third factor is that Iraqi Shi'is have always felt marginalised and isolated, even in a country where they considered themselves to be the majority.

These factors have impacted upon the dynamics of Shi'i political Islam in post-Saddam Hussein Iraq. These Islamists, who have looked to this new political phase as an opportunity to seize power, constitute several groups and parties. The main three of these parties, which will be discussed below, are the al-Da'wa Party, the Supreme Council for Islamic Revolution in Iraq (SCIRI) and the followers of al-Sadr.

The al-Da'wa ('Call to Islam') Party

The al-Da'wa Party is one of the oldest Shi'i Islamist parties in Iraq. Credit for its foundation in 1957 is generally given to Sayyid Muhammad Baqir al-Sadr, who joined the party despite objections from the *marji'iyya* in Najaf, particularly from the top Shi'i cleric in Iraq – at that time, Sayyid Abdul Muhsin al-Hakim. Al-Hakim strongly supported the traditional Shi'i doctrine that clerics should not get involved in politics (until the appearance of the hidden imam, al-Mahdi). However, in allowing himself to become such a figurehead for al-Da'wa, al-Sadr clearly rejected this stand, as evidently did al-Hakim's own sons, one of whom, Abdul Aziz al-Hakim, was the head of the Islamic Supreme Council of Iraq (ISCI), while the other, Mohammed Baqr (a later head of the Supreme Council for Islamic Revolution in Iraq [SCIRI], who was killed in 2003) had already joined al-Da'wa despite his father's objections.

Al-Da'wa has called since its inception for the establishment of an Islamic state. The party was founded as a Shi'i copy of the Muslim Brotherhood, and its members were very much influenced by Muslim Brotherhood literature – particularly Sayyid Qutb's 'The Milestone'. The party resorted to the use of violence against the regime of Saddam Hussein, starting in the 1970s,[5] and in

role of Najaf clerics in theorising a synthesis of Shi'i Islam and Western-style constitutionalism in 1905–1911.'

4. Hanna Batatu, *The Old Social Classes and the Revolutionary Movement in Iraq*, Arabic translation by Afif al-Razar, vol. 1, Arab Researches Foundation, 1995.
5. Fuller, *Islamist Politics*.

response the Baathist regime, which was alarmed by the Islamic Revolution in neighbouring Iran, responded fiercely, cracking down heavily on the party and other Shiʻi political movements. Saddam Hussein outlawed the al-Daʻwa Party, and made it a capital crime to be a member, arresting its leading figures and forcing others to flee to Tehran.[6]

Due to its resistance and struggle to constitute an opposition, the al-Daʻwa Party earned a great deal of respect among Shiʻi Iraqis. After the Americans overthrew the Baathist regime in 2003, the leaders of the party rose to top posts, and two of them became prime ministers of the new Iraq: first Ibrahim al-Jaʻfari, a former high-ranking leader of al-Daʻwa, and then Nouri al-Maliki.[7]

The Supreme Council for Islamic Revolution in Iraq (SCIRI)

SCIRI was founded in 1982 as an umbrella organisation for Iraqi Shiʻi groups, in direct response to Khomeini's encouragement. In 1986, after al-Daʻwa left the alliance, Muhammad Baqir al-Hakim became its leader. Until 2003 SCIRI

6. Cole, 'The Ayatollahs and Democracy', p. 8.
7. It is worth mentioning that in 1982, when Khomeini meant to create an umbrella for Iraqi Shiʻi groups, the al-Daʻwa Party had joined in the founding of the Supreme Council for Islamic Revolution in Iraq (SCIRI) in Tehran, but due to differences in the political attitude towards *wilayat al-faqih* (the guiding principle of Khomeini) and 'against Iranian efforts to control the al-Daʻwa Party', they later broke ranks. Since then the al-Daʻwa Party has remained split between a faction in Iran that is part of SCIRI and calls itself the Islamic Daʻwa-Iraqi Organisation, and a more independent London-based branch that is more 'Iraqi' in character, and largely responsible for fundraising. See Fuller, *Islamist Politics*. The al-Daʻwa Party (both factions), along with the SCIRI and other Shiʻi parties, allied during the 2005 elections into the United Iraqi Alliance List. Later on, however, cracks started to appear in this Alliance which would lead to a complete split. Al-Daʻwa itself has suffered from some splintering, as prominent members have become more attached to the London or Damascus branch activities, and a sub-group evolved in Iraq led by Hashim Naser al-Musawi, which maintained more sympathy with the Iranian *wilayat al-faqih*, and has counted among its members several current ministers in the Iraqi government. There have also been other even more purely Iraqi al-Daʻwa splinter groups, who have come to resent the perceived domination of al-Daʻwa by foreign members. Even as recently as May 2008, the prominent al-Daʻwa figure Ibrahim al-Jaʻfari, who in 2005 had suffered a vote of no confidence by all Sunni, Kurdish and secular groups in parliament for his failure as prime minister to end the violence in Iraq, was expelled from al-Daʻwa for declaring a new sub-party.

was based in Tehran and enjoyed 'the support of the Iranian government which aided him in establishing the Badr Brigade (currently called the Badr Organisation), of some 10,000-man Iraqi exile militia forces'.[8]

After the overthrow of the Baathist regime, SCIRI became a major political force in the new Iraq. On 28 August 2003 Muhammad Baqir al-Hakim was assassinated in a suicide bombing allegedly committed by al-Zarqawi's second wife's father, Yassen Jarad. Abdul Aziz al-Hakim succeeded his brother in the leadership of the SCIRI. Although the Badr Brigade, the military wing of the SCIRI, played a major role in establishing the Iraqi security forces, it was accused of committing sectarian violence against Sunnis.

The Followers of the second al-Sadr (the Sadrists)

The term 'Sadrists', often used in the media, refers to the group led by Muqtada al-Sadr, son of Sayyid Muhammad Sadiq al-Sadr, a prominent Shi'i scholar and thinker who was assassinated by the Saddam regime in 1999. The Sadrists militia, Jaysh al-Mahdi, has also been accused, like SCIRI's Badr Brigade, of committing sectarian violence against Sunnis. Meanwhile, for the young Muqtada al-Sadr, although lacking strong clerical credentials, his family name has played a major role in creating him as popular leader and positioning his Ansar al-Mahdi party as a major opposition group in Iraq, after quitting the government in 2006. The majority of Muqtada's followers are young people based in poor areas of Iraq, reflecting the legacy of his father and uncle in cultivating strong support in populous areas.

While Muqtada is the best-known representative of the Sadrist movement in Iraq, there are two other groups that have claimed to be the 'real representatives' of the Mohammad Sadiq al-Sadr movement: the al-Hasani group, founded after the invasion of Iraq in 2003, and al-Ya'aqoubi (later the al-Fadillah Party), founded in the same year. The al-Hasani group is led by Ayatollah Mohammad Hasani al-Surkhi, an engineer in his forties. This group has refused to participate in the Iraqi government, is opposed to the American troops' presence in Iraq and is against the Iranian influence in Iraq.[9]

Ayatollah Mohammed al-Ya'aqoubi (b. 1960), who was an engineer and became a cleric in 1992, has claimed to have been close to Mohammad Sadiq

---

8. Fuller, *Islamist Politics*.
9. See *Asharq Alawsat*, 17 August 2006.

al-Sadr.[10] His party participated in the 2005 elections on the United Iraqi Alliance List, and won fifteen seats in the parliament. The party's stronghold is Basra city, in southern Iraq. In 2006 the al-Fadillah Party split from the Shi'i bloc (those groups who had participated in the election on the United Iraqi Alliance List) in the Iraqi parliament. Later, on 16 April 2007, the al-Sadr bloc quit the Iraqi government.

The Sadrists have relied on the legacy of al-Sadr, claiming to represent the Arabic *marji'iyya*, as opposed to the other Shi'i clerics of non-Arab (i.e. Persian/Iranian) origin. This explains the critical and independent attitudes that al-Sadr's followers have been keen to display towards Iran, the Iraqi government and the presence of American troops in Iraq. However, these positions have usually come into conflict with political realities on the ground, and the al-Sadrists seem to have been compelled to make compromises. For instance, Muqtada al-Sadr allied himself with Iran when he was unable to challenge the government in 2007, and also had to tone down his opposition when the Iraqi government cracked down on his movement in 2008.

This was a case in which political realities forced ideological Islamist movements to change their political behaviour, in contradiction of their original ideological proclamations. It is true in the Iraqi case that the 'sectarian atmosphere' in post-Saddam Iraq has turned Shi'i Islamist groups, and Sunni groups as well, into representatives of religious groups or communities rather than nationwide political parties.

The influence of this sectarian orientation on the Shi'i movements was clearly demonstrated when Paul Bremer, the head of the Coalition Provisional Authority between 11 May 2003 and 28 June 2004, suggested a complex caucus system based on regional caucuses for the election of the government (this was proposed on a geographical basis that guaranteed the rights of minorities). The plan intended to ensure the protection of the rights of the minority Sunnis and Kurds.[11] But the plan was never accepted by the Ayatollah Ali Sistani, because for him it was not based on 'one man, one vote'. Making this protest public, he mobilised the Shi'i street in January 2004 against the proposed plan, calling 'tens of thousands of demonstrators into the streets of Basra and Baghdad, demanding direct elections. The demonstrations were supported by the al-Da'wa Party and the Supreme Council for Islamic Revolution in Iraq, though

---

10. See his website at www.yaqoobi.com.
11. 'Paul Bremer's Rough Ride', *Time*, 20 June 2004.

secular parties were absent.'[12] While the position of Shi'i groups justified their preference for direct democracy, this position was seen widely as a reflection of the desire of the Shi'is to control power in the new Iraq.[13]

Furthermore, the sectarian orientation of Shi'i groups became more obvious with the Ibrahim al-Ja'afari government, which came to power in April 2005, as the Shi'is dominated government and its security apparatuses, which were infamously involved in sectarian violence. While such violence was partly a response to the violence that had been perpetrated by extremist Sunni groups (mainly al-Qaeda and its derivatives) against the Shi'is and their holy places, that violence was nevertheless an indication of how these Islamist groups were shaped by, and shaping, the volatile 'sectarian atmosphere'.

It should be added that Jaysh al-Mahdi (or JaM), the military wing of the Sadrist movement, was greatly used by Iran to form what are now called 'Special Groups', which have targeted Iraqi security forces and politicians in addition to the multinational forces in Iraq. Since Muqtada al-Sadr moved to Iran, the Sadrist movement has started to split into two wings. One side appears to be following certain Sadrist figures, such as Salah al-Ubaidi, the spokesman for the Sadrist movement in Najaf, who is supported by Liwa' Simaisim (Muqtada al-Sadr's brother-in-law). These two formed the al-Ahrar List, which participated in the last provincial elections on 31 December 2008. The other wing, which is considered to take a harder line, has coalesced around some Sadrist MPs, such as Baha' al-'Araji and Ahmad al-Mas'udi; this wing is called the Sadr City Group.

Sunni Islamists

While the occupation of Iraq played a major role in the emergence of militant Sunni groups, part of the momentum of today's Sunni Islamism in Iraq goes back to the mid-1990s, when Saddam Hussein, a secular nationalist, launched the so-called 'Faith Campaign' in order to strengthen the declining legitimacy of his weakened regime in the wake of the First Gulf War in 1991. In that campaign bars were closed, alcohol banned, hundreds

---

12. Cole, 'The Ayatollahs and Democracy', pp. 16–17.
13. Author interview with Rafid Jabbori, the London-based Iraqi journalist who is well informed about Iraqi religious and political groups, London, 21 December 2008.

of mosques opened and a major new theological school established called Saddam University, teaching only 'the Sunni version of Islamic theology', since the 'Faith Campaign' was directed at Sunni Muslims and excluded Shiʻi theology.[14]

This environment played a role in the emergence of Sunni groups in Iraq, and later assisted in the absorption of Salafi-Jihadist ideology. The Sunni Islamists in Iraq are represented, generally speaking, by the Muslim Brotherhood, Salafis and Sufis. The Muslim Brotherhood is the oldest Islamist formation in Iraq, established in the 1940s but operating secretly for most of its political life, and thus already involved in politics in various forms. The Salafis, however, have emerged more visibly only in the wake of the invasion of Iraq in 2003, joining either the insurgency or Sunni political organisations (Islamist and non-Islamist). The Sufis have mostly adhered to their traditional position of non-involvement in politics.[15]

The discussion below will focus on three of the best-known Sunni Islamist formations: al-Hizb al-Islami (the party of the Muslim Brotherhood), the Association of Muslim Scholars in Iraq and the Sunni militant groups (al-Qaeda and the like).

Al-Hizb al-Islami (the Islamic Party)

Establishment of the first branch of the Muslim Brotherhood movement in Iraq began in the late 1940s, when Shaykh Mohammed Mahmoud al-Sawaf applied to the government to register his party under that name. The government rejected his application. In 1961 the Muslim Brotherhood became a legal party under the name of al-Hizb al-Islami. The Iraqi Muslim Brothers won the Iraqi High Court's permission to operate in Iraq in 1961, largely because the Iraqi government at the time, and particularly president Abdul Karim Qasim, wanted them to weaken the pan-Arab and communist movements that were very active during this period. But the latter were strong enough to confront the Muslim Brothers, who as a result lost many members, and the party was forced to close its offices, thereafter working underground. However, during the last few years of Saddam's

14. See Laura Sheahen, 'Saddam Plays the Faith Card', March 2003, at www.beliefnet.com/Faiths/Islam/2003/04/Saddam-Plays-The-Faith-Card.aspx. See also Fuller, *Islamist Politics*.
15. Author interview with Rafid Jabbori.

regime, benefiting from the 'Faith Campaign', the party reactivated itself in several areas of the country.[16]

The party's objectives focus, as in the case of other Muslim Brotherhood organisations in the region, on education and the implementation of Islamic values among Muslim youth in order to prepare a generation capable of creating an Islamic state. The Iraqi Muslim Brothers have also pronounced their belief in political participation.

Based on this position, the party participated in Iraqi opposition meetings in London and Kurdistan, in 2001 and 2002 respectively. More importantly, however, the party participated in the new Iraqi political process initiated after the American invasion in 2003, and wanted to represent Iraqi Sunnis in the new political framework. The party has been heavily criticised by other Sunni groups because it has participated in the political process 'under the occupation umbrella'. Its leader is Tariq al-Hashmi, who is also one of the Iraqi president's two deputies.

The Association of Muslim Scholars in Iraq (AMSI)

With a reformist Salafi inclination, the Association of Muslim Scholars in Iraq (AMSI) was founded after the invasion of Iraq on 14 April 2003 as an umbrella for Sunni activists from different backgrounds (the Muslim Brotherhood, Sufis and Salafis, as well as non-Islamists). AMSI is an alliance between two entities: '(The Association of Legislation Scholars) which was founded by a number of legislation scholars and students, [o]n the [western bank of Dijle river, which is known as] al-Karkh. The other entity (The Society of Muslim Scholars) [was founded by mosques, imams and students of science on the eastern bank of the same river and known as] al-Rusafa.'[17] The major figures behind the foundation of AMSI were Shaykh Ahmad al-Kubaisi, a leading Sunni shaykh who has since left the Association, and Shaykh Harith al-Dhari, who became the secretary-general of AMSI and remains in post at the time of writing.

The top priority of AMSI, as repeatedly declared by its leaders, is the withdrawal of occupation forces from Iraq. Although AMSI claims to

---

16. Lo'ay al-Mahmoud, 'Islamic Sunni Forces in Iraq and their Positions toward Occupation' (in Arabic), 13 April 2008, at www.islamonline.net/servlet/Satellite?c=ArticleA_C&cid=1203758980232&pagename=Zone-Arabic-Daawapercent2FDWALayout.

17. See the AMSI website (English version), at www.heyetnet.org/eng/amsi-news/22-heyet/45-a-brief-description-of-amsi.html.

represent a nationwide project, and indeed has denounced the killing of Shiʻi civilians, it is in fact a body that represents only Sunnis in Iraq. Like al-Hizb al-Islami, AMSI has failed to produce a nationwide political discourse, as the vast majority of members of both organisations and their rhetoric are Sunni-centred.

One of the major criticisms that has been directed at the Sunni Islamists, and at AMSI in particular, relates to their ambiguous position towards al-Qaeda and its practices. Although AMSI has denounced al-Qaeda attacks against Iraqi Shiʻis, it has nevertheless identified al-Qaeda in Iraq and its foreign fighters, including their leader Abu Musʻab al-Zarqawi, as a legitimate part of the Iraqi resistance.[18] The ambiguity and ambivalence that have marked the position of the Sunni Islamists – mainly AMSI and al-Hizb al-Islami – towards al-Qaeda and its attacks against the Shiʻis have echoed the attitude of mainstream Shiʻi groups towards attacks against Iraqi Sunnis. Both positions have their roots in the changing context of sectarian tension (and conflict) in today's Iraq.

Militant Sunni groups

The occupation of Iraq has inflamed the insurgency, and armed groups have mushroomed all over the country to fight against American troops and the Iraqi government. The insurgency's bases have mainly been in the Sunni areas, although they have conducted attacks all over Iraq.[19] The membership of the insurgency groups is a mixture of Salafis, Muslim Brothers, Sufis (from the Jaysh Rijal al-Tariqa al-Naqshbandiyya [The Men of the Army of Naqshbandiyya Order], Iraqi tribesmen and Baathist ex-military officers.

The best-known groups are the 1920 Revolutionary Brigades, the Ansar al-Sunna Army, al-Jaysh al-Islami in Iraq, al-Qaeda in Mesopotamia (later the Islamic State of Iraq), the Islamic Front for Iraqi Resistance (JAAMI)/Salah al-Din Brigades, the al-Rashidin Army and some other, smaller, groups.[20] These groups have reflected a combination of two sentiments. On the one

---

18. See AMSI statement no. 157, released on 15 September 2005, at www.iraq-amsi.org (in Arabic).

19. See Murad Batal al-Shishani, 'The Iraqi Resistance between Terrorism and National Liberation: A Quantitative Study', *Iraq Studies*, Fifth Issue, Gulf Research Centre, Dubai, November 2005 (in Arabic).

20. See detailed list of militant Iraqi groups in Abdul Hameed Bakier, 'Iraq's Islamic Mujahideen Profiled by Jihadi Websites', *Terrorism Focus* (Jamestown Founda-

hand, they have embodied the feelings of isolation and exclusion prevalent among Iraqi Sunnis but, on the other, they have been mostly driven by the determination to end the American occupation of Iraq, and the rejection of the new political arrangements. Most of the attacks conducted by these groups have been directed either at American troops or at Iraqi government forces.[21]

By 2005 the sectarian tension in Iraq had dramatically increased, mostly because of the attacks of some of the insurgent groups, particularly al-Qaeda. These insurgent groups and their military activities have certainly exacerbated the sectarian atmosphere in Iraq, as much as they have been influenced by it. These groups have therefore focused their political and military activity on two fronts. They have either directed their violence towards the Shi'is – most of al-Qaeda's action has been on this front – or, in the case of the anti-al-Qaeda groups, associated themselves with the Awakening Councils that were founded by Sunni tribes in 2006 to confront al-Qaeda, as the alliance between the al-Qaeda and the Sunni community in Iraq has weakened.

The switch in either direction, in favour of or against al-Qaeda, indicates the strong role of the sectarian atmosphere in shaping political positions and behaviours in the new Iraq.

Kurdish Islamists

The collapse of Saddam Hussein was a golden opportunity for the Kurds to assert their historical demand for the creation of a national entity. The Kurds have achieved several political gains in the new Iraq: the head of the Iraqi state is now a Kurd; Kurdistan, in the northern part of Iraq, is considered the most secure area of the country, and is witnessing strong economic development and, more importantly, enjoys sovereignty, self-determination, and a wide degree of autonomy.

In this context, the political programme of the Kurdish Islamists confirms the absence of a nationwide Iraqi national project. With the exception of the Kurdish Salafi-Jihadist Ansar al-Islam group, which was suppressed by the US air force with the assistance of the (Kurdish) *peshmerga* forces in 2003

---

tion, Washington, DC) – two parts: vol. 5, no. 40, 26 November 2008, and vol. 5, no. 41, 3 December 2008.

21. Al-Shishani, 'The Iraqi Resistance'.

(and whose founder and spiritual leader, Mullah Krekar, is now in exile in Norway) and, more recently, the 'Kurdistan Islamic Brigades', affiliated to al-Qaeda in Iraq, the Kurdish Islamists have associated themselves with the Kurdish national aspiration, have opposed the insurgency and have engaged with the new status quo in Iraq.

According to the Iraqi analyst Fadhil Ali, the major Islamist forces in Kurdistan, and their current positions, can be characterised as follows.[22]

The Islamic Union of Kurdistan (IUK)

The Islamic Union of Kurdistan (IUK) is the biggest Islamic party in Kurdistan, and represents the Muslim Brotherhood in Kurdistan. The IUK is headed by Salah al-Din Muhammad Baha'a al-Din, and is considered the third party in Kurdistan, with members in both the central and regional parliaments.[23] The party won 1.3 per cent of the vote in the December 2005 elections, and five out of 275 seats.

The IUK, as a branch of the Muslim Brotherhood, is active at the grass-roots level, mainly among students (reportedly winning nearly 40 per cent of the vote in the Dahuk University student elections). The party also has an adult political base, particularly in Arbil.[24] In relation to the Kurdish national cause, the IUK says it will defend the rights and the constitutional achievements of the Kurds.[25]

The Islamic Movement in Iraqi Kurdistan (IMIK)

Formed in 1987 in Halabja, the Islamic Movement in Iraqi Kurdistan (IMIK) fought against Saddam's regime in the 1980s. In the 1990s the IMIK engaged in fighting with Jalal al-Talabani's Patriotic Union of Kurdistan (PUK). The movement is led by Mullah Ali Abd al-Aziz Halabji.[26]

---

22. Fadhil Ali, 'Kurdish Islamist Groups in Northern Iraq', *Terrorism Monitor*, vol. 6, no. 22, 25 November 2008.
23. Ibid.
24. See, 'Iraqi Opposition' at www.globalsecurity.org/military/world/iraq/opposition.htm.
25. See the party's website, at www.kurdiu.org/ara/about.aspx.
26. Ibid.

The Islamic Group of Kurdistan (IGK)

Headed by Mullah Ali Bapir, the Islamic Group of Kurdistan (IGK) was formed in 2001 as an offshoot of the IMIK. The movement participates in the regional government and parliament. It does not currently advocate *jihad*, and has announced its willingness to work with Sufi as well as Salafist forms of Sunni Islam.[27]

Al-Qaeda in Iraq and the Sunni Arab Society

Al-Qaeda in Iraq (or in Mesopotamia) and later the 'Islamic State of Iraq', referring to the self-declared state in al-Anbar province in 2006, has played a major role in the dynamics of the transformation in Iraq and in the region since the invasion of Iraq in 2003.

By virtue of its strong ties with the Sunni community in Iraq, at least in the initial phase of its formation in 2004/05, al-Qaeda provides an example of the important role of local communities in the new Iraq as an incubator of political and militant organisations. The Sunni community in Iraq has played a crucial role in the rise and fall of al-Qaeda in the country. This implies that this group could re-emerge, depending on the socio-political conditions and how they affect the 'incubator', taking into consideration that the rule of law, democracy and stability all remain fragile in the new Iraq.

The importance of Iraq in al-Qaeda's perspective

Most ideologues of the Salafi-Jihadi stream insist that their conflict (*jihad*) against the US is a religious one, and that the war in Iraq is part of that conflict. Osama bin Laden, the leader of al-Qaeda, has said that the conflict 'is a religious conflict and there is a clash of civilizations. [The Americans and their allies] aim to eliminate Islam in all directions, and it has nothing to do with the weapons of mass destruction, but it is a very obvious occupation in all the senses of the word.'[28] Yusuf al-Ayiri, the leader of al-Qaeda in Saudi Arabia, and one of the significant ideologues of Salafi-Jihadists, whose writings have influenced jihadists all over the world – and Iraqi insurgents

27. Ibid.
28. Osama bin Laden's speech directed to the Iraqi people on 6 May 2004. The transcript can be found at www.tawhed.ws.

in particular[29] – has divided the American motivations behind the invasion of Iraq into those of religion and those of economics. The religious motives, in his opinion, reflect the presence of 'an extremist ideology governing the White House ... which aims to accelerate the battle of Armageddon in the interest of Israel and to distort Islam in the name of democracy and reform'. The economic motivation for invading Iraq, in al-Ayiri's opinion, is to control the region's oil.[30]

The Saudi Abu Omar al-Saif, who was the Arab fighters' ideologue in Chechnya until he was killed by Russian troops on 12 December 2005, disseminated several writings regarding the jihadist movements, including those in Iraq.[31] He perceived the war against Iraq as the third cycle in a series of crusades against Muslims. The first cycle corresponded to the wars from 1096 to 1291, and the second to the colonial movement of the nineteenth century. In his writings Abu Omar, like al-Ayiri, makes it clear that he believes that the West aims to destroy, in the name of its 'War on Terrorism', the Muslim way of life by spreading 'infidel democracy', 'empowering Jews' and 'looting Muslims' wealth'.[32]

In the context of a religious interpretation of the Iraqi conflict, the Salafi jihadists have viewed the American presence in Iraq as a golden opportunity to 'transfer the battle into the heart of the Muslim world instead of [it remaining] in the margins'.[33] Salafi-jihadist literature therefore focuses on encouraging

---

29. Al-Ayiri was killed in May 2003 by Saudi security forces. For further information on his writings, see Roel Mejir, 'Rereading al-Qaeda: Writings of Yusuf al-Ayiri', *ISIM Review* (The International Institute for the Study of Islam in the Modern World, Netherlands), no. 18, Autumn 2006, pp. 16–17.

30. Yusuf al-Ayiri, 'Silsilat al-Harb al-Salibyah 'ala al-'Iraq' ('The Crusader War against Iraq' Series), 2003, from author's archive.

31. Murad Batal al-Shishani, 'Portrait of a Chechen Mujahid Leader', *Terrorism Monitor*, vol. 2, no. 8 (23 April 2004), and 'Abu Omar al-Saif: His Life and after His Death', *Chechnya Weekly*, vol. 7, no. 3 (19 January 2006).

32. Abu-Omar al-Saif, 'Al-'Iraq wa Ghazu al-Salib: Durus wa Ta'amulat' ('Iraq and the Invasion of the Cross: Lessons and Meditations'), 2004, from author's archive.

33. Fawaz A. Gerges, 'The Iraq War: Planting the Seed of al-Qaida's Second Generation', Silver City. NM and Washington, DC: *Foreign Policy in Focus*, 27 October 2005; Reuven Paz, 'The Impact of the War in Iraq on the Global Jihad', in Hillel Faradkin, Husain Haqqani and Eric Brawn, eds, *Current Trends in Islamist Ideology*, vol. 1, Center on Islam, Democracy and the Future of the Muslim World, Hudson Institute, Washington, DC, 21 March 2005, p. 39.

young Muslims to join in a *jihad* in Iraq as a launching pad aimed at taking the battle to neighbouring 'infidel' regimes one after another. In bin Laden's words, 'defending the rest of Muslims countries, and the two mosques in particular [the holy places in Saudi Arabia], starts by fighting in the front lines in the land of Mesopotamia'. Bin Laden considers the *jihad* in Iraq to be a 'rare and precious opportunity' to mobilise Muslims to fight against the US.[34]

Salafi-jihadist ideologues have preferred to mobilise young Muslims from Iraq's neighbouring countries. Abu Omar al-Saif has urged 'the *mujahidin* from the Levant countries, the Arabian Peninsula, Iraq, Turkey, and from other areas to join the *jihad* against the conspirator alliance: Christian-Jews with *murtadin* [apostates]'.[35]

Furthermore, while al-Ayiri has identified the Shi'is as 'more dangerous than Jews',[36] al-Saif has divided the 'enemy' in Iraq into four categories:

> [First], the original Kuffar [infidels], like the Americans, the British, the Australians, and other Christians. [Second], the *murtadin*, Muslim secularists such as some Arabs and Kurds whose principles were a cross between secularism and nationalism. [Third], *rafidah* (rejecters) [the Salafi name for the Shi'is, considered to be aberrant Muslims], who will collaborate with the Americans as their predecessors did when the Mongolian Tartars invaded Iraq [in the thirteen century]. [Fourth], *munafiqin* [hypocrites] serving Americans and their allies either with their words or by fighting on their side.[37]

With such an ideology, Iraq has become a breeding ground for Salafi-jihadists from all over the world, fuelled by the occupation of Iraq but mobilised equally against Shi'i Iraqis. Their leader was the Jordanian Ahmed Fadel Nazal al-Khalayleh, better known as Abu Muss'ab al-Zarqawi, who became one of the most influential Salafi-jihadist leaders. His name still attracts admiration within the circles of jihadists, even after his killing by American forces in June 2006. Al-Zarqawi and his

---

Al-Ayiri wrote that 'the fall of Saddam's regime has served Islamists' interests to raise their banner and fill the vacuum of power' – al-Ayiri, 'Silsilat al-Harb al-Salibyah 'ala al-'Iraq'.

34. See bin Laden's speech, 6 May 2004.
35. Al-Saif, 'Al-Iraq wa Ghazu al-Salib: Durus wa Ta'amulat'.
36. Al-Ayiri, 'Silsilat al-Harb al-Salibyah 'ala al-'Iraq'.
37. Al-Saif, 'Al-Iraq wa Ghazu al-Salib: Durus wa Ta'amulat'.

organisation were responsible for the most brutal attacks in Iraq,[38] and more significantly played a central role in provoking sectarian violence there. Al-Zarqawi was succeeded by the Egyptian Abu Hamza al-Muhajir, who announced in October 2006 the formation of the Dawlat al-'Iraq al-Islamiyya (the Islamic State of Iraq [ISI]), and named Abu Umar al-Baghdadi its *amir*.

The strategic vision of the Salafi-jihadists includes the creation of a safe haven for al-Qaeda's operations in the region and beyond, transcending their immediate political objectives in Iraq. According to Zarqawi,

> We do not fight for a fistful of dust or illusory boundaries drawn by 'Sykes-Picot'. We are not fighting so that a Western evil would replace an Arab evil. Ours is a higher and more sublime fight. We are fighting so that Allah's word becomes supreme and religion is all for Allah. Anyone who opposes this goal or stands in the way of this aim is our enemy and will be a target for our swords, regardless of their name or lineage ... a Muslim American is our dear brother: an infidel Arab is our hated enemy, even if we both come from the same womb.[39]

He also commented, 'We have revived the jurisprudence of our good ancestors in fighting heretics and enforcing Allah's law on them. *Jihad* will be continuous, and will not distinguish between Western infidels and heretic Arabs until the rule of the caliphate is restored, or we die in the process.'[40]

Membership and structure

Al-Qaeda's attempts to urge young Muslims to join a *jihad* in Iraq have shaped its social structure there. Based on a list of *mujahidin* in Iraq posted on the *jihadi* web forums, the ranks of the Salafi-jihadists fighting in Iraq – most of whom are part of Zarqawi's al-Qaeda in Iraq organisation – come from

---

38. For quantitative analysis of al-Zarqawi's attacks, see Murad al-Shishani, 'Al-Zarqawi's Rise to Power: Analyzing Tactics and Targets', *Terrorism Monitor*, vol. 3, no. 22, 18 November 2005.

39. Abu Musab al-Zarqawi's letter, 'Mawqifuna al-Shar'i min Hukumat "Karzai al-Iraq"' ('Our Legal Standpoint on Iraqi Karzai's Government' [meaning Iyad Allawi]), which is undated, published on several jihadist web sites on 2005, from author's archive.

40. Ibid.

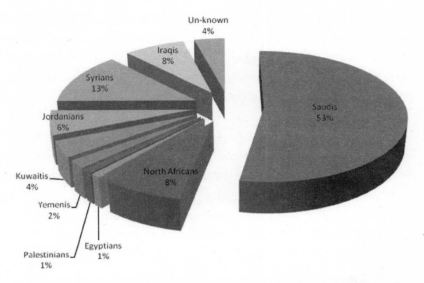

Fig. 6.1: Foreign Volunteers in Iraq to Percentage of Iraqis, data compiled by author

all over the Arab world. Of these members, 53 per cent are Saudi nationals, 13 per cent are from Syria, 8 per cent are from Iraq, 5.8 per cent are from Jordan, 4 per cent from Kuwait, and 3.8 per cent from Libya, with the rest distributed among other countries (see Fig. 6.1).[41]

While these figures are not comprehensive, they do give an idea of the complexion of the jihadists in Iraq, and indicate that the largest percentage belong to countries surrounding Iraq, presumably because accessing Iraq is easiest for these fighters. Moreover, the clashes that took place from 2003

41. See Murad al-Shishani, 'The Salafi Jihadist Movement in Iraq: Recruitment Methods and Arab Volunteers', *Terrorism Monitor*, vol. 3, no. 23, 2 December 2005. One of the most recent studies, based on list of 700 foreign fighters in Iraq, concluded almost similar results to those mentioned above. According to this study Saudis comprised about 41 per cent of Arab fighters in Iraq; Libya was the next most common country of origin, with 18.8 per cent of the Arab fighters. Syria, Yemen, and Algeria were the next most common countries of origin with 8.2 per cent, 8.1 per cent and 7.2 per cent, respectively. Moroccans accounted for 6.1 per cent of the fighters and Jordanians 1.9 per cent. The major difference between the author's analysis, mentioned above, and this study was the number of Libyans. See Joseph Felter and Brian Fishman, 'Al-Qa'ida's Foreign Fighters in Iraq: A First Look at the Sinjar Records', December 2007, CTC Harmony Project (Combating Terrorism Center, US Military Academy, West Point, New York).

to 2006 between the Saudi regime and the Saudi branch of the al-Qaeda network forced many young Saudi Salafi jihadists to migrate to Iraq. Many of these *jihadis* are prominent fighters and ideologues, a good example being the Salafi-jihadist ideologue Abdullah Rashid al-Rashoud, whom Zarqawi eulogised after he was slain by American forces near al-Qaim.

In addition there are many North Africans – principally Moroccans, Algerians and Libyans – among Arab fighters. This is because local Salafi-jihadist movements in these countries are in conflict with their governments. As in Saudi Arabia, overwhelming security pressures have therefore forced fighters to seek out new havens.

The rise and fall of al-Qaeda in Mesopotamia

Interestingly, the number of local Iraqis among the Salafi jihadists is very low (around 8 per cent),[42] reflecting an Iraqi unwillingness to join foreign-led extremist ideological movements. Joseph Felter and Brian Fishman have rightly noted that al-Qaeda in Iraq 'worked hard to recruit Iraqis and build cordia relationships with nationalist and Baathist insurgents in Iraq, but its brutal tactics and religious conservatism alienated more Iraqis than it attracted'.[43]

Al-Qaeda has struggled hard to appeal to Iraqis, and it is widely believed that the recent appointment of al-Baghdadi as the *amir* of the Islamic State of Iraq (ISI) emerged out of this struggle.[44] It is also worth mentioning that a very influential Salafi-jihadist ideologue such as Abu Mohammad al-Maqdisi[45] urged that the leadership of the *mujahidin* in Iraq should be

42. Al-Shishani, 'Al-Zarqawi's Rise to Power'.
43. Felter and Fishman, 'Al-Qa'ida's Foreign Fighters in Iraq', pp. 3–4.
44. Ibid, pp. 3–5.
45. Abu Muhammad al-Maqdisi was al-Zarqawi's mentor. Both had been arrested by the Jordanian authorities in the mid-1990s, after the formation of what became known as the Baya'at al-Imam Group. Al-Maqdisi's real name is I'sam Mohammad Tahir al-Barqawi. He was born in Nablus in 1959, and moved during childhood with his family to Kuwait. He studied at the University of Mosul in Iraq, then travelled to Saudi Arabia, Pakistan and Afghanistan, where he met various jihadist groups and wrote some of his most famous books, including *Millat Ibrahim* (Ibrahim's Creed) and *Kawashif al-al-Jalliyya fi Kufr al-Dawla al-Sa'udiyya* (The Shameful Actions Manifest in the Saudi State's Disbelief). West Point Combating Terrorism Center, in its comprehensive study on the 'Militant Ideology Atlas', 2006, concluded that al-Maqdisi is one of the most influential jihadist ideologues 'who has the most impact on other *jihadi* think-

in Iraqi hands – an issue that was an area of disagreement between him and al-Zarqawi before the latter's death.[46]

Al-Qaeda in Iraq is mindful of the importance of its relations with the Iraqi Sunni community, and al-Zarqawi underlined this in his letter to al-Qaeda leaders that was intercepted and leaked by American forces in 2004. In that letter, which came to be known as the 'letter on sectarian war in Iraq', al-Zarqawi talked about the sectarian war as a strategic option, depicting the Shi'is as a greater danger than the Americans. He believed that this threat provided the most effective way of galvanising Iraq's embattled Arab Sunni community against the new Iraq.[47]

Al-Zarqawi had hoped to manipulate Sunnis into involving themselves in the fighting by pushing Shi'is to attack Sunnis in response to his attacks against them. At that time, the Iraqi Sunnis had started to join the Iraqi security forces, partly with increasing tendency to participate in the new political process. These changes alarmed al-Zarqawi, and he indicated in the same letter the difficulty his organisation would face if he lost the sympathy of Sunnis. He talked about the difficulty of inciting people to fight the police, with whom they shared kinship and other relationships. This created a dilemma for the faction: they now had either to force their local Iraqi recruits to fight their relatives, or to 'pack their bags and search for another land that would repeat the sad story in the fields of *jihad*'.[48]

For their part, the Sunnis of Iraq, who felt isolated and marginalised after the fall of the Saddam regime, initially incubated al-Zarqawi and al-Qaeda. This took place at a time when sectarian violence against them had increased. This relationship and the feeling within the Sunni community explain the reluctance of Sunni political forces to criticise al-Zarqawi and his project publicly, until the Awakening Council Forces were formed in 2006 and engaged in fighting against al-Qaeda.

Furthermore, the brutal tactics and religious conservatism of al-Qaeda have backfired and isolated them from Sunni Arabs in Iraq. Iraqi Sunnis have ultimately realised that boycotting the political process has made them

---

ers and has been the most consequential in shaping the worldview of the *jihadi* movement'.

46. See al-Maqdisi's open letter to al-Zarqawi, 'Munasara wa Munasaha' ('Advocating and Advising'), June 2005, at www.tawhed.ws.

47. Zarqawi's letter on the sectarian war in Iraq, *Al-Hayat*, 12 February 2004.

48. Ibid.

absent themselves from the decisions affecting them and the areas in which they live. They have also come to believe that Zarqawi's operations in Iraq were doing harm to the reputation of Iraqi resistance, on the one hand, and targeting Sunnis themselves, on the other.

January 2006 was a turning point in the relation between al-Qaeda and the Sunnis of Iraq. The alliance between both parties has gone on to break down; both the Sunni tribes and the Iraqi resistance started to confront al-Qaeda.

On 23 January 2006 the press reported a statement by six major Iraqi resistance groups – the most important of which were the Islamic Army, the Brigades of the 1920 Revolution, and the Regiments of Ramadi Revolutionaries – announcing that they had formed a group in the Anbar province, a stronghold of Sunni Arabs. The group, called the 'People's Cells', consists of 4,000 people, and its aim is to maintain the security of the province. In their founding statement, the groups condemned the targeting of civilians and called for the necessity of putting an end to the attacks against Shi'is.[49]

Moreover, Sunni Arab tribes had already started to stand up to Zarqawi. The Albu-Fahd tribe, the largest Dulaim tribe in Ramadi, and the al-Bubaz tribe from Samarra, formed local committees to 'chase foreigners away'.[50] On 12 January 2006, the *New York Times* reported armed attacks against Zarqawi's faction by the resistance, which was confirmed by Arab and Iraqi newspapers. The attacks took place in several regions, including Ramadi, Hassiba and Dlou'iah, forcing Zarqawi to move to Diala, according to media sources.[51]

The divergence in tactics between the Iraqi nationalist 'resistance' and al-Qaeda is rooted in the vast difference in their strategic objectives. The nationalist Iraqi 'resistance' has a realisable political aim – that is, to end the occupation and participate in ruling the country. Meanwhile, al-Qaeda in Iraq sees the Iraq conflict as a temporary (albeit the most important) arena in which the greater struggle between the Salafi jihadists and the United States is unfolding.

In addition, clerics have called on young people to volunteer and join the tribal–religious coalition against al-Zarqawi's faction in the Sunni Arab regions. Zarqawi's operations enraged Sunni Arabs: they were targeted by assassinations

---

49. *Al-Hayat*, 23 January 2006.
50. *Al-Hayat*, 18 January 2006.
51. *New York Times*, 12 January 2006, and *Al-Zaman*, 16 January 2006.

that claimed the lives of important figures among Sunnis, such as Shaykh Iyad al-Izzi, Shaykh Hamza Issawi, Shaykh Abdul-Ghaffar ar-Rawi, university professor Hamad Faisal and the Albu-Fahd tribe's chief, Nasr Abdul-Karim al-Hindawi – all of whom were in support of the political process.[52] Furthermore, Sunni Arabs were targeted by suicide bombings. Al-Qaeda targeted volunteer centres for the Iraqi army and police in Sunni Arab regions, especially Ramadi. This drove Sunni Arabs to make a deal with the Iraqi government and American forces to handle the security in their region. As a result, the rates of enlistment in the army and police increased in Ramadi and Fallujah, and it was agreed that Sunni Arabs would be responsible for the security of their own areas in return for the withdrawal of coalition forces from their region.[53]

All these incidents led ultimately to the formation of the Awakening Councils in January 2007, in the predominantly Sunni al-Anbar province, by Shaykh Abdul Sattar Abu Risha, with the aim of confronting al-Qaeda. After their success in forcing al-Qaeda out of al-Anbar, other Sunni provinces and areas started to form their own councils, often incorporating former Iraqi insurgents. Although Abu Risha was assassinated by a suicide bomber in September 2007, one can safely conclude that the Awakening Councils were the main factor behind the reduced threat posed by al-Qaeda in Iraq, as indicated by the decline in its attacks over the three following years.

The main factor behind the successful Awakening Councils was their representation of the Sunnis of Iraq, which demonstrated the crucial role played by sectarian factors in the new Iraq. The setback experienced by al-Qaeda therefore indicates that its fortunes were correlated with the support and incubation provided by the local Sunni community, or the lack of it.

The Islamists of Iraq have clearly been seriously affected by the sectarian atmosphere that has dominated Iraq since the US invasion, and sometimes the Islamists have been responsible for creating it. These Islamists, despite their claim to offer a nationwide ideology and/or political project, have been reduced in this atmosphere to community-focused groups advocating their own sectional interests.

The sectarian effect is rightly seen as the major obstacle to the creation of a nation state in Iraq. Recently, Prime Minister Nouri al-Maliki has made several attempts to bridge the gap with the Sunni community. One of those

---

52. *Al-Hayat*, 16 January 2006.
53. *Al-Hayat*, 14 January 2006.

was the crackdown on the Shi'i al-Mahdi militia in March–April 2008. Some observers[54] have suggested that this political decision was an important step for al-Maliki in presenting himself as a national leader and represented the start of a national political project. For such purposes, that step seems to have been insufficient. A reintegration process is required that will include all Iraqi people and communities.

For instance, the US announced in September 2008 that responsibility for 54,000 of the roughly 100,000 members of the Awakening Councils would be handed over to the Iraqi government. The government has pledged to absorb just 20 per cent of these members into the police and armed forces[55] – and as the Iraqi government has all along done little to support the Awakening Councils, the movement's leaders have concerns about the government's will to commit to its pledges.

Al-Sahwat members think that the Iraqi government is reluctant to accept them because of the influence of Shi'i militants on the security forces.[56] This situation indicates that the state institutions – and organs of security in particular – need to be re-established on a national basis. This situation could also create a fertile environment for the driving of the Awakening Councils' members into the arms of al-Qaeda, or other Iraqi insurgent factions, which would promote the re-emergence of al-Qaeda and the possible re-launching of sectarian violence.

In the final analysis, al-Qaeda's strength has been associated with the extent to which it is accepted by the Sunni community in Iraq, which means that it could certainly re-emerge as a significant force given the current fragile socio-political balance in Iraqi politics. At the same, in the context of al-Qaeda's declining fortunes in Iraq, it is worth reiterating the seriousness of the threat posed by al-Qaeda returnees from Iraq to neighbouring countries.

---

54. Author interview with Rafid Jabbori.
55. *Al-Hayat*, 19 October 2008.
56. *Al-Hayat*, 7 October 2008.

SEVEN

Islamism in the Gulf Region

Abdullah Baabood

Islamism in the Gulf is best seen in the context of the global resurgence of religion and the revival of Islam in the latter part of the twentieth century. Global religious resurgence, in the post-Cold War period, has challenged the expectations of the modernisation theory of the progressive secularisation and Westernisation of developing societies. Indeed, religion has become a major ideological, social and political force, appealed to by governments, political parties and opposition movements alike, a source of liberation and violent extremism.[1]

There is generally a conceptual muddle around the understanding of 'political' Islam, which not only undermines any deeper understanding of the phenomenon but adds to an overall misconception and analytical confusion on how to explain Islamism. The complexity of the subject has also been compounded by the very nature of Islamism: by its own dynamics, its varied manifestations, its causes and the reasons for its ascendancy.

The political ideology of Islamism takes various forms. It is a broad term that embraces a body of diverse and even contradictory political, social, psychological, economic and even class functions, and it is represented by different types of social movement that draw general inspiration from Islam. However, for the sake of simplicity and generalisation, the definition of Islamism used here is 'Islam used to a political end'.

As these issues have been discussed in depth elsewhere and in some of the early chapters in this book, this chapter will concentrate on Islamism in

---

1. For background see Martin Riesebrodt, 'Fundamentalism and the Resurgence of Religion', *Numen International Review for the History of Religion*, vol. 47, no. 3; Marcel Gauchet, *The Disenchantment of the World: A Political History of Religion*, Princeton: Princeton University Press, 1997; Jeff Haynes, *Religion in Third World Politics*, Buckingham and Philadelphia: Open University Press, 1993; John L. Esposito, 'Religion and Global Affairs: Political Challenges', *SAIS Review*, vol. 18, no. 2 (Summer–Fall 1998), pp. 19–24.

the Gulf region, and especially the countries of the Cooperation Council for the Arab States of the Gulf (GCC): Bahrain, Kuwait, Qatar, Oman, Saudi Arabia and the United Arab Emirates. The chapter will provide a historical account of Islamism in the region, with its own local characteristics and idiosyncrasies. It will consider the causes of the rise of Islamism among the different Sunni, Shi'i and Abadhi sects. It will also survey the range of interpretations of this central issue, including that which forms part of a system supporting and supported by states; that of traditionalists, who believe that Islamic codes must be introduced gradually, and who advocate a peaceful approach to socio-political transformation through preaching; that of the Salafis, who believe that all necessary law is contained in traditional Islamic legal codes, and take the pious ancestors of the patristic period of early Islam as exemplary models; and that of the jihadists, who believe that only violent revolution will achieve the desired goal. I will conclude by suggesting that – while there are generalities across the Gulf region relating to Islamism – there are many nuances and differences as Islamist movements in this region are largely home grown, respond to varying challenges at the national level and meet with different institutional and official responses to their demands and aspirations.

Reasons for the rise of Islamism in the Gulf region

In addition to the conceptual confusion around the nature of Islamism, there is also no consensus on its causes – especially in accounting for the extraordinary speed of its evolution and ascent to become what is probably the fastest-growing force in Muslim world politics.

The gathering power and deepening reaffirmation of the faith have causes that are both internal and external to Islam. There is a widespread acceptance in the literature that the surge in Islamism appears to be an outcome of a host of historical, political, economic, cultural and social developments in Muslim countries. The colonial legacy, the accountability of rulers, rapidly deteriorating social conditions, the marginalisation of large sections of societies, intergenerational conflict, globalisation, modernity and Westernisation, mass media and mass communication, Western cultural hegemony and the fear of losing identity and values, and rising inequalities and the failure of earlier, secular attempts at solutions (primarily pan-Arab nationalism and socialism) have all been among the main causes of the rise and appeal of Islamism.

While these factors provide the background for the rise of Islamism in the Gulf region as well as in other Arab and Muslim countries, other domestic, regional and global factors have also played a central role.

The government co-optation and manipulation of religion

Gulf state governments have mastered the art of co-opting and manipulating religion and its ideas for the purposes of bolstering state power and consolidating national identity in order to win legitimacy for ruling dynasties.[2] Indeed, all Arab governments, with the notable exception of Lebanon, have constitutions or basic laws that explicitly proclaim Islam as the official religion of the state, as well as the main – if not the sole – source of legislation. Religious teaching at schools and mosques is a central element of educational curricula, while preaching at mosques and other social and religious gatherings has become a socio-political phenomenon aimed at Islamising the population, in a context of a fear of the spread of other ideological movements, including communism, socialism and even Arab nationalism. Given the lack of other venues for public speeches, gatherings and political meetings, mosques have become the only channel open to the population for public assembly. This is an essential issue as far as political development in the Muslim world is concerned, and has much to do with the politicisation of religion by both regimes and opposition groups.

Meanwhile, the governments of the Gulf states have used Islamic tenets to create their own ideology and self-avowed identity in order to enhance their own legitimacy and to fend off other ideologies. Gulf regimes have sought to respond to Islamist groups' challenges by espousing the same ideology, and by lending support to their activities both at home and abroad in an effort to tame and co-opt them.

Unlike other ideologies that have been experimented with in the Arab region, Islam forms an essential part of people's consciousness, and is inherently embedded in the very fabric of Arab Muslim society. On a personal level, Islam constitutes a crucial element of identity. Islamism, however, was

---

2. Joseph Nevo, 'Religion and National Identity in Saudi Arabia', *Middle Eastern Studies,* vol. 34, no. 3 (July 1988), pp. 34–53.

held at bay by Arab nationalism, which reigned supreme in the 1950s and 1960s, until its downfall in June 1967, when Arab armies were defeated in the Six Day War by Israel. In the search for alternative models to that offered by the increasingly discredited secular movement, Islam provided a ready answer, redirecting people's attention to the glory of the Islamic past, to Muslim *esprit de corps* and to an era of supposed authenticity untouched by corrupting foreign values.

The accountability of rulers

To many Islamists, the governments of the Gulf states fall short in their strict application of Islamic principles and *shari'a* law, and are regarded by them as tainted by human reasoning and thus unfaithful to the true teaching found in the Qur'anic text and the *sunna* ('the way of the Prophet'). This is especially true in Wahhabism in Saudi Arabia, which adheres to a strict transcription of the religious texts and rejects the practice of modern reasoning and interpretation.[3] This brings into question the legitimacy of the ruling regimes, which are mainly autocratic monocracies ruled by hereditary dynasties. Opposition groups judge the performance of these states harshly, exposing what are perceived as untenable shortcomings in both domestic and foreign policy. The question of legitimacy is thus sharpened by what opponents perceive as incompetent governments involved in corruption and the mismanagement of states' resources.

The relationship between the ruler and the ruled

In Islam, politics and government are viewed as constituting a single sphere of the religion. Among the precepts of Islam that govern the relationship between the ruler and the ruled are such issues as the duty of hearing and obedience (*al-ama 'wa' l-ta'a*), the pledge of allegiance (*al-bayah*), and the promotion of virtue and prevention of vice (*al-amr bi'l-ma'ruf wa'l-nahy 'an al-munkar*). Equally, there is an obligation to observe the *shari'a* (God's law), engage in consultation (*shura*) with the people and put into practice the concept of holy war (*jihad*). Opposition groups have used such

---

3. See Roel Meijer's chapter in this volume.

politico-ideological concepts to Islamise the population and spread the religion, and occasionally to challenge their own regimes.

Failures of foreign policy

In foreign policy, domestic opposition stems from the inability of Gulf regimes to resolve the Arab–Israeli conflict and ease the plight and the suffering of the Palestinians. The defeat of Arab armies at the hands of Israel and the continuing Israeli occupation of Arab land – including that of Jerusalem, Islam's third-holiest site – as well as unchecked and unchallenged Israeli intransigence, have exposed these regimes' ineptness and demonstrated their failure to defend Arab and Islamic causes. The policies of Western governments – and especially the US, which unequivocally and uncritically supports Israel – are seen by many as applying double standards, and as being directed against Arab and Islamic causes and interests. The utility of the Gulf state governments' close relations with the US is therefore questioned by restive populations, and especially by Islamist groups. Their relationships with the West have become a liability and a burden for those governments, which have become defensive, while Islamist groups calling for more action and opposing such close relations have become popular, and their message has won greater public appeal.

Regional radicalisation

As the Gulf states gradually expanded their contacts with the outside world from the 1960s onwards, they exposed their citizens to broader political debates at a time of regional radicalisation and politicisation. Moreover, the Gulf states urgently needed well-trained professionals at a time of rapid, oil-induced modernisation. The Muslim Brotherhood came to play a key role in the new and expanding administration – especially in education, where it designed school and university curricula and provided the bulk of faculty members. The Gulf state regimes became host to a large number of Syrian and Egyptian Muslim Brothers and their leaders, who were persecuted in their home countries by the Baathist and Nasserist regimes.[4]

---

4. Adeed Dawisha, *Arab Nationalism in the Twentieth Century: From Triumph to Despair*, Princeton and Oxford: Princeton University Press, 2003. p. 278.

These religious leaders brought about the formation of the Muslim Brotherhood in the 1950s and 1960s, and subsequently the ancestral and Salafi movements in the 1980s. The Gulf states used the Muslim Brothers' politicised version of Islam as a weapon in their political–ideological dispute with their Nasserist and Baathist neighbours. For example, King Faysal of Saudi Arabia (ruled 1964–75) used religion effectively to ward off Arab national-ism, Nasserism and communist attempts to spread into the kingdom and the Gulf region. Faysal made Saudi Arabia – the birthplace of the Prophet Muhammad and home to Islam's two holiest sites, Mecca and Medina – a haven for disgruntled, expelled and hounded Islamic fundamentalists. This was especially the case for members of the Egyptian Muslim Brotherhood fleeing Nasser's oppressive rule. Faysal and other Gulf rulers welcomed these disaffected religious militants, activists and teachers with open arms, and used them to fill influential posts in key ministries and to manage and staff schools and universities. They managed to guide the formation of Saudi Islamic policies both at home and abroad. In particular, King Faysal and his successors embarked on enhancing the state power and regional position of Saudi Arabia by using religious precepts, and by supporting the propagation of a global Wahhabist version of Islam and *da'wa* (the Islamic call to win converts and adherents) through financial aid. The creation in 1962 of the Muslim World League, based in Mecca, and in 1971 of the Organisation of the Islamic Conference in Jeddah, can be seen as components of an effort to thwart other regional arrangements influenced by Nasserim, enhancing instead Saudi stature in the region, and to proselytise the Saudi strain of Wahhabi Islam around the world.[5]

The reaction to modernisation and development

Financed by their oil income, the Gulf states took the fast track to moderni-sation and development, viewed by many as 'Westernisation'. This subjected their traditional tribal systems of social life to enormous strain, resulting in unprecedented individual disillusionment, economic imbalances and political alienation. The breakneck pace of modernisation appeared to challenge the status of mosques as social centres, while capitalism and globalisation emerged

---

5. As'ad Abukhalil, *The Battle for Saudi Arabia: Royalty, Fundamentalism, and Global Power*, New York: Seven Stories Press, 2004, p. 104.

to contest the role of Islam as a guiding ideology. In the Gulf, perhaps more than in any other part of the world, modernisation and economic growth have far surpassed social and political development. As the socio-cultural fabric began to unravel, the ensuing disaffection gave rise to a yearning for familiar, traditional values. The failure of capitalist modernity and social utopia has made the language of morality, articulated through religion, into a substitute politics.[6] As the public became more contemptuously dismissive of modernity, with its alien ideas of 'sovereignty' and 'nationalism', it rejected and condemned such notions as imported ideas (*hulul mustawrada*). 'Islam is the solution' (*al-islam huwa al-hal*) became the prevalent slogan of Islamism. With the threat of globalisation and its cultural impact in the age of mass communication, Islamism gained greater appeal in defence of the identity and values of Arab Muslims. The champions of both official Islam and popular Islam – those who defended the system and those who challenged it – justified their policies and demands in terms of the Islamic faith.

Demographic and social change

Empowered by their oil wealth, the Gulf states embarked on the consolidation of state power and an expansion of welfare benefits and programmes throughout the region, in an attempt to gain legitimacy. Benefits were, however, unevenly distributed, making material inequities and social imbalances greater and more visible than ever before. As population growth outstripped the economic prosperity of these *rentier* states, whose economic well-being was largely dependent on the vagaries of the oil market, the unwritten social contract – generous welfare in exchange for political acquiescence – began to come under stress. Falling oil prices in the 1980s and 1990s resulted in economic austerity and stagnation and rising unemployment, especially among young people. With the lack of successful economic diversification, less disposable income was available to Gulf state governments to distribute among their citizens and to continue with welfare programmes. The failure of other ideological forces to solve equity and distribution issues invariably led Islam to take on that task, and followers of other failed ideologies were quickly won over by it. Deteriorating socio-economic conditions at times of growing

---

6. Asef Bayat, *Making Islam Democratic: Social Movements and the Post-Islamist Turn*, Stanford: Stanford University Press, 2007.

populations, highly skewed towards a young population with rising expectations, caused both social unrest and an ideological void, which provided fertile ground for calls for political participation and increased opposition. Moreover, the appeal of Islamism was partly the result of a reaction against official corruption and repression which, in the minds of many citizens, had reached intolerable levels in their societies. Issues of inequality and injustice are debated across the Gulf by those who contrast the sometimes objectionable realities of everyday life with the Islamic ideals of equality, justice and alms-giving. The distressed, dispossessed and alienated have chosen Islamism as a means to express discontent, and Islam's social promise suddenly has a political relevance.[7] This has been accentuated by the official support that the religion has gained from governments, and by the political space and sanctuary available for Islamic activism.

Islamic Revolution in Iran

The success of the 1979 Islamic Revolution in Iran provided a strong boost to the attractiveness of Islamism in the Gulf region. It created a rival voice speaking on behalf of Muslims worldwide, especially with its initial call for the export of the revolution to other Muslim countries, and particularly to the Gulf states. Although it was Shi'i in sectarian affiliation – in contrast to Sunni Islam which is dominant in the Gulf states – the Iranian Revolution succeeded in inspiring religious advocates and triggering religious organisation throughout the region. The Iranian Revolution presented a model of revolutionary Islam, in contrast to the conservative model observed by the regimes in the Gulf states. To respond to the perceived threat of the export of the Iranian Islamic version of revolution, conservative Gulf-state governments gave an extra measure of support to the Sunni camp at a time when Islamism was gathering momentum. Indeed, rivalry between Saudi (Sunni) and Iranian (Shi'i) versions of Islam, and competition for leadership and cultural and political hegemony in the Gulf region and beyond, should be understood within this context.[8]

---

7. C. Benard and Z. Khalilzad, '*The Government of God*': *Iran's Islamic Republic*, New York: Columbia University Press, 1984, p. 25; Ø. Noreng, *Oil and Islam: Social and Economic Issues*, Chichester, New York: Wiley, 1997, p. 272.
8. See, for example, F. Gregory Gause III, 'Saudis Aim to Roll Back Iranian Influence', Council on Foreign Relations, 16 March 2007, available at www.cfr.org;

The Soviet invasion of Afghanistan

The Soviet invasion of Afghanistan in the early 1980s, and the subsequent support from Gulf states and Western governments for the *jihad* in Afghanistan against the Soviet army and the communist regime in Kabul, provoked significant support for a wide network of Islamic groups and organisations fighting against the occupation. They received substantial financial, logistical, political and moral support; citizens of the Gulf states were recruited as *mujahidin* and participated in the struggle in Afghanistan where, for example, bin Laden and his al-Qaeda organisation were established. These groups were emboldened by the success of the *mujahidin* in Afghanistan, while the cross-border experience that Islamists gained in Afghanistan, Bosnia and Chechnya, and their struggle in areas where Islam and Muslims were seen to be under attack, gained them much popular support, especially among the alienated youth.

The Iraqi invasion of Kuwait

The Iraqi invasion of Kuwait resulted in a growing presence of American (non-Muslim) troops in the region – particularly in Saudi Arabia, which is home to Islam's most holy sites. This was seen as heretical; it undermined the Gulf-state regimes and strengthened the case of the opposition – especially of the Islamists. The Gulf states were portrayed as American protectorates, and the vulnerability and dependence of these states on the West was highlighted, with the insinuation that the billions of dollars paid in arms purchases and large defence contracts had been misspent. Washington's Middle East policies – especially those relating to the Arab–Israeli conflict, Palestine and Iraq – cast its allies in the region in a bad light. Thus, in the eyes of the opposition, the Islamic credentials of these states had been called into question, and the continuing presence of Western troops in the region (despite the US redeployment out of Saudi Arabia) was viewed as a prop for what had become illegitimate governments.

---

and Henner Fürtig, *Iran's Rivalry with Saudi Arabia between the Gulf Wars*, Reading: Ithaca Press, 2002.

US Middle East policy and the 'war on terror'

There is general dissatisfaction in the region with US Middle East policy, which is criticised as being overwhelmingly influenced by the strong Israeli lobby in Washington. Many questions are also raised about the 'double standards' of US policy in the region – including its attitude towards the various conflicts, its support of undemocratic regimes, and its ideological stance against Islamists.[9] Against this background, US policy and the rhetoric of 'the war on terror' – following the al-Qaeda attack on US soil on September 11, 2001 and the subsequent US attack on Afghanistan to destroy al-Qaeda's network and the Taliban government which acted as its host – was perceived as a 'crusade' directed against Muslims. This alienated many Muslims, and their rage was further fuelled by images from the Guantánamo Bay detention camp and the rise of xenophobia and Islamophobia in the West that coincided with neoconservative warnings of the rise of Islam and a looming 'clash of civilisations'.

Iraq: US sanctions and military invasion

The US sanctions imposed on Iraq from the 1990s until the 2003 invasion and occupation of the country were only possible because the US and its allies were able to use Gulf states' land and draw on their logistical support. Similarly, the acquiescence of Gulf regimes was crucial in mounting the invasion of Iraq. The drastic consequences of this invasion in terms of the loss of life and suffering of the Iraqi people, the destruction of an Arab Muslim country and the treatment of Iraqi prisoners at Abu Ghraib fuelled discontent and angered the public, leading to a further rise in the appeal of Islamism. Indeed, the resulting Shi'i control of Iraq and Iranian support for Shi'i communities in Iraq gave rise to more radical Sunni elements from the Gulf states joining the Iraqi resistance to the occupation.

---

9. Ramin Ahmadov, 'The US Policy toward the Middle East in the Post-Cold War Era', *Alternatives: Turkish Journal of International Relations*, vol. 4, nos 1–2 (Spring/Summer 2005), pp. 138–50.

Survey of Islamist groups and movements

Islamic groups and movements are not new phenomena, having existed in the Arab Mashriq well before the 1980s, where they were mainly quietly occupied in teaching, preaching and proselytising. While other political and ideological forces, such as liberals, nationalists, Baathists or Nasserists represented stronger trends, Islamist groups barely existed at the political level, and were largely confined at the fringes of political and ideological confrontation. Islamist groups nevertheless began to take centre stage as other competing secular ideologies began to wane, helped along by the changes in the social environment outlined above.

In the Gulf region, the growing power of Islamist groups began to be noticeable from the 1980s. Although they share much common ground in their beliefs and aspirations, Islamist groups in the Gulf are far from monolithic or homogeneous, and are not bound by any central organisation or hierarchical structure. Far from being uniform, they take various forms according to the particular needs and circumstances of local areas. They are commonly loose, fragmented and decentralised groups divided between various religious sects and factions; their aims and objectives are diverse, and their methods are often poles apart. They emanate from the three main sects of Islam: Sunni, Shi'i and Abadhi (the dominant sect in Oman), and they are composed of a varied mix of workers, university students, intellectuals, religious scholars, businessmen and even royal princes.[10] Women, although not active participants, still play an important supporting role in the Islamisation of society. Their goals and demands vary from the call for such far-fetched aims as the overthrow of the incumbent government and the replacement of the ruling elite, or the creation of an Islamic state under *shari'a* law, to the opposition of official corruption and the call for good governance, greater social justice, and political reform.

Sunni Islamist groups

The Sunni sect, being the largest, constitutes the main group, and is itself divided. There are three major Sunni movements extending from

10. Abdulaziz O. Sagar, 'Political Opposition in Saudi Arabia', in Paul Aarts and Gerd Nonneman, eds, *Saudi Arabia in the Balance: Political Economy, Society, Foreign Affairs*, London: Hurst, pp. 234–70.

mainstream movements to traditional fundamentalism, which can be categorised as follows.

The Muslim Brotherhood

The Muslim Brotherhood comprises al-Ikhwan, which is its most mainstream and moderate branch; the Salafi movement, which is traditional and ancestral; and the slightly less dogmatic Islah (reform) fundamentalism.[11] All three Sunni movements share a strong dislike for the Shi'i sect within Islam.[12]

Ikhwan, the mainstream Muslim Brotherhood, now has a small but active following among urban-educated Gulf citizens. Following early Salafi Wahhabism, which brought religion to the forefront of politics in the early eighteenth century, the Ikhwan marked the start of the new wave of Islamism in the Gulf, which began in 1980s. The Muslim Brotherhood began after the migration of its leaders from Nasserist Egypt and Baathist Syria to the Gulf, where they were welcomed by the region's rulers, who co-opted them to take over religious education and confront new revolutionary ideas emanating from Arab nationalism and from liberal and leftist circles.

Ikhwan adopted the method of preaching in favour of, and carrying out, philanthropic activities while working alongside incumbent governments to achieve gradual reform in the direction of Islamic principles. Ikhwan began to lose its appeal among the restive youth as a result of its long-term strategy of pursuing gradual change and the perception that it appeased rulers in exchange for attaining high government offices for its leaders, who in the process had become corrupt.

The Muslim Brotherhood has followers in almost all the Gulf states. In Saudi Arabia, for example, it has given way to the Salafi and neo-Salafi movements, but still has its own followers among the urban-educated Saudis. In Qatar, though it is no longer an organised movement, it was mainly active through the Youth of Doha Society, which it subsequently dissolved; but

---

11. There is also a fourth Sunni group that is part of resurgent populist Islam in the Gulf. This is populist Sufism, represented by the mystical movements such as the al-Rifai brotherhood in Kuwait. This mystical component of Sunni populist Islam is especially strong in North Africa, but currently has only a limited presence in the Gulf. The Sufi groups that do exist are sharply opposed both to the Salafi movement and to Shi'ism.

12. See, for example, Laurence Louer, *Transnational Shia Politics: Religious and Political Networks in the Gulf*, London: Hurst, 2008.

it is well represented within Islamic banking and Islamic financial services organisations. It has influence in the Al-Jazeera Channel and other media, educational and religious institutions.[13] With its small Qatari following, it does not constitute political opposition, and its leaders enjoy high status and wide influence, as well as close relations with government. In the UAE it was represented by the Society of Social Reform (*al-Islah al-Ijtima'i*), which was dissolved in the mid-1990s; it now concentrates on preaching and charitable work, though it used to have influence in the education sector before the government decided to curb its role. In Bahrain it is active through the Reform Movement (*al-Islah*) and the National Islamic Forum. The Bahrain Islamic Society and *Al-Tarbiya al-Islamiyya* were splinters off the Muslim Brotherhood, and they concentrate on preaching, while the *al-Shura* group is the political wing of the Islamic Society.

In Kuwait the Brotherhood is represented through the Social Reform Society and the Islamic Constitutional Movement (ICM), which acts as the political front for the organisation.[14] The ICM, which was established in 1991 after the liberation of Kuwait, is in fact a local restructuring of the Kuwaiti branch of the Muslim Brotherhood, marking its split from the global Muslim Brotherhood because of the latter's position on the Iraqi invasion of Kuwait, which was deemed by Kuwaiti branch to have been supportive of the invasion.[15]

In Oman, where political association is outlawed, the government uncovered an Islamic cell of about 130 people believed to be members of the Muslim Brotherhood in 1994.[16] The group consisted of high-ranking government officials, as well as security and army personnel, and they were charged with forming an illegal political party to undermine state security, and with subversion. They were sentenced by a state security court to imprisonment and

---

13. Mamoun Fendy, 'Al-Infisam al-Qatari bain Ruayat al-Amir w'al Agendat al-Jazeera', [Qatari Schizophrenia between the Amir and the Aljazeera Vision], *Asharq Alawsat*, 4 October 2004, available in Arabic at www.aawsat.com.

14. For background see, Falah Abdullah Al-Mudaires, *Jama'at al-Ikhwan al-Muslimin fi 'l-Kuwait* [Islamic Brotherhood Group in Kuwait], Kuwait: Qurtas Publishing, 1999. See also Shafeeq N. Ghabra, 'Balancing State and Society: The Islamic Movement in Kuwait', *Middle East Policy* vol. 5, no. 2, May 1997, pp. 58–71.

15. Falah Abdullah Al-Mudaires, *Jama'at al-Ikhwan al-Muslimin*, pp. 46, 47.

16. N. Janardhan, 'Islamists Stay Clear of Terrorism in Oman', *Terrorism Monitor* vol. 4, no. 9, March 2006, available at www.jamestown.org.

death sentences; but the sultan reduced their sentences to imprisonment, and freed them in 1995.

The Salafi movement

The Salafi movement began partly as a response to Ikhwan's limited credibility. However, while the Muslim Brotherhood, which began in the different environments of Egypt and the Levant, was generally flexible and tolerant, and recognised women's rights and other social issues, the Salafis – mainly of the Wahhabi movement of the Arabian Peninsula – were generally intolerant scriptural literalists, some of whom were even violent. The Salafi movement is made up of a number of groups.

1. Wahhabism

Wahhabism, a conservative and non-violent Salafi interpretation of Islam, could be seen as the official religious school of thought that is firmly rooted in Saudi society, and among its religious scholars (*'ulama*). The term 'Wahhabi' refers to a religious tradition developed over the centuries by the *'ulama* of the official Saudi religious establishment.[17] The term is now so overused that it has lost much of its meaning, serving to describe disparate groups and individuals across time and space, so long as they adhere to an austere or conservative view of Islam.

This revivalist movement – initiated in Najd, in central Arabia, in the early eighteenth century by Muhammad ibn 'Abd al-Wahhab – has been continued by its followers, who consider themselves to be the legitimate guardians of the tradition. Indeed, in seeking to spread his *da'wa*, 'Abd al-Wahhab found an ally in Muhammad ibn Saud, head of the small town of Dir'iyya (near modern-day Riyadh). Their pact in 1744 marked the foundation not only of the first Saudi state,[18] but also of a local religious establishment entrusted with developing and spreading 'Abd al-Wahhab's puritanical ideas.

---

17. For more on Wahhabism and the history of Saudi Arabia, see Roel Meijer's contribution in this volume; Madawi al-Rasheed, *Contesting the Saudi State: Islamic Voices from a New Generation*, Cambridge: Cambridge University Press, 2007; and Madawi al-Rasheed, *A History of Saudi Arabia,* Cambridge: Cambridge University Press, 2002.

18. Although both the first (1744–1818) and second (1823–91) Saudi states eventually collapsed as political entities, the alliance between the al-Saud family and Wahhabi preachers remained the basis for the formation of the modern Kingdom of Saudi Arabia in 1932.

Wahhabism and the Saudi religious establishment historically constitute the core of the Saudi intellectual field. The influence of Wahhabism extends far beyond the religious establishment's official role. Since the state's foundation, it has shaped its religious culture, education and judiciary.[19] As a result, it has had an impact – to a greater or lesser degree – on all the kingdom's Sunni Islamist trends.

However, after decades of relative autonomy, the religious establishment has developed a striking political pragmatism. To preserve its alliance with the rulers, it has supported Saudi policy even when it diverged from the movement's religious convictions:[20] it has been used by the ruling elite to rubber-stamp official decisions, issuing religious rulings to validate the regime's political stands.[21] Among these, the *fatwas* authorising the presence of foreign troops (1990)[22] and peace with Israel (1993)[23] cost the Wahhabi establishment much credibility, to the extent that many Saudis now view it as a mere extension of the regime. However, while it continues to provide indispensable legitimacy to the Saudis' rule, and acts as a guardian of the country's official Wahhabi doctrine, its perceived alliance with the rulers has caused a neo-Wahhabism to emerge. The movement's pragmatism has repeatedly led to 'radical Wahhabis' opposing the official religious establishment and accusing it of being corrupt and subservient to the regime.[24] While early Wahhabism was unified, it has now fractured into different strands.

---

19. Wahhabism is by no means the only Muslim denomination in Saudi Arabia. In fact, the country's population is one of the most diverse in the Middle East in this respect: Saudi Arabia has Sunnis belonging to all four jurisprudential schools, Sufis, and separate branches of Shi'ism.
20. Guido Steinberg, 'The Wahhabi Ulama and the Saudi State: 1745 to the Present', in Aarts and Nonneman eds., *Saudi Arabia in the Balance*, pp. 11–34.
21. The nomination of Shaykh ibn Baz as the head of the Wahhabi establishment in 1967, under the reign of King Faysal (1964-1975), may be considered the turning-point in its subordination to the regime.
22. This first ruling was given in August 1990, a few days after Saddam Hussein's invasion of Kuwait, by the Council of Senior 'Ulama (*haya kibar al-'ulama*), the highest institution in the Wahhabi religious establishment.
23. This ruling was provided by the Kingdom's top *mufti*, Shaykh ibn Baz himself, on 13 September 1993.
24. Guido Steinberg, 'The Wahhabi Ulama and the Saudi State', in Aarts and Nonneman eds., *Saudi Arabia in the Balance*, pp. 11–34.

2. *The Salafi reformers: Sahwa*

The term *al-sahwa al-islamiyya* refers to the fomentation of religious activism and enthusiasm that gripped Saudi universities in the 1970s and 1980s, rather than to any specific, formal movement. Ideologically, the young Sahwa Islamists advocated a blend of the traditional Wahhabi outlook (mainly on social and cultural issues) and the more contemporary Muslim Brotherhood approach (especially on political issues). They distinguished themselves from the Wahhabi establishment, which concentrated on abstract theological debates, by their readiness to discuss issues of contemporary significance. Unlike their official counterparts, they were also open to modern technology such as the cassette tape – which rapidly became their principal means of communication – as well as faxes and extensive use of the internet.

A turning-point in the evolution of Sahwa was the 1979 take-over of the mosque in Mecca by Juhayman al-'Utaybi and his group of neo-Salafis, who were motivated to a large extent by anger at perceived immorality and societal changes in Saudi Arabia, which the conservative and moderate religious establishment could not address.[25] The regime, rather than use the opportunity to initiate long-overdue political and social changes, responded by strengthening the religious establishment and pouring additional money into religious institutions as a means of co-opting its critics and bolstering its legitimacy. The unintended consequence was to strengthen the Sahwa, which was not at that time considered an autonomous movement and had largely assimilated into the margins of the official establishment. The Sahwa used its strong presence in the educational sector to take advantage of government support.

With this newfound impetus, Sahwa clerics grew increasingly confident and began to participate in public debates. They took issue with both liberals, whom they accused of undermining Saudi society through secularisation,[26] and the Wahhabi establishment, which they criticised for its lack of interest

---

25. Thomas Hegghammer and Stephane Lacroix, 'Rejectionist Islamism in Saudi Arabia: The Story of Juhayman al-'Utaybi Revisited', *International Journal of Middle East Studies* vol. 39, no. 1 (2007) pp. 103–22.

26. The 1980s were marked by the so-called 'modernism' debate, which opposed a group of writers and poets calling for a reform of Islamic literary tradition with the Sahwa, which accused them of trying to destroy the foundations of Saudi society. See Mamoun Fandy, *Saudi Arabia and the Politics of Dissent*, Basingstoke: Palgrave MacMillan, 1999, p. 48.

in contemporary issues and its unconditional – albeit still veiled – support for the regime.

This neo-Wahhabi reformist strain was composed of self-styled '*ulama of the centre*' – centrist religious scholars – who had emerged from the Sahwa. In the 1990s, beginning with the Gulf War, Sahwa clerics like Salman al-Awdah, Safar al-Hawali, Ayed al-Qarni and Nasir al-Omar became more vocal, denouncing the state's failure to conform to Islamic values, its corruption, and its subservience to the US, while also condemning official Wahhabi clerics for their silence on all of these issues.

But the Sahwa clerics never constituted a uniform group. From the outset, because of their background, they represented a variety of undercurrents – some closer to Wahhabism, others to the Muslim Brotherhood.[27] Such divisions remain apparent today in the conflicting positions they espouse on issues such as relations with liberal reformers, Shi'is and Sufis, and in their attitudes toward al-Qaeda and other violent Islamist groups.[28] Both the Sahwa and neo-Sahwa tendencies accepted the legitimacy of the Saudi state as a political structure, and were only to demand a reform of Saudi politics after the first Gulf War in 1990.

In Kuwait Salafism is more marginal, and has its base in the Heritage Group (*al-Turah*) – an influential Islamic association that gained strength from the 1970s – and the Islamic Popular Alliance (IPA), better known as *al-Salaf* ('ancestry'), which has its roots in the Society for the Rebirth of Islamic Tradition. This group, which has been attracting followers since the 1980s, is more literalist in its interpretation of Islam than the Islamic Constitutional Movement (ICM), formerly known as the Kuwaiti Muslim Brotherhood.[29] Linked to the Social Reform Society, it is a non-governmental association formed to practise religious policing, which is similar to the official Saudi 'Committee for the Prevention of Vice and

---

27. Among the latter are subdivisions between so-called Bannaists and Qutbists. Bannaism and Qutbism refer to the two main ideologues of the Egyptian Muslim Brotherhood, Hasan al-Banna and Sayyid Qutb. See also Kamal Helbawy, 'The Muslim Brotherhood in Egypt: Historical Evolution and Future Prospects', Chapter 4 in this volume.

28. International Crisis Group, *Saudi Arabia Backgrounder: Who Are the Islamists? ICG Middle East Report* 31 (21 September 2004), available at www.crisisgroup. org>.

29. Shafeeq N. Ghabra, 'Balancing State and Society: The Islamic Movement in Kuwait', *Middle East Policy* vol. 5, no. 2 (May 1997), pp. 58–71.

Promotion of Virtue'. However, the government intervened and banned the practice.[30]

3. *The Salafi rejectionists*

Rejectionist Islamists (sometimes referred to as neo-Salafists) first appeared in Saudi Arabia in the 1970s on the margins of the Sahwa, though they regarded the Sahwa as excessively preoccupied with politics, just as they considered the jihadists to be ignorant of religious affairs. Unlike the Sahwa reformers who were dominant in schools and universities, the rejectionists avoided official education altogether, seeking religious instruction elsewhere. They focused on questions of individual faith, morals and ritual practices, as opposed to broader social, cultural or political issues. They were hostile to the very concept of the nation-state, regarding the state as illegitimate, and seeking not to modify it but to break with it – most often through withdrawal, but sometimes by means of revolt.

Rejectionist Islamists do not constitute a homogenous social or political movement. Indeed, there has been far more diversity among them in terms of approach and organisational structure than among the Sahwa. Saudi rejectionist Islamism, for example, has been variously represented by organisations such as the one led by Juhayman al-ʿUtaybi, which seized Mecca's Great Mosque in 1979; by fringe communities, which typically withdrew from society and adopted a very conservative, puritan lifestyle; and by informal religious study circles, which rejected both mosque-based Wahhabism and the school and university-centred Sahwa teachings.[31]

Juhayman al-ʿUtaybi founded a group known as the al-Jamaʿa al-Salafiyya al-Muhtasiba (JSM). The JSM movement was one of the Saudi rejectionists' most visible and organised manifestations. The JSM began in Medina in the mid-1970s, and was inspired partly by the views of Nasr al-Din al-Albani (1914–99), a Syrian Salafi scholar.[32] The JSM rejected all schools of Islamic

---

30. Ibid., p. 63.
31. Hegghammer and Lacroix, 'Rejectionist Islamism in Saudi Arabia', pp. 103–22.
32. Nasr al-Din al-Albani was a Syrian scholar of Albanian origin who was born in 1914. He founded a school of Islamic thought that views the Qur'an and the *hadith* as the sole bases for religious decisions. Al-Albani taught at the University of Medina in the late 1950s, but was compelled to leave due to his many disagreements with Saudi scholars, notably on ritual issues. Nevertheless, he

jurisprudence (*fiqh*), including Wahhabism, on the grounds that each involved a degree of human judgment, adhering instead to a literal reading of the *hadith* (traditions of the Prophet's life) as the sole source of religious truth. Disagreements with the Wahhabi establishment initially turned on ritual questions; over time, however, the JSM evolved into a full-scale socio-political protest movement of some significance.

For example, a radicalised faction of the JSM, under the leadership of Juhayman himself, seized the Mecca mosque in a 1979 uprising. The reasons behind the violent and surprising step taken by Juhayman and his group included a protest against the 'un-Islamic' aspects of the Saudi state and the public declaration that one of Juhayman's companions, Muhammad al-Qahtani, was the Mahdi (the Islamic equivalent of the messiah), and that the Mecca operation would bring about the end of the world. Many others took part in order to precipitate radical political and social change.[33]

Juhayman and his companions were either executed or imprisoned, and the JSM as an organisation disappeared after the Mecca events; but most of Juhayman's basic ideas – notably the critique of social corruption and moral decadence articulated in his writings – outlived him.[34] Remnants of the JSM sought refuge in Kuwait, Yemen and the northern Saudi desert regions in the 1980s. A decade later, groups of young Islamists calling themselves 'students of religious knowledge' (*talabat 'ilm al-din*) and viewing themselves as direct heirs of JSM could still be found seeking out the remaining companions of Juhayman among desert Bedouins. Shunning mosques and universities, they formed religious study groups in their homes, and had for all practical purposes withdrawn from a society they deemed sinful. Juhayman al-'Utaybi's letters were republished in Kuwait years later, and inspired a younger generation of neo-Salafi ideologues. One of those introduced to Juhayman's writings in Kuwait was Abu Muhammad

maintained close ties with Saudi Arabia, and particularly to the city of Medina, until his death in 1999. ICG, *Saudi Arabia Backgrounder*.

33. Hegghammer and Lacroix, 'Rejectionist Islamism in Saudi Arabia', pp. 103–22.

34. While living in the desert, Juhayman wrote a series of articles known as the 'Seven Letters of Juhayman', to justify the attack, as well as much religious poetry. He also made tape-recordings of his speeches, some of which still circulate in Saudi Arabia. See Hegghammer and Lacroix, 'Rejectionist Islamism in Saudi Arabia'.

al-Maqdisi, who in the 1990s became a leading ideologue of the so-called Salafi-jihadist trend.[35]

In direct challenge to the Saudi authorities, in May 1993 six prominent Islamists announced the formation in Riyadh of Saudi Arabia's first human rights organisation – the Committee for the Defence of Legitimate Rights (CDLR). The CDLR is a loosely knit political reform group that began to assert itself after the 1991 Gulf War. Its intention was to place its struggle against the regime within the context of the worldwide human rights movement. Although the CDRL's declarations defined human rights in terms of the legitimate confines of *shari'a* law in its specific (and strict) interpretation of individual rights, rather than the universal standards accepted by global human rights organisations, international human rights organisations rushed to support the Saudi association and it was disbanded by the authorities two weeks after its formation, and its spokesman, Muhammad al-Mas'ari, was jailed. [36] CDRL members were nevertheless among the signatories of the 1992 Memorandum of Advice addressed to the Saudi king, calling for the eradication of corruption and the application of *shari'a* law. Mas'ari was freed in 1993 and clandestinely went to London, and re-founded the CDRL with Sa'ad al-Faqih in April 1994. Through a series of communiqués faxed to Saudi Arabia and throughout the world, the CDRL sought to mobilise public opinion against the Saudi regime and its human rights record. Despite bitter attacks, the CDRL advocated moderation and peaceful change in the kingdom on the basis of *shari'a* principles. In 1996 the CDRL was split because of disputes between Mas'ari and al-Faqih, and the Movement of Islamic Reform in Arabia (MIR), which espoused more radical views, was created as a result.[37] Until this split, the CDRL had been one of the most organised and professional Saudi political opposition groups.

4. The Salafi jihadists

Salafi jihadism is a loose term used to designate an outlook that invokes Wahhabi theology to advocate the resort to violence. In effect, Wahhabism provides jihadists with a more sophisticated theological framework for their

---

35. Stephane Lacroix, 'Islamo-Liberal Politics in Saudi Arabia', in Aarts and Nonneman eds., *Saudi Arabia in the Balance*, pp. 35–56.

36. R. Hrair Dekmejian, 'The Rise of Islamism In Saudi Arabia', *Middle East Journal* vol. 48, vol. 4 (Autumn 1994), pp. 627–43.

37. Sagar, 'Political Opposition in Saudi Arabia'.

activism. This more violent version, with followers among radical youth, enjoyed (overt and covert) support from some *'ulama*.[38] While both Salafi reformers and rejectionists are at pains to distinguish themselves from those they refer to as jihadists, there have been instances of rejectionists gravitating toward *jihadi* circles, whose activities occurred with increasing frequency from the early 1980s onwards. In the mid-1990s, the *jihadi* movement, of which al-Qaeda is the most prominent radical group, was split into two main branches: the 'classical jihadists', and the more radical and marginal 'global jihadists'.[39] The distinction between the two branches is that the classical jihadists prefer to wage semi-conventional warfare within confined theatres of war, while global jihadists are prepared to use all means in all locations. This was the main reason for the separation of Khattab, the Saudi commander of the Arabs in Chechnya, from Osama bin Laden, the Saudi jihadist leader in Afghanistan.[40]

The origins of today's jihadism can be traced back to the participation – actively encouraged and facilitated by Gulf regimes and western governments at the time – of thousands of Saudis, and to a lesser extent other Gulf nationals, in the Afghan war against the Soviet Union. These governments offered logistical and financial assistance to prospective *mujahidin* – for example, subsidised flights to Pakistan – and the official religious establishment declared it a collective duty (*fard kifayah*) for Muslims to fight in Afghanistan.[41]

There is no satisfactory comprehensive analysis of the motivations and socio-economic background of the Saudis and other Gulf nationals who went to Afghanistan in the 1980s and 1990s. Although their motivation was not clear, they appear not to have been driven by any particular political project or set of religious beliefs: most were teenagers; for most participation was purely symbolic; their trip rarely lasted longer than the summer holidays; and many never made it across the border from Pakistan to Afghanistan. For those who remained, the experience was profoundly transformative, as they became part of the romanticised culture of violent resistance that flourished within the Arab contingent of the Afghan *mujahidin* war.[42] These militants developed

---

38. Ibid.
39. Thomas Hegghammer, 'Islamists and Regime Stability in Saudi Arabia', *International Affairs* vol. 84, no. 4 (2008), pp. 701–15.
40. Ibid. p. 706.
41. For example, 'Abd al-'Aziz bin Baz, the Mufti of Saudi Arabia at the time, issued a *fatwa* decreeing *jihad* in Afghanistan a collective duty.
42. ICG, *Saudi Arabia Backgrounder*.

an ultra-masculine, militaristic and violent worldview, and they experienced their initial political awakening outside their own country. Moreover, the so-called Afghan Arab jihadists, who retained a base at home, were given virtually free travel in and out of their country during the 1990s and were in a position to influence youth in the Gulf region.[43]

By the end of the Afghan war against the Soviet army, a global jihadist culture had already spread to many Islamist circles in the Gulf, while many of its youth continued to leave their countries in search of military training and to gain combat experience throughout the 1990s – particularly once al-Qaeda had established an infrastructure of training camps in Afghanistan in the mid-1990s.[44]

The US-led invasion of Afghanistan in the aftermath of 11 September 2001 – which precipitated the fall of the Taliban and the beginning of the 'global war on terror' – denied al-Qaeda its safe haven, thus removing the basis of its unique organisational structure and resulting in the decentralised and multi-polar nature of the global jihadist movement.[45] With the *mujahidin* recruits returning home, al-Qaeda began to change its tactics and perspectives, and started its war against the 'crusaders' in the Arabian Peninsula. In addition, the US-led invasion of Iraq in March 2003 gave the global jihadist movement a strategic and emotional focal point at a time when the movement was strategically disorientated, having lost its territorial base in Afghanistan. A splinter-group of al-Qaeda known as 'al-Qaeda in the Arabian Peninsula' (QAP) launched a violent campaign in 2003 with a series of large-scale attacks against Western targets in Saudi Arabia, pitting themselves against Saudi security services and undermining and diverting attention from another al-Qaeda splinter-group in Iraq, known as *al-Qa'ida fi Bilad al-Rafidain* ('al-Qaeda in the Land of the Two Rivers'). This latter group was involved in fighting against US troops and Shi'i domination in Iraq. This rekindled the ideological conflict between classical and global jihadists, as this develop-

43. So long as they were not involved in domestic militant activities – with some notable exceptions, such as Osama bin Laden – they were rarely prosecuted. Saudi officials acknowledge this – see 'Interview with Jamal Khashoggi', 7 July 2004, available at www.jamestown.org>.

44. In addition to attending training camps in Afghanistan, global *mujahidin* fought in places such as Bosnia and Somalia in the early 1990s and in Chechnya in the late 1990s.

45. Thomas Hegghammer, 'Global Jihadism after the Iraq War', *Middle East Journal*, vol. 60, no. 1 (Winter 2006), pp. 11–32.

ment was considered to drain crucial human and financial resources.[46] The invasion and occupation of Iraq led to a channelling of radical forces to Iraq, possibly at the expense of other fronts in the global *jihad*. It also modified the jihadists' conception of the enemy, and placed the Gulf countries, and even Europe, more clearly in the spotlight. This development explains the number of terrorist attacks in Europe, and the increase in the number of violent incidents in Gulf countries such as Kuwait and Qatar.[47]

Shi'i Islamists[48]

Shi'i Islamists' presence as a political movement in the Gulf is more recent than that of the Sunni Muslim Brotherhood. They first emerged as the al-Da'wa Party in Iraq in 1958, which rapidly formed branches in the Gulf and other Arab countries in the 1960s and 1970s.[49] Learning from Ikhwan's organisational and political experience, the al-Da'wa Party opened affiliated branches in Bahrain, the Eastern Province of Saudi Arabia and Kuwait. While political openness in Kuwait helped it to operate in a relatively public manner, political conditions in Bahrain and Saudi Arabia prevented it from doing so, despite the fact that some of its leaders and iconic figures came from these countries.[50]

---

46. Thomas Hegghammer, 'Islamists and Regime Stability in Saudi Arabia', *International* (2008), pp. 701–15.

47. Thomas Hegghammer, 'Global Jihadism after the Iraq War'.

48. Shi'ism originated in the dispute over the Prophet Muhammad's succession. 'Ali, the Prophet's cousin and son-in-law (as husband of his daughter Fatima) claimed to be the Prophet's rightful successor, but was repeatedly passed over before eventually becoming the fourth caliph. His position was soon challenged by Muawiyya, the founder of the Umayyad dynasty, and 'Ali was killed in 661 ce. His supporters, *Shai'at 'Ali* ('the partisans of Ali'), were those who accepted the argument that the leadership (*al-imama*) of the Muslim community combined spiritual and temporal responsibilities, and required divine inspiration, and should therefore be drawn from the Prophet's line alone. They subsequently supported the claims of 'Ali's sons, Hassan and Hussayn, as his rightful successors, in opposition to the line of Sunni rulers; both sons led unsuccessful revolts against the Umayyads and were killed (Hassan in 671, and Hussayn in 680). Thereafter, the Shi'is regarded all Sunni rulers as illegitimate usurpers, and recognised only their own imams in the line of descent from the Prophet through 'Ali's children.

49. Baqer S. Al-Najjar, *Al-Haraka al-Diniyyah fi al-Khalij al-'Arabi* [Islamic Movements in the Arabian Gulf], Saqi, London, 2007, p. 61.

50. Ibid.

Whereas Sunni Islamism has fragmented into rival tendencies with distinctive worldviews, as well as different strategies and forms of organisation, Shi'i Islamism has remained impressively integrated. There is, however, no such thing as Pan-Shi'ism, or even unified leadership.[51] Shi'i Islam is better organised than Sunni Islam, sharing a coherent religious view based on a distinct conception of Islamic laws and practices. Specifically, it is not divided into separate political, missionary and jihadist forms of activism. This fact is ultimately rooted in Shi'ism's historic status as the minority form of Islam; more immediately, it is closely connected with a remarkable feature of Shi'i Islamism – namely, the leading political role of the *'ulama* or the *marji'iyya*.[52] Historically, the *'ulama*'s influence has been based on their autonomy from the state. But their authority within the Shi'i community also owes a great deal to the fact that, unlike their Sunni counterparts, the mainstream Shi'i *'ulama* have never stopped practising *ijtihad* – the intellectual effort involved in the interpretation of scripture. Notwithstanding the images of bearded and turbaned clerics commonly associated with them, the activist Shi'i *'ulama* have been far more modernist in this sense than most of their Sunni counterparts. The result is that the divisions within Shi'i Islamism are quite different from those within Sunni Islamism, in terms of their bases, nature and implications.

Although reliable data are not available, Shi'i Muslims are estimated to amount to roughly 10 per cent of the population in Saudi Arabia, 30 per cent in Kuwait, 15 per cent in the UAE, between 50 and 70 per cent in Bahrain and a smaller percentage in the other Gulf states.[53] Because of their status as the minority, and as politically marginal or even oppressed communities (whether or not they have formed absolute numerical minorities), in most of the states in which they have found themselves, communalism – the defence of community interests in relation to other populations and the state – has become the most natural form of Shi'i political activism.[54] This has been the case for Shi'i activism not only in Gulf states (Kuwait, Saudi Arabia, the UAE), but

---

51. Vali Nasr, 'When the Shi'i Rise', *Foreign Affairs*, vol. 85, no. 4 (July/August 2006), pp. 58–74.

52. See Chapters 6 and 10 in this volume.

53. Louer, *Transnational Shia Politics*.

54. International Crisis Group, *Understanding Islamism*, ICG, *Middle East/North Africa Report 37* (2 March 2005), available at <www.crisisgroup.org>.

even in Lebanon and Pakistan. It has also been the tendency in states where Shiʿites have become the numerical majority – namely Iraq and Bahrain.

Although Shiʿi movements in some Gulf states were relatively active in the past because of certain socio-economic and political grievances, it was the Iranian Revolution of 1979 that gave a strong political and moral boost to the movement. The success of the Shiʿi revolution in Iran was a turning-point not only for the entire Islamist movement in the region, but it had even more relevance for the Shiʿi sect. The revolution introduced an entirely new lexicon based on the use of religion as a political tool, and inspired more populist movements throughout the region, where the Shiʿi now had a more powerful neighbour – Iran – to support their cause. Khomeini's pronouncement of an intention to export Iranian-style revolution to the Gulf monarchies gave the Shiʿi an ally and supporter, and Shiʿi uprisings began to gather momentum all around the Gulf.

In Saudi Arabia, the Shiʿis are mainly concentrated in the oil-rich Eastern Province, which was integrated into the Saudi state in 1913. Since then, Shiʿis have complained of not being allowed to practise their faith freely and of being treated as second-class citizens.[55] In fact, Shiʿi Islamist organisations began to emerge in the Eastern Province in the 1970s, enraged by their socio-economic and political marginalisation. The process accelerated with the 1979 Iranian Revolution; invigorated by that uprising, thousands celebrated the Shiʿi Ashura festival despite an official ban. The heavy-handed response led to violent confrontations and disturbances in 1979 and 1980, which were crushed by the National Guard.[56] Few Shiʿi activists remained in Saudi Arabia, and those who did were co-opted and silenced by the regime; most fled to Syria, Iran, the UK or the US. Significant mass civil disobedience lasted less than a decade, but the leadership gradually moderated its views, recognising the limitations of agitation and violence and seeking improved ties with a regime whose legitimacy it came to acknowledge, and whose role as a bulwark against more extreme Sunni militants it came to accept. By the late 1980s, many had moderated their views, distancing themselves from Khomeini's agenda and embracing principles of political pluralism and democracy.[57] In 1993, the

55. Fouad Ibrahim, *The Shiʿis of Saudi Arabia*, London: Saqi, 2007, p. 7.
56. See Madawi al-Rasheed, 'The Shia of Saudi Arabia: A Minority in Search of Cultural Authenticity', *British Journal of Middle Eastern Studies*, vol. 25, no. 1 (1998).
57. 'The Shiite Question in Saudi Arabia', *Middle East Report*, no. 45 (19 September

Saudi government reached an agreement with the exiled activists, as a result of which many returned.[58]

The attacks of 11 September 2001 and the QAP's subsequent terror campaign inside the Saudi kingdom focused government attention on the most militant forms of religious extremism. They also spurred *rapprochement* between non-violent Islamists and liberals, both Sunni and Shi'i, who, faced with the threat of violent Sunni militancy, joined in calling for political and religious reform. But if al-Qaeda's activities offered a chance to improve sectarian relations, the war in Iraq has pulled in the opposite direction. Emboldened by the example of their Iraqi coreligionists, some Saudi Shi'is believed they ought to press further, while the sight of Shi'i dominance in yet another neighbouring country has heightened Sunni suspicion. A rising number of Saudi Sunni jihadist militants seeking new battlefields and threatening Western and government targets, as well as the Shi'i minority, have been drawn to Iraq, motivated by opposition not only to the US but also to the increased role of the Shi'is.[59]

While Shi'i activists periodically express community grievances, they are at pains to make clear their loyalty to the nation. They openly display their hostility to any alliance with an outside power, and – in an effort to pre-empt an obvious regime concern – show their determination not to take advantage of the situation in Iraq. Some explicitly deny the existence of a 'Shi'i question', in so far as 'the problems affecting Shi'is are those that affect the Saudi nation as a whole'.[60] Thus, in April 2003, three weeks after the fall of Iraq's Baathist regime, 450 activists signed a letter to the crown prince requesting an end to religious discrimination and the establishment of a religious authority to regulate their affairs in Saudi Arabia. Equally, by demonstrating their clear nationalist stance, some fifteen Shi'i intellectuals – mainly Islamists – were able to join the centrist coalition that issued the January 2003 petition. Among them were Jaafar al-Shayeb, a long-time campaigner for Shi'i rights, and Muhammad al-Mahfuz. Hasan al-Saffar, the long-time leader of the Saudi Islamist movement, welcomed the initiative. While some liberals balked at the

2005), available at merln.ndu.edu>.

58. In a 1993 meeting, King Fahd promised Shi'i leaders that political restrictions would be relaxed in exchange for their ending active opposition from abroad. See Mamoun Fandy, *Saudi Arabia and the Politics of Dissent*, pp. 198–99.

59. 'The Shiite Question in Saudi Arabia'.

60. Ibid.

December 2003 petition's overly 'Islamist' overtones, and the presence among the signatories of prominent Sunni Islamists from the Sahwa, Shi'i Islamists remained. This represented a significant evolution in Saudi Islamism, in so far as Sahwists and Shi'i Islamists had traditionally considered each other to be enemies, and avoided any cooperation on political projects.[61]

Anxious about the Sahwists, but far more fearful of any potential Shi'i separatism, the regime appears to view the Sahwist–Shi'i *rapprochement* as the lesser of two evils. This explains why, for the most part, it spared Shi'i Islamists during the 2007 crackdown: none of their leaders was arrested, and the only Shi'i who remains in jail, 'Ali al-Dumayni, is a liberal activist who did not formulate his political demands within a Shi'i framework.

By most accounts, community leaders such as al-Saffar have persuaded the vast majority of the Shi'i movement of the wisdom of this conciliatory approach. More radical factions have in effect been silenced. Modest as they may be, the achievements of the Shi'i community – most notably the achievement in March 2004 of the right to celebrate Ashura in relative freedom – have strengthened al-Saffar and the moderate leadership, while winning over some residual sceptics. The Saudi government has conceded more Shi'i rights, most importantly by promoting inclusive national dialogues and bringing along key members of the Sunni clergy. However, after the sectarian clashes in Medina in March 2009, Saudi police were reported to have arrested at least eleven Shi'is in eastern Saudi Arabia after a firebrand preacher attacked the Sunni authorities over recent sectarian clashes.[62]

It is worth noting that, while there are no legal Shi'i political organisations or societies in Saudi Arabia, informal networks do exist. The Shi'i Islamic Reform Movement – the most powerful and popular religious–political network – is led by activists who helped transform Shi'i religious and political authority in the late 1970s, and who share personal bonds and a common experience in confronting the regime. It is a loose network that lacks central coordination, an office or official membership. While its popular support cannot be precisely assessed, its unofficial candidates swept the 2005 municipal elections in predominantly Shi'i communities. The group has abandoned its 1970s radicalism, and focuses chiefly on education, charities, counselling programmes and mosque maintenance. Its most prominent leaders, including al-Saffar, aspire

---

61. Ibid.
62. Reuters, 'Saudi police arrest Shi'is, search for preacher', 22 March 2009, available at www.alertnet.org.

to a national role as interlocutors between the rulers and Shi'is. In recent years, they have registered some success, carving out space for Shi'is.[63]

Saudi Hizbullah is the next-largest Islamist group, and is also known locally as the Followers of the Line of the Imam (*Ansar Khat al-Imam*), in reference to Khomeini. Founded in 1987 by several prominent clerics, it is a clergy-led religious–political organisation whose leaders come from the Eastern Province.[64] Saudi Hizbullah is distinguished from the Islamic Reform Movement in two important ways. First, it espouses Khomeini's principle of *wilayat al-faqih* ('guardianship of the Islamic jurists'), and most members emulate the *marja'iyya* of Iran's Supreme Leader Ayatollah Khamenei. There is also a small but important difference in juridical theory. While the Shi'i Islamic Reform Movement calls for greater clerical involvement in politics, it does not insist that the clergy supervise political affairs. Secondly, the Followers of the Line of the Imam reject the Shi'i Islamic Reform Movement's more conciliatory approach, wholly distrusting the ruling family and government. For the most part, that sentiment has translated into the movement's isolation (in contrast to al-Saffar's engagement), though it has reportedly also slipped periodically into violence. The Khobar attack of 1996 is typically cited, despite continued uncertainty as to whether that organisation was behind the bombing and whether, even assuming the perpetrators belonged to Hizbullah, they were directed by its leaders. The government cracked down in the wake of the Khobar bombing which led the movement to focus on social and cultural activities to the exclusion of politics, resulting in its increased influence.

Traditionalists and rejectionists constitute the smallest Islamist political grouping. They include a limited number of independent clerics who, lacking any genuine organisation, play a marginal role as opponents of the Shi'i Islamic Reform Movement and other advocates of national integration. They include quietist religious figures displaced by followers of other Shi'i religious and political trends who fundamentally distrust the Sunni-dominated regime, hold

---

63. Notably through their leader al-Saffar's efforts, Shi'is have been permitted to observe Ashura publicly (albeit only in predominantly Shi'i towns and villages, not in mixed cities such as Dammam).
64. Current leaders include Shaykh Hashim al-Shukus, Shaykh Abdulrahman al-Hubail and Abduljalil al-Maa, Shaykh Hashim al-Hubail, Shaykh Hassan al-Nimr and Sayyid Kamal al-Sada.

that the community ought to avoid national politics altogether, and advocate an exclusive focus on community affairs.[65]

The Shi'i community in Kuwait accounts for around 20 to 30 per cent of the population, including thousands of Iranian origin, who form the majority, while the rest originate from the Eastern Province of Saudi Arabia.[66] Iraqi and Lebanese Shi'is who had a connection to Iran were arrested following the 1983 bombings in Kuwait, and the attempted assassination of the Emir of Kuwait. Kuwaiti violence was sparked in January 1987 by domestic extremist groups after eleven Kuwaiti Shi'is were arrested following bomb attacks on oil installations. Sixteen Kuwaiti Shi'is, a majority of whom were of Iranian origin, were executed in Saudi Arabia in September 1989 after being convicted by a *shari'a* court of causing bomb explosions in Mecca during the Hajj of July 1989. Intercommunal tension eased following a Shi'i demonstration of loyalty during the Iraqi occupation of Kuwait in 1991. The National Coalition (*al-Italaf al-Watani*) is the main framework under which the Shi'i have functioned since the liberation of Kuwait, and the Society of Social Culture (*Jami'iyya al-Thaqafa al-Ijtimiyya*) is the social and cultural front for the coalition. The few Shi'i groups that are susceptible to Iranian influence include *Hizb al-Da'wa* (the Islamic Call Party). The National Coalition claims to be independent from any outside influence, and that its framework allows for differences between its members with no hierarchy of authority. It shares many views with other Sunni groups, with few ideological and religious differences, and it calls for respect for the constitution and for reform, as well as for women's rights.[67]

In Bahrain the relative proportion of the Shi'i population is far higher than in any other Gulf state, making up more than half of the population. The Shi'i religious movement therefore occupies a far more important social role than its Sunni counterpart by its very nature, and because of its relationship with the state,[68] from which its relative autonomy gives it

---

65. One such rejectionist cleric, Shaykh Nimr al-Nimr, head of a mosque in the village of 'Awamiyya, north of Qatif, typically speaks against any engagement with the al-Saud family.

66. Filah A. al-Mudaires, *Al-Tjamua'at al-Siyasiyya al-Kuwaitiyya, Marhalat ma ba'ad al-Tahrir* ('Kuwaiti Political Groups: the period after liberation', (in Arabic), second edn, Kuwait: Al-Manar, 1996, p. 25.

67. Ibid., pp. 28, 29.

68. Abdulhameed al-Ansari, '*Al-Jama' at al-Dinniyya wa Taathiruha 'ala al-Istiqrar al-Siyasi (Mantaqa al-Khalij Numudja'* [Religious Groups and their Impact on Political Stability (the Gulf Region as an Example)], (Arabic) conference

more credibility and impact. The Shi'i movement in Bahrain is divided into two main groups: the first is more conciliatory and more integrated within the system, while the second is in opposition to and critical of the Sunni-secular government, and resorts to political discourse rather than religious preaching. It makes extensive use of the mosque, Hussaynyat (regular Shi'i religious gatherings) and Ashura in disseminating its ideology and demonstrating its influence.

The Shi'is have repeatedly descended into the streets of Bahrain to protest against various government policies, and to press demands for change. While some of these demands overlap with those of the secular and Sunni opposition in their objective of constitutional change, not all do; in many cases the Shi'i go further, addressing social and economic concerns as well.[69] Dissident Shi'i groups such as the Islamic Call Party and the Islamic Front for the Liberation of Bahrain (IFLB) have periodically challenged the government. Following the Iranian Revolution, a large number of IFLB members were arrested in December 1981 on the charge of supporting an Iranian-backed plot to overthrow the Sunni regime, and subsequent plots have been forestalled. Since then several Shi'is have been arrested and killed by riot police.[70]

Since the Gulf crisis, the Shi'is have agitated mainly on issues of human rights and democratisation, using persuasion and advocacy, and operating through international media and human rights organisations such as Amnesty International to air their grievances. The Shi'i religious leadership has also established a substantial organisational framework both within and outside the island state, though it has provided a home for contradictory political and religious tendencies. The largest of these is Jam'iyya al-Wifaq al-Watani al-Islamiyya (generally known as al-Wifaq), which is an amalgam of a variety of personalities and movements with different ideologies and outlooks. Although it may appear to be representative of the Shi'i community, its confrontational stances demonstrate the problems associated with the composition of its leadership and their inherent differences, which resulted in its boycotting of the 2002

paper delivered at Religion and Society in the Arab World, Al-Itihad Annual Forum 2008, Abu Dhabi, 20–21 October 2008.

69. Louay Bahry, 'The Opposition in Bahrain: A Bellwether for the Gulf', *Middle East Policy*, vol. 5, no. 2 (May 1997), pp. 42–57.

70. Ibid.

elections.[71] Despite its shortcomings, al-Wifaq calls consistently for equality among citizens, fair and equitable power sharing, redistribution of national wealth, and fair employment opportunities.

Similarly, Jam'iyat al-'Amal al-Islami (the Islamic Action Society), whose chairman Habib al-Jamri calls for a real democracy, focuses on reshaping legal and state institutions. It aims to promote constructive dialogue between the king and the people, and advocates a return to the 1973 Constitution as well as resolution of the problems of unemployment and discrimination. Many leaders and members of the movement, including al-Jamri himself, returned to Bahrain in a reconciliation agreement with the government, and some of its leaders were even given top government jobs, including ministerial positions.

Outside Bahrain, two political opposition organisations dominate Bahraini Shi'i activities. The first is the Harakat Ahrar al-Bahrayn al-Islamiyya (the Islamic Freedom Movement of Bahrain), which was founded in 1981 and is based in London, headed by Said al-Shihabi and Mansour al-Jamri. The Bahrain Freedom Movement, as it is known in the West, has moderate Islamic views; it does not demand the application of *shari'a* law, but calls for the application of the 1973 Constitution and for fair distribution of wealth among Bahrainis. The second group, founded in 1976, is al-Jabha al-Islamiyya li Tahrir al-Bahrain (the Islamic Front for the Liberation of Bahrain), which has offices in Damascus, London and Tehran. The Front advocates more radical views, calling for the application of *shari'a* law and the replacement of the al-Khalifah royal family if they refuse to abide by a constitution limiting their powers. A smaller organisation, called the Committee for Human Rights in Bahrain, operates in England and Denmark.[72]

Other Gulf states have small unorganised Shi'i groups that are not necessarily active, or are not in opposition to national governments.

Abadhi Islamists

Oman is the only country in the world with a sizable Abadhi sect, which constitutes the majority of the population, the rest of which is of various Sunni schools, with a small number of Shi'is. Abadhism rejects primogeniture, and asserts that the leadership of Islam should be upheld by an imam who is capable and elected by the people, and in whom both political and

---

71. Al-Ansari, 'Religious Groups and their Impact on Political Stability'.
72. Louay Bahry, 'Opposition in Bahrain'.

religious leadership would be vested.[73] The ruling al-Said family is from the Abadhi sect.

Given the nature of Omani internal politics, in which no parties or political association are allowed, there are no political groups to speak of. However, some Abadhi conservatives still harbour dreams of the restoration of the Imamate – the religiously dominated but elected form of government that preceded the establishment of the present al-Said dynasty in 1741, and which operated in the interior of Oman until the decisive establishment of al-Said rule over the whole of Oman in the 1950s.[74]

Moreover, some Abadhis fear that the tenets of the sect are under attack, especially from Sunni extremists from Saudi Arabia.[75] Others object to the speed of modernisation, and the loss of the values and national identity of the conservative country. Hence, in late December 2004 and early January 2005, a plot was reported to have been discovered, leading to the detention of thirty-one men, including civil servants, military personnel, preachers, Islamic scholars and university professors from the Abadhi. They were charged with joining a secret organisation first set up in 1982, forming the al-Bashaer military group, raising funds, conducting military training, convening secret meetings, smuggling and possessing arms and seeking to overthrow the regime. On May 2005, in an open court, they were convicted and given sentences ranging from one to twenty years – but were pardoned on June 2005 by the sultan.[76]

Islamism in the Gulf region is a many-branched movement that began to gain momentum in the 1980s, after the governments of the region failed to secure fair distribution of wealth, freedom from Western control, prosperity and good governance. Although Islamism in the region is heterogeneous and largely home-grown, and responds to the varied domestic, regional and international issues in each country, there are some commonalities in its causes and manifestations.

---

73. For background see Hussein Ghubash, *Oman: the Islamic Democratic Tradition*, Abingdon: Routledge, 2006.
74. Jeremy Jones and Nicholas Ridout, 'Democratic Development in Oman', *Middle East Journal*, vol. 59, no. 3 (Summer 2005), pp. 376–92.
75. Mark Katz, 'Assessing the Political Stability of Oman', *Middle East Review of International Affairs*, vol. 8, no. 3 (September 2004), available at meria.idc. ac.il.
76. See Janardhan, 'Islamists Stay Clear of Terrorism in Oman'.

The movement is part of the resurgence of religion in the Third World, where modernisation, Westernisation and secularism were adopted at the expense of traditional Islamic values. Frustration over the failure to meet post-independence aspirations, the effects of the population explosion, the impact of rapid urbanisation, the imbalance in the distribution of wealth, the culmination of failed policies and the problems derived from Western (and Soviet) economic exploitation and cultural domination, all created opposition to Western capitalism, Marxist socialism and other national secular ideologies. Globalisation, coupled with the impact of a consumer society and social permissiveness, were seen to be corrupting Islamic morality, destroying the social fabric, and threatening the identity of Islamic countries.

Within this general trend towards the increasing rise of Islamism, there are national peculiarities that have contributed to the spread and growth of this phenomenon in the Gulf states. The nature of the political systems and the *rentier* economic structures that underlie them have resulted in the unfair distribution of wealth and unfulfilled aspirations among a young and growing population, all of which has added to Islamism's momentum. Other regional factors have played a role in the rise of Islamism in the Gulf, including the sense of Arab defeat and disillusionment with Arab nationalist ideology, as well as the Iranian Revolution which inspired both the Sunni and Shi'i variants of Islam. The perceived attack against Islam and the invasion and occupation of Arab and Muslim lands have also been factors motivating the use of Islam as a unifying force. This call gained resonance in the traditional and conservative societies of the Gulf states, where Islamism was used by groups to challenge or lobby incumbent governments, invariably on issues of political, social or economic discontent. However, given the nature of the religion and its division into Sunni, Shi'i and Abadhi schools, there have been clear differences in the outlooks of the followers of each of these sects. There have even been vast differences within each of these Islamic schools in relation to their own goals and methods.

The majority, though, favour further reform, designed to ensure political and economic participation as well as social equality and good governance. These groups from all sects of Islam tend to work within the system to achieve peaceful transformation while adhering to Islamic principles. Other minority Islamist groups, though more vociferous, wish to change the status quo and are not reluctant to use violence and force to achieve their goals. Where there has been political space and greater freedom of action, even radical groups have changed their views and participated in the political process. But the opposite is also true: other governments' repression has led to more subversion and violence. The Gulf states' resilient regimes have, however, been largely able to co-opt Islamist opposition groups; having begun to open up the political arena through national dialogue and greater political participation, they appear to be riding out the storm.

EIGHT

Hamas: Conflating National Liberation and Socio-Political Change

Khaled Hroub

Contemporary Islamist movements are the product of political, social and economic developments which themselves force further adaptations, using (and misusing) historical, religious and cultural legacies at each stage of their development. These adaptations have been scrutinised, publicised and reproduced as no other political phenomenon has in our modern world. Understanding the context within which a certain Islamist movement has evolved is essential if one is to comprehend its component parts and its attractions for its supporters. The Palestinian Islamism of the twentieth and twenty-first centuries – in particular the Palestinian Muslim Brotherhood and its offspring, Hamas – is a case in point.

Using context as its principal analytical tool, this chapter discusses the evolution and structural transformations which occurred within the Palestinian Islamist movement, from its early inception in the 1940s until the electoral victory of Hamas in January 2006 and its military take-over of the Gaza Strip in June 2007. Although the focus will be on recent history from the establishment of Hamas in 1987 onwards, the study also examines the evolutionary phases that preceded this fundamental turning-point. It traces the long journey of Palestinian Islamists, from their beginnings as a weak and marginal force, sometimes accused of acquiescing in the Israeli occupation and marginalised beyond what would be considered the 'Palestinian revolutionary legitimacy', to their relentless struggle to secure a place for themselves at the very heart of this 'legitimacy' – a struggle fought with both bullets and the ballot box. During this long journey, the Islamists have adopted various goals and strategies, reacted differently to external events, and have maintained shifting relationships with different local, regional and international actors. All these nuances deserve to be addressed. A crucial question in almost any discussion of Hamas, as in that of any other Islamist movement, is whether the movement is religious or political. A similarly fundamental question that must be addressed – and that affects policies on, as well as perceptions of, political Islam movements – is that of the engagement in political processes which would initially appear unreceptive to Islamists. The issue of engagement is actually more pressing in cases where Islamist movements are capable of winning free and fair elections, or winning a major share of popular votes that implies (or even requires) a power-sharing arrangement. What further compounds this issue is the perception among the Islamists, as well as many others, that the terms of engagement and isolation are debated and effectively made or unmade by Western powers who still have huge leverage over countries where these Islamists exist. This results in sheer frustration since even though power might be won through democratic elections, 'Western legitimacy' still has to be bestowed on the winners if their victory is to be endorsed. In particular, considerable frustration is felt towards European equivocation because Europe is seen by the Islamists and others as more pragmatic and 'principled', and less ideological than the US.[1]

Early emergence, late influence

The historic roots and causes behind the emergence of Palestinian Islamism as a powerful political, military and social force share some common features with those that have been behind the rise of other Arab 'Islamisms'. In a typical Arab/Muslim societal setting, the surfacing of any Islamist movement is a reaction to a blend of processes including; the challenge of Western modernity; the failure of other reformist or revolutionary ideologies to tackle social, economic and political challenges; the predicament of the post-colonial state; and/or simply the politics of opposition against an oppressive status quo. In the Palestinian case, an additional factor has played a crucial role in the formation and orientation of Islamist movements: the Zionist project which gathered momentum in the country in the early twentieth century and the Israeli military occupation and control over Palestine and the Palestinian people which followed, resulting in the establishment of

---

1. On the question of Western policy toward Hamas in particular and with reference to the issue of engagement see the insightful analysis of Nathan J. Brown 'Principled or Stubborn? Western Policy Toward Hamas', *The International Spectator*, vol. 43, no. 4, December 2008.

a Jewish state in Palestine in 1948. This Israeli occupation has, in fact, been the greatest shaper of most, if not all, Palestinian political formations that have appeared since 1948. Resisting the occupation has become not only the catalyst behind many political and armed movements, but is also the prime measure of their popular legitimacy and the justification for their very purpose. In the context of 'resistance' the Palestinians have imported various ideologies – Marxism, Pan-Arabism, nationalism and finally Islamism – all moulded and reproduced in tandem with nationalist aspirations and meant to help in fighting against the Israeli occupation. At least in part, therefore, the late employment of Islamism in the Palestinian territories in 1980s and onwards replicated the earlier use of other ideologies to achieve Palestinian self-determination which had failed.[2]

The term 'Palestinian Islamism' could be used to describe a broad spectrum of various groups and ideologies but in this chapter, however, the focus will be on Hamas and its mother organisation, the Muslim Brotherhood in Palestine (MBP) since groups and manifestations of Palestinian Islamism other than the MBP have always been weaker and less influential than the Palestinian Muslim Brothers. The other three main formations of Palestinian Islamism with any prominence are Hizb al-Tahrir, the Islamic Jihad Movement in Palestine and the Salafi groups. Hizb al-Tahrir, the second-oldest Islamist party in Palestine, was established in Jerusalem in 1952 as a splinter group of the MBP but is nowadays incomparable in strength and popularity with the MBP/Hamas.[3] The Islamic Jihad Movement in Palestine, another splinter group of the MBP that was formed in the early 1980s, enjoys only meagre support when measured against Hamas's broad support.[4] Salafi groups in

2. For broader perspectives on Palestinian nationalism and its variants, see Yezid Sayigh, *Armed Struggle and the Search for State: The Palestinian National Movement, 1949–1993*, Oxford: Clarendon Press, 1997.

3. In a November 2008 poll conducted by the Jerusalem Media and Communication Centre in the West Bank and the Gaza Strip Hizb al-Tahrir was not specified as an answer to the question 'Which Palestinian faction do you trust most?'. It was instead included with other small Islamist groups in the category 'Other Islamist Factions' which only scored 3.9% of the pollsters, compared to 16.6% for Hamas and 2.4% for Islamic Jihad. See http://www.jmcc.org/publicpoll/results/2008/index.htm. On Hizb al-Tahrir in Palestine see Beverly Milton-Edwards, *Islamic Politics in Palestine*, London: I.B. Tauris, 1996, pp. 64–72.

4. See *Islamic Politics in Palestine* for the levels of popularity. For more on the Islamic Jihad Movement see Meir Hatina, *Islam and Salvation in Palestine:*

Palestine are so far weaker than all the above. They are marginal in terms of popular support, take no part in any electoral process and have no record or experience of resisting the occupation.[5]

The MBP goes back to the late 1930s when the Egyptian Muslim Brotherhood in Egypt (MBE), founded in 1928, started to send envoys and leaders to surrounding countries with the mission to spread the movement by setting up local branches. Representatives of the Egyptian organisation visited the Palestinian cities of Gaza, Jerusalem, Jaffa, Haifa and Nablus in the late 1930s and early 1940s. By then, the MBE was very popular in Egypt, functioning in public and attracting members from all strata of society.[6] In May 1946, the Palestinian members of the Muslim Brotherhood inaugurated their official headquarters in Jerusalem.[7]

Palestinian cities in the 1920s, 1930s and 1940 – especially Jerusalem, Jaffa and Haifa – were vibrant with political activism mostly in opposition to the British mandate and fuelled by the looming threat of the Zionist movement in Palestine.[8] Political activism was intense but most activists were unarmed, including those belonging to a newly established association, the 'Muslim Brotherhood Association' in Palestine as it was originally called. Also noteworthy is that most Palestinian associations at the time did not represent society as a whole; their leaders and most of their members were 'notables' or drawn from the upper middle class. Some activism was more of an assertion of the social position and prestige of these notables than any sincere political effort or sacrifice.[9] To a certain extent, this was also true of the

The Islamic Jihad Movement, Tel Aviv: the Moshe Dayan Centre for Middle Eastern and African Studies, 2001.

5. On the weakness of the Salafis in Palestine see Khaled Hroub, 'Salafi Formations in Palestine and the Limits of a De-Palestinised Milieu' in Roel Meijer, *Global Salafism: Islam's New Religious Movement*, Hurst/Columbia University Press, 2009.

6. For the history of the MBE, see B. Lia, *Society of the Muslim Brothers in Egypt: The Rise of an Islamic Mass Movement 1928–1942*, Reading: Ithaca Press, 1998.

7. A. Al-F. M. El-Awaisi, *The Muslim Brothers and the Palestine Question 1928-1947*, London: Tauris Academic Series, 1998, pp. 150–71.

8. See Rashid Khalidi, *Palestinian Identity: The Construction of Modern National Consciousness*, New York: Columbia University Press, 1998, especially chapters 6 and 7; and Basheer M. Nafi, *Arabism and Islamism and the Palestine Question 1908–1941*, London: Ithaca Press, 1998, especially chapter 6.

9. For more on the composition of these formations, see B. N. Al-Hout, *Political*

MBP whose first leaders, especially those from Jerusalem and Gaza, already enjoyed an elevated social position. Rather than entailing sacrifice and hardship, joining the MBP during the 1940s bestowed additional social status on its members.[10] From the early 1950s onwards a split between the leadership and rank-and-file membership occurred as the ranks of the MBP started to be filled by supporters drawn from the lower classes and refugee camps (after the expulsion of Palestinians from Israeli-occupied land before, during and after the 1948 war). In comparison, when Hamas emerged in the late 1980s and 1990s, its membership was more diverse. Most members and leaders of Hamas were drawn from either the lower middle class, the poor from rural areas who had settled on the poorest parts of Palestinian cities or those who had now lived for a long time in refugee camps. But, at the same time, there were still members and leaders with urban and upper-class backgrounds who were playing a no less important role.[11] Between these two time periods, a rapid process of internal mobility had displaced the prestige-oriented leadership in favour of more 'revolutionary' and disadvantaged groups.

From another angle, what has differentiated the composition of the Islamist movement from nationalist and leftist movements has been the continued co-existence between the well off and the poor within the ranks of the MBP. Any 'class-based' analysis was criticised as implying a Marxist and anti-religious understanding of the structure of society. The MBP, and later Hamas, have therefore managed to keep a healthy circle of wealthy landlords and businessmen around themselves, who have through religious practice, even if not always through active membership, found in the MBP (and then Hamas) clean hands to channel assistance to poor Palestinians.[12]

The MBP remained a marginal force on the Palestinian scene from its inception in the 1940s until the late 1970s. One major explanation for this

---

Leadership and Institutions in Palestine 1917–1948 [in Arabic], Beirut: Institute for Palestine Studies, 1986.

10. Unpublished archival papers of the 1940s MBP, retained by the author, inform of this mostly upper middle-class to upper-class cross-sectional formation of the society.

11. See S. Mishal and A. Sela, *The Palestinian Hamas. Vision, Violence, and Coexistence*, New York: Columbia University Press, 2000, pp. 13–26.

12. Based on the author's personal contact and knowledge of Hamas leaders and members over the past two decades. See also K. Hroub, 'Historic Roots', in K. Hroub, *Hamas. Political Thought and Practice* , Washington: Institute for Palestine Studies, 2000, pp. 11–41.

is the apolitical approach that it adopted over a long period of time. It was mostly engaged in religious and social activism, ensuring the 'comprehensiveness' of the ideology of its Egyptian mother organisation, the Muslim Brotherhood. The Egyptian movement had always aspired to reinstate what Hasan al-Banna, the movement's founding leader, perceived to be the holistic nature of Islam, encompassing the mundane and the divine. Al-Banna promoted activism in all spheres – the social, cultural, religious, political and military – in an effort to return Muslim society to its original ethos.[13] In practice the MBP chose to advance one form of activism while slowing down another, a policy it believed to be justifiable in adapting it to its particular set of conditions, confirming a contextual perception of the evolution and practice of the MB in general.

The adoption by the MB in Egypt, and later in Palestine, of military activism was therefore based on careful contextual calculations, mostly capabilities and cost-benefit analysis. As a result, the strategy of the Palestinian branch of the Brothers was based on the postponement of military activism until the 'conditions are ripe'.[14] Instead, they focused on the Islamisation of society. Indeed, the path adopted by the Brothers, with some occasional exceptions, was therefore marked by non-violent and non-confrontational approaches to Israeli occupation: from the time of the establishment of Israel in 1948 to the founding of Hamas in 1987, the 'Islamisation of society' through social, religious and charitable work was the focal strategy of the MBP. The MBP attributed the Palestinians' 1948 defeat to society's deviation from the true path of Islam and therefore believed that bringing society back to Islam was the key to being able to fight back and liberate Palestine.

After the 1948 war and the creation of Israel, what remained of the land of 'historic Palestine' was administered by Egypt in the Gaza Strip, and Jordan

13. H. Al-Banna, *Memoirs of the Preaching and the Preacher* [in Arabic], Cairo: Islamic House of Publishing and Distribution, no date [1st edn, 1947].

14. It should be noted here, however, that the engagement of the Egyptian MB in the Palestine issue and resistance against the British mandate were strong in the 1930s, leading to the 1948 war, and widely acknowledged. One of the best detailed accounts of the participation of the MB in 1948 is K. Al-Sherif and M. Al-Sibae, *The Muslim Brothers in the Palestine War* [in Arabic]Cairo: Islamic House of Publishing and Distribution, 1984. Both authors were senior members of the movement and engaged on the Egyptian and Syrian fronts respectively. See also El-Awaisi, *The Muslim Brothers and the Palestine Question*, chapters 1 and 2.

in the West Bank (of the River Jordan). Due to geographical proximity and ease of access, the MBP in the Gaza Strip was closer in organisational ties and influence to the MB in Egypt, whereas the MBP in the West Bank became part of the MB in Jordan.

With the 1967 War, Israel occupied the Gaza Strip and the West Bank, ousting Egypt and Jordan respectively, and the entire territory of mandated Palestine fell under the military control of Israel. The MBP in both areas drew closer and later formed one organisation. Yet the MBP's notions of confronting the Israeli occupation even in the Gaza Strip and the West Bank remained postponed until such time as Palestinian society was 'changed and become ready' for the war of liberation.

During the Jordanian rule of the West Bank between 1949 and 1967, the MBP had allied themselves to the Jordanian regime on the grounds of a common enmity to President Nasser of Egypt. The Jordanian King Hussein tolerated activities of the MB in Jordan and Palestine in order to keep a check on leftist and pan-Arab nationalists seeking to topple his rule and create a republic. Their alliance with King Hussein had the effect of making the MBP less popular with many Palestinians.[15]

The prioritisation of the MBP agenda under the overarching mantra of first morally (spiritually) 'preparing the generations for the battle', cost the Islamists dearly. In the decades in which the MBP adhered strictly to this 'avoidance' of confrontation with the Israeli occupation, the Palestinian national cause was vehemently fought for by nationalist and leftist forces using armed resistance.[16] From the early 1950s, armed groups of varying

---

15. On the relationship between Jordan and the MB before and after the 1967 War, see A. Cohen, *Political Parties in West Bank under Jordanian Regime, 1949–1967*, Ithaca: Cornell University Press, 1982; see also B. Milton-Edwards, *Islamic Politics in Palestine*, London: Tauris Academic Studies, 1996, pp. 84–90.

16. Later, Hamas leaders justified the strategy of their brothers during that period as being part of the resistance since it was meant to confront the 'bad influences of the Israeli occupation on Palestinian society'. This is, for instance, the account of Khaled Mishael, head of Hamas's Political Bureau. See K. Mishael, 'Hamas Movement and the Liberation of Palestine. Interview with Ghassan Charbel' [in Arabic], *Al-Hayat*, 10 December 2003, p. 29. In a detailed document issued by Hamas's Political Bureau in June 2000, Hamas chronicled the movement's evolution into five successive phases, as follows: The Movement's Historic Roots (1946–1967); The Phase of Preparation for Launching the Movement's Project (1967–1980); The Founding Phase (1980–1987); The Phase of the Launch (1987–1994); The Post-Oslo Phase (1994–2000). This chronology,

political orientation started to emerge and fight under the banner of the 'liberation of Palestine'. Therefore, the leadership of Palestinians who wished to assert their national rights landed in the hands of those groups that fought Israel militarily from the beginning, the very same groups that would, in the mid-1960s, unite to form the Palestine Liberation Organisation (PLO), an umbrella front for all Palestinian resistance movements. The Islamists excluded themselves from the PLO, even before being excluded by others, showing little interest in joining a coalition of communist and secular nationalist parties. Their weakness, together with their marginalisation and refusal to engage in armed resistance, hardly gave the MBP a ticket to join the PLO at its inception.[17]

The PLO soon became the embodiment of Palestinian legitimacy and leadership. Staying outside the PLO umbrella, the Islamists had to fight on more than one front, always desperate to gain popular legitimacy without involving itself in active resistance to the Israeli occupation. During the 1960s and 1970s, the PLO managed to capture the imagination, support and even revolutionary romanticism of the Palestinians, their aspirations for the liberation of Palestine. By adopting the 'popular war for liberation' as its strategy, it chose a policy that both reflected and built the Palestinian psyche in a way that was extremely difficult to challenge. Without being democratically elected, the PLO not only enjoyed legitimacy uncontested by any rivals and claimed to be the representative of the Palestinian people,[18] but also became the source of any legitimacy

---

although helpful especially because it is the official Hamas version, should be seen with a critical eye. Examining the details of each phase, one gets the sense of a pervasive attempt to re-construct the near past to serve the present image of Hamas; see the full text of this document in A. Tamimi's *Hamas: A History from Within*, Northampton: Olive Branch Press, 2007, pp. 271–83.

17. In the late 1960s and the 1970s, Palestinian Islamists saw the PLO as a collection of atheists and secularists who would gain nothing for Palestine because of their anti-religious beliefs. An example of this widespread view is found in Abdualla Azzam's writings, speeches and sermons. Azzam was a leading MBP figure before leaving to join the *jihad* in Afghanistan in the early 1980s. He was assassinated in Pakistan in 1989.

18. Although no single internal Palestinian political body could compete with the PLO on the issue of representation of the Palestinians, Jordan managed to rival the PLO strongly up until 1974. Shortly after the 1948 war and the establishment of Israel the West Bank was united (or in fact annexed) to the East Bank of the River Jordan. Since then Jordan claimed to represent the Palestinians.

for any emerging faction which was based on fighting Israel. Thus, the Islamists were perceived by many Palestinians, and certainly by nationalist (Fatah) and leftist parties, as having placed themselves completely outside the collective national effort against the Israeli occupier. In later stages, the issue of legitimacy and representation of the Palestinian people became the most contested issue between Hamas and the PLO, even more so after Hamas's victory in the 2006 general elections in the West Bank and the Gaza Strip.

Another factor that weakened the political and popular influence of the MBP after the mid-1950s was their bloody confrontation with Egyptian President Gamal Abdel Nasser. Nasser, with his pan-Arabist ambitions, was perceived by many Arabs and most Palestinians as the quintessential pan-Arab leader and hero who stood fast in the face of Israeli and Western imperial policies in the Middle East. The indigenous Arab forces that confronted Nasser the most – the MB organisations, some Arab communist parties and conservative regimes in the Gulf – suffered great blows to their popular appeal in the Arab world, and perhaps beyond. The MBP's conflict with Nasser and their reluctance to engage in armed struggle against the Israeli occupation combined to create the perception among many Palestinians that the MBP were not only accommodating the ongoing occupation but were also interested only in attacking nationalist and leftist Palestinian groups, those who had carried the flag of resistance against occupation since 1948. This negative perception of the MBP's policies persisted until the second half of the 1980s, when the Brothers decided, under a multiplicity of pressures, to undertake a major shift in their strategy: to engage in the confrontation against the Israeli occupation using all means, starting with their participation in the first *intifada* (uprising) in December 1987. A new context was once again to impose its diktats, compelling the Palestinian Brothers to acquire a new image and approach.[19]

When Israel occupied the West Bank in the 1967 War it was under Jordanian rule and sovereignty. As a result of the 'unification' the Palestinians of the West Bank were considered Jordanian citizens.

19. The Palestinian Islamists responded almost immediately to the *intifada*. Intense internal and external debates and unbearable pressure to take part in the *intifada* all contributed to the Brothers' decision to form Hamas. See, on this, Hroub, *Hamas: Political Thought and Practice*, pp. 36–42.

'Neo-Islamism': the emergence of Hamas

The Iranian revolution of 1979 influenced Palestinian Islamists deeply, as it did many other Islamists (and non-Islamists) around the world. It injected a great sense of determination to effect change through political revolution and resistance rather than through slow social change. By the early 1980s, many members of the MBP wanted their organisation to adopt the Iranian model and engage in full-scale confrontation against the Israeli occupation. While the leadership insisted on adhering to the same old strategy of effecting bottom-up change, angry members split and formed an organisation of their own: the Islamic Jihad in Palestine. This group, although it has remained small in size and influence to this day, became a catalyst in the MBP's internal transformation into Hamas in 1987.[20]

Many leaders of the MBP thought that if they persisted any longer with their non-confrontational strategy they would lose more people to either the Islamic Jihad or other emerging groups. In the summer of 1985, an internal deliberation acknowledged the need to adopt a major shift in strategy and called for preparations – but left the timing of implementation open – for confrontation with the Israeli occupation.[21] Two years later, when the Palestinian *intifada* began in December 1987, the MBP decided the time was right. A few days after the *intifada* erupted, Hamas was declared the military branch of the MB. By internally transforming themselves and creating Hamas, the Palestinian Islamists were responding to surrounding pressures and giving up some of their traditional ideology. A few years after the inception of Hamas, around 1992/3, the Izz Eddin Al-Qassam Brigades were formed as the military wing of Hamas, and so another transformation took place that was to turn Hamas into a political party.[22]

In contrast with the traditional thinking of the MBP, the emerging Hamas in 1987 reshuffled priorities, ushering in a new phase in Islamist activism in

---

20. The first writings of Fathi Al-Shikaki, the founder of the Islamic Jihad in Palestine, praised the Iranian revolution as a model for the Palestinian; see F. Al-Shikaki, *Khomeini: The Islamic Solution and the Alternative* [in Arabic], Occupied Territories: no publisher, 1979. For a fuller analysis of the formation of the Islamic Jihad Movement, see M. Hatina, *Islam and Salvation in Palestine. The Islamic Jihad Movement*, Tel Aviv: The Moshe Dayan Center for Middle Eastern and African Studies, 2001.
21. Hroub, *Hamas: Political Thought and Practice*, p. 35.
22. Ibid., p. 242.

Palestine termed 'neo-Islamism'. The notion of resistance against the Israeli occupation lay at the heart of this reshuffling, sometimes in parallel with and sometimes at the expense of social change priorities. Islamists realised that by adopting military and confrontational stances against Israel, they would be welcomed into the hearts of the people. Therefore, after the emergence of Hamas a process began of conflating military resistance *with* social change and Islamisation. It was as if a strategy already embraced, but long shelved, was activated, rather than a completely new one introduced. The 'dormant' and much-praised history of the Islamists' participation in the 1948 war now became a reference point from which Hamas declared its descendancy.[23]

The Palestinian Islamists were anxious to rid themselves of their past image of being inactive against the occupation, and started amassing 'resistance legitimacy', competing with PLO factions on their historical ground. Ironically, by the end of the 1980s, the PLO had started to make a major shift in its own strategy in the opposite direction: from armed struggle to peace negotiation. In 1991, the PLO attended the Madrid Peace Conference, which was sponsored by the United States in the aftermath of the first Gulf War with the aim of promoting peace between the Arab countries and Israel. The PLO initiated negotiations with Israel and in 1993 the Oslo Agreements were concluded. By then, Hamas had fully developed into a resistance movement, effectively inheriting the strategy of the armed struggle from the PLO. Having acquired this new resistance capital, 'Hamas began to compete with the PLO over Palestinian legitimacy and the representation of the Palestinian people and became louder in its refusal to acknowledge the PLO as the sole and legitimate representative of the Palestinians'. The Oslo process was meant to conclude with a Palestinian state in the West Bank and the Gaza Strip by 1999, but it failed to do so. Instead, another *intifada* erupted in 2000, giving Hamas another chance to enhance its 'resistance' image and to build further its political and military capabilities.

A large part of Hamas's success was due to the PLO's failure to bring about tangible solutions for the Palestinian people. Since 1988, the PLO has officially agreed on the principle of a two-state solution, confirming its *de*

---

23. In Hamas's Charter, made public in August 1988, there is much emphasis on the 'links of the same *jihad* chain', where Hamas is the natural heir to the struggle and military resistance of the Muslim Brothers and their participation in the 1948 war.

facto recognition of Israel.[24] Risking its legitimacy and gambling its long-term legacy, in 1993 the PLO signed the Oslo Accords, seen by many Palestinians to compromise basic and minimum Palestinian rights. By the time the second *intifada* took place in 2000, giving Hamas life blood for many years to come, the peace process on which the PLO had gambled its legitimacy and reputation, was a complete failure. For example, the settlements in the West Bank that were supposed to be dismantled as a result of Oslo had in fact doubled in size during the five-year phase of Oslo. The situation of the Palestinian people had worsened in almost all aspects. All this had weakened the legitimacy not only of the PLO but also of the peace process itself. And Hamas was there, cultivating the 'fruits' of these successive failures from 1991 onward. By exerting no pressure on Israel, Western policies contributed to weakening the moderate camp within the Palestinians. Out of the debris of this series of failures, Hamas's rise was inevitable.

Liberation and social change

While the PLO and the peace process foundered, the Palestinian neo-Islamists, capitalising on their achievements in the resistance struggle represented by the first and second *intifadas* in 1987 and 2000, never stopped their bottom-up social and religious work. The process of the re-Islamisation of Palestinian society and identity has moved forward hand in hand with resisting the occupation. This has included gradual attempts, both direct and indirect, to replace notions, concepts and symbols that used to be the accepted manifestations of 'Palestinianism'. In tandem with the reshaping of their role and image within the wider Palestinian arena, Islam as understood by Palestinian neo-Islamists has been brought to centre stage, not only as it is related to the conflict with Israel, but also to the shaping of the future of Palestine and Palestinian society.[25]

---

24. In Algeria in November 1988, the Palestinian National Council, the Palestinian parliament in exile controlled by the PLO, issued a 'Declaration of Independence'after intense deliberations. The declaration called, officially and collectively, for the first time, for the creation of a Palestinian state on the West Bank and Gaza Strip only, covering an area of 22% of the historic land of mandatory Palestine. The declaration represented a historic turning-point in the struggle of the Palestinian national movement, as it indirectly acknowledged the existence of Israel on the remaining 78% of the land.

25. See I. Barghouthi, *Religion and State in Palestine* [in Arabic], Ramallah:

In this process, the drive towards liberation has become further inter-mingled with the drive towards social change. The political capital that the Islamists have been accumulating through their new resistance strategy has been used to achieve aspects of their agenda for social and religious change. The degree of compatibility between liberation and social change therefore keeps changing and sometimes becomes extremely blurred.

Such changes in the degree of compatibility between these two priorities correspond to two modes of reception within Palestinian society. The mode of resisting Israeli occupation is positive and gains the Islamists credit. The trade-off is that Palestinians appear to grant their Islamists generous margins within which to operate and tolerance with respect to their agenda for social change, yet, if the Islamists were to press the idea of Islamising in the narrow sense of the word too strongly, the mode of reception in the rather compos-ite Palestinian society would change in ways that would not necessarily be favourable to the Islamists. Similarly, if there were to be a concrete solution to the conflict of the kind desired by the majority of the Palestinians, the two modes of reception would most likely change in a way that would be unfavourable to the Islamists.

The shifting dynamics between resistance/national liberation and social change has its time/space, power/actor and context/pressure variations. The policies and strategies of Hamas between 1987 and 2007 have differed – sometimes sharply – according to these variations. Hamas opposed the Oslo Agreements of 1993-4 and insisted on holding onto its resistance strategy, even though this was perceived by the PLO and the Palestinian Authority after 1994 to be detrimental to Palestinian national aspirations.[26] But the elected Hamas, in power since 2006, has shown a completely different policy. Effectively, it has stopped its military 'resistance project' to give its government

---

Ramallah Center for Human Rights, 2007, p. 4; also on the general theme, see L. D. Lybarger's insightful account, *Identity and Religion in Palestine. The Struggle between Islamism and Secularism in the Occupied Territories*, Princeton and Oxford: Princeton University Press, 2007, especially chapter 1, pp. 1–26.

26. Hamas has outlined its rejection of the Oslo Agreements in numerous statements. Among the most important official statements of Hamas are 'Memorandum from Hamas about the Latest Development' on 8 February 1993; 'Resistance and Struggle will Remain the Only Dialogue with the Occupier Enemy', on 20 February 1994; 'No for Compromises, Yes for Retreating from the Sin of Oslo', on 28 February 1994; and 'Hamas's Position of Self-Rule Authority', on 7 July 1994. These statements were issued in Arabic.

time and space for political success. Two years after assuming power, Hamas went so far as to accuse those groups and factions that kept launching rockets against Israeli towns after the June 2008 ceasefire of damaging the national Palestinian interest and serving the Israeli occupation.[27] This position has stunned many Palestinians because this specific action – rocket launching – was exactly what Hamas had done in previous years while the PLO/PA was attempting to achieve the 'national interest' by non-military means.

Such a trajectory represents a sharp turn from those long periods when the Islamists were either a secondary force in the Palestinian polity or were in the opposition after the 1993-4 Oslo Agreements. This is not to say that the social change agenda has enjoyed more space since Hamas has assumed power. In fact, Hamas's religious and social concerns have been toned down in order to fend off fears among many Palestinians that Hamas-in-power could mean a forced Islamisation of society. Also, the pressures on the Hamas government, regionally and internationally, which culminated in an almost total blockade, left Hamas with other major pressing concerns to deal with. What is significant to bear in mind, perhaps as a summation of what seem to be sharp oscillations between opposing approaches, is that Hamas and the earlier Palestinian Islamists of the MBP have shown a great measure of context answerability. They have promoted a multi-track agenda combining social change, religious propagation, political participation and military engagement, although not necessarily with the same momentum at any given time. The flexibility of moving back and forth between these tracks and across them, speeding one up and slowing another down, while justifying all manoeuvres by religious rulings and *fatwas*, is one of the most salient conclusions of the study of Hamas's political behaviour.

The Palestinian Islamists' views of the West, like those of other Islamists in general, have shown variations and change, manifesting ambivalent opinions. There is the conventional tension between the West as the source of science, advancement and modernity and the West as the colonial project that never stops imposing its hegemony on Arab and Muslim countries. But in the Palestinian case, Islamists also see the West as the main backer of Israel, something which further complicates their understanding of various Western manifestations. What has been remarkable, however, is the rapid moderation

---

27. Leaders of Hamas issued several statements to this effect after the ceasefire; see *Al-Jazeera* net: http://www.aljazeera.net/NR/exeres/E20B985E-F67C-4062-8F70-3A834EE966AE.htm, 26 June 2008.

of Hamas's discourse on the West over the past few years, particularly after winning the 2006 elections. In the first place, a clear and favourable view of Europe has been formulated as compared with a persistently negative one of the United States. Then, and as a result of becoming a leading party deeply engaged in politics, Hamas has faced the intractability of international affairs and their bearings on the Palestine cause. This has led to a more nuanced discourse and even-handed policies toward Western powers. The chances of a new Palestinian Islamism evolving, more moderate and less ideological – Erdogan rather than Taliban in bent (as some Hamas leaders keep reiterating)[28] – have thus increased. The rhetorical language of Hamas's 1988 Charter, in which all Western powers were portrayed as conspirators with the Zionist movement against the Muslims, the Arabs and the Palestinians,[29] has been replaced by more rational and critical discourse.

Post-2006 Hamas and the 'new Palestinian legitimacy'

Palestinian legitimacy has always been the product of tacit agreement and coercion among Palestinians over the decades. As a result, the terms 'legitimate' and 'legitimacy' have become integrated with the national cause and involve furthering national goals and enhancing resistance strategy against the Israeli occupation. The legitimate leader (or organisation) is the one who holds the banner of resistance and revolution, advancing and bringing the goals of liberation closer. Thus, the identifier of legitimacy is the measure of its resistance against the occupier. A leader or a party would suffer great damage to its legitimacy if it were perceived as non-resistant, as was long the case with the Palestinian Islamists. Sets of mechanisms and practices, as well as symbolism, bureaucracy and evolved norms and modes of conduct had all institutionalised the 'Palestinian legitimacy' in and around the PLO until the Palestinian Authority (PA) was created after the Oslo Agreements of 1993-4.

A part of the Oslo Agreements was to organise presidential elections and parliamentarian elections to elect a Legislative Council (with limited powers)

---

28. Ahmad Yousef, advisor to Ismail Haniya, Hamas's prime minister, invokes this comparison to assure all parties that Hamas's line is moderate and closer to the experience of the Turkish Islamists than to that of the Taliban. Interview in Gaza City, 7 March 2007.
29. See the part of the Charter entitled 'Forces Abetting the Enemy'.

in the West Bank and Gaza Strip, bringing the Palestinian polity, or most of it, into a new phase of legitimacy in terms of definition and source. For the first time since 1948 and the displacement of the Palestinians, the national Palestinian legitimacy became based on popular will expressed via democratic electoral process, not exclusively on revolution and revolutionaries, albeit with the major flaw of excluding the Palestinians in the Diaspora. In theory, the source of this legitimacy is supposed to be the people rather than guns (the revolution). In practice, Palestinian legitimacy has since moved to integrate electoral legitimacy with the legitimacy of resistance.

It has been argued above that the Islamists' strategy of morally 'preparing the generations' without engaging in resisting Israel created a devastating image of them among broader Palestinian constituencies. In those days, of course, the Islamists had no illusion about daring to claim either to represent the Palestinian people or to be a part of the Palestinian (resistance) legitimacy. Yet the infrastructure of social and organisational work that the Islamists had been creating for almost three decades yielded very powerful grassroots networks. Those networks, in the late 1980s, gave Hamas the base from which the movement was able to challenge the PLO factions in fighting the Israeli occupation. It took Hamas almost twenty years – from the transformation of the Islamists into Hamas in late 1987 to the 2006 Hamas victory in the elections – to cross the resistance threshold and move to the heart of Palestinian legitimacy. In two decades, it had to build up enough resistance capital to erase the idle past of its founding MB fathers who had opted for a non-violent approach.

During these long years, Hamas's discourse and practice evolved from the rhetorical and ideological to the more pragmatic and political. 2005 and 2006 can perhaps be seen as the time in which Hamas showed its most moderate and pragmatic face. In 2005, Hamas decided to run for the elections in January 2006, the same elections that it had denounced in 1996 as part of the rejected Oslo Agreement. Along with that decision, Hamas declared its willingness to join the PLO, dropping a number of old and classic reservations, including the objection that the PLO is a secular organisation. Moreover, it agreed to a unilateral truce, stopping all suicide attacks inside Israel and giving the movement the space to breathe and prepare for the electoral battle.[30] The

---

30. These were three decisions that shaped the following course of developments on Hamas's side. The author has discussed them in detail elsewhere; see K. Hroub, 'Hamas's Path to Reinvention', *Open Democracy*, 10 October 2006.

electoral platform of Hamas's 'Reform and Change' list was surprising in terms of its new discourse – a maximum of realistic politics (compared to the movement's previous literature) and a minimum of religiosity.[31] Throughout all of the above, a process of continuous negotiation between the political and the religious seemed to be taking place within the movement.

Only by accounting for these changing contextual determinants is one able to understand certain, sometimes surprising, moves of Hamas. Any attempt to understand them solely from an ideological perspective by, say, measuring them against Hamas's 1988 Charter would be greatly misleading.

In those two years, Hamas's cost–benefit calculations led the movement to reconsider major strategies and make the necessary shifts to meet emerging circumstances. At every sudden bend in the course of events, Hamas would respond more according to objective elements, than to a pre-set ideological or religious catalogue. The tension inside Hamas between the political and the religious has been there since the movement first appeared; however, it has been more or less visible depending on the political conditions. In certain periods, Hamas could ease the tension, allowing the movement's political and religious drives to complement each other. At other times, this coexistence between the two has proved difficult, forcing Hamas to give priority to one or the other, conditioned by the issue at hand. This process has, however, never involved consciously choosing between two competing options. If it had, it would have faced strong opposition as many people in Hamas would have argued that there should be no decoupling between politics and religion and that, if a seemingly political decision were taken, it should not be seen as religion-free.

As a result, the decision-making process is very subtle and there is no sifting of the political and religious components of a certain move, nor a way of comparing them, followed by the advancement of one or other in a mathematical kind of way. In fact, negotiating the political and the religious takes place within Hamas (and many other Islamist movements for that matter) at the subconscious level, gradually and indirectly. It involves tacitly approving the continuous process of smuggling the political into the realm

---

31. For extended analysis of Hamas's electoral platform, see Hroub, 'A "New Hamas" through its New Documents', *Journal of Palestine Studies*, vol. 35, no. 4 (Summer 2006), pp. 6–28 (http://www.palestine-studies.org/journals.asp x?id=7087&jid=1&href=fulltext); and for the full text of the document, see Tamimi, *Hamas: A History from Within*, appendix VI, pp. 292–316.

of the religious, in response to new pressures and circumstances. The process therefore combines rational calculations about political options, spontaneous acceptance of non-religious assessments or alliances and a parallel justification and legitimisation process that reproduces political choices and decisions in religious clothing so they can be sold to Hamas's supporters and constituencies. This process of prioritising the political over the religious reached a peak when Hamas won the elections and faced the dilemma of forming an exclusive Hamas-led government.

Since Hamas's victory in the 2006 elections the Palestinians have come into a new phase in their internal politics: a new Palestinian legitimacy has come into being. The principal marker of this new legitimacy is the fact that Hamas has become an integral part of it. Despite all the great losses that Hamas has suffered and the number of strategic mistakes that it has made, it is now a powerful movement that competes and claims to represent all Palestinians. Both in resistance as well as in democratic elections, it has accumulated sufficient legitimacy capital to prevent its staunchest enemies questioning its central role in the Palestinian polity. Any reunification of the West Bank and the Gaza Strip (after Hamas's military takeover of the Strip in June 2007) will necessitate having Hamas at the heart of the political process and decision-making. In fact, many Palestinians and other regional and international players have come to believe that after the 2006 elections the days when the PLO enjoyed an exclusive monopoly over Palestinian legitimacy are over. It is a new reality that external actors can do little about; they can ignore it, but they cannot change it.[32]

The implications of the formation of a new Palestinian legitimacy with Hamas as a part of it are many. These could be discussed at the level of Hamas itself, at the wider Palestinian national level and at the level of the conflict with Israel in general. Internally and over the past two years, Hamas has been undergoing the greatest phase of tension yet between its constituent political and religious drives. A more political role of the movement governed by being part of the 'Palestinian legitimacy' has resulted in increased

---

32. The author has analysed elsewhere the detailed implications of Hamas's victory for all parties concerned, including Hamas itself; see Hroub, 'Hamas in and out of power' in A. Elshobaki, K. Hroub, D. Pioppi and N. Tocci eds. *Domestic Change and Conflict in the Mediterranean: The Cases of Hamas and Hezbollah*, EuroMeSCo Paper No. 65, Lisbon: EuroMeSCo, January 2008 (http://www.euromesco.net/images/65eng.pdf).

politicisation of its programmes and members. The political realities of the Palestinian situation, with all their compromising and less religious dimensions, have made further and wider inroads to the heart of the rank and file of the organisation.

At the national level many Palestinians see in Hamas's participation in the political process and decision-taking that pertains to the national cause an injection of strength in the collective position. The 'chain of concessions' that the PLO has been making to Israel over the past two decades would have come to an end, as Hamas argues with the support of many Palestinians. Yet, others consider Hamas's elevation to occupy a central place on the top of the Palestinian political hierarchy to be a measure of radicalisation that will further complicate future Palestinians choices. Whatever the case, what is almost certain is that the make-up of the Palestinian leadership and its legitimacy have changed.

But the most important implication of the post-2006 elections relate to the future of the conflict and/or peace between Israel and the Palestinians. Any process that is to go ahead and conclude in a sustained peace deal between the two parties has to be legitimised and approved by the Palestinians. Since January 2006 and Hamas's victory in the Legislative Council elections, it is inconceivable that any partisan consensus or referendum towards any agreement can proceed without the endorsement of Hamas.

Before the elections, especially during the days of Arafat, one of the premises upon which the peace process (of Oslo Accords 1993-4) was built was that by using and relying on Arafat who wielded charisma, power, money and influence, a peace deal could be concluded without the need for a Palestinian consensus. Arafat had the leadership, legacy and aura to sell any deal to (or impose any deal on) the Palestinians. Things have changed. Arafat is no longer on the scene to impose deals on the Palestinians and in the meantime Hamas has become far stronger and is now backed by electoral as well as resistance legitimacy. The logic of imposing a deal should be substituted by the logic of building broader consensus that must include Hamas. Any move forwards must start from this point if it is to secure the required collective consensus and legitimacy of the Palestinians.

The context post-January 2006 (Hamas's winning of the elections) and post-June 2007 (Hamas's military take-over of the Gaza Strip) has also had various consequences for Hamas's social and religious thinking and practice. Some segments within the movement, the more conservative and religiously rigid, have thought that by acquiring further power that is mandated by popular electoral support Hamas could and should press on for more Islamisation of society. These strata of Hamas understood its victory more as public support for the social and religious ideals of the movement, while other more sophisticated leaders of Hamas have been aware that many Palestinians have voted in favour of Hamas's political and military stand, and are not particularly impressed by its social and religious agenda. A considerable number of Palestinians have in fact punished Fatah, Hamas's main rival, by casting their angry votes for Hamas – a fact that many Hamas's leaders are fully aware of. These occasional and temporary voters have tipped the balance of power to give Hamas an unexpected and surprising victory. Thus, it would be a grave strategic mistake to build on this fragile victory and make hard choices that require a more solid and broad ground of support. This awareness explains, at least in part, Hamas's reluctance to advance any social and religious agenda overtly, even in the Gaza Strip where they dominate all aspects of public life.

On the ground there was a certain (ironic) social reality in play. While the sophisticated view within the Hamas which advocated non-aggressive social and religious policies seems to have gained the upper hand, refusing to impose laws or start official or semi-official Islamisation campaigns, the atmosphere in the Gaza Strip in particular has shifted towards conservative views and practices. In the first place the economic embargo has worsened the daily life of ordinary Palestinians, driving them closer to religion as the only refuge when the entire outside world has turned its back on their misery.[33] Those who support Hamas have tended to manifest more 'Islamic' appearances and behaviour, while those who fear Hamas have started to adapt their behaviour to appease local Hamas elements as a strategy to avoid harassment. While no regulations have been drafted by the Hamas-controlled Legislative Council to superimpose any codes of religious practices, the brutality with which Hamas controls the Gaza Strip militarily has created

---

33. Reports about the magnitude of the humanitarian disaster in the Gaza Strip resulting from the Israeli and international embargo are numerous. See for example Oxfam's report 'Gaza Strip: Humanitarian Implosion', March 2008, http://www.oxfam.org.uk/resources/policy/conflict_disasters/downloads/gaza_implosion.pdf. In April 2008 the former American President Jimmy Carter described the blockade imposed on the Gaza Strip as a 'crime and an atrocity'; see http://www.globalresearch.ca/index.php?context=va&aid=8739.

a great sense of intimidation in the area. Many ordinary Palestinians have therefore opted not to irritate Hamas's men by wearing clothes or behaving in ways seen by these men as un-Islamic. A *de facto* Islamisation of the Palestinian society in the Gaza Strip has thus taken place – a process that deserves special research on its own, identifying the elements of indirect pressures and agencies that have operated under the aegis of Hamas power yet without being officially linked to it.

NINE

The Islamic Movement in the Jewish State

Tilde Rosmer

During the war in 1948 more than 700,000 Palestinian Arabs – or seven-eighths of the inhabitants of the territories that became the state of Israel after the war – were expelled or fled.[1] Today, approximately 20 per cent of the Israeli population is not Jewish, but indigenous Arab Palestinian.[2] Ian Lustick describes the predicament of the Palestinians who remained in the state of Israel as that of an 'instant minority' whose lives were in 'complete disarray':

> Fragmented along geographical, religious, and familial lines, it was entirely devoid of leadership above municipal level ... Their economic situation was desperate; their immediate concerns were the integrity of their property and the safety and unification of their families.[3]

Until 1966 all Palestinians in Israel lived under military government, under which more of their land was confiscated and expropriated, and their freedom of movement and economic opportunities were severely restricted. In terms of citizenship, according to David Kretzmer:

> Of the 150,000 Palestinians who remained in the territory of the state of Israel at the conclusion of the 1948 war, about 60,000 were granted immediate citizenship, and the rest were entitled to it if they met certain conditions stipulated in the Nationality Law of 1952. These

---

1. B. Morris, *The Birth of the Palestinian Refugee Problem, 1947–1949*, Cambridge: Cambridge University Press, 1987.
2. According to the Israeli Bureau of Statistics, 75.5 per cent are Jewish, 20.2 per cent are Arab, and 4.3 per cent are 'other' – latter defined as immigrants and family members who are not registered as Jewish with the Ministry of Interior. Population of Israel on the eve of 2009: 7.4 million (Central Bureau of Statistics, 30 December 2008, available at www.cbs.gov.il).
3. I. Lustick, *Arabs in the Jewish State: Israel's Control of a National Minority*, Austin, TX: University of Texas Press, 1980, p. 51.

conditions prevented many Palestinians from becoming citizens until the Nationality Law was amended in 1980.[4]

The inferior position of these non-Jewish citizens of the Jewish state is well documented, in particular with regard to the continuous appropriation of their land, discrimination in the education system and economic disadvantages.[5] According to Gershon Shafir and Yoav Peled, although Palestinian citizens of Israel formally enjoy civil and political rights as individuals, they are excluded from equal membership in the political community as non-Jewish citizens.[6] Consequently, they are 'more or less secure in the exercise of their individual rights, as long as these rights do not conflict with the national goals of the Jewish majority'. The tensions between these national goals and the rights of non-Jewish citizens are today made visible in the recent banning by the Central Elections Committee of all Arab parties from running in the Israel parliamentary elections of 2009.[7]

---

4. D. Kretzmer, *The Legal Status of the Arabs in Israel*, Boulder: Westview, 1990, pp. 36–40, cited in Y. Peled and G. Shafir, *Being Israeli: The Dynamics of Multiple Citizenship*, Cambridge: Cambridge University Press, 2002, pp. 110–11.

5. See Lustick, *Arabs in the Jewish State*; Peled and Shafir, *Being Israeli*; N. N. Rouhana, '"Jewish and Democratic"? The Price of a National Self-Deception', *Journal of Palestine Studies*. vol. 35, no. 2 (Winter 2006); I. Abu-Saad, 'Education and Identity Formation among Indigenous Palestinian Arab Youth in Israel', in *Indigenous and Minority Education – International Perspectives on Empowerment*, Be'er-Sheva: Ben-Gurion University of the Negev, 2005; M. Al-Haj, 'Israeli "Development" and Education Policies and Their Impact on the Negev Palestinian Bedouin: Historical Experience and Future Prospects', *Holy Land Studies*, vol. 2, no. 1, (September 2003); M. Al-Haj, 'The Status of the Palestinians in Israel: A Double Periphery in an Ethno-National State', *Association for Israel Studies* Conference, on-line paper from the 2004 Association for Israel Studies Conference, The Hebrew University, Jerusalem, www.aisisraelstudies.org/2004papers.htm, 22.02.2007, 2004; S. Payes, *Palestinian NGOs in Israel: The Politics of Civil Society*, London: Tauris Academic Studies, 2005; S. Swirski, *Politics and Education in Israel: Comparisons with the United States*, London: Falmer Press, 1999. See also documents from non-governmental organisations in Israel, such as Adalah, the Legal Centre for Arab Minority Rights in Israel (www.adalah.org); Ittijah, the Union of Arab Community-based Associations in Israel (www.ittajah.org); and ADVA, a non-partisan policy analysis institute (www.adva.org).

6. Peled and Shafir, *Being Israeli*, p. 111.

7. 'The Central Elections Committee voted overwhelmingly in favour of the motions, accusing the country's Arab parties of incitement, supporting terrorist

Thus, in Israel, 'national' distinctions separate Jews from the Palestinian Arab minority, whereas 'ethnic identity' is used to describe divisions among Jewish Israelis; Palestinian citizens[8] of Israel do not belong to the Jewish nation, and are systematically discriminated against.[9] According to Thomas Hylland Eriksen, in developing their policies towards minority groups, states generally choose between strategies of assimilation, segregation and multiculturalism.[10] From previous analyses of the situation of Palestinians in Israel, the Israeli state's policy towards its Palestinian minority appears to be characterised by an attempt simultaneously both to assimilate and to segregate this community.[11] With regard to the Muslim minority in particular,

---

groups and refusing to recognize Israel's right to exist.' ('Israel bans Arab parties from running in upcoming elections', *Ha'aretz*, 13 January 2009.)

8. In this chapter the term 'Palestinian citizens of Israel' will be used to describe Arab Palestinians living inside Israel (excluding the approximately 170,000 Palestinian inhabitants of occupied East Jerusalem). The very act of naming minorities is political, and I have opted to use the term 'Palestinian citizens of Israel' as it is the term preferred by my sources. The Israeli government and Israeli media usually use the terms Arab Israelis and Israeli Arabs.

9. The Israeli geographer Oren Yiftachel describes Israel as an 'ethnocracy', which he defines as a 'regime governed by two main principles: (a) despite several democratic features, ethnicity (and not territorial citizenship) is the main organising logic for the allocation of state resources; and (b) a dominant "charter group" enjoys a superior position over other ethnic groups; this group appropriates the state apparatus, and dictates the nature of most public policies. The combination of the two principles typically generates ethno-class stratification and segregation. Given these "ethnic rules of the game," and given the dominance of the Ashkenazim [Jews of European origin] as the Israeli "charter group," the Israeli polity has been characterised by ongoing practices of ethnic control over both Arab and Jewish minorities.' O. Yiftachel, 'Nation-Building and the Division of Space: Frontiers and Domination in the Israeli "Ethnocracy"', 1991, available at www.geog.bgu.ac.il. The first person to describe Israel as an ethnocracy was the Norwegian political scientist Niels Butenschøen, in 1988. See 'State, Power, and Citizenship in the Middle East, A Theoretical Introduction', in N. Butenschøen, U. Davis, and M. Hassassian, eds, *Citizenship and the State in the Middle East: Approaches and Applications*, New York: Syracuse University Press, 2000.

10. T. H. Eriksen, *Ethnicity and Nationalism: Anthropological Perspectives*, London: Pluto, 2002, p. 123.

11. For example, in the analysis of Lustick, *Arabs in the Jewish State*, and Alisa Rubin Peled, *Debating Islam in the Jewish State: The Development of Policy Toward Islamic Institutions in Israel*, New York: State University of New York Press, 2001.

Israel's policies are designed to advance what I characterise as 'controlled autonomy'.[12] As described by Alisa Rubin Peled, whereas the state provides some autonomy for religious communities, this policy is combined with control over religious offices:

> The state supported communal autonomy in realms perceived as purely religious, such as personal status and freedom of worship. At the same time, the government suspected an intrinsic link between Islam and Arab political nationalism, its greatest concern. Thus, Israel implemented a system of strict central controls to prevent the emergence of a national Muslim leadership or an independent religious education system.[13]

Eriksen suggests further that the response of minorities towards the state generally takes one of three forms: acceptance of assimilation, opting for coexistence, or calling for independence or autonomy.[14] Al-Haraka al-Islami fi Isra'il – the Islamic Movement in Israel – emerged in the early 1980s, and is today one of the main non-Jewish opposition groups among Israel's citizenry, promoting and protecting the interests of the Palestinians in Israel. In the case of this movement, which split in 1996, two responses are discernible. Both the Movement of Shaykh Darwish and the Movement of Shaykh Salah are rebuilding a Palestinian Muslim identity for their constituents, and attempting to construct an autonomous infrastructure for Palestinians in Israel. While the Movement of Shaykh Darwish and its representatives in the Knesset attempt to integrate into the state apparatus, the Movement of Shaykh Salah rejects such integration. As the Movements do not operate with registered membership, it is difficult to determine exactly the number-balance between them.

Based on interviews with the leading *shaykhs* (religious leaders) of the Islamic Movement in Israel, conducted in the summer of 2008, this chapter

---

12. The state's policy towards the Palestinian Christian minority has been different, and the state has generally favoured the Christian community over the Muslim community in its policies on minority religious affairs (Peled, *Debating Islam in the Jewish State*, p. 5). According to Peled, 'Israel tended to give preference to Christian affairs in order to gain the regard of the largely Christian West, particularly since most of the Muslim world was inherently opposed to the existence of the Jewish state' (p. 4).

13. Ibid., p. 3

14. Eriksen, *Ethnicity and Nationalism*, pp. 123–4.

will examine the trajectory and predicament of the Movement, and consider its current political positions. I will focus on the Movement's defining
moments and analyse how they influenced its present character and shaped
its development, while investigating its leaders' attitudes to assimilation,
coexistence and autonomy.

Representing an indigenous and national–religious minority in a conflict
zone, the Islamic Movement campaigns for the rights of Palestinian citizens
of Israel on many levels, including those of religion, territory, law, civil life
and human rights. Its situation is particularly complex, due to the ongoing
conflict between the state of Israel and Palestinians represented by the Palestine Liberation Organisation (the PLO), including those living in worldwide
exile, and by Hamas and other political groups based in the Israeli-occupied
territories of the West Bank, including East Jerusalem and the Gaza Strip.
Moreover, Palestine and al-Aqsa (the third-holiest site in Islam) are the foci
of much global attention (and contention), and their symbolic and religious
value to Muslim communities worldwide should not be underestimated. This
positions the Islamic Movement in Israel in a particularly central situation. The
Movement represents Palestinian Muslims with access to al-Aqsa, a mosque
located in their historic homeland (Palestine), and in an area that is currently
under military occupation (East Jerusalem) by the state to which they hold
citizenship (Israel). Thus, the Islamic Movement in Israel is conducting its
political and religio-cultural struggle in the religious and geographical nexus
of Islamic movements worldwide.

According to Nikki Keddie, there have been three watersheds in recent
political–religious history in the Middle East: 1928, which marked the establishment of the Muslim Brotherhood in Egypt; 1967, when Israel defeated the
Arab states, bringing to an end the ascent of pan-Arabism and Arab nationalism; and the 1979 Iranian Revolution.[15] For Palestinian citizens of Israel and
for the Islamic Movement, I would add three further significant dates: 1983,
when the Islamic Movement was established;[16] 1996, when it split over the

---

15. N. Keddie, 'The New Religious Politics: Where, When, and Why Do "Funda-
    mentalisms" Appear?' *Comparative Studies in Society and History*, vol. 40, no.
    4 (October 1998), pp. 696–723.

16. Because of the nature of this Movement's gradual formation, some say that it
    was established in the early 1970s, and others at the beginning of the 1980s.
    The date used to mark its establishment here is the date when its leader, Shaykh
    Darwish, was released from prison, and upon his release established the Shabab

issue of parliamentary participation; and 2000, when the killings of several Palestinian citizens by Israeli police sparked the al-Aqsa *intifada*.

Between 1948 and 1966, the particular context of Palestinian citizens of Israel was largely governed by their isolation from the Palestinians in the West Bank and Gaza, as well as from the wider Arab world. This chapter contends that it is largely as a result of this background that the Movement developed in the way that it did. Unlike most other Sunni Islamist movements in the Middle East, whose leaders have been schooled within a secular educational system, the leaders of the Islamic Movement in Israel are *shaykhs*.[17] Another unusual feature of the Islamic Movement in Israel, as compared with other Sunni Islamist movements in the region, is the predicament of Palestinian citizens of Israel as an indigenous minority within a non-Muslim state. These complex circumstances have several implications for the identity, goals and practices of the Movement, providing both limitations and possibilities that sometimes create paradoxical situations. Perhaps the most striking example of the paradox inherent in this predicament is the opportunity of participating in Israeli elections at all levels. Some members of the Movement seized this opportunity and stood for national elections in 1996 – a decision that provoked the Movement to split. Furthermore, the perennial challenges experienced by Palestinian citizens of Israel became heightened following the outbreak of the al-Aqsa *intifada* in October 2000. The events of autumn 2000 marked the formal end of the years of peace negotiations of the 1990s, and saw a return to violent confrontation between the Israeli military and Palestinians in the occupied Palestinian territory; but the violence was not confined to that territory. During the events of autumn 2000, thirteen Palestinian citizens were shot dead by Israeli police while demonstrating in support of the Palestinians in the occupied territory.[18] This was the single bloodiest

---

al-Muslimin, which soon became the al-Haraka al-Islami fi Isra'il – the Islamic Movement in Israel.

17. The early Algerian Islamist movement may offer a further exception since *shaykhs* there played an important role, in response to the French colonial powers, in formulating the early Salafi-inspired calls for reform and national assertiveness in the first half of the twentieth century. The Association of Algerian 'Ulama linked religious reform and Islamic education with the promotion of Algerian nationalism. E. Shahin, *Political Ascent: Contemporary Islamic Movements in North Africa*, Boulder, CO: Westview Press, 1997, pp. 161–2.

18. Adalah, 'Special Report, October 2000 Killings', available at www.adalah.org/eng/october2000.php.

event for Palestinian citizens of Israel since the Kufr Qasim massacre of 1956, when forty-nine villagers were killed by Israeli police for breaking a curfew they had not been informed about.[19] This chapter examines the reactions of the leadership of the Movement to these events and their consequences.

The emergence of the Islamic Movement in Israel: Islam is the answer[20]

The Islamic Movement in Israel was established in 1979/80 by Muslim clergy holding Israeli citizenship who were educated in West Bank institutions after Israel occupied the area, along with other Arab territory, in the 1967 war. Upon their return to Israel, these men established study centres and set up their own movement. According to Peled,[21] the movement inside Israel crystallised in 1979, and 'Abdullah Nimr Darwish from Kufr Qasim quickly became its leader. Knesset Member for the Islamic Movement, Shaykh Ibrahim Sarsour, explained:

> The 1967 War was a Holocaust from a military point of view, but it was the beginning of the reawakening of the Arab population inside Israel. For the first time we felt that we had found the other part of our nation. I mean those Palestinians who lived in the occupied territories ... And I must confess to you that the Palestinian people who lived inside the occupied territories were more educated than we were. They were in direct connection with the Arab world, with the Muslim world, and with the international community. Shaykh 'Abdullah [Nimr Darwish] was the first Arab Israeli citizen to go and study in one of the famous colleges in Nablus.[22]

To appreciate the particularities of the context in which the Islamic Movement in Israel developed, it is necessary to consider the establishment of the state of Israel in 1948. As described above, seven-eighths of the Arab inhabitants in the land that became the state of Israel after the war were expelled or fled, and of those who remained, less than half were granted immediate citizenship. Between 1948 and 1966, Palestinians inside Israel lived under a military government (*memshal tzvai* in Hebrew). This was part of what Ian Lustick described in his seminal study *Arabs in the Jewish State* as 'a highly

---

19. Peled and Shafir, *Being Israeli*, p. 232.
20. 'Islam is the Answer' is the slogan of the Islamic Movement of Israel.
21. Peled, *Debating Islam in the Jewish State*.
22. Author interview.

effective system of control'.[23] According to Lustick, this system comprised three interacting processes: segmentation, dependence and cooptation. Lustick argues that it was due to the effectiveness of this system that there was no significant political or communal organisation among Palestinians in Israel until the 1970s. During the period of military rule, Israel confiscated more than half of the land belonging to the Palestinians remaining in Israel, in addition to that belonging to those who were living in exile and denied their right of return, and the state systematically marginalised the remaining Palestinian population both economically and politically.[24] The abolition of military rule finally gave Palestinian Arabs in Israel the opportunity to travel freely within the country, to organise themselves politically, to be tried in the same legal system as Jewish citizens, and to participate in the country's economic and social life.

With the war in 1967, which resulted in Israel's occupation of the West Bank and Gaza, Palestinians inside Israel gained access to the Palestinian population and religious teaching institutions in the occupied Palestinian territories. In her analysis of the turn towards political Islam taken by Muslim Palestinians in Israel after 1967, Alisa Rubin Peled argues that, in addition to the region-wide trend towards Islamism and the access to Islamic teaching provided by Israel's occupation of the West Bank, other scholars have overlooked the influence of the weakening state of the Muslim establishment and education inside Israel.[25] According to Peled, the shortage of *qadis* (religious judges) and religious functionaries became pressing in the 1960s due to a combination of factors: the vacuum left after the 1948 war, when most of the Palestinian intelligentsia fled; the ageing of those who remained and reached retirement age; and the failure of the state to ensure proper recruitment procedures for Muslim religious leaders. According to Peled, the state based its religious appointments on the political acceptability, rather than on the religious expertise, of the individuals concerned. The consequence of this approach was that there were few suitable individuals inside Israel to

---

23. Lustick, *Arabs in the Jewish State*, p. 5.
24. See Peled and Shafir, *Being Israeli*; Abu-Saad, 'Education and Identity Formation', pp. 235–56; Rouhana, '"Jewish and Democratic"' pp. 64–7; Ghanem, *The Palestinian-Arab Minority in Israel, 1948–2000, A Political Study*, New York: State University of New York Press, 2001; Lustick, *Arabs in the Jewish State*.
25. Peled, *Debating Islam in the Jewish State*, pp. 129–30.

replace retired *qadis*.[26] The Muslim community had raised the problem of recruitment since 1948, but the state had failed to address it adequately.[27]

It was the vacuum that had been created by the lack of religious expertise in Israel that the *shaykhs* who had been educated in the West Bank began to fill from the late 1970s. These same individuals later became the leaders of the Islamic Movement. As Shaykh Ra'ed Salah explained:

> The Islamic Movement started in the early seventies and the beginning, in my opinion, was due to two factors. The first factor was the arrival of a group of Muslim scholars from the West Bank and Gaza Strip who personally initiated and started to give lessons in our mosques, which originally lacked an Islamic revival. Their role developed into giving lessons in homes and at public gatherings in the streets. The second factor was that in that period, we learned, for the first time, that there are Islamic institutes in which we could study Islamic studies, whether in Hebron, Jerusalem or Nablus. This was the first time in our history that we had the opportunity to learn about Islam according to its principles as stated in the Holy Qur'an.[28]

According to Peled, the Israeli Ministry of Religious Affairs initially encouraged Muslim students from Israel to study in the West Bank, and even subsidised their tuition.[29] It also assisted in establishing the Hebron Islamic Studies Centre. The reason for this policy was the belief that increased contact between Muslims from inside Israel and Palestinians in the West Bank would demonstrate to the latter the advantages of the former's situation, and thereby reduce local opposition to the military occupation.[30]

Member of Knesset Shaykh Sarsur recalled his experience of being a young teenager when Shaykh Darwish returned to Israel from his studies in Nablus in the occupied West Bank. Both Sarsur and Darwish are from Kufr Qassim, where, according to Shaykh Sarsur, the Movement began after Shaykh Darwish returned in 1972:

> In 1969, that means two years after the 1967 War, the imam of the village – who was an old man – encouraged that young, charismatic

---

26. Ibid., p. 121.
27. According to Peled (p. 122), Muslim religious leaders in Israel had already called for the establishment of a seminary in 1950.
28. Author interview.
29. Peled, *Debating Islam in the Jewish State*, p.128.
30. Ibid.

man [Darwish] to go and study Islam in Nablus. There was no alternative. Even during the years of his study in that college he used to come at the weekends to the village. And we were, at that time, pupils in the elementary school – in the eighth grade, ninth grade. And I was raised in a very conservative family. I used to go with my father to the mosque and we used to see that young charismatic man who preached on Fridays, in the only mosque at those times in our village. And when he looked at us, he saw that there were tens of pupils coming to the mosque. That's why he began to create that kind of connection between him and us. And that was the beginning, the first step towards becoming the Islamic Movement, which was established after Shaykh 'Abdullah finished his studies in Nablus in 1972. So I was raised – I can say that I grew up – with the Islamic Movement since I was a child of thirteen or fourteen years.[31]

Later, Shaykh Sarsur became one of the leading figures in the Movement. In 1988 he was appointed spokesman of the Movement, and in 1989 he became the first mayor of the exclusively Palestinian town Kufr Qassim to be elected while representing the Movement. In 1989 the Movement ran and won in local elections in several municipalities of Palestinian-inhabited villages and towns. Shaykh Sarsur described this year as 'a kind of revolution – an Islamic Revolution – I mean a peaceful Islamic Revolution in Israel'.[32] Shaykh Sarsur was elected head of the Movement of Shaykh Darwish in 1998, and has been a Member of Knesset for the Islamic Movement since 2006.

Knesset Member 'Abbas Zakur emphasised that the primary agenda of the Movement was to introduce Islam to the Muslims in Israel – to teach them about Islam. To this end, they used to invite male and female preachers from the West Bank and Gaza, until the late 1980s, to give talks at mosques about Islam. As'ad Ghanem divides the history of what he described as 'the Islamic religious organisations in Israel' into two periods. The first period spans the years 1979–81, which were dominated by the paramilitary underground organisation Usra al-Jihad ('Family of Jihad') set up with the aim of waging a war in Israel. After the leaders were imprisoned and their centres attacked by the Israeli security forces, the Movement changed focus towards legal and social activities aimed at their community and local politics. The second period, which commenced in 1983 and runs to the present, began when Shaykh Darwish became the leader of a new organisation, called

31. Author interview.
32. Author interview.

Shabab al-Muslimin – the Young Muslims – which became the Islamic Movement in Israel.[33]

Muhammad Hasan Amara explains that Darwish's imprisonment with the rest of the members of the Family of Jihad in 1980 marked an early shift in his – and the Movement's – development from a small activist group to a grassroots movement.[34] According to Amara, prior to his imprisonment, Shaykh Darwish spoke about his antipathy to Western culture and imperialism, and presented Islam as a complete, liberal, humanist way of life for all mankind. By contrast, after his release in 1983, Darwish emphasised the importance of following Israeli law and avoided making public calls for an Islamic state. From then on, the Movement was modelled on the Muslim Brotherhood of Hassan al-Banna, and focused on youth education and the teaching of Islam, collecting *zakat*, organising volunteer work camps across the country, and other initiatives whose goal was to provide pastoral care for the Palestinian Muslim community in Israel.[35] Shaykh Kamel Khatib also noted[36] that the *da'wa* (advocacy) work of the Islamic Movement began following the release of Shaykh Darwish in 1983. He mentioned building kindergartens and clinics, sports clubs and other communal leisure facilities for communities; publishing a magazine called *Al-Sirat* ('The Way');[37] holding Islamic weddings; and organising volunteer work camps around the country. In other words, since the 1980s the Movement has been in the process of building the infrastructure for an autonomous network of institutions to serve Muslim Palestinian citizens of Israel.[38]

This infrastructure has first of all been constructed at a local level. To indicate the success of the Movement on a local level, in 1989 the Movement ran for elections in fifteen Arab locales, gaining fifty-one seats and six chairmanship positions, and in the 1998 municipal elections, the Movement

33. Ghanem, *The Palestinian-Arab Minority in Israel*, p. 124.
34. M. H. Amara, 'The Nature of Islamic Fundamentalism in Israel', *Terrorism and Political Violence*, vol. 8, no. 2 (Summer 1996), pp. 156–7.
35. Ibid.
36. Author interview.
37. Today the Movement has several publications catering for a mixed audience, including a magazine by and for women.
38. The Islamic Movement's institutions are open for use by all Palestinians in Israel, and their leisure centres, clinics and other amenities are used by Christian and Muslim Palestinians.

gained forty-seven membership seats and seven chairmanship positions.[39] Until the 1970s, Palestinian citizens voted for Jewish Zionist parties, most for the Labour-forerunner Mapai, or the Jewish–Palestinian Communist Party. This changed with the emergence of Palestinian secular parties – in particular Rakah, the Sons of the Village, the Progressive List for Peace, and Balad. These are now challenged by the Islamic Movement. In addition to party politics, local elections in Palestinian towns and villages have been strongly connected with *hamula* politics.[40]

For example, Um al-Fahm, the Palestinian town that has been the centre of Muslim religio-political activism in Israel, has seen great improvements since the Islamic Movement took over the running of the municipality in 1989. According to Maha al-Taji, the Islamic Movement won the support of the inhabitants because it was delivering what neither the state nor previous local authority administrations had previously delivered: 'Garbage collection, the sewage system, schools, and commercial space, all improved under the tenure of the Islamic Movement.'[41] Al-Taji argues further that, since the Islamic Movement entered municipal politics in Um al-Fahm in 1983, the city has been able to rid itself of traditional *hamula* politics, which had been an obstacle to effective government. She credits the Islamic Movement with this development, and identifies its ideological appeal and its success in delivering services to local residents through its voluntary organisations as the tools that were employed in order to overcome narrow *hamula*-driven interests.

The Movement's split

The Movement's split in 1996 was caused by a disagreement regarding its participation in parliamentary elections, and resulted in two branches,

---

39. M. T. al-Taji, 'Arab Local Authorities in Israel: Hamulas, Nationalism and Dilemmas of Social Change', PhD, University of Washington, 2008, p. 155.

40. 'The *hamula* (literally, an extended family), a traditional kinship social structure, plays an important part in the internal affairs of the Arab minority in Israel and provides the basis for the patronage system that pervades the Arab minority's local politics. *Hamula*-dominated local authorities, rife with patronage and serving narrow personal interests, have had a detrimental effect on the well-being of Arab residents, leaving them with financially dilapidated local authorities and deficient local services.' Al-Taji, 'Arab Local Authorities in Israel', abstract.

41. Ibid., p. 277

which have subsequently become known to their members as the Islamic Movement of Shaykh Darwish and the Islamic Movement of Shaykh Salah.[42] The Islamic Movement headed by Shaykh Salah opposed participation in national elections for ideological and political reasons. Ideologically, Shaykh Salah argued that the Movement should not participate in a political system that is not based on *shari'a*. His political concern was that participation in national elections would weaken the Movement's unique contact with the people by making it 'just another Arab party'; that it would mean getting into the 'dirty business' of politics; that it would make the Movement dependent on government resources, and thus provide the state with control over its activities; and, finally, that it would force the Movement to swear allegiance to the state, and to its (Jewish) symbols and (Zionist) agenda.[43]

On the other hand, Shaykh Darwish argued that, on the ideological level, there was room for a political compromise to be made with non-Islamic actors if they constituted the local context in which politics were conducted.[44] Thus, according to Shaykh Darwish, the Islamic Movement in Israel should be able to engage in national politics if this is the best way to promote and protect the interests of the Palestinians in Israel.

Shaykh Abbas Zakur, a Member of the Knesset for the Movement of Shaykh Darwish, described the years between 1989 and 1996 as the peak of the Movement's general management of national activities. It was during this period that the Movement established a National Consultative Assembly (*shura*), headed by Shaykh Darwish. In discussions about entering national elections, Shaykh Darwish was the leading supporter of such participation, whereas Shaykh Salah was against it. Zakour recalled that, in a vote on the issue in the *shura* in 1996, with representatives of all Palestinian towns,

42. In Hebrew, and often also in English, the Islamic Movement of Shaykh Ra'id Salah is referred to as the 'Northern wing/branch' of the Islamic Movement, and the Islamic Movement of Shaykh 'Abdullah Nimr Darwish is referred to as its 'Southern wing/branch'. The division into northern and southern refers to the localities of the towns in which these two leaders live in the so-called Triangle – an area of central Israel primarily inhabited by Palestinian citizens of Israel, and does not represent a real geographical division between Palestinians inside Israel.

43. I. Aburaiya, 'The 1996 Split of the Islamic Movement in Israel: Between the Holy Text and Israeli–Palestinian Context', *International Journal of Politics, Culture and Society*, vol. 17, no. 3 (Spring 2004), pp. 450–51.

44. Ibid., p. 449.

villages and cities inside Israel, the majority was in favour of participation in national elections.[45]

Shaykh Kamil Khatib of the Movement of Shaykh Salah explained why he did not consider it appropriate for the Movement to join the Knesset:

> The Islamic Movement initially depends on the service of our people through associations that we established and these associations set up institutions all over the country. For example, this place we are in here [the interview took place in Kufr Kanna] is a complex in which there is a public library for the residents of the village and a kindergarten, and nearby we have a new elementary school. We have a clinic, ambulances, and a sports club for karate and for football. This exists in many Arab villages. We seek to serve our people through the establishment of these institutions and this is what Shaykh Ra'id Salah called for. I am sure he told you about what is called a 'self-reliant society' – that is, we do not expect to cry on the doorsteps of the ministries. We seek, with the abilities of our people, to build our own institutions to maintain our identity.

When asked about the differences between the two parts of the Movement, Shaykh Khatib identified the disagreement over parliamentary participation as the main source of difference, and put this in a larger context:

> Israel was, in fact, interested in the entry of the Islamic Movement into the Knesset. It sought to make the Islamic Movement a bridge to connect with other Muslim peoples. This would contribute to the normalisation of relations between Israel and the Muslim and Arab peoples. In addition, another of the benefits of our entry into the Knesset would be to beautify Israel's ugly face, as if it is in actuality a democracy. [46]

Despite the split, all leaders of the Movement emphasise that they are united on religious issues. According to Shaykh Zakur of the Movement of Shaykh Darwish, even though there is a division in the Islamic Movement, it is united in its approach as a moderate Islamic Movement. He qualified 'moderate' by stressing that the focus of the Movement is not on the way in which people dress, such as whether the women wear headscarves or the men wear a robe or have a long beard, as is the case with some other Islamist movements, such as

45. Author interview.
46. Author interview.

the Salafi and Tabligh: 'The important thing to us, as an Islamic Movement, is what should be important in a modern lifestyle. We want Islam to present good manners, the good side of Islam and not superficial things.'[47]

Shaykh Khatib makes the point that, despite his criticism of the participation in the Knesset of the Movement of Shaykh Darwish, and his and Shaykh Salah's choice to remain outside the Knesset, this did not prevent their shared presence in other bodies representing Palestinian citizens of Israel, such as the High Follow-up Committee for Arab Citizens in Israel.[48] Making a similar point, Shaykh Salah disagrees with how the Hebrew Israeli media presents the so-called 'northern' and 'southern' wings of the Movement as opposites:

> The press exaggerates things so that it will have some material. This is not strange or new, but in fact, we have many things that bring us together that are principles we have agreed upon. Alongside these principles, there have been some views which ... have made it impossible to combine the different ideas in one position. This is what caused the presence of two views on the ground. Each tried to adopt his idea and work with it. Therefore, there were two Islamic views at the same time. Perhaps the most notable is the subject of the Israeli Knesset and the feasibility of participation in this Israeli institution. There are no differences in fundamental issues ... The main difference is the political position, not the fundamentals.

One of the tangible consequences of the split in 1996 was the establishment of a parallel Al-Aqsa Association by the Movement of Shaykh Salah. The original Al-Aqsa Association was established in 1989 by Shaykh Kamil Rayan of the Movement of Shaykh Darwish, in order to document and preserve Palestinian religious sites inside Israel. According to Shaykh Rayan, Palestinians in Israel 'are at war' with the Israeli authorities over the demolition of Palestinian monuments and landmarks in Israel.[49] Shaykh Rayan described this war as manifest in every stone, every wall and every bone and skull buried in Muslim and Christian graveyards. He put this into a larger perspective using a triangle to illustrate the main issues in the conflict between the Israeli Zionists and the Palestinians. First, there is the struggle over land; second, there is the struggle over religious sites;

---

47. Author interview.
48. The High Follow-Up Committee for the Arab Citizens in Israel was established in 1976 after the first Land Day demonstrations. It is a non-partisan organisation representing all Palestinian citizens of Israel.
49. Author interview.

and third, there is the struggle over the protection and rights of human beings (the Palestinians). Shaykh Rayan explained his belief that the Israelis want to empty the land of Arabs and remove all signs of Arab history. Through the Al-Aqsa Association, the Islamic Movement tries to protect existing religious sites such as Al-Aqsa, and to fight for the right of Muslims to access sites that have been demolished and/or appropriated by the state. Shaykh Rayan gave the example of the Muslim cemetery upon which the Hilton Hotel in Tel Aviv now stands. In 2000, the new Al-Aqsa Association of Shaykh Salah was established with the same focus and agenda as the original association. It is not clear to what degree the two associations cooperate or compete, but Shaykh Rayan appeared unimpressed by the establishment of the second association.

Another consequence of the split, according to Shaykh Zakur, was the loss of public support, and what he describes as

> a great reduction in the level of religious people. Between 1996 and today, over the past ten to twelve years, there has been a great withdrawal from an Islamic way of life even from religious people. They are no longer as strong in religion as they used to be. Religious women are not at the same level as they were in 1996. You can see that from the way they dress.[50]

According to Zakur, the Islamic Movement's leadership lost some of its prestige as a result of the internal split in 1996. People now have less respect for the *shaykhs*, he explained. Without mentioning any specific groups, Shaykh Zakur claims that, in the vacuum created by this disappointment, other groups have emerged in place of the Islamic Movement.

Since 1996, the Movement of Shaykh Darwish has participated in parliamentary elections in 1999, 2003 and 2006 in a coalition called the United Arab List (UAL), together with the Arab Democratic Party and three other smaller Arab parties. Of the total of 120 parliamentary seats, the UAL gained five seats, two seats, and four seats in those three election years respectively.[51] The leaders of the Movement of Shaykh Darwish who support participation in the Knesset, and who emphasise the necessity of integration into the Israeli state and society, also stress the paradox of their situation as an indigenous

---

50. Author interview. The last remark about how women dress seems to contradict Shaykh Zakur's earlier remark that the Movement is not interested in how people dress.
51. Knesset website: www.knesset.gov.il.

minority. They express concern that, despite holding citizenship, they do not 'belong' to the nation of the state in which they hold citizenship and in whose parliament they serve as elected representatives. Both Shaykh Kamil Rayan, who today holds the position of Deputy Manager of the Union of Local Authorities in Israel, and Member of Knesset Shaykh Ibrahim Sarsur, admit that they are disappointed with their inability to make any changes to the political system after having joined the Knesset. Both state that now, with hindsight, they do not think that their presence in parliament has made much of a difference for their constituents. However, they both consider it important to keep their parliamentary positions and to continue to voice their opinions and protests. According to Shaykh Sarsur, their aim is to relay a message to the (Jewish) Israelis:

> There is no alternative for you but to accept us. We are here. We were here. And we will go on living here. And we will never quit the parliament – whether you like that or you do not like that; whether you love it or you do not love it. We are a part of this country. You have really to decide that you accept this reality and you are ready to live with this reality. Going on living in a confrontation in the parliament will never serve what you always say or speak about – coexistence. Coexistence is really based on mutual respect. Without mutual respect do not think … that we, the Arab population, may raise the white flags … may submit and so on. We go on struggling within the limitations of your law. And we hope one day that our cause will come to a certain kind of solution.[52]

Shaykh Sarsur provides two examples as further illustrations of the difficulties he and his colleagues face as Muslim Palestinian Members of the Israeli Knesset. The first example is a new law enacted in the Knesset that bans any person who wants to run for the parliamentary elections from doing so if he or she visits one of the countries defined as 'enemy countries' by the Israeli authorities.[53] To date, the list of such countries includes Syria, Yemen, Saudi Arabia, Sudan, Afghanistan and Uzbekistan, according to Sarsur. However,

---

52. Author interview.
53. Also, Attorney and Director of Adalah, Hassan Jabareen, has expressed concern with regard to this and other laws that, according to him, target the Arab minority in Israel. For details see 'NEWS UPDATE, 19 November 2008, At Briefing for Embassy Representatives from 23 Countries, Adalah Urges Participants to Raise Issues Regarding Racist Anti-Arab Laws and the October 2000 Killings with their Governments and with Israel', available at www.adalah.org.

he explains, the Israeli authorities can, at any given moment, declare any country to be an enemy country. Thus, he fears that if he were to visit, for instance, one of the states in the Gulf area, which today is not defined as an enemy country, he might be penalised if it were decided to change the status of the country, and the penalty is applied retroactively.

Another example of the intimidation of Palestinian Members of Knesset that Sarsur provides is the accusations levelled at them by other Knesset Members that they are traitors. Sarsur describes the reaction to protests voiced by himself and others Palestinian members of Knesset against the war in Lebanon during the summer of 2006:

> When the Israelis launched the second Lebanon War in 2006, the vast majority of the members of the parliament supported the Israeli government in that bloody war. The only members of parliament who declared their opposition to this kind of war were the Arabs. The vast majority of the members of parliament, even the government, did not deal with this position of the Arab members of Knesset as legitimate. They accused us of betraying [Israel].

At the heart of the dilemma that Palestinian representatives in the Knesset face lie the reasons for the Movement's split in 1996: disagreement over how the Movement can best represent and protect the rights of its constituency. Is the constituency best served by being represented in Israeli state institutions, thus lending legitimacy to these institutions and to the state? Or are the constituency's best interests served by the creation of alternative institutions, and the fighting of state institutions from the outside? This is a general dilemma faced by all organisations and activist groups working to advance and protect the rights of Palestinian citizens of Israel, and not a problem confined to the Islamic Movement alone.[54]

Relations with Jewish citizens and the events of October 2000

The complex predicament of Palestinian citizens of Israel has influenced the character of this Islamic organisation and the views it expresses, and has imbued it with nationalist perspectives. As Peled notes, 'With the rise of Islamism, for the first time in Israeli history, an Arab political movement openly promoted a

---

54. For a further discussion of this problem with other Palestinian organisations in Israel, see S. Payes, *Palestinian NGOs in Israel*.

dual nationalist and religious agenda.'⁵⁵ This mixture of an Islamist and national agenda is not unique to the Islamic Movement in Israel, or, indeed, to Islamist Movements. Fred Halliday has warned against '"regional narcissism" (the belief that ... everything that happens in the region is somehow dissimilar to that which takes place elsewhere, and is singularly evil or angelic as a result)'.⁵⁶ As with other liberationist and nationalist ideologies, Islamism has usually developed in a context where there are highly pronounced tensions between state and society.⁵⁷ Thus, Islamism overtly appeals to colonised and exploited Muslims, and shares many characteristics with nationalist movements.

As an indigenous minority in a state whose nation and symbols are not Muslim, and which discriminates against its non-Jewish citizens, the national Palestinian identity of this Islamic Movement constitutes an essential part of its ideology. When asked about the goals of the Movement, Shaykh Kamel Rayan of the Movement of Shaykh Darwish used personal examples when referring to the triangular goals of protecting land, people and religious sites:

> It lies under this triangle; land, people and landmarks. We want our land and we will not allow it to be confiscated and stolen; they stole 700 dunums from my father and I will not forget them. People: they expelled my uncle from the country, and it is his right to return. Landmarks: the mosques should not be touched. This is the goal in short.

The pragmatic perspective of the Movement of Shaykh Darwish is evident in the reply of Shaykh Ibrahim Sarsur. When asked about the main goals of the Islamic Movement in Israel, he says:

> Let me answer this question in an ironic way. Once, a journalist asked me: 'What do you, as an Islamist and a leader of the Islamic Movement, think about creating an Islamic state within the state of Israel?' Maybe he expected me to say 'No,' directly. I said to him, 'Yes, but on one condition. If I wake in the morning and switch on the radio and hear that 75 per cent of the Jews embraced Islam. Only in those circumstances might I think of having an Islamic state inside of Israel.' So, it is a naive idea to think about creating an Islamic state or looking

---

55. Peled, *Debating Islam in the Jewish State*, p. 122.
56. F. Halliday, *The Middle East in International Relations: Power, Politics and Ideology*, Cambridge: Cambridge University Press, 2005, p. 10.
57. Ibid., p. 310.

forward to having an Islamic state inside Israel. Because we are aware of the limitations – we are aware of the realities on the ground. We are aware of the fact that we are a part of the Israeli Jewish state. The vast majority of the inhabitants of this state are Jews. The Israeli state was established to be the aspiration of the Jewish people in the entire world, especially those who immigrated to this part of the world – they created the state and they want to live in a Jewish state. We are aware of this fact; but regardless of this fact, we want to be a part of this state, but not a part of the identity of this state.

When asked a similar question, Shaykh Salah, who heads the other branch of the Movement, does not mention the establishment of an Islamic state as a goal, but emphasises strengthening 'an Islamic way of life' for Palestinian Muslims in Israel, maintaining Palestinian presence on the land, and preserving holy sites. He describes a bleak reality in which Palestinian citizens of Israel face constant hostility from the Israeli establishment, and offers no vision for the future. He emphasises that he does not consider it appropriate to ask Palestinians to speak of the future while Israel continues to act in a manner he considers oppressive:

> This suffering is escalating, and the [international] parties are asking our Palestinian people, 'What do you suggest?' 'Do you agree to the establishment of two states for two peoples?' While the suffering of our Palestinian people continues! There have been agreements such as the Oslo Agreement, and the Oslo Agreement has been destroyed and our Palestinian people have remained under the imposed logic of choices: 'What do you choose?' Then there was the incursion of the Israeli establishment in the West Bank where it is Judaizing the West Bank and Jerusalem, while this logic continues to be proposed to the Palestinian people: 'What do you, the Palestinian people, choose?' ... What I mean is that, to date, the Zionist scheme persists and continues. Palestine's Nakba[58] began in 1948, and to date the consequences of this Nakba are still reverberating for our Palestinian people. The Nakba of Palestine did not occur once, the Nakba of Palestine is still happening and the Israeli side continues to strive to double the size of this Nakba and its effects. Naturally, our Palestinian people continue to suffer.

On the other hand, Shaykh Darwish, who heads the other branch of the Movement, is reported as speaking of coexistence in the Israeli media, such

---

58. *Nakba* means 'catastrophe' in Arabic, and is the term used to describe the consequences for the Palestinians of the 1947–49 war.

as in response to riots in Acre in October 2008, which were sparked when a Palestinian citizen drove through a Jewish neighbourhood on the Jewish holiday of Yom Kippur. Following the riots, Shaykh Darwish himself participated in the Peace Sukkah,[59] which was set up in Acre as a venue for its Jewish and Arab residents to meet and seek understanding. Shaykh Darwish made the following address in Hebrew to those present and to the press:[60]

> Bless all those who have come here to help and strengthen the coexistence in Acre, but those who have come from outside Acre – whether they be big or small, bearded or not – those who have only come to incite and come between the residents are an unwelcome presence in this city. We have learned from you, Acre, how to live together.

However, in interviews with other leaders of the Movement of Shaykh Darwish, coexistence is expressed as an aspiration, but they do not describe present relations between Jews and Palestinians in Israel as constituting coexistence.

When considering the different attitudes towards the Israeli state and its institutions, as expressed by leaders of the two branches of the Movement, the repressive treatment of the Movement of Shaykh Salah must be taken into consideration. Shaykh Salah and his Movement have been closely monitored by the Israeli authorities, and the Shaykh was imprisoned in May 2003 charged with supporting 'terrorism' because he had participated in fundraising for charities in the West Bank linked with Hamas.[61] Salah was released in July 2005. Recently, in autumn 2008, the offices of the Movement in Um al-Fahm were closed, and documents and computers confiscated by Israeli police due to suspicion of the organisation's cooperation with Hamas.[62]

Whereas the religious goals of the two branches of the Islamic Movement are presented as being the same (to protect the holy sites and revive observance of Islam among Palestinian Muslims), their political responses to Israeli policies and to the predicament of Palestinian citizens as a

---

59. A *sukkha* is a hut built as part of the Jewish holiday Sukkot to commemorate the wandering of Moses in the Sinai desert.

60. H. Einav, 'Hundreds Gather at Akko "Peace Sukkah"', *Ynet*, 15 October 2008.

61. J. Dakwar, 'The Islamic Movement Inside Israel: An Interview with Shaykh Ra'id Salah', *Journal of Palestine Studies*, vol. 36, no. 2 (Winter 2007), pp. 66–76, esp. p. 67.

62. E. Ashkenazi and Y. Stern, 'Police Close Islamic Institute Suspected of Aiding Hamas', *Ha'aretz*, 24 August 2008.

minority group sometimes differ. In broad terms, the Movement of Shaykh Salah advocates autonomy, or a self-reliant society as described by Shaykh Khatib above, whereas the Movement of Shaykh Darwish advocates participation in the state and the advancement of a multicultural society. These differences are evident in the strategies and approaches chosen by the two branches.

Shaykh Sarsur of the Movement of Shaykh Darwish identified three main challenges facing Palestinians in Israel that are directly connected with relations with the state and/or with its Jewish citizens:

1. Israelisation/Zionisation (the pacification of Palestinian citizens and their assimilation into Israeli society and culture through education and language, and by denying them their own religious and cultural institutions);

2. The threat of population transfer;

3. Violence against Palestinians by state agencies and by Jewish citizens.

All interviewees raised these issues, but with differing emphases and attitudes concerning how to act towards the Israeli state and its Jewish citizens. Addressing the first challenge of Israelisation and Zionisation, Shaykh Sarsur relates the strategies employed by the Movement for developing a Palestinian Muslim identity, including strengthening the attachment of the Muslim population inside Israel to their cultural roots and national history. He emphasises that, as Palestinian citizens of Israel, they do not wish to be the target of the Israelisation and Zionisation policies that their population has been exposed to since 1948. Rather, they want to be active citizens whose citizenship is acknowledged for its civic value. They have no interest in becoming part of the Israeli Jewish Zionist identity:

> I think Israelisation, Zionisation, direct interference of the Israeli minister of education and other ministers in our schedules, in our schools, in our programmes and so on, creates a very serious danger [for our] identity. So we have, as an Arab minority – Muslims, Christians, and others – as a whole, we have plans to oppose such kinds of Israeli interference in our daily lives. So I am not exaggerating by saying to you that in the last twenty years, we speak courageously about the necessity of having a certain kind of cultural autonomy. We are Arabs, we are Muslims, we are Christians, and we have our own identity. And

the Israelis must really support our efforts to crystallise, to maintain our identity as a part of this kind of ... multicultural life inside Israel. It is for the sake of the Israelis, really.[63]

Sarsur suggested that he would like the Palestinians in Israel to play a role in Israel analogous to that of Jews in Europe and the United States. He believes that European and North American Jews now enjoy full citizenship in the countries in which they are living, but at the same time are able to actively support the Israeli state. Similarly, Sarsur envisions a future in which Palestinian citizens of Israel enjoy full citizenship in the state of Israel, but are able to actively support an independent Palestinian state without calling into question their loyalty to Israel or undermining their rights as citizens.

By contrast, while he agrees with Sarsur on the need for the development and strengthening of Muslim Palestinian identity in Israel, Shaykh Khatib did not refer to a need or desire to be part of the state. In his explanation of the predicament of a Palestinian Islamic Movement in Israel, Khatib spoke about safeguarding his followers from assimilation:

> First, when we define ourselves, when I define myself as a person, when I am asked who I am, I answer that I'm a Muslim first, an Arab second, and thirdly a Palestinian who lives in my homeland, in the land of my fathers and forefathers, in the state of Israel. This means that my goals, when I am asked about the goals of the Islamic Movement, are to serve Islam as a religion and convey its faith, manners, ideas and morals among people and among Muslims. This does not contradict, but runs in parallel with serving my homeland and my people as Palestinians who live here in our country in the land of Palestine, even though it was later named the state of Israel. Specifically, we consider the Islamic Movement's mission to be to assist the Palestinians who remained inside Israel to maintain their religious and national identity, and to preserve their land in order to remain steadfast and endure, because with their Islamic identity they can be protected from assimilation in Israeli society.

According to the Palestinian journalist Qassem Khatib, it is this call for autonomy, especially as it is espoused by the Movement of Shaykh Salah, that concerns the Israeli authorities. This concern is related to the so-called

63. Author interview.

'demographic threat' often referred to in Israeli media and politics. Ideas about how to maintain an optimal demographic balance between Jews and Arabs in Israeli-controlled territory (which includes the Arab territories occupied by Israel since 1967) have been debated since the establishment of the state of Israel. At the heart of the discussion is a fear that the 'Jewish character' of the state might be challenged, undermined or even overwhelmed should demographic trends result in non-Jewish Arabs forming a majority of the population living under Israeli rule.[64] This topic was a central issue in the debates and campaigns that took place prior to the Knesset elections of 2006. The 'demographic threat' was also used as a principal argument during Ariel Sharon's unilateral disengagement from the occupied Gaza Strip in 2005, which Sharon presented as a policy designed to preserve and increase a Jewish majority in the state.[65] With the rise of the party Israel Beitenu ('Israel Our Home'), the demographic debate has taken centre-stage in some political circles. The party's chairperson, Member of Knesset Avigor Lieberman, explicitly advocates a population exchange of Palestinian citizens with a future Palestinian state in order to engineer two relatively homogenous populations: a Jewish population in Israel and a Palestinian population in Palestine.[66]

Thus, the second challenge facing Palestinians in Israel identified by the Islamic Movement – namely, the threat of a population transfer of Palestinian citizens of Israel into the occupied Palestinian territory – is perceived by many Palestinian citizens as very real, and provides a further indication to them of the fragility of their citizenship. Shaykh Salah spoke with concern about this issue, and the degree to which population transfer

---

64. Israeli demographers Arnon Sofer and Sergio DelaPergola write about this 'threat' academically, demonstrating an open ideological commitment to the Jewishness of the state of Israel. See L. Galili, 2002, 'A Jewish Demographic State', *Journal of Palestine Studies*. vol., 32, no. 1 (Autumn 2002), pp. 90–93.

65. Ilan Pappe, *London Review of Books*, 20 April 2006, available at lrb.co.uk.

66. See for example an interview with Lieberman in the *New York Times* – G. Myre, 'Israeli Official Discusses Iran and His Controversial Agenda', 7 December 2006: 'Mr Lieberman calls for a land and population exchange that would seek to reduce significantly the number of Arabs who are Israeli citizens. They currently account for more than a million of Israel's 7 million people. Under the plan, several Arab towns in northern Israel would become part of the Palestinian areas in the West Bank. The major Jewish settlement blocs in the West Bank would become part of Israel.'

is accepted by the Jewish Israeli majority. According to him, the idea of a population transfer is now openly discussed by Israelis, suggesting that it has become an accepted idea. He cited recent polls indicating that more than 70 per cent of Jewish Israelis support a transfer of Palestinian citizens.[67] To Salah, such statistics indicate that the Israeli state's approach and attitude towards its Palestinian minority is representative of public opinion.[68]

The third challenge facing Palestinian citizens that was identified by leaders of the Islamic Movement is the increasing violence and discrimination they face. Several *shaykhs* describe this challenge in their interviews. When asked about the consequences of the killing of thirteen unarmed Palestinian citizens by Israeli security forces in October 2000, most *shaykhs* reply that this event represented a deterioration of the situation, but none of them sees this as an entirely new development. Rather, the events of October 2000 were described as marking a new extreme in the already difficult predicament of Palestinians in Israel.

Shaykh Salah emphasises that October 2000 was not a turning-point, because the relationship between Palestinian citizens and state authorities had not been positive prior to these events. In Salah's explanation, in the past the Palestinian minority had suffered from religious persecution, from discrimination based on their nationality and from historic injustice. While these difficulties continued, the situation deteriorated further following the events of October 2000. To contextualise his analysis, Salah emphasises that the Palestinian people inside Israel did not feel any positive change during the so-called 'Oslo years', or under Labour rule:

> Suffering remained suffering and even increased, and this presented to me the conclusion which I, personally, am still convinced of today – namely, that the nature of dealing with us is not subject to the understanding of a particular Israeli party as much as it is part of the notion

---

67. These numbers are supported by the recent polls: 'Poll: Israelis favour Arab transfer to Palestine', *Jerusalem Post*, 31 March 2008: 'The poll, conducted over the Internet, included 668 adult Israeli Jews representing the entire political spectrum, cites a 3.7% margin of error. The poll asked participants whether as part of an agreement to establish a Palestinian state there would be justification to demand that Arabs with Israeli citizenship relocate to Palestinian territory. Only 24% were totally against the idea.'

68. Author interview.

of the Zionist scheme. Once again, I confirm that the change that was reflected in the Israeli political scene did not positively affect us; on the contrary, the suffering increased and continues to increase. Quite the opposite! Unfortunately, I see that some of the ideas that were previously unspoken are now acknowledged by the Israeli establishment, such as the call for our transfer, which has [come to be] stated openly by different Israeli leaders.

Salah divided the manifestations of injustice and violence experienced by Palestinians inside Israel into two sources: those originating from the state and those originating from the Jewish public. In his view, the Israeli establishment incites violence against Palestinians at the popular level and the Israeli public responds by supporting the injustices authorised by the Israeli establishment.

Conclusion: the fear of the fear of Israelis

Context seems to weigh more heavily than ideology on the development of the Islamic Movement in Israel, and on the choices of its leaders. This is not to say that the leaders' religious commitment is in any way inferior to their national commitment. The paradoxical context of the Islamic Movement in Israel is reflected in the unique circumstances of Palestinian citizens of Israel generally: their status as citizens provides them with certain individual rights and affords them the opportunity of promoting an Islamist agenda, yet their identification as an indigenous national and non-Jewish minority creates legal, distributional and communal limitations. Because the movement represents an indigenous minority in a state whose nation and symbols are not Muslim, and which discriminates against its non-Jewish citizens, the Palestinian national identity of this Islamic movement is an essential part of its ideology. This is reflected in the three principal goals of the Movement – protecting land, people and religious sites – whereas other Islamist Movements often prioritise the establishment of an Islamic state. Instead of speaking of transforming the Jewish state into an Islamic state, leaders on both sides of the 1996 split emphasise the need for strengthening 'an Islamic way of life' for Palestinian Muslims in Israel, maintaining Palestinian presence on their land, and preserving holy sites.

The specific context of the Islamic Movement in Israel also appears to be the overriding factor in the way that the leaders shape the Movement's political positions. It is evident that many of the policies adopted by the Movement arise from the leaders' fear of the fear of the Israelis. In the leaders' reactions to the defining moments of October 2000 and the al-Aqsa *intifada*, the war in Lebanon in 2006, and the siege imposed on Gaza since 2006, the *shaykhs* interviewed expressed concern for their constituents' physical and legal security, as well as for their rights as citizens. This is evident in the three primary challenges identified by all the leaders interviewed: Israelisation/Zionisation, the threat of population transfer, and threats of violence against Palestinians by state agencies and Jewish citizens. The Movement as a whole can claim two notable successes. It has been successful in raising awareness domestically and abroad about the predicament of Palestinians inside Israel, and it has succeeded in renewing Muslim Palestinian identity. As for the threats of population transfer and violence, the tools available to the Movement in opposing these threats are few, according to its leaders.

As one group, the Movement has responded to state policies by rejecting assimilation – in their words, 'Israelisation and Zionisation'. Both branches of the Movement have opted for autonomy by establishing their own institutions and developing a Palestinian Muslim identity for their followers; but they differ both in their interactions with the state and its institutions, and in their messages to the Jewish and Palestinian populations in Israel. Whereas the Movement of Shaykh Darwish participates in elections at all levels of the Israeli political system, and has two representatives in the Israeli parliament, the Movement of Shaykh Salah refuses to participate in state-wide elections; the first argues that this integration into the Israeli state is conducive to the protection and promotion of the rights of Palestinian citizens of Israel, whereas the second holds that accepting elections to parliamentary positions means accepting the Zionist political system, and thus legitimising institutionalised discrimination against Palestinians. Similarly, in their public discourse, the leaders of the Movement of Shaykh Darwish speak of coexistence as a goal, whereas the leaders of the Movement of Shaykh Salah emphasise the continued suffering of the Palestinians at the hands of the Israelis.

Yet, despite these differences, the two branches of the Movement appear to cooperate with each another and work in a similar fashion at a grassroots level, supplying social services to the local population through their organisations and volunteer work camps. All leaders interviewed emphasise support for the Palestinians living in the occupied Palestinian territories,[69] and insist that the differences between the two branches of the Movement are political, and not ideological or religious. The Islamic Movement in Israel may therefore represent an exemplary case study of Islamist compromise and pragmatism. Both branches of the Movement demonstrate pragmatism, not only in their ability to cooperate with each other despite internal differences, but also in their non-violent, law-abiding responses to the Israeli political context.

However, pragmatism should not be confused with efficacy. By their own admission, the representatives of the Movement of Shaykh Darwish do not yet consider their involvement in parliamentary life to have reaped any rewards for their constituency. Conversely, the Movement of Shaykh Salah rejects participation in state-wide elections in favour of promoting a 'self-reliant society', though it also underplays its agency by focusing on the oppressive environment in which it operates. It is therefore unclear how successful this branch of the Movement considers its approach to have been. It is perhaps too early to determine which approach – the integrative or the rejectionist – has been more successful in promoting and protecting the rights of Palestinian citizens of Israel. But both branches of the Islamic Movement in Israel have clearly demonstrated that, for many Palestinian citizens of Israel, Islamism is indeed the answer.

---

69. As an example of this Palestinian solidarity, Shaykh Salah and Shaykh Sarsur, Member of Knesset for the Movement of Shaykh Darwish, both joined a boat with provisions headed for Gaza in December 2008, organised by the Committee against the Siege (S. Roffe-Ofir, 'Arab MKs to Sail to Gaza', 3 December 2008, available at YNet.news.com).

TEN

The Making of Lebanon's Hizbullah

Ibrahim Moussawi

Although the 1982 Israeli invasion of Lebanon proved to be the main impetus that gave rise to Hizbullah, Lebanese citizens living along the southern border area had endured decades of aggression since the creation of the Zionist entity in May 1948. Indeed, one of the earliest recorded Israeli attacks on Lebanese territory claimed seventy civilian victims in a gruesome massacre in the village of Houla on 31 October 1948.[1] The Israeli incursions, attacks and military operations continued, and later increased in frequency and intensity during the decade that preceded the 1982 Israeli invasion. While these activities were ostensibly aimed at Palestinian guerrilla fighters operating in the country,[2] they brought tremendous hardship and suffering to Lebanese citizens, especially those living along the southern border, a predominantly Shi'i region.

This tumultuous period coincided with the emergence of an active clerical movement in Lebanon during the late 1960s and 1970s, and Hizbullah would later both draw ideological inspiration and attract cadres from the ranks of the organisations that grew up out of this movement. Among the most influential of these groups was Haraka al-Mahrumin ('Movement of the Deprived') and its military wing, Amal (the 'Battalions of the Lebanese Resistance'), both of which Imam Mussa al-Sadr played a principal role in founding during the early 1970s. Haraka al-Mahrumin aimed at alleviating the dire poverty and hardship befalling citizens in the south of the country,

---

1. For more on this, see an article based on interviews with the survivors of that attack Nicholas Blanford, '50 Years On, Questions Still Surround Massacre at Houla', *Daily Star*, 31 October 2003.
2. The government of Lebanon had granted the Palestine Liberation Organisation (PLO) licence to launch attacks from South Lebanon against Israel under the terms of the Cairo Agreement, which was signed on 3 November 1969. The agreement was later annulled by law number 87/25, passed by the Lebanese parliament and published in the Official Gazette on 18 June 1987.

the eastern Bekaa, and the so-called 'boroughs of misery' around the capital, Beirut, which had become inhabited mostly by southern Lebanese refugees.[3] Amal focused on the primary mission of resisting Israeli aggression and occupation, a cause that Imam al-Sadr ceaselessly advocated. A second organisation that provided Hizbullah with ideological inspiration was the Islamic Da'wa Party in Lebanon, founded by Najaf-educated clerics under the spiritual guidance of the late Ayatollah Sayyid Muhammad Baqir al-Sadr, who was executed by Saddam Hussein's regime in the early 1980s.[4] Among its spiritual leaders was the prominent Lebanese cleric, the Grand Ayatollah Sayyid Muhammad Hussain Fadlallah. A third group from which Hizbullah drew cadres and inspiration was the Lebanese Union of Muslim Students, which initially comprised university students who had formed committees and begun to engage in public life through the creation of congregations that engaged in mostly religious activities.

During the late 1970s, however, the Shi'i Lebanese community also drew considerable inspiration from the 1979 victory of the Islamic Revolution in Iran, led by Ayatollah Khomeini. The success of the Revolution and the empowerment of the masses in Iran led to a thirst for political revitalisation in Lebanon, where the Shi'i community had been relegated to the status of second-class citizens within the existing sectarian political order. The Iranian Revolution saw the emergence in Beirut of 'supportive Committees to the Islamic Revolution in Iran' – groups that later served as a conduit of communication with the newly installed Islamic leadership in Tehran. More importantly, however, the Iranian Revolution, which saw the toppling of the Shah's regime and the empowerment of the citizenry through the creation of an Islamic Republic, resonated in the southern suburbs of Beirut and began

---

3. Sadr initially established Haraka al-Mahrumin in 1974 together with Gregoire Haddad, a Greek Catholic archbishop, to provide relief and services to impoverished Lebanese, regardless of their sect. However, after the outbreak of the Civil War, it developed under Sadr's leadership into a mostly Shi'i movement.

4. For more than a millennium, Najaf was the pre-eminent seminary centre of study for Shi'i clergymen. However, after the end of the Gulf War in 1991, popular revolts in the area were met with a severe military response from Saddam Hussein's regime and the ensuing decade saw the arrest and assassination of senior clerics in Najaf, including Muhammad Sadiq al-Sadr, who was killed along with his two sons in 1999. During this period the Iranian city of Qom became the pre-eminent religious centre, but Najaf has regained prominence since the fall of Saddam's regime in 2003.

to transform the resigned political thinking of the Shi'i citizenry. Moreover, the military victories of the young republic against invading Iraqi forces on the battlefield in late 1980 and early 1981 helped forge an unshakable belief among the Shi'i Lebanese population that the liberation of occupied territories was possible.

All of these developments were in play in Lebanon when Israel invaded the country on 6 July 1982, with the stated aim of annihilating the PLO, which had been operating in the south of the country after being expelled from Jordan in July 1971. The operation, dubbed 'Operation Peace for Galilee', was launched on a flimsy pretext – the attempted assassination in London of Shlomo Argov, the Israeli ambassador to the United Kingdom, on 3 July 1982. The following day, Israel announced that the attack had constituted a breach of the ceasefire agreement concluded with the PLO in 1981 and began launching air strikes on Palestinian targets in Beirut, drawing retaliatory missile and mortar fire on Israeli settlements in the occupied Golan. The full-scale Israeli invasion of Lebanon was launched on 6 July with the aim of annihilating the Palestinian resistance – an objective that won tacit approval from the US government.

What the Israelis did not anticipate, however, was that the invasion, which aimed to secure their northern border and crush Palestinian resistance, would set into motion a chain of events that would give rise to a Lebanese resistance movement that would eventually pose an even greater obstacle to their aim of asserting military domination over Lebanese territories. During the course of the invasion, small groups of Lebanese resistance fighters began to take shape, executing more than one successful operation against the advancing Israeli troops. Acting at times alongside the Palestinian *fedayin*, these groups of devote individuals succeeded, despite their limited resources, in crippling the Israeli advance towards the Lebanese capital, with fierce battles taking place in towns on the outskirts of Beirut such as Khaldeh and Hadath, and daring attacks being launched subsequently on the occupying forces. The first known martyrdom attack was carried out by Ahmad Kassir on 11 November 1982, targeting the Israeli military headquarters in Tyre, South Lebanon.[5]

---

5. The details of this operation were disclosed only after the Israeli withdrawal of 1985, when video recordings of the operation's details were broadcast in Kassir's native village of Deir Kanoun al-Nahr. Other early operations that occurred in 1982 included an ambush in the Msaitbeh area, an ambush of an infantry patrol in the vicinity of the Parliament building in Beirut, confrontations in

Segments of this nascent Lebanese resistance movement would later coalesce around a new social movement that would take the name Hizbullah, or the 'Party of God', and would receive military instruction from the Iranian Revolutionary Guard after Ayatollah Khomeini ordered troops to Lebanon. After conducting clandestine resistance operations against Israeli forces for two-and-a-half years, the movement was announced publicly in an Open Letter in 1985. This document marked the first public articulation of a political ideology but did not represent a serious attempt to assert a comprehensive political programme:

> We are the sons of the *umma*, the party of God (Hizb Allah), the vanguard of which was made victorious by God in Iran ... [W]e do not constitute an organised and closed party in Lebanon, nor a narrow political framework. Rather, we are an *umma* linked to the Muslims of the whole world by the solid doctrinal and religious bond, namely, Islam.

The letter goes on to outline the movement's objectives, which were primarily to confront Israel and its allies – the United States, France, the Lebanese Phalanges – and to attack the existing sectarian–confessional system. Thus, Hizbullah's first public message asserted rather clearly that the movement was not a political party, and that it harboured no ambitions as such but, rather, that at this stage it more closely resembled other rejectionist and reactionary Islamist factions. [6]

Although the group continued to focus mostly on resistance activities for the next few years, it also began to expand its role by providing social services to the people, with its efforts focused initially almost entirely on the Shi'i community – since it was the most deprived and was bearing the brunt of Israeli aggression – but with services not excluding non-Shi'i residents of the same areas. Hizbullah helped rebuild destroyed houses in South Lebanon, and

---

the old Saida Boulevard in Beirut and along the road leading to Saadiyat, and a number of ambushes in South Lebanon.

6. The Open Letter was read by the official party spokesman, Sayyid Ibrahim Amine al-Sayyed, on 16 February 1985, the day of the first commemoration of the assassination of Shaykh Ragheb Harb, a prominent cleric from Jibsheet who had begun to promote the mobilisation of armed resistance among the populace. Harb had been assassinated on 16 February 1984. The Open Letter was published on 17 February 1985, both in the *As-Safir* newspaper and as a pamphlet.

constructed a huge social and humanitarian network to alleviate the suffering of the people – especially the poor in various regions of the country. These efforts would later prove to have established a grassroots base that would serve as a launch-pad from which the movement would enter the political sphere and develop a working political agenda and vision for the country.

National versus global attitudes towards the movement

In its local context in Lebanon, Hizbullah has been perceived from its inception as a legitimate resistance movement – a perception that gained greater currency over the decades as the armed wing of the party achieved successive military victories against the Israeli occupation, earning the group increasing public support among a majority of the Lebanese populace. In fact, Hizbullah fighters were so successful against the Israeli occupation forces that it was not uncommon to read reports in the Israeli media, and even assessments published by the Israeli military, that acknowledged Hizbullah's courage and achievements, and heaped scorn on the Israeli side for being humiliated on the battlefield. Several Israeli operations directly targeted the resistance, including 'Operation Accountability' in 1993 and 'Operation Grapes of Wrath' in 1996 – from both of which Hizbullah emerged intact, and therefore victorious. From the latter, Hizbullah gained international recognition with the 'April Understanding', which came as a result of international mediation and negotiations in which Hizbullah took part. The Lebanese public perception that the armed resistance was the only effective way to counter Israeli aggression was reinforced, because this resistance could yield concrete results such as the swap deals that Hizbullah concluded with the Israelis through indirect negotiations brokered by UN and German mediators in 2003 and 2008, as well as the liberation of South Lebanon[7] in 2000 after seventeen years of resistance operations.

Hizbullah's behaviour after the liberation in 2000 also served to reinforce further the positive public perception of the resistance movement. After the Israeli withdrawal, many speculated about what Hizbullah would do with its newfound authority in the South; but initial fears that the group might

---

7. The UN initially verified Israel's full withdrawal from Lebanese territory but the Lebanese government rejected the assessment, insisting that the Shebaa farms and Kfar Shouba Hills are Lebanese and thus still occupied by Israel.

terrorise the population were quickly dispelled. The resistance movement dealt with collaborators by handing them over to the army and diligently maintained the ceasefire with the Israeli enemy.

Formal recognition of the armed wing of Hizbullah as a legitimate resistance movement was first enshrined in the Taif Agreement of 1989, which ended Lebanon's fifteen-year civil war.[8] The document, which called for the disarmament of the parties that had participated in the internal conflict, drew an important distinction between 'militias', which were to be disarmed and disbanded under the accord, and the 'resistance', which was permitted to continue activities aimed at driving out the Israeli occupation. Hizbullah had not taken part in the civil war and was therefore not considered a militia; rather, its military actions had always been devoted to the fight against the Israeli occupation and it was thus considered a legitimate resistance movement. Successive cabinet policy statements, including the 2005 and 2008 ministerial policy statements, would reiterate this distinction by mentioning the right of armed resistance.

Hizbullah's military victories also helped win the resistance movement considerable support among the peoples of the Arab and Islamic worlds. In fact, Hizbullah's standing in the Arab and Muslim worlds reached its zenith in the wake of the 2006 War, when pictures of Sayyid Hassan Nasrallah, the leader of the party, could be found in the capitals of Arab countries across the region and comparisons abounded between the Hizbullah leader and the late Egyptian president, Gamal Abdel Nasser. Even Sunni Islamists celebrated the movement's military exploits, including some in countries whose regimes had been critical of Hizbullah at the onset of the 2006 War. The perception that Hizbullah was both repelling invading forces and defying US attempts to reshape Lebanon's political identity in a more pro-Western direction continues to elevate the group's status among the people of the Arab world, as has been reflected in various opinion polls.[9]

---

8. The agreement was negotiated in Ta'if, Saudi Arabia, in September 1989, and approved by the Lebanese parliament on 4 November 1989. The Lebanese civil war had devastated the country between 1975 and 1990.

9. An ABC/BBC poll published in April 2008 revealed that eight out of ten people in the Arab world had a negative view of the United States and that Nasrallah was the most admired leader in the Arab world – followed by Syrian President Bashar Assad and Iranian President Mahmoud Ahmadinejad, both of whom also earned admiration for their willingness to stand up to Washington. A separate poll, published in July 2008 and conducted by the Saban

In the West, however, the perception of Hizbullah was quite different from the outset. A number of high-profile bombings and kidnappings during the civil war years were attributed to the group, though it has denied direct involvement in these attacks, some of which were claimed by other groups that were operating in the country at the time. These attacks included the targeting of multinational forces and the bombings of the US Marine barracks and the US embassy in 1983, as well as a number of hostage-taking incidents.

These attacks, which were widely blamed by the West on Iranian-linked militants – a vague label that later became associated with Hizbullah – fuelled the misperception of the resistance movement as a fanatic terrorist group. The misperception was later codified into law in the United States, and a handful of other states that have branded the resistance as a terrorist group.[10]

The contrast between Western and local perceptions of Hizbullah is all the more stark when viewed in the light of the movement's gradual entry into Lebanese politics. In politics Hizbullah, like other parties in Lebanon, forged a wide array of alliances and proved itself skilled at adapting to its environment, as will be discussed below. But, broadly speaking, Hizbullah gained legitimacy in its local context at the same time that it was de-legitimised externally by Western governments; in fact, the West's attempts to demonise the group have in some respects served to bolster its standing further among Arab and Muslim publics, as it is viewed as thwarting Washington's perceived attempts to dominate the region.

It is important to note, however, that exceptions have arisen in both the local and external contexts. Segments of Western societies whose governments have branded Hizbullah a terrorist group have rejected that label, and have expressed limited support for the movement on the basis of concepts like social justice.[11] Meanwhile, segments of Lebanese society have in the years since Israel's withdrawal from South Lebanon grown increasingly critical of the Lebanese government's recognition of Hizbullah's armed wing.[12]

Center at the Brookings Institution in Washington, also showed Nasrallah to be the most admired Arab leader in the region.

10. The US Department of State first listed Hizbullah as a foreign terrorist organisation on 18 October 1999, as stated by Secretary of State Madeleine Albright.

11. For example, the UK-based Stop the War Coalition has hosted Hizbullah members at speaking events in Britain.

12. Leaders of the Christian Lebanese Forces and Phalange Party factions, for example, have expressed growing concern about Hizbullah's arsenal.

The ideology of Hizbullah

Hizbullah's ideology is built upon three basic pillars: Islam, *jihad* and *wilayat al-faqih*. This section will explain each of these three concepts. It is important to note, however, that while these concepts are viewed as sacred principles, they do not constitute a tyrannical, fanatical, static set of precepts that confine the evolution of the movement, but rather are fluid, and can be adapted to existing socio-political circumstances.

Belief in Islam as a comprehensive religion is perhaps the most funda-mental characteristic that defines the movement. In the view of the party, Islam is not confined to the mosque, but rather is perceived as having direct relevance both to the individual and to society in every aspect of life. Con-temporary Shi'ism is firmly grounded in immutable edicts, but it is also adaptable to changing socio-political circumstances. This can be attributed to the concept of *ijtihad* (independent reasoning), which is specific to Shi'i *fiqh*, and provides space for rethinking religious edicts and injunctions taking into consideration time, place and the prevailing circumstances. Shi'i jurisprudence has thus proved to be dynamic and progressive, leaving ample space for flexibility in interpretation and compromise, as long as it does not encroach upon the immutable set of principles (*thawabt*). Shi'ism holds that Islam leaves room for two things: an immutable space that cannot be changed regardless of the prevailing developments and circumstances; and a second, mutable space that is closely related to changing circumstances and prevailing objective conditions on the one hand and the principles of religious legislation on the other.[13]

This room for interpretation stems from the fact that there are two types of verse in the Qur'an: *ayat muhkama* or 'verses that are unequivocal in meaning', and *ayat mutashabiha*, 'verses that require allegorical interpre-tation'. While the first are unalterable edicts pertaining to prayer, fasting, pilgrimage, alms-giving and similar practices of worshipping, the latter are open to interpretation that takes new circumstances into consideration. The *shari'a* – the body of Islamic law that addresses societal issues – is similarly regarded as open to reinterpretation, creating a space in which adherents to the faith can keep pace with rapid social and political changes.

---

13. Interview with Shaykh Muhammad Shqayr, an Islamic scholar who teaches Islamic history at the Lebanese University in Beirut, 15 January 2007.

The second concept that constitutes a basic pillar of Hizbullah's ideology is that of *jihad* – a word that has its origins in the root of the verb 'to struggle' or 'to strive'. It therefore has a broader meaning than 'holy war' or 'military combat' and embraces all forms of struggle, including the internal struggle against one's own temptations to do evil. This notion is expressed in a *hadith* that relates the story of the Prophet Muhammad receiving a soldier after he had returned from combat: 'Welcome to a troop that has fulfilled that smaller *jihad* and for whom the bigger *jihad* still awaits.' When asked about the bigger *jihad*, the Prophet answered: '*jihad* with the soul'.[14] *Jihad* thus bears direct relation to the daily struggle with one's own soul, and the struggle to choose virtue over vice, as well as to military confrontation with an enemy. The *hadith* also defines the *jihad* with the soul as the larger of the two challenges, while the military battle with the enemy is a lesser test.

The military form of *jihad* is also considered a religious duty – though religious clerics draw a distinction between two types of military *jihad*. The first is offensive, or initiative *jihad*: the entry into others' lands for reasons not related to the reclamation or liberation of occupied land. This type of *jihad* is considered the sole prerogative of the Prophet Muhammad; it ceased to be permissible after his death and would only be viewed as legitimate in the present day upon the appearance of the Imam al-Mahdi.[15] The second type of military *jihad* is defensive *jihad*: the defence by Muslims of their land and the confrontation of aggression or occupation. This type of *jihad* is viewed as a religious obligation, which must be fulfilled by devout Muslims and be carried out without hesitation with whatever means are available. The determination of what constitutes defensive *jihad* is entrusted to the jurist–theologian, or *wali al-faqih*.

This brings us to the third pillar of Hizbullah's ideology, which is the concept of *wilayat al-faqih*. Literally translated, *wilayat al-faqih* means 'mandate of the (Islamic) jurist' or 'guardianship of the jurist' – *wilaya* meaning 'government' or 'legal authority', combined with *faqih*, which is the standard Islamic term for someone who interprets the law. The concept as elaborated by Ayatollah Khomeini is a forthright attempt to legitimise governance by Shi'i clergy in the temporal as well as the spiritual realm. Concretely speaking,

---

14. Abdul Razaq Kilani, 'Jihad: A Misunderstood Aspect of Islam', *Islamic Culture* vol. 70, no. 3 (1996) pp. 35–46.

15. This view of offensive *jihad* represents the overwhelming consensus of clerics and there are only very few exceptions to this rule.

it implies that the highest authority of Islam – the guide or leader (*rahbar*) – should be both one of the highest religious authorities (*marja' al-taqlid* or 'authority of emulation') and the political leader, who 'understands his time' and can therefore lead a mass movement. The leader is one who has dedicated his labours to understanding *shari'a* jurisprudence, and who is distinguished by his piety, diligence, justice, and devotion to Islam. The qualities of such a *marja'* are illustrated in what Shaykh Tubrusi states in his book *Al-Ihtijaj*, quoting an anonymous imam: 'He of the *fuqaha*, or legal experts, who is self-preserving [*sanan linafsihi*], religion preserving, against his desires, conforming to God's will, then the lay people should emulate him.'[16] Such a leader is one who naturally emerges from among the *fuqaha*, or religious clerics, and gains the approval of his followers. As the most learned and trusted Islamic authority, the *wali al-faqih* becomes the custodian of the Islamic nation and sets the guidelines for the Islamic community, with the aim of preserving their interests in accordance with Islam.

Some observers have pointed to Hizbullah's adherence to the concept of *wilayat al-faqih* as evidence that the party secretly aims to topple the government of Lebanon and replace it with an Islamic state governed directly from Tehran. From this perspective it is impossible to imagine that Hizbullah could both embrace such an ideology and simultaneously participate in democratic governance in Lebanon. But, as we shall see in the following section, the commitment to the jurist–theologian does not limit the scope of Hizbullah's internal direction, the party's ability to forge relations with the various powers and constituents of Lebanon or its ability to operate within its democratic system. Indeed, the very notion of imposing an Islamic form of governance is anathema to the concept of *wilayat al-faqih*. As Ayatollah Khomeini asserted in his book on Islamic government, 'since *wilayat al-faqih* is something decreed by God, do not be afraid of it. The *faqih* cannot treat people with force or power; if any *faqih* wanted to do so, he would be denied his *wilaya*'. According to Khomeini,[17] the responsibility of governance is mutual and reciprocal between the government and populace, both of which

16. Ali Ahmad Al-Bahadli, *Al-Hawza al-'Ilmiyya fi al-Najaf: Ma'alimaha wa Har-akataha al-Islahiyya (1920–1980)* ('The Religious Seminary in Najaf: Features and Reformist Trends'), Beirut: Dar Al-Zahra, 1993, p. 201.

17. Ayatollah Khomeini, *Al-Hukuma al-Islamiyya* ('Islamic Government'), second edn, Beirut: Markaz Baqiyyat Allah Ala'zam, 1999.

are ultimately viewed as subject to the *shari'a*, or Islamic law. Moreover, the concept of *wilayat al-faqih* is not rigid, and is subject to reinterpretation.

Hizbullah's adoption of a post-Islamist outlook

For the first few years after the publication of its Open Letter, Hizbullah's activities remained focused almost entirely on military resistance and the provision of social services to the deprived. But that was to change in 1992 with Hizbullah's first entry into politics, a development that would see the evolution of its ideology from that of a nascent Islamist faction into one of a fully fledged political party with public stances on a wide range of issues. This development was made possible by the adoption of the Taif Accord, which ended the civil war by redistributing power among Lebanon's sects, and introduced a blueprint for reform aimed at creating a more equitable political system.

In its early years, Hizbullah's only discernible political aspiration was the realisation of an Islamic system of governance, though the party never advocated the imposition of such a system by force – which, indeed, would run counter to the commandments of the Qur'an, which stresses freedom and rejects the imposition of one's own doctrine on others: 'Let there be no compulsion in religion: Truth stands out clear from error: whoever rejects evil and believes in God has grasped the most trustworthy hand-hold that never breaks. God is All Hearing and All Knowing' (2: 256). This message was incorporated into Hizbullah's Open Letter, which both openly stated the party's aspiration to achieve Islamic governance in Lebanon and emphasised its commitment to arriving at such a state through the free choice of the people:

> Where the freedom of choosing a governing system is attributed to our people in Lebanon, they will not find a better alternative to Islam. Hence, we call for the implementation of the Islamic system based on a direct and free choice of the people, and not through forceful imposition as may be assumed by some.[18]

The post-Taif order, however, saw the transformation of Hizbullah's approach to politics. Arguably, this shift in thinking can be described as the onset of

---

18. 'Open Letter', drafted by Hizbullah to the oppressed in Lebanon and throughout the world, p. 20.

pragmatic attempts to construct an 'alternative modernity' incorporating both religious and modern democratic principles. Asef Bayat has described this metamorphosis, as it occurred in Iran in the late 1980s, as the onset of 'post-Islamism'. By post-Islamism, he means both a political and social *condition* in which Iranian Islamists became aware of their system's inadequacies, and were thus compelled to reinvent it; and also a *project* or conscious attempt 'to turn the underlying principles of Islamism on its [*sic*] head by emphasising rights instead of duties, plurality in place of a singular authoritative voice, historicity rather than fixed scriptures, and the future instead of the past'.[19] As we shall see, a similar transformation, brought about through pragmatic introspection and a willingness to experiment with incremental adjustments, took place within the ranks of Hizbullah.

Hizbullah's first foray into Lebanese politics occurred during the 1992 parliamentary elections. The decision to participate was made after considerable debate among the party's leadership about the implications of taking part in a political process that did not represent its view of an ideal system. The discussions between the members of Hizbullah's executive council centred on the question of whether participating in the polls would signal the abandonment of its commitment to Islamic governance, or whether the party could embrace its commitment to Islam and all of its principles while simultaneously engaging in a political system that was inherently un-Islamic. Other questions that were raised included whether participation in such a system would have a corrupting influence on the party that would lead to the reordering of its priorities; whether the party would be granting legitimacy to a non-Islamic order through its involvement in parliament, and thereby facilitating its own entrapment in the existing political structure; and whether it would be indirectly responsible for the passage of un-Islamic laws or other objectionable decisions taken by the national legislature, despite its own opposition. A similar internal debate would take place in 2005, when Hizbullah took the further incremental step of deciding to participate in the executive branch of government for the first time.[20]

---

19. Asef Bayat, 'Islamism and Democracy: What is the Real Question?' Amsterdam: Amsterdam University Press, pp. 18–19. See also Bayat's 'The Coming of a Post-Islamist Society', *Critique: Critical Middle East Studies*, vol. 5, no. 9 (Fall 1996), University of Hamline (Minnesota), pp. 43–52.

20. For more on the internal debate that preceded Hizbullah's decision to participate in parliament, and later the municipalities and the executive branch of

After engaging in this debate, the council's leadership ultimately decided in 1992 to take part in the parliamentary elections and sought the approval of Ayatollah Ali Khamenei, who conferred legitimacy on the project through a formal legal opinion (*fatwa*). Shortly thereafter, on 3 July 1992, Nasrallah announced that the party would take part in the elections, which were to be held on 23 August of the same year. Despite the fact that this gave the inexperienced party less than fifty days to prepare, the results were remarkable, with vigorous campaigning, high turn-out and surprising electoral victories, reflecting the extent to which Hizbullah had succeeded in creating a powerful grassroots movement.[21]

But what was perhaps most noteworthy about Hizbullah's involvement in the 1992 polls was the publication of a comprehensive political platform ahead of the vote, as this signalled the emergence of a qualitative shift in discourse. Whereas the movement had previously focused almost entirely on resistance and charitable activities, Hizbullah's entry into the parliamentary arena had necessitated that the party turn its attention to more practical political concerns. Whereas the Open Letter had gone no further than setting out a political ideology, the 1992 platform articulated a pragmatic political programme for the country, touching on a wide range of practical issues such as the electoral law, public administration, social and economic development, job creation and education.[22]

The party platform also suggests that Hizbullah had at this stage begun to posit a new interpretation of *wilayat al-faqih*. This shift in outlook would allow Hizbullah to operate within an increasingly pluralistic public sphere and demonstrate greater openness towards other political parties and groups from a variety of religious communities. In the following years Nasrallah would reiterate the party's stance on this matter in an increasingly unequivocal way:

---

government, see Naim Qassem, *Hizbullah: The Story from Within*, London: Saqi, 2005, and *Hizbullah: al-Manhaj, al-Tajriba, al-Mustaqbal* ('Hizbullah: The Approach, the Experience and the Future'), Beirut: Dar Al-Hadi, 2002. Qassem is the deputy secretary-general of Hizbullah.

21. The elections saw the birth of the Loyalty to the Resistance Bloc, with twelve members of parliament out of a total of 128 – eight Shi'i, two Sunni, one Roman Catholic and one Maronite Christian.

22. The full text of the 1992 Election Programme is published in the appendix of Qassem, *Hizbullah*.

We want neither authority, nor monopoly, nor to impose our ideology or agenda on the Lebanese nation. We believe such a diverse country could not be governed without the participation, cooperation, unity and solidarity of all its public components ... Many tried, through their media to twist this truth. They say that Hizbullah follows *wilayat al-faqih* – the just authority, the jurisprudent authority, the wise authority, the brave authority, the honest authority and the loyal authority. I declare today, as I did many times before, that I am proud of being one of the individuals in the party of *wilayat al-faqih*. I would also say that Lebanon is a diverse and pluralistic country and we must preserve it as such.[23]

Hizbullah's unlikely alliance

Perhaps nowhere is Hizbullah's transformation in outlook better illustrated than in its formation of an unlikely alliance with the (mostly Christian) Free Patriotic Movement (FPM). The two parties signed a joint memorandum of understanding during a meeting between Nasrallah and MP Michel Aoun at St Michael's Church in Shiah, a suburb of Beirut, on 6 February 2006. The accord was viewed as surprising for a number of reasons, which will be discussed in this section. It also serves to demonstrate that the party had by this time undergone a reordering of priorities and adaptation to Lebanon's pluralistic political culture.

Among the many elements that made the agreement with the FPM surprising was the fact that Aoun had long been a staunch opponent of the Syrian regime, with which Hizbullah had over the years cultivated a strong relationship on the basis of a shared strategic perception of the conflict with Israel. In 1989, Aoun, who was then commander of the Lebanese Armed Forces, had launched a failed 'war of liberation' in a bid to oust the Syrian military from Lebanon. His efforts earned him exile for fifteen years in France, from where he continued to oppose the Syrian presence fiercely through his political activities. Indeed, on 17 September 2003 Aoun joined a roundtable discussion on Syria held by members of the US House Subcommittee on the Middle East and Central Asia, thereby lending his backing to efforts to draft HR1828, or 'the Syrian Accountability and Lebanese Sovereignty

23. Nasrallah made the remarks during a televised speech on 28 May 2008 to mark the eighth anniversary of Liberation Day, or Israel's withdrawal from most of South Lebanon, in the year 2000.

Restoration Act of 2003', which was passed into law by the Congress on 12 December 2003.[24] The legislation called upon the government of Syria to 'immediately and unconditionally halt support for terrorism' and 'immediately declare its commitment to completely withdraw its armed forces, including military, paramilitary, and security forces, from Lebanon, and set a firm timetable for such withdrawal.' It also strangely demanded that the government of Lebanon 'evict all terrorist and foreign forces from southern Lebanon, including Hizballah'.[25] Aoun similarly lent his public backing to UN Security Council Resolution 1559, which, echoing the Taif Agreement, called for the withdrawal of Syrian troops and the disarmament of all domestic and foreign militias in Lebanon.[26]

Hizbullah's alliance with the FPM was all the more unusual in light of the latter party's generally secular and pro-Western outlook. Moreover, the FPM, while ostensibly open to participation from among all sects, primarily comprises Christians and representatives of Christian interests. In fact, during the 2005 parliamentary elections the FPM had swept predominantly Christian districts, allowing Aoun at the time of the inking of the memorandum to assert himself as the most authoritative representative of the Christian community and the leader of the largest single Christian bloc in parliament, the Change and Reform bloc.[27]

---

24. The roundtable discussion was organised by Rep. Ileana Ros-Lehtinen, who was one of 297 co-sponsors of HR 1828, sponsored by Rep. Eliot L. Engel of New York. Aoun's testimony was later cited by both lawmakers during the Congressional discussion that preceded the passage of the legislation. See the Congressional Record, vol. 149, 15 October 2003 and 20 November 2003, available at wais.access.gpo.gov.
25. The full text of the resolution can be viewed online at www.congress.gov.
26. The resolution's use of the term 'militia' is somewhat ironic, in view of the Taif Accord's distinction between a militia and a resistance force, since the Security Council was presumably trying to push for the disarmament of Hizbullah.
27. Election results for the predominantly Christian parties in the 2005 vote were as follows: the Change and Reform bloc secured twenty-one MPs, comprising fourteen for the FPM, five for the Skaff bloc, and two for the Murr bloc; the Christian parties of the March 14 coalition (the rival camp to the Hizbullah/ FPM alliance) won twelve seats, with six for the Lebanese Forces and six for the Qornet Shewan Gathering, which comprised Phalangists and independents. The FPM later won another seat from the Phalange in the 2007 by-election in the Metn district, though the party won the contest by a narrow majority, suggesting that it is unclear to what extent Aoun has retained his support among the Christian community.

Clearly, the FPM's Christian affiliations did not make it a suitable partner with which Hizbullah could pursue the objective of creating an Islamic order in Lebanon. The memorandum therefore signified a reordering of priorities in which a nationalist outlook would take precedence over Hizbullah's previously expressed Islamist goals, as well as the party's adaptation to a political culture of pluralism and adoption of a more democratic vision of its Islamist project. In fact, the text of the accord provides ample evidence of the party adapting to the political reality in Lebanon and gradually transcending its exclusivist Islamist platform in favour of pursuing a pluralist strategy.

Some of the items in the ten-point accord are unsurprising, given Hizbullah's previous stances, and mark, if anything, only a slight shift in stance. These include the two parties' expression of commitment to dialogue, to determining the status of those who went missing during the civil war and to introducing a modern electoral law that 'guarantees the accuracy and equity of popular representation' and serves to 'limit the influence of political money and sectarian fanaticisms'. However, a few items in the memorandum, as well as some of the terminology employed in the document, warrant further discussion, as they signal a significant transformation in Hizbullah's approach and thereby serve to illustrate the party's ongoing attempts to revise its Islamist outlook.

In the second item of the memorandum, the two parties expressed their commitment to consensual democracy, stating that it 'remains the fundamental basis for governance in Lebanon, because it is the effective embodiment of the spirit of the Constitution and of the essence of the pact of shared coexistence [the Taif Accord]'. They also affirmed that 'any approach for resolving national issues according to a majority–minority formula remains dependent on historic and social conditions for practising effective democracy in which the citizen becomes a self-standing value'.

Similar themes are reiterated in the fourth clause of the memorandum, which deals with the need to build 'a modern state that enjoys the trust of its citizens and is able to meet their needs and aspirations and provide them with a sense of security and safety as related to their present and future'. To achieve that goal, the two parties called for adoption of 'the standards of justice, equality, parity, merit and integrity'; the creation of an 'equitable and impartial judiciary [as this] is the essential condition for creating a state of rights, laws and institutions'; and the addressing of corruption through, among other measures, the activation of oversight bodies and the issuing of a 'demand of the government that Lebanon signs the United Nations Treaty for Combating Corruption'. Hizbullah's endorsement of these two points in the memorandum in particular suggests the party's ability to incorporate a focus on issues such as democracy, rights, liberties and secular law alongside its Islamic ideology.

An emphasis on a commitment to rights, personal freedoms and pluralism is detected again in point seven of the agreement, which deals with security issues and condemns 'any form of political assassination' on the basis that such killings are 'a violation of basic human rights, the most important foundations of the existence of Lebanon represented by difference and diversity, and the essence of democracy and its practice'. The two parties also asserted that 'security measures must not be in conflict with the basic freedoms guaranteed by the Constitution, with first the freedom of expression and political action that do not threaten security and public stability'.

Perhaps what is most interesting about the agreement is its demonstration of a new measure of flexibility with regard to the issue of conducting armed resistance. Point ten of the document states that the 'protection of Lebanon and the preservation of its independence and sovereignty are a national public responsibility and duty, guaranteed by international treaties and the Human Rights Charter, particularly in confronting any threats or dangers from any source that could harm them'. Interestingly, although this certainly does not represent Hizbullah's abandonment of its religious principle of *jihad*, the agreed source of legitimacy for the resistance here is the UN Human Rights Charter. The two parties went on to affirm that armed resistance 'is an honourable and sacred means that is exercised by any group whose land is occupied, in a manner identical to the methods of political resistance', but also called for addressing the issue of Hizbullah's arms within two boundaries: 'reliance on justifications that meet a national consensus for keeping the weapons' and 'the definition of objective conditions that would lead to a cessation of the reasons and justifications for keeping those weapons'. The 'objective conditions' here are defined in the document as Israel's continued occupation of Lebanese territories, imprisonment of Lebanese citizens and threats to Lebanese sovereignty.[28] Thus, the weapons of the resistance are perceived as legitimate not only in light of the prevailing *conditions* on the ground – a stance that is in

---

28. After the conclusion of the last prisoner swap between Hizbullah and Israel on 16 July 2008, there were no longer any Lebanese prisoners in Israeli jails.

keeping with Islam's injunction forbidding pre-emptive *jihad* and permitting defensive *jihad* – but also in view of national *consensus* on the issue.

Until now, the prevailing consensus in Lebanon has been that Israel's continued aggression and violation of Lebanese sovereignty represent conditions that constitute ample justification for maintaining the resistance in its current form. However, were those conditions to change dramatically in the future, there is reason to believe that consensus on the matter of Hizbullah's weapons might also shift in response. In view of Israel's decades-long track record of showing little interest in respecting Lebanon's sovereignty, that is unlikely to happen in the immediate future.

Whither the resistance?

Hizbullah's alliance with the FPM grew stronger in the context of a protracted political crisis that unfolded in Lebanon between November 2006 and May 2008, and from which the country has not yet fully emerged. When the two parties signed the memorandum of understanding in early 2006, Hizbullah was a member of the cabinet, whereas the FPM had rejected participation in the executive branch of government, arguing that the number of ministerial portfolios offered to it did not reflect its national standing, or indeed its level of representation in parliament.

Hizbullah's participation in the cabinet was partly the result of the 'Quartet agreement' struck during the 2005 parliamentary elections between Hizbullah and Amal, on one side, and Future Movement leader MP Saad Hariri and Progressive Socialist Party leader MP Walid Jumblatt on the other. That alliance won the latter two parties Shi'i votes and led to a political understanding regarding the resistance that was later enshrined in the cabinet statement, which read:

> The government considers that Lebanon's resistance is a sincere and natural expression of the Lebanese people's right to defend its land and dignity in the face of Israeli aggression, threats, and ambitions as well as of its right to continue its actions to free Lebanese territory.

But the alliance between the four parties began to unravel during the 2006 War with Israel, and when talks to expand the government unravelled in November 2006, the five Hizbullah and Amal ministers resigned, along with one other minister, and joined the FPM in a new opposition alliance.

The power struggle between what remained of the governing coalition and the newly formed opposition dragged on for over a year, with the latter staging a sit-in protest outside the government headquarters at the Grand Serail. The opposition argued that the government was no longer legitimate by virtue of its exclusion of Shi'is, as this constituted a violation of the Constitution, which states: 'There is no constitutional legitimacy for any authority which contradicts the "pact of communal coexistence".' It was also viewed as a violation of Article 95 of the Constitution, which reads: 'The confessional groups are to be represented in a just and equitable fashion in the formation of the Cabinet.' But the governing coalition refused to back down and carried on with its usual business in the absence of Shi'i participation, thereby exacerbating the divisions between the two camps. The government camp justified its position on the grounds that less than one-third of the ministers had resigned; Article 69 of the Constitution states that the cabinet will be considered to have resigned if more than one-third of its members has quit. Amid the crisis, the term of President Emile Lahoud came to an end; but parliamentary Speaker Nabih Berri, the leader of Amal, refused to call a session to elect a replacement so long as the cabinet rejected calls to resign.[29] When Lahoud left office at the end of his appointed term, the presidency therefore was left vacant.

The crisis intensified further on 3 May 2008, when the cabinet issued two controversial decisions to remove Hizbullah's telecommunications network and fire the Shi'i head of security at Rafik Hariri International Airport, claiming that Hizbullah had set up a surveillance camera to monitor a runway. Shortly thereafter, on 7 May 2008, a labour strike began, which had been planned in advance, demanding higher wages. The opposition had given its backing to the strike and had urged its supporters to participate. But during the course of the protest, which saw demonstrators block the road towards the Beirut airport, clashes erupted when government supporters attacked the protestors – at first with stones, and later with gunfire and grenades. On 8 May 2008, Nasrallah delivered a speech in which he said the two controversial government measures amounted to a 'declaration of war', and that the opposition would take measures of 'self-defence', adding: 'We will not be killed in the streets. We will not be shot at. We will not accept for our resistance and military to be targeted.' Almost immediately after Nasrallah

---

29. According to the Lebanese Constitution, the parliament elects the president.

spoke, clashes erupted across the capital, pitting opposition fighters against pro-government gunmen. The opposition rapidly seized control of West Beirut, capturing rival gunmen and fighting later spread to the Chouf mountains. The opposition fighters swiftly handed control of the areas it captured over to the Lebanese Armed Forces.

The dramatic turn of events prompted the Arab League to intervene, and from 16 to 21 May Qatar hosted a national dialogue conference of Lebanese leaders in Doha. The parties agreed to a six-point document known as the Doha Accord, which called for all parties to issue a call within twenty-four hours for parliament to convene and elect Michel Sleiman as consensus president; for a national unity government to be formed by expanding the number of cabinet seats to thirty, with sixteen to go to the governing coalition, eleven to the opposition, and three to the president; for all parties to commit not to resign or obstruct the government's work; for the adoption of a new electoral law based on a modified version of the 1960 law; for all parties to agree to refrain from using weapons to make political gains; for national leaders to launch a national dialogue on promoting the Lebanese state's authority over all its territory and maintaining the security of all citizens; and for all political leaders to refrain from using sectarian rhetoric and mutual accusations of treason. The accord has so far been partially implemented, with the election of Sleiman and the creation of a unity government; the national dialogue was set to begin on 16 September.

Interestingly, the unity government saw the reduction of Hizbullah's share of ministers from three to one, and the FPM increasing its representation from zero to three. Hizbullah had long argued that its objective was not to increase its own share of power, but rather to have a more representative government, and backed these statements by giving up its own cabinet shares to its allies in the opposition. This development provides further evidence of the party's adaptation to Lebanon's pluralistic political process and of the increasing pragmatism of its own behaviour within that system.

The new electoral law is expected to be more representative of popular sentiment and could dramatically alter the current parliament's composition in favour of the opposition alliance.[30] However, the elections will be preceded

---

30. A 2007 Beirut Center for Research and Information opinion poll predicted that the opposition would win an election with 58 per cent of the popular vote. The survey was conducted between 19 and 31 October using a simple random sample of 5,000 respondents, stratified by sect and region.

by the national dialogue sessions, which are expected to address the matter of the weapons of the resistance with a view to improving national security and defence, as well as enhancing the authority of the state. It is possible that these discussions could see the introduction of incremental measures that would place new boundaries on the resistance's activities, such as the creation of a coordination committee that would better facilitate communication with the Lebanese Armed Forces, or an agreement about the types of activities that can be conducted. However, in view of the overwhelming public support for the resistance, as well as the broad participation of opposition parties in the national talks, it would be highly unlikely that the dialogue sessions would lead to major changes such as the disarmament of the resistance. Thus, both the resistance and political arms of Hizbullah are likely to continue to play important roles in the Lebanese national arena.

ELEVEN

Al-Qaeda in the Middle East, North Africa and Asia: Jihadists and Franchises

Camille Tawil

Created by Osama bin Laden in late 1980s, the al-Qaeda organisation is the result of a set of complicated factors that have shaped this group, in a very short period of time, to become one of the best-known 'terror' groups in modern history. In fact, the story of al-Qaeda is inseparable from the story of its 'sisters': the 'jihadist' groups that were formed around the same time as al-Qaeda, and which led a series of failed attempts to topple governments described as 'apostate' in the Arab world. It was the failed attempts of these 'sister organisations' to achieve their stated goals – of the establishment of governments ruling according to the Islamic *shari'a* – that led to the creation of al-Qaeda, which evolved into the group we know today.

This chapter aims to examine al-Qaeda's evolution over four stages of its formation, showing how it progressed, and how much it was transformed in each of these stages, in structure as well as in method. The first stage lasted for about two-and-a-half years, from the time al-Qaeda was created, in 1988 until shortly after the second Gulf War – after the Iraqi invasion of Kuwait in August 1990, and its defeat by the American-led coalition in March 1991. This stage, which lasted until the end of 1991, can be called 'the formation years' – al-Qaeda was not a properly structured group, but more a coalition of like-minded jihadists who fought in the Afghan *jihad*.

The second stage covers the relocation of al-Qaeda leadership to Sudan between 1992 and 1996. It was a period that witnessed the re-launching of al-Qaeda, and the cementing of its relationship with various jihadist groups in the Middle East.

The third stage lasted from 1996 until 2001, with al-Qaeda moving countries again and returning to Afghanistan during the Taliban era. It was a period when al-Qaeda started to focus its operations against a single 'enemy' – the West in general, and America in particular. It is that 'enemy', according to al-Qaeda, that was to blame for the failure of the jihadists to topple the Arab regimes which they considered 'apostate' – such as those in Egypt, Algeria and Libya. These three countries were the main battleground between the jihadists and Arab regimes during the 1990s. This stage culminated in the spectacular terrorist attacks of 11 September 2001.

The final stage began just after the defeat of the Taliban regime at the hands of the Americans in November 2001, and lasts to this day. It is a period in which al-Qaeda has launched a 'global *jihad*', and, instead of remaining as one group, it has operated through a network of franchises – in the Gulf area, North Africa, the Levant and Iraq, and even in Europe.

The first stage: al-Qaeda is born

Al-Qaeda describes itself as a Sunni group that applies *jihad* 'as a means of change, in order to make God's word supreme'.[1] It defines *jihad* as 'fighting in the manner of God', not participating in charitable works. It also stresses that it seeks to 'encourage' people to become jihadists, stating that it 'prepares for it [*jihad*], and starts it, when it is able to do so'. This indicates that al-Qaeda, at the time of its formation in 1988, was still not engaged in *jihad* outside Afghanistan, the place where its founders had met.[2] Al-Qaeda was

---

1. Al-Qaeda has never published a set of principles defining its ideology and policies. But a document exists that was written by the founders of al-Qaeda, in which they set out their goals and state how they hope to achieve them. A copy of this eight-page document is retained by the author; it is written in Arabic, with some changes made by hand to the typed text (which indicates that this was still a preliminary draft of the final document), and contains the principles upon which al-Qaeda was formed, its organisational structure and its goals. The American government released it, among other documents that it confiscated in the aftermath of the war against al-Qaeda and the Taliban in Afghanistan in 2001.

2. Court papers presented by the American government in January 2003 assert that the work on establishing the al-Qaeda organisation 'commenced' in September 1988. See the case presented on 6 January 2003 before the Federal Northern District Court of Illinois, outlining the evidence against Mr Enaam Arnaout, the head of the Benevolence International Foundation (BIF), an Islamic charity with alleged ties to al-Qaeda. news.findlaw.com/hdocs/docs/bif/usarnaout10603prof.pdf. However, Noman bin Othman, a Libyan who participated in the Afghan *jihad* at the end of the 1980s, told this author that al-Qaeda was created either in December 1988 or January 1989. Although bin

at that time more or less a coalition of like-minded jihadists who were in Afghanistan fighting with the *mujahidin* against the Soviet occupation that had started in 1979. Those jihadists were, to be precise, a small band of people who fought mainly on the side of Osama bin Laden – a young, wealthy Saudi who was among the first Arabs to go to Afghanistan to participate in the *jihad* – especially in the battle of Jaji in Paktia, in south-east Afghanistan, in spring 1987, when bin Laden and his men ambushed soldiers from an elite Soviet unit. Jaji was the first battle fought solely by Arab fighters in the Afghan *jihad*,[3] and bin Laden's victory there gave him and his group wide publicity throughout the Arab world.

The creation of al-Qaeda coincided with the withdrawal of the Soviets from Afghanistan – something that was widely seen as a victory for the Islamist insurgency and its American backers, despite the fact that the Soviets left a communist government in Kabul, led by their ally, President Mohammed Najibullah, who survived there until the spring of 1992.[4]

There are two things that should be said about this newly created organisation. First, it was clear that al-Qaeda was a grouping of jihadists from different locations – the Gulf countries, the Levant, Iraq, North Africa, Egypt and Sudan, among others. Its multinational nature was one of its defining features, especially when compared with other jihadist groups that were being established – or re-established – during the same period, marked by the end of the *jihad* against the Soviets. Among these were two Egyptian organisations: the Jihad Group (Tanzim al-Jihad, or Islamic Jihad) and the Islamic Group (al-Jama'a al-Islamiyya). These two groups had been in existence in Egypt in the 1970s, but were crushed by the security forces after they assassinated the Egyptian President Anwar Sadat in October 1981 for

---

Othman was not a member of al-Qaeda, he is known to have been close to some of its founders, and is very knowledgeable about jihadist organisations. In fact, he was a leading member of one of al-Qaeda's 'sister' organisations – the Libyan Islamic Fighting Group – from the early 1990s until after the war on terror.

3. Until that day, the Arabs who wished to participate in the Afghan *jihad* had to do so alongside one of the Afghan factions, such as the Hezb-i-Islami group led Gulbuddin Hekmatyar, or the Jamiat-e Islami of Burhanuddin Rabbani, or the Islamic Union for the Liberation of Afghanistan (Ittihad-i-Islami) of Abdul Rabi Rasul Sayyaf, among other groups.

4. The Soviets announced their withdrawal in April 1988, and pulled their troops out in February 1989.

signing a peace treaty with Israel.[5] By the second half of 1980s, the remnants of these two factions regrouped on the Afghan–Pakistani borders. Their re-creation was not a laborious job, for both groups already had a defined set of common texts that formed the bases of their thinking and ideology. This did not apply to other groups that were being established around the same time in that area, such as the Libyan Islamic Fighting Group (LIFG) and the Algerian Armed Islamic Group (GIA), whose respective countries would become their theatres of operations.[6] These two groups were created mostly by Libyan and Algerian 'Afghans' who were not formerly part of a known jihadist group in their own countries,[7] and therefore had to create a group almost from scratch (having to define their ideology and objectives, and determine how to achieve them).

Each of these four groups – two Egyptian, one Libyan, and one Algerian – had a national agenda to topple what they considered 'apostate' governments in their own countries, and to establish 'Islamic' ones in their place. The respective membership of these groups was exclusive: Egyptian, Libyan or Algerian. Al-Qaeda, on the other hand, adopted a different recruitment strategy from its inception, projecting itself as a multi-national group and not limiting itself to operating for or in a single country, but rather concerning itself with the whole Islamic world.

For al-Qaeda's ideologues, the *raison d'être* of the organisation was to establish a 'state of Islam' through the spreading of the ideology of *jihad*, from Afghanistan to the rest of the Arab and Muslim world, and through helping 'oppressed' Muslims wherever they happened to be.[8] It clearly stated

5. The Jihad Group and the Islamic Group briefly united in 1981, and members of this unified group led the attack against President Sadat in October of that year. However, ideological differences were soon to appear in the Egyptian prisons among the arrested leaders of this unified group, which led them to split once more into two groups.

6. The Libyan Islamic Fighting Group was established in the beginning of the 1990s, although its name was only officially adopted in 1993. The Algerian Armed Islamic Group was also created by Algerian Afghan jihadists, in 1991, but did not start operating under this name inside Algeria until October 1992.

7. Some of those jihadists were in fact members of local jihadist cells that were active in various Algerian and Libyan cities, before they went to join the Afghan *jihad*.

8. Before it became an organisation, al-Qaeda began as a 'registration office' for young people, especially from the Gulf, who came to fight with bin Laden, in case they were killed and their families needed to be informed.

that its policy was to seek 'cooperation' with other Islamic groups in order to 'unite and merge'. Al-Qaeda was prepared to fight a *jihad* 'in any place in the Muslim countries, in case that was needed and [al-Qaeda] was capable of doing so'.[9] It did not name any of the Muslim countries in which it was ready to engage in *jihad*, but it was known that bin Laden, by the end of the 1980s, was preparing for *jihad* in South Yemen, which was ruled by a Marxist government – the only one of its kind in the Arab world.[10] The Hadramout region of Yemen[11] was also the birthplace of bin Laden's father – which may have given him another incentive to work against the communist rulers in Aden. But bin Laden's involvement in supporting the jihadists in South Yemen does not seem to have lasted long – any plans he may have had for Yemen had to be postponed in the aftermath of the Iraqi invasion of Kuwait in August 1990. Immediately after the invasion, bin Laden's attention was diverted by Saddam's (apostate) regime's threat to the holy places in Saudi Arabia; his intentions and proposals to fight Saddam will be discussed below.

Second, it was clear from the beginning that al-Qaeda had a large proportion of Egyptians among its ranks – especially those surrounding bin Laden and controlling his training camps. An Egyptian member of the Jihad Group, Abu Ubaida al-Banshiri, became the first military chief of al-Qaeda. Upon his death in 1996, al-Banshiri was succeeded by a fellow member of Egyptian Jihad, Abu Hafs al-Misri, who remained military chief until he died in 2001.[12]

---

9. See document referred to in note 1.

10. Bin Laden's involvement, in 1989 and 1990, in the fight against the communist leaders of South Yemen is well documented. For example, Abu Musab al-Suri, who was one of the trainers at al-Qaeda camps (at the end of the 1980s and the beginning of the 1990s), says that bin Laden 'formed al-Qaeda for *jihadi* goals, in Afghanistan and outside Afghanistan ... in order to support the *jihad* and the groups which are carrying this *jihad* in various places [around the world]. He [also] had a private *jihadi* project in South Yemen against the former communist government, but the goals of this project expanded later to cover the whole of Yemen.' Al-Suri's 'The Global Islamic Resistance Call', released (in Arabic) in December 2004, pp. 710–11 – a copy of this document is retained by the author.

11. The Hadramout region was part of the People's Republic of South Yemen (the Communist South Yemen) when it gained its independence in 1967, before becoming part of the Republic of Yemen in 1990, after the unification of North and South Yemen.

12. Ali Amin al-Rashidi (Abu Ubaidah al-Banshiri) was al-Qaeda's military chief, until his death in Lake Victoria in May 1996. His successor, Mohammed Atef

The influence of the Egyptians caused some irritation at that time among other jihadists, who found that they now had to go through them in order to reach bin Laden – something they had not had to do before.

The Egyptian role inside al-Qaeda was no accident, as was subsequently demonstrated. It was the result of a policy adopted by the leaders of the Islamic Jihad group, which wanted to influence bin Laden by inserting some of their men at the top of his newly created organisation. The Egyptian jihadists intended to give bin Laden a helping hand in creating his own group, and in return expected to profit from spreading their ideology among al-Qaeda's recruits, and to benefit financially from an influx of donations they thought that they would surely receive from wealthy Islamists in the Gulf, because of their support for bin Laden. The influence of the 'Egyptian brigade' inside al-Qaeda was soon to be felt, when they assumed the lead role in al-Qaeda's training camps, spreading their ideology among those who trained to become jihadists.

This final point may need further clarification. Almost everyone who went to Afghanistan at that time – around the end of 1980s and the early 1990s – had in mind participation in what they saw as *jihad* – performing duties to help the oppressed Muslims of Afghanistan. Many of those new recruits had never belonged to any particular group, and different Islamic groups were competing to include the newcomers within their own ranks. Both Saudi Salafists and the Muslim Brotherhood were competing to win over recruits from this mass of Islamists helping the Afghans. There was also the Egyptian Jihadist school of thought, which came to Afghanistan in the 1980s, emerging out of a history of friction and rivalry with the Muslim Brothers, who favoured a less confrontational struggle against the regime in Cairo. With the re-establishment of the Jihad Group on the Afghan–Pakistani borders, the old rivalry that it had had in Egypt with the Muslim Brothers was reignited. Among the first steps taken by the newly re-established Jihad Group in Afghanistan was the publication of a book criticising the Muslim Brothers – *Al-Hasad al-Murr: al-Ikhwan al-Muslimun fi Sittin 'Aman* (The Bitter Harvest, the Muslim Brotherhood in Sixty Years).[13]

(Abu Hafs al-Misri), was military chief until November 2001, when he was killed in an American strike in Afghanistan.

13. *Al-Hasad al-Murr* was written by Dr Ayman al-Zawahiri, a leader of the Jihad Group at the end of the 1980s. At that time, Zawahiri was not the 'amir' of his group, although many thought that he was (the Jihad Group was in fact headed

It is now widely believed that it was the influence of those Egyptian Jihad-ists on bin Laden, among other factors, that precipitated the split between bin Laden and the late Dr Abdullah Azzam, the 'father' of the Arab Afghans. When the Egyptians took over the management of al-Qaeda's camps, they were able to indoctrinate the recruits according to their specific interpretation of Islam. Within the following couple of years, these jihadists were to gain the upper hand in the struggle for supremacy with the rival Islamist currents operating on the Afghan–Pakistani borders.

After the end of the *jihad* in Afghanistan, it was thought that al-Qaeda, still only a very small group, would have no clear idea of what to do next. The Gulf Arabs had no problem returning to their own countries, whose regimes were not seen as un-Islamic, despite their alliance with the Americans; Islamic *shari'a* was applied, to varying degrees, in all the Gulf countries.[14] But outside the Gulf, the picture was more complicated. Many of the 'Arab Afghans' who had left their countries to fight in Afghanistan were not welcomed back in their countries. This was especially the case for the Egyptian and Algerian jihadists, but also, to varying degrees, for Arabs from other countries.

Al-Qaeda was still only in its second year when, in August 1990, Iraq invaded Kuwait. Osama bin Laden was quick to offer the Saudi government a helping hand – he said he was willing and ready to form an Islamic army of jihadists to fight a guerrilla war against the Iraqis and drive them out of Kuwait. What he had in mind was the role that was played by the *mujahidin* in Afghanistan against the Soviets. However, the Saudi government did not take his offer seriously and instead accepted help from an American-led coalition. But the stationing of American forces on Saudi soil was something that triggered great hatred in bin Laden towards the Saudi government and against the Americans themselves, for he saw their presence as defiling the purity of the Muslim holy lands.[15] There are two *hadiths* by the Prophet Mohammed that are taken to mean that 'no two [different] religions can

at that time by another 'doctor', Dr Fadl, or Sayyid Imam Abdel-Aziz el-Sherif, who led this group until 1993, when he was replaced by Zawahiri).

14. Saudi Arabia comes top, among the Gulf States, in applying the *shari'a* to all fields of life.

15. In fact, by then, bin Laden had already set himself against the US (and the UK), even before they stationed their troops in Saudi Arabia. He was openly critical of both, calling for a boycott of American and British products because of their support for Israel.

coexist in the Arab Peninsula', which is understood by the jihadists to mean that Islam should reign alone in the Arabian peninsula.[16]

By the end of the Gulf War and the liberation of Kuwait, in March 1991, the al-Qaeda organisation was beginning to disintegrate. Bin Laden was put under *de facto* house arrest in Saudi Arabia, and his passport was confiscated. Some of al-Qaeda's founding members returned to their own countries and started new groups, or went on to other countries to start a new life. This was especially the case after the defeat of the Najibullah government in Kabul in the spring of 1992, when many Arabs saw no reason to stay in Afghanistan and continue fighting. The spectacle of the Afghan *mujahidin* factions fighting fiercely with each other immediately after the fall of the communist regime provided another reason for frustration and discouragement.

By the end of the *jihad* in Afghanistan, lacking an opportunity to repeat that experience against Saddam's troops, al-Qaeda seemed a weak and fragmented organisation and the people who had helped to create the group had opted to take divergent paths in other parts of the Muslim world.

The second stage: al-Qaeda revived in Sudan

Sudan played an important role not only in bringing al-Qaeda back from the dead, but also in cementing its relationship with other jihadist groups that were active in the first half of the 1990s. The importance of Sudan to al-Qaeda and its sisters stemmed from a number of factors that deserve a closer look.

The first concerns the fact that the Sudanese government at the time was more than willing to host bin Laden and his colleagues. Sudan was then ruled by a young Islamist government led by President Omar al-Bashir and Hassan al-Turabi, which had come to power by military coup in 1989.[17] In the first half of the 1990s the Sudanese government in Khartoum was engaged in a full-blown war with the South, whose population is partly Christian and partly Animist. Thus the Islamist government tended to portray its war with

---

16. The two hadiths are: 'Two religions shall not co-exist in the Arabian Peninsula' and 'Expel the polytheists out of the Arab Peninsula'.

17. Although the Bashir–Turabi alliance seemed to start strong, they fell out in 1999 and became bitter enemies, with Bashir remaining in power and Turabi marginalised in the opposition.

the South as a religious struggle, and referred to what its army was doing as *jihad*. It was therefore no surprise that this Islamist government sought, and eventually received, help from jihadist groups. Bin Laden was one of those invited to settle in Sudan – an invitation that he happily accepted after some hesitation. He was quick to offer help to the Sudanese government in its *jihad* against the Southern rebels. Soon after leaving Saudi Arabia in 1991 (where he had been under a *de facto* travel ban because of his opposition to the presence of the American troops on Saudi soil), he moved to Pakistan, and then to Afghanistan – but enjoyed comfort in neither. On the one hand, he found that the Afghan Mujahidin were fighting among themselves for power, and on the other he feared that the Saudi government might try to kidnap him back to Saudi Arabia since he had left the kingdom illegally. When the Sudanese government invited him, he was more than happy to oblige. He moved to Sudan with many of his supporters, and offered the Sudanese government help in its war with the South. In return, the Khartoum government furnished the 'safe haven' he craved.

The second factor is that Sudan was at the heart of several developments in the Arab world at that time. Unlike Afghanistan, Sudan borders Egypt, Libya and Algeria – three countries whose governments al-Qaeda's 'sister groups' were fighting, separately, to topple. In Egypt, the Islamic Group and the Jihad Group were heavily engaged in a vicious struggle with the Egyptian security forces. In Algeria, the Armed Islamic Group (GIA) launched a bloody insurgency against the government, which had prevented an Islamic party, the Islamic Salvation Front (FIS), from assuming power when it cancelled the elections the Islamists had been on the verge of winning in January 1992.[18] In Libya, the Libyan Fighting Group (LIFG) was in turn preparing to launch a *jihad* against Colonel Gaddafi's regime. Bin Laden maintained a good relationship with the leaders of this group, which was actively providing help to the GIA in Algeria, in the hope that, if it succeeded in toppling the Algerian regime, a domino effect would be created, leading to the fall of other neighbouring regimes, such as those in Libya and Egypt. Indeed, the Algerian government at that time was on the defensive, and members of the LIFG who went to Algeria to help the GIA became convinced that the Islamists could topple it, if a decision was taken to attack the Algerian

---

18. Several jihadist groups were engaged in the fight against the Algerian government, but bin Laden's support went specifically to the GIA, which the Algerian members of al-Qaeda played an important part in forming.

capital.[19] Later, in 1995 and 1996, when the Libyans had fallen out with the GIA leadership, it was bin Laden who came to the rescue. He sent a Libyan member of al-Qaeda to Algeria to examine what was happening, but he was soon captured by the GIA and sent to one of its bases, while a decision on his fate was awaited. But bin Laden's envoy managed to escape by mid-1996, subsequently finding his way out of Algeria and rejoining al-Qaeda.[20]

The presence of bin Laden in Sudan enabled him to forge strong links with many Islamists, especially the groups fighting a *jihad* in Egypt, Libya and Algeria. But his involvement with them and their attempts to topple the ruling regimes was later to have a strong influence on his thinking, as will be seen in the third stage of al-Qaeda's development under the Taliban regime in Afghanistan.[21]

However, by June 1996 al-Qaeda and its sisters had lost almost everything they had worked for during their time in Sudan. The Algerian security forces were able to deal a big blow to the GIA, which became involved in a vicious internal struggle between competing currents within its ranks. Less than a year after the start of the *jihad*, the Libyan security forces were also able to crush the LIFG following some major confrontations, especially in the east of the country.[22] The jihadists' battle in Egypt was also lost in 1996, after

---

19. This author knows from leaders of the LIFG that some of its leaders who went to Algeria to aid the GIA said that the Islamists were camping outside Algiers in their hundreds, and that the Algerian capital could be overrun if the Islamists were to make a decision to attack it. That decision was never taken, and the Algerian government was given time to start a counterattack against the GIA positions in the areas around the capital.

20. The story of this envoy, Atiya Abdelrahman, is now well known, and he is known to be active in Waziristan. See the letter he wrote in 2005 to Abu Musab al-Zarqawi, which was released in September 2006 by the Combating Terrorism Centre, the United States Military Academy at West Point, NY, a copy of which can be found at ctc.usma.edu.

21. It should be noted that not everything that bin Laden did in Sudan was directly connected to military activities, either in support of the government's *jihad* against the South, or in his aid to the jihadists in Egypt, Libya and Algeria. In fact, bin Laden ran various profit-making projects employing many people who were not necessarily members of al-Qaeda or the other jihadist groups active in Sudan.

22. In fact, the LIFG did not initiate the *jihad* against the regime in 1995, but was almost forced to do so when Libyan security started dismantling its 'sleeper cells'. It was clear by mid-1996 that the group was no match for the security forces. It should also be mentioned that the LIFG was busy, at that time, on

the security forces had crushed the militants, forcing the Jihad Group of Ayman al-Zawahiri to order its members to halt the fight, recognising that it was no longer capable of carrying out further attacks. That decision was taken by the end of 1995, but was never made public.[23] As for the Islamic Group, which was active mainly in Upper Egypt, a rift started to appear, as a result of its defeat, between those who wanted to continue the fight (who were mainly located outside Egypt) and those wanting to stop and carry out a 'rethinking' (*muraja'a*) of their ideology, and of why they had failed to achieve their goals (they consisted mainly of the leaders of the group who were imprisoned inside Egypt).

As if all these defeats of the jihadists were not enough for bin Laden and his allies, the Sudanese regime came to realise that the 'guest' and his activities were no longer bearable, asking him, as politely and circuitously as they could, to leave. For al-Zawahiri, there was no politeness: the Sudanese government was so angry with him that it gave him little time to pack. His group had killed two teenagers it had found spying, without informing the Sudanese authorities. These killings had taken place despite the fact that it was Sudanese intelligence that had handed the two boys to the Egyptian Jihad Group, not knowing that they would be tried and executed. Al-Zawahiri was seen by the Khartoum government as running a 'state within a state', and was told to leave immediately. But, despite being kicked out of Sudan, al-Qaeda had ample time to begin anew, and rebuild an organisation that seemed to have died in the aftermath of the 1991 Gulf War. Afghanistan would once more provide the stage for al-Qaeda.

The third stage: al-Qaeda goes global

Bin Laden flew out of Sudan in July 1996, travelling straight to Jalalabad in the south-east of Afghanistan, as did many of his al-Qaeda followers who had

---

another front. Some of its best fighters were in Algeria fighting alongside the GIA, before 'disappearing' in mysterious circumstances after a quarrel with the GIA leadership.

23. Al-Zawahiri ordered the halt in operations on the pretext that the group had lost the capacity to do so, after the security forces had arrested hundreds of its members. That decision was kept secret, and only became known years later. It seems that al-Zawahiri did not want to announce his decision in case it was interpreted as a recognition of defeat.

been with him in Khartoum. Afghanistan was then witnessing a tremendous transition – the Taliban were emerging as the real power, at the expense of the old *mujahidin* factions that had driven the Soviets out of Afghanistan in the late 1980s, before fighting amongst themselves. Bin Laden was soon to become a guest of the Taliban, who considered him an 'inherited guest' and promised him shelter.[24] Bin Laden was grateful for their gesture, and was soon to repay his debt to the Taliban: it was his fighters who were to play an important role in defending Kabul from a massive attack by the Northern Alliance, which ensured the Taliban's retention of power in 1998.

In Afghanistan, bin Laden was quick to resume his activities.[25] Among his first actions in Afghanistan was to reorganise al-Qaeda, in an effort to win more recruits. Before that, however, he needed to understand why the jihadist movements he had backed in Egypt, Libya and Algeria had failed in their attempts to topple what he and they still considered 'apostate' regimes. In reaching an understanding of the causes of this failure, bin Laden had to seek help from one of his most trusted friends: al-Zawahiri. The leader of the Jihad Group in Egypt had also been kicked out of Sudan, but he had decided to go to Chechnya instead of Afghanistan – though he proved unable to make it to that destination: he was arrested by the Dagestani authorities and imprisoned because his entry papers were forged. He spent several months in prison, before bin Laden and several other people in Afghanistan who knew where he was were able to bribe the Dagestani police – who did not know his true identity. Al-Zawahiri was set free, and was now able to find his way back to Afghanistan. Once there, his close relationship with bin Laden became even stronger, and al-Qaeda and the Jihad Group came to operate as a single organisation – although their formal merger was not completed until June 2001. Having nowhere else to go, bin Laden and al-Zawahiri

24. When bin Laden returned to Afghanistan from Sudan in 1996, he was protected by the Nangarhar Shura in Jalalabad, a local council of Islamic leaders that was not aligned with either the government of Burhanuddin Rabbani in Kabul or the Taliban in Kandahar. When Jalalabad fell to the Taliban in September 1996, bin Laden offered his support to the new rulers, who in turn accepted him as an 'inherited guest'.

25. Bin Laden gave some television interviews with the international media. It could be argued that he was keen on a quick resumption of his activities in order to show his former hosts – the Sudanese – his displeasure at being told to leave (having previously kept quiet in Sudan in order not to upset its government).

reached the conclusion that the jihadists needed to go global; there was no longer any point in fighting the local 'apostate' regimes in the Middle East, such as in Egypt, Algeria and Libya. The West, according to this analysis, would never allow them to fall.[26] Thus, instead of fighting a losing battle against these regimes, the fight should aim at their backers – the West in general, and America in particular. This conclusion was made crystal clear in the formation of a new group in February 1998, which was dedicated to fighting the Americans – the 'World Islamic Front for Jihad against Jews and Crusaders'.

This 'World Islamic Front' which issued a *fatwa* making the killing of Americans 'an individual duty for every Muslim who can do it in any country in which it is possible to do it', included, in addition to bin Laden and al-Zawahiri, Rifa'i Ahmad Taha (Abu-Yasir), from the Egyptian Islamic Group; Shaykh Mir Hamzah, secretary of the Jamiat-ul-Ulema-e-Pakistan; and Fazlur Rahman, *amir* of the Jihad Movement in Bangladesh. The signature of Rifa'i Taha, in particular, on this *fatwa* by the World Islamic Front, caused uproar within his organisation, the Islamic Group. Rifa'i was the leader of the group in exile, but the rest of the leadership was mostly imprisoned inside Egypt. The two sides already had different opinions on many issues in the second half of the 1990s, especially when it became clear that the jihadists had lost the battle against the regime. The leadership of the Islamic Group inside Egypt decided to announce a total halt to operations in the summer of 1997,[27] but Rifa'i replied by claiming responsibility for a massacre against tourists visiting Luxor in November of that year.[28] Rifa'i's position became untenable when he went further, joining bin Laden and al-Zawahiri in the

---

26. Although bin Laden supported the jihadists in Algeria, Egypt and Libya, he had one reservation about their work in Libya: he argued that the Gaddafi regime was at odds with the US government, and that it would therefore be wrong to fight against it. Some Libyan members of al-Qaeda, while based in Sudan in 1995, asked him to allow them to leave his organisation in order to join the LIFG, which was engaged in *jihad* against the Libyan government. He did allow them to do so, and they joined the LIFG's fight against Colonel Gaddafi's regime.

27. It should be noted that the leaders of the Islamic Group stress that their decision to end the fight was not related in any way to their defeat at the hands of the security forces. They say that their decision resulted from internal debates in the first half of the 1990s.

28. In this massacre, fifty-eight tourists were killed at the hands of four members of the Islamic Group.

World Front. But the imprisoned leaders of the group had the upper hand, and forced him to clarify that his signature on the Front's *fatwa* did not represent the Islamic Group. Soon after that, Rifa'i stepped down from his position in the Islamic Group, and was replaced by a supporter of the policy of halting operations inside Egypt.[29]

Bin Laden and al-Zawahiri had lost Taha's Islamic Group of Egypt, but equally important was the absence of the Algerian and Libyan jihadists, whose failure in their *jihad* was to lead to the creation of the World Islamic Front. The Algerian group leading the *jihad*, the GIA, seems not to have been consulted by bin Laden and al-Zawahiri about the creation of the new 'Front for Jihad against Jews and Crusaders', apparently because of the infighting within the GIA, which led to the creation of more than a dozen splinter groups that were busy deciding what direction to take, after it had become clear that they were no longer able to topple the government. The fact that the leadership of these splinter groups was still based inside Algeria may also have hindered any proper consultation in person with bin Laden and al-Zawahiri, both of whom were based at that time far away, in Afghanistan. However, a small group of Algerian Islamists, disillusioned with what had happened in their country, did travel to Afghanistan to work with bin Laden and al-Qaeda – but it is not known whether they tried to create a group to re-launch the *jihad* in Algeria.[30]

As for the LIFG, its relationship with bin Laden and those around him was always good. However, the group – despite its defeat in Libya – was still able to resist bin Laden's invitation to join him in the newly formed World Islamic Front, with al-Zawahiri and Taha. The big difference between the LIFG and the Algerian GIA was that, while the Algerian group splintered after its defeat, the splintered groups remained inside Algeria, whereas the defeat of the Libyan group at the hands of Gaddafi's security forces did not

29. Rifa'i Taha was replaced as head of the Islamic Group in exile by Mustapha Hamza, the leader of the June 1995 assassination attempt against President Mubarak in Addis Ababa. By the time Hamza replaced Taha, the former was a supporter of the peace initiative the Islamic Group had launched in 1997. Hamza and Taha are now being held in Egypt.

30. Some of the Algerians who went to Afghanistan became disillusioned with the GIA's *jihad* and the allegations that it was 'infiltrated' by the security services, especially after the group claimed responsibility for killing hundreds of innocent Algerians during 1997 and 1998. Some of those Algerian jihadists later decided to join the fight against the Russians in Chechnya.

lead to the splintering of the group. Its leadership relocated to Turkey, from which it reviewed its policies and mistakes. It decided to call a halt to its operations inside Libya. It stayed in that country until 1999/2000, when it relocated again to Afghanistan. But, even there, it still persisted in its resistance to making its struggle a global one, as al-Qaeda was trying to do. It stated clearly that its fight was confined to Libya; it may have shared bin Laden's hate for the American government, but it decided that its war was with Gaddafi and not the Americans.

Meanwhile, bin Laden was actively pursuing his goal: fighting the Americans. His World Islamic Front was soon to translate its threats against the Americans into action; in August 1998, bin Laden's organisation blew up the US embassies in Nairobi and Dar es Salaam, before attacking the USS *Cole* in Aden in October 2000, and then moving on to its biggest attack ever – the 9/11 *ghazwa* ('raid') against New York and Washington in 2001.With these attacks, a new stage in the history of al-Qaeda would dramatically unfold.

The fourth stage: al-Qaeda's franchises

The attacks of 9/11 drew a quick response from the Americans, which bin Laden may not have expected to unfold in the way it did – especially in relation to Washington's ability to bring the Pakistanis on board for its declared 'Global War on Terror'. It took the Americans only a few weeks to drive the Taliban government out of Kabul,[31] at which point al-Qaeda and the other jihadist groups based in Afghanistan found themselves on the run. Their best option was the tribal territory of Pakistan and the big cities, where it was thought to be easy to hide. However, with the Pakistani security organisations working with the Americans, hiding was not easy. Hundreds of suspected al-Qaeda activists were arrested, some ending up in the Guantánamo Bay detention camp in Cuba.

Al-Qaeda and the Egyptian Islamic Jihad (the Jihad Group) paid a heavy price in America's response to 9/11; but the Americans seem to have made a mistake in the way they reacted against all jihadists, not only those connected to the attacks on American soil. The Americans, in their angry response, considered most jihadists based in Afghanistan as one single group. Al-Qaeda operatives were pursued in the same way as were other jihadists.

---

31. The Taliban government withdrew from Kabul on 13 November 2001.

For example, the leaders of the LIFG who managed to flee Afghanistan in 2001 were followed all over the world, despite the fact that they were not part of al-Qaeda's war against the Americans. The Libyan group's two most important leaders were caught and handed over to Libya.[32] Egyptian jihadists were also followed and arrested, and many were rendered to their country of origin. On the face of it, the Americans seemed to have achieved successes in fighting against al-Qaeda and its sisters on more than one front.

Then, in March 2003, came the invasion of Iraq, by which the Americans eventually came to feel trapped. Not only did they misjudge the Iraqi response to their invasion, they made the fatal mistake of going to war based on two lies that discredited them: the claims of Iraq's WMD capabilities and of a link between Saddam and al-Qaeda, both of which turned out to be false. What made things even worse for the Americans was the reaction of ordinary young Arabs, who were even more outraged by the revelations of what some American soldiers had done at Abu Ghraib prison. Many young men from across the Arab world showed a keen desire to go to Iraq and join what they considered to be a *jihad* against the occupiers of a Muslim country.[33]

Al-Qaeda took advantage of the fact that America was focusing on Iraq, and started to reorganise itself somewhere on the Afghan–Pakistani borders, especially in the tribal areas of Pakistan. But because the security situation was still very risky, al-Qaeda was confined mostly to the tribal 'Pashtun belt' along the borders (especially the Federally Administered Tribal Areas and the North-West Frontier Province), with bin Laden and his deputy al-Zawahiri moving between the two sides of the border.

This fact led to al-Qaeda becoming more decentralised; it could no longer have overall control of what its operatives were trying to do. But al-Qaeda was desperate to launch more operations against the Americans, in order to prove that it was not defeated. For that reason, it had to accept help from people who were not even members of al-Qaeda, but who were willing to extend a helping hand to bin Laden. Abu Musab al-Zarqawi made his name in Iraq. A Jordanian Islamist, he had been in Afghanistan at the time of 9/11, and had to flee when the Americans began their invasion. At that time, however,

---

32. Abu Abdullah al-Sadek and Abu al-Mundhir, the *amir* of the LIFG and head of the religious committee, were held in Thailand and China, respectively, in 2004, and then handed back to Libya.

33. It is estimated that hundreds of young Arabs went to Iraq as early as 2003 to join the war against the Americans.

al-Zarqawi was still working as an independent jihadist, having turned down an invitation from bin Laden to join al-Qaeda. Zarqawi found his way to Iraq just before the Americans started their war in 2003. He created his own organisation (Al-Tawhid wa'l-Jihad), and began his attacks against the Americans and other Iraqis he saw as collaborating with them – the Shi'is in particular. But Zarqawi was not Iraqi, and he represented only one faction of what became known as the Resistance. He therefore decided to join forces with bin Laden. This alliance would channel recruits to his organisation in Iraq – especially from among the young Saudis who were volunteering to become suicide bombers in Iraq, al-Zarqawi's deadliest weapon. Swearing allegiance to bin Laden also brought al-Zarqawi financial help from those in the Gulf who wanted to give money to the Resistance. What better 'display of piety' could there be other than giving help to an organisation 'blessed' by bin Laden? The latter, in return, would be credited for the operations carried out by al-Zarqawi in the name of al-Qaeda, which were already causing the Americans considerable pain. Al-Qaeda would be seen as making the Americans suffer in their Iraqi quicksands.

What was correct in Iraq was also correct in other countries. Thus, in addition to the creation of al-Qaeda in Iraq, other franchises of al-Qaeda also appeared: al-Qaeda in the Arab Peninsula, al-Qaeda in the Islamic Maghreb (North Africa), al-Qaeda in Ard al-Kinana (Egypt), and al-Qaeda in the Bilad al-Sham (Syria, Lebanon, Jordan and Palestine), as well as the 'military wing' of al-Qaeda in Europe. Some of these franchises managed to launch attacks, but some were more successful than others.

In Egypt there were few attacks, but those that occurred – in Sinai in 2004 and 2005 – caused significant loss of life, though al-Qaeda never took credit for them. In Saudi Arabia, the al-Qaeda branch was very active between 2003 (when it launched its first attack) and 2005; but the Saudi security forces seem to have been able to dismantle much of the al-Qaeda hierarchy and its 'sleeper cells'. Today, either al-Qaeda seems to have decided to halt its operations and regroup in the kingdom, or the security forces have always been successful in pre-empting its attacks and arresting its members or supporters. In 2008, the remnants of the dismantled branch of al-Qaeda in Saudi Arabia joined forces with al-Qaeda's branch in Yemen and re-launched the group under the title al-Qaeda in the Arabian Peninsula (AQAP).

Al-Qaeda has also been very active in North Africa – especially since the summer of 2006, when it became clear that the Salafist Group for Preaching and Combat (GSPC) was seeking to become part of bin Laden's group. It did so in January 2007, and soon started a campaign of suicide bombings against government and foreign targets. This branch of al-Qaeda was thought to be operating across North Africa, but its base was certainly in Algeria. In 2007, a leader of the LIFG also announced that it had merged with al-Qaeda, though the leaders of the group inside Libyan prisons were known to have objected to that.[34]

However, al-Qaeda's biggest dilemma was the prospect of facing possible isolation somewhere on the Afghan–Pakistani borders, and thus losing direct control over the activities of its franchises. The clearest example of this was al-Qaeda's first franchise – the Zarqawi-established branch of al-Qaeda in Iraq.

Al-Zarqawi is understood to have concluded that the Americans' Shi'i allies presented the biggest danger to his plans in Iraq, and started directing his attacks against them and their leaders. These attacks may not have met with the approval of al-Qaeda's main branch (spanning Pakistan and Afghanistan), but it was powerless to restrain al-Zarqawi. He was the '*amir*' in Iraq, and it was his right to choose the policies he deemed effective. Al-Qaeda might have been worried that al-Zarqawi's actions could drive the Iranians to react – Shi'i Iran was an important transit route for al-Qaeda operatives, and also held some important al-Qaeda leaders who it refused to hand over either to their own countries or to the Americans.

But al-Zarqawi's actions became intolerable to the al-Qaeda leadership on the Afghan–Pakistani borders when he began a campaign against Sunni tribal leaders and other insurgent groups who refused to join him, and when he tried to extend his sphere of influence outside Iraq. He sent suicide bombers who blew themselves up in Amman in November 2005, causing outrage among Muslims when it became clear that ordinary Muslims had died in these attacks. The al-Qaeda headquarters in Waziristan immediately sent him a letter, threatening to sack him if he conducted any further such operations without prior consultation with them.[35] It was this rebuke that forced

34. In November 2007, Abu Laith al-Libi announced the merging of his group, LIFG, with al-Qaeda. He was killed in an American raid in Pakistan in January 2008. In the summer of 2009, the leaders of the LIFG in Libyan prisons issued a 417-page document ('Corrective Studies on the Doctrine of Jihad, Hesba and Ruling') in which they distanced themselves from actions claimed by extremist Islamist groups, including groups influenced by al-Qaeda's ideology.

35. Atiyeh Abdelrahman, the al-Qaeda member who was bin Laden's envoy to

al-Zarqawi to make some important changes to his policies: he had to allow the Iraqis to take the lead role in his organisation, which was re-branded as *Shura al-Mujahidin* (Council of Mujahidin) in Iraq; al-Zarqawi's actions had alienated many of the resistance factions in Iraq and much of the population. The Americans were able to kill him in June 2006, from which point al-Qaeda in Iraq seems to have gone downhill. Although it remained able to launch attacks, they were not on as large a scale as they had previously been. Nevertheless, this group remains undefeated.

It seems clear that al-Qaeda might not have become the worldwide Islamic movement that it is today, had the Americans not gone into Iraq based on a set of justifications which turned out to be pure lies, and had they taken a different approach in dealing with the jihadist groups that I term al-Qaeda's 'sisters'. Those jihadists, I would argue, were products of their own circumstances in their own countries. They rose against governments they accused of being 'apostate', but they were never an integral part of al-Qaeda, despite supporting the 'Islamic' aims bin Laden claims to defend. Their focus was local – limited to fighting Arab rulers in order either to topple them or to force them into applying *shari'a* law. The American Global War on Terror, which tended to lump them together with al-Qaeda, had the effect of giving them almost no choice but to become part of bin Laden's worldwide struggle against the West.

In fact, the Arab jihadists were, by the end of the 1990s, more or less a defeated force. They had launched what they thought was a *jihad* against their 'apostate' rulers, but had met a similar fate to al-Qaeda's branches: defeat. In Algeria, Libya and Egypt – the three main battlegrounds for the jihadists during the 1990s – the security forces had gained decisive victories against the Islamic fighters, forcing them to analyse the reasons for the setbacks in their *jihads*.

In Algeria, that reassessment led the Islamists into splitting into two main camps. One was led by supporters of the Islamic Salvation Front (FIS), the party that was deprived of victory in the 1991 general elections by the military-backed government. This camp decided to lay down arms and begin peace talks with the authorities, which granted amnesty to those who surrendered.

---

the GIA in Algeria, sent a letter to al-Zarqawi from al-Qaeda's headquarters in the Waziristan region of Pakistan, dated 11 December 2005, in which he said he risked removal as al-Qaeda's leader in Iraq if he continued his policies. Atiyeh had been a friend of al-Zarqawi when the latter had been based in Herat (Afghanistan) in the late 1990s.

The other camp was led by remnants of the Armed Islamic Group (GIA), the most extreme of the militant groups active in Algeria, which decided to continue its *jihad*. This camp was fragmented and weak, however, and was losing ever more support from among the population because it was pursuing a policy that went against the wishes of the general public, who were clearly in favour of a peace settlement between the government and the Islamist opposition. This resulted in the marginalisation of the Islamists who rejected the peace efforts, who were led by a splinter group of the GIA, the Salafist Group for Preaching and Combat (GSPC). But the GSPC was still, at the time of 9/11 attacks, a 'local' jihadist group whose aims were more or less limited to Algeria, and had not become part of al-Qaeda's war against the West.

In Libya, the LIFG followed a similar path to that of the Algerian Jihadists. The Libyan Islamists realised that they were a defeated force by the end of the 1990s, but their reassessment of why their *jihad* had failed led them only as far as calling for a cessation of any operations inside Libya, and a reloca-tion into the 'safe haven' of Afghanistan. By the time of the 9/11 attacks, the LIFG was a group whose aim was still 'local' – limited to Libya – and it was not part of al-Qaeda's struggle against the West.

In Egypt, the defeat of the jihadists at the hands of the security forces led the militant Islamists into a further reappraisal of their aims, which resulted in their dividing into two broad camps. The 'Islamic Group' concluded that it had been wrong all along in declaring a *jihad* against the regime, and retreated from its past assertions of the regime's apostasy. In contrast, the 'Jihad Group' refused to back away from its accusation that the regime was apostate, making it lawful for its members and supporters to fight a *jihad* against the government. However, despite sticking to this policy of consid-ering the Egyptian regime as 'apostate', the Jihad Group realised that it was a defeated organisation inside Egypt, and ordered a ceasefire on the part of its members. By the time of the 9/11 attacks, the main militant group, the Islamic Group, had already sought reconciliation with the regime, despite the insistence of the Jihad Group of Ayman al-Zawahiri on the regime's apostasy. Nevertheless, the latter group, by its own admission, was a defeated organisation, unable to launch any attacks inside Egypt.

But all these 'defeated' organisations seem to have been able to repopu-late their ranks as a result of the American reaction to the 9/11 attacks, and the 'adventure' that led them into Iraq in 2003. They did so by allying themselves with al-Qaeda's worldwide war against America and the West, instead of focusing on their local aims in their own countries. The Algerian GSPC was quick to use the war in Iraq, in particular, to its own advantage, by recruiting many of the frustrated Algerian youth who wanted to fight the 'American occupiers' in Iraq, as well as to start a new campaign against the government – this time in the name of al-Qaeda's franchise in North Africa. Some elements of the Libyan LIFG, in turn, tried to use the war in Iraq to their advantage by mobilising the Libyan youth who also wanted to fight the Americans. But the LIFG had an internal problem that prevented it from taking full advantage of the Iraq War: its main leaders, including the group's *amir*, his deputy, and the heads of the military and religious committees, had all been captured and were imprisoned. So, when the leader of the LIFG in Afghanistan, Abu Laith al-Libi, announced in 2007 that his organisation had merged with al-Qaeda, his announcement lacked the credibility of having the backing of the group's known leadership, which was held in Libyan prisons. This ambiguity regarding the real position of the LIFG leadership on the merger with al-Qaeda seems to have left the jihadists inside Libya with no proper jihadist organisation to lead and direct them.

This leaves the Egyptian jihadists. Despite the 9/11 attacks and the American war against Iraq and the jihadists in general, the 'Islamic Group' remained true to its 'rethinking' (*muraja'a*): it never wavered in condemning any use of violence against the Egyptian regime, going as far as promising to deliver to the authorities any of its members who proposed resuming the fight against the government. The 'Jihad Group' also suffered a setback when one of its former leading members – Dr Fadl – attacked what he called the misuse by certain groups of the word *jihad* as a universal Islamic justification for carrying out attacks that are not sanctioned by the Islamic religion, and even goes as far as violating its teachings. However, the top leader of the 'Jihad Group', Ayman al-Zawahiri, seems to be sticking to his ideology that considers the regime in Egypt – along with the rest of the regimes in the Arab world – as 'apostate', and favours a continuation of the war against the West. Although the attacks against the tourist sites in Sinai that took place in 2004 and 2005 have never been linked officially to al-Zawahiri's group, it is almost certain that those who carried them out were influenced by this ideology, if not directly connected with it.

If this is the current situation of these jihadist groups in the Middle East today, then it seems clear that al-Qaeda, as a result of the American 'War on Terror', has been able to transform itself into a global movement, with branches and franchises all over the world. Different jihadist groups have been forced to join bin Laden's struggle against the West, using the Iraq War – a war based on lies – to revive their depleted ranks. However, despite this expansion of bin Laden's organisation, there seems to be an inherent weakness in this 'new' al-Qaeda: the franchises of bin Laden's group can certainly continue to launch attacks against 'Western interests', but they seem unable, on their own, to topple the 'apostate' governments against which they took up arms in the first place. Another difficulty is illustrated by al-Qaeda's franchise in Iraq, governed by al-Zarqawi's 'independent' policies: the authority and control of bin Laden over his franchises can become weak, allowing some to operate in a way with which he himself would not necessarily feel comfortable.

TWELVE

Islam and Muslims in Europe: Changes and Challenges

Tariq Ramadan

Over the past generation a profound change has been taking place among younger Muslims in Europe. Fifty years ago, most Muslims were immigrants who came looking for work and a new future. They had made no great study of Islam and continued religious practices they used to conduct back in their countries of origin. Their plans were to work briefly in Europe, save money and return home as soon as they could. For the most part, this first generation came from simple backgrounds heavily marked by their culture of origin, whether Indo-Pakistani, North African or Turkish.

Assuming that their stay was temporary, parents at first tried to protect themselves from this unfamiliar European environment rather than integrate themselves into it. But most of these original immigrants never left. Their children were born in Europe, became fluent in their national language and became better educated than their elders. The parents' dream of going home faded. Religious leaders, who had tended to be either appointees of governments or Islamic militants in exile, found themselves obliged to adapt to the situation of their young people, speak their language, reshape the format of religious education and redefine their structures of social and cultural activity. The emergence of this new generation of European Muslims has resulted in a new way of thinking and talking about the nature of Islamic communities here.

Changes

The last fifteen years have seen an enormous change within Europe's Muslim communities. There is upheaval as generations of children born here move to the fore: associations of Muslim activists have increased in size and number, and there are new voices talking about citizenship and political participation and claiming inherent rights to nationality. There is also a more visible commitment to fighting discrimination in areas such as employment, places of worship, state subsidies and so on. This is happening throughout Europe, though it varies according to how long there has been a Muslim presence. But in the end, Muslim integration into the fabric of Europe will have three main strands – straightforward taking-on of citizenship, involvement in society and politics at all levels and the demand for financial and political independence.

Europe is not virgin territory, however. Integration may be becoming a reality, yet the Muslim communities settled in Europe are still seen by some of the countries of origin as their own private preserve, where they mean to act on the same principles and use the same methods they apply to their own citizens at home.

The 1960s to 1980s saw associations for Algerians, Moroccans, Tunisians and Turks spring up all over Europe. They brought expatriates together, with the aim of making it possible for them to meet each other – but also for their embassies to keep a closer eye on them. One might have expected that, with the changes taking places in Europe, practices like this would have decreased and that surveillance – if there had to be any – would henceforth be a matter just for the European states. Not a bit of it. In fact, the reverse is true.

In the name of security, a close watch is being kept all over Europe. There is a sophisticated set-up of surveillance and intelligence-gathering. It is aimed primarily at 'national dissidents'. Tunisian (undoubtedly the most efficient), Moroccan, Algerian, Turkish and even Saudi intelligence services, sometimes directly connected with their embassies, gather information, infiltrate associations, keep watch in the mosques and attend conferences and symposiums where they make sure that – with varying degrees of subtlety – their voice is heard. Playing on the sensitive issue of the 'Islamic threat', official and unofficial agents of the countries of origin also do a particularly effective PR job on journalists, local councillors and up to the highest levels in the government.

These local agencies of the foreign powers are legion throughout Europe and they use the pretext of their interest in the Islamic question to exert a major political influence. Monitoring their own dissidents does not satisfy their obsession with security. Often, British, Italian, French or Belgian nationals will – because of their parents' origins – be subjected to the same surveillance. And if they visit their families' home country (of which they may no longer be nationals), they are questioned at length about their activities and contacts.

Besides this interference by security authorities on European soil, there is another source of concern: the countries of origin still seek to wield exclusive control over the major Muslim institutions in Europe. Beyond the financing of the great mosques, like those in Rome, Madrid, Paris, Lyon, Brussels, Geneva and London, this involves keeping a tight political hold over them. The official pronouncements of these outposts follow the dictates of the authority financing them. What can be said is controlled, and those in charge are supervised.

What is Europe doing?

Faced with this strategy of surveillance, and keeping a tight hold over European Islam, what is the attitude of the European countries – since this is plainly interference in their internal affairs? The official line seems clear. Britain, France, Germany and Belgium all say they now recognise Islam as a fact of European life, that they hope to see the emergence of European citizens who have Islam as their religion and take charge of their future, who organise their own representation and achieve political and financial autonomy.

However, European countries seem to be being taken hostage by foreign states, who are making use of the religion of their own people to impose policies favourable to themselves. So it is a struggle for power as well as for religious belief. But a closer analysis shows this conflict is not quite so clear cut. Even though the discourse on citizenship for the Muslims of Europe is being raised more and more by the political actors (who have to concern themselves with the number of potential voters), the fact remains that Islam in Europe is prey to an obsession with security and a desire to control.

Far from providing reassurance, the fabric of Muslim associations that has grown so much denser over recent years, with a new generation of Muslims demanding citizenship and rights and an active part in politics, is generating fear. These new Muslims may be European, but they are still Muslim. And they are upsetting the old lines of demarcation – they are not like the old Muslim leaders who were so docile and so little nuisance.

Against this background, intervention from abroad, rather than being a problem, could be in the short-term interest of the European states. The latter could profit from the surveillance carried out by foreign agents on their territory, as well as from the indirect hold the Muslim states have over the mosques and other large institutions. In both cases, this would ensure political and religious control of the situation. The various intelligence services are in permanent contact with each other, and where the organisation of Islam is concerned, the European countries have everything to gain from doing deals with the agencies of foreign states; it makes it easier for them to negotiate, or indeed lay down, rules of conduct as part of friendly exchanges between governments.

As it is, many European countries still see Islam as something not only foreign, but dangerous to boot, and at all events a source of instability. They prefer to deal on the quiet with the dictatorships of the Muslim-majority countries, which may not observe the law, but serve the strategies of Western governments and protect their interests. Virtually all the European states want autonomy from their countries of origin for their Muslims and yet they pursue a policy based on affiliations and allegiances with the governments of origin (and on information gleaned from the various intelligence services).

In the years ahead, the states of Europe are going to have to rethink how they cope with their Muslims and with Islam. The associative movement proliferating all over Europe is producing full Muslim citizens of those countries – citizens who are politically and financially independent and are already beginning to ask questions about the justification for the Europeans' links with the dictatorships of the Muslim world. Already, they are claiming the right to organise themselves on their own and decide for themselves the legitimacy of their religious representation. This is a fast-growing phenomenon. Whatever the countries of origin may want, they are losing ground, and second- and third-generation Muslims feel fewer and fewer ties with the countries their parents and grandparents came from.

If Europe is to succeed in the tricky venture of achieving cultural and religious pluralism in its societies, then there is an urgent need for it to move away from security-based thinking, in order to encourage dialogue, negotiation and confidence between states and their citizens: the only democratic way is one that respects both the law and its citizens.

New societies, new Europe

A silent revolution is taking place. Old concepts that divided the world into two hostile camps – Islamic versus non-Islamic – are outdated and need to be reviewed. European constitutions allow Muslims to practise their religion, and should therefore be respected. Religious principles should not be confused with culture of origin: European Muslims should only be Muslim, instead of forever remaining North African, Pakistani or Turkish Muslims. Active citizenship has to be encouraged and a European Islamic culture needs to be created. How? By respecting Islamic principles while adopting European tastes and styles.

Mentalities are changing fast. Islamic associations are active at the local level, building bridges and encouraging Muslim citizens to vote. New artistic voices are being heard. Although this energy and vitality are particularly visible in countries with the oldest Muslim presence, the same phenomenon is underway elsewhere too. But numerous challenges remain and the day when Muslims and their fellow citizens can live together in harmony is still far off. A series of stumbling blocks exists within Muslim communities that need to be reformed.

Too many Muslims are getting things mixed up. Problems of discrimination in housing or the workplace should not be taken as 'attacks on Islam', but as the effects of social policies that we must commit ourselves to changing, as citizens demanding equal rights. Muslims must not fall into a 'victim mentality', and the alibi that Islamophobia is preventing them from flourishing. It is up to Muslims to assume their responsibilities, construct clear arguments, engage in dialogue both within their own communities and with their fellow citizens and reject the simplistic vision of 'us versus them'.

Common values of equality, justice and respect should be promoted in the name of a shared 'ethic of citizenship'. Over time, Muslims must do away with the temptation to shut themselves off as an isolated minority, for otherwise they offer encouragement to those extremist voices that argue: 'You are more Muslim when you're against the West.' The Muslims of Europe must be more self-critical.

But their non-Muslim fellow citizens need to make an effort too. They need to accept that Europe's population has changed, that it no longer has a single history and that the future calls for mutual understanding and respect. They need to face up to their ignorance and reject the clichés and prejudices that surround Islam. They must start discussing the principles, values and forms that will enable us to live together.

The new Muslim presence poses a series of unavoidable questions to all the citizens of Europe. Are you prepared to study the history of a civilisation that is present in your lives and which forms part of your pluralistic society? Do you sincerely believe that Muslims – with their spirituality, ethics and ·creativity – have a positive contribution to make?

The future of Europe will be built by all those who accept this challenge. It will be based on self-criticism, lasting and demanding dialogue, respect for diversity and the expression of common values. The path leads from simple integration to mutual enrichment. It is going to take time and, above all, it means that we are going to have to start trusting each other. After September 11, that is the biggest single challenge we face.

What is common? What is diverse? Some essential questions

The presence of millions of Muslims in Europe has begun to raise a series of questions that are being asked in similar ways in each country: Are Muslim citizens about to change our culture and our traditions? Are our Greco-Roman and Judeo-Christian values under threat? How do we define and protect our identity? With their long history of welcoming immigrants, and due to the nature of their Muslim populations, European societies are at the forefront in addressing these issues, as well as in putting forward new answers that are emerging from these Western Muslim communities.

It is important to begin by specifying the fundamental nature of the problem: the increased visibility of Muslims in European society is leading towards a genuine crisis of identity. As old reference points seem to disappear it becomes harder to believe that Muslims can be fully Europeans. A feeling of confusion has emerged among 'ordinary people', oscillating between doubt over their ability to preserve their culture and fear of being invaded by the customs and values of the other: the European citizens with a Muslim background. Doubt and fear commonly provoke reactions of shutting out or of rejection, both of which are characteristics of an identity crisis.

European Muslims need to pay more attention to the doubts and fears that their fellow citizens have. They should become aware that those of their fellow citizens who are not Muslims are not comfortable with the way that

Muslims define themselves, or with their own relationship towards Islam. While the general atmosphere is full of suspicion, Muslims have a duty to establish intellectual, social, cultural and political spaces for the development of trust and appeasement. This has to begin with an engagement in a clear discussion of Islam and about the practices and the values that Muslims promote. Islam is not a culture but a body of principles and universal values. One should not mix up these universal principles with a Pakistani, Turkish or Arab way of living them. In this way, Islam allows Muslims to adopt aspects of the new cultures and environments they find themselves in, as long as it does not oppose any clear prohibition specified by their own religion. Thus, while practising their religion, they can preserve certain features of their own culture of origin in the form of richness and not dogmas. At the same time, they can integrate themselves into European cultures, which become a new dimension of their own identity. This is a process that is not only normal, but desirable.

European Muslims need to find again this intellectual, social and political creativity that has been missing (and sometimes killed) for so long in the Islamic world. What the Muslims' consciousness here has yet to learn and to formulate in a confident manner is an acceptance of European cultures through a process of making them their own and not to keep perceiving a contradiction in being both Muslim and European, as long as freedom of conscience and freedom of worship are protected. European legislations recognise and protect the fundamental rights of all citizens and residents. This common legal framework needs to be pushed forward, because it allows equality within diversity. Common European citizenship does not prevent a diversity of cultures and of belonging. European societies have been changing and the presence of Muslims has forced them to experience an even greater diversity of cultures. As a result, a European identity has evolved that is open, plural and constantly in motion, thanks to the cross-fertilisation between reclaimed cultures of origin and the European cultures that now include new (Muslim) citizens.

Multicultural societies

Seen from this perspective, the new European Muslim citizenship is enriching for the whole of society. Muslims should live it and introduce it in this manner to their fellow citizens. Of course, this compels them to come out from the intellectual and social ghettos within which they have lodged themselves, often in a complacent manner. Living together and building a truly multicultural society does not mean merely being satisfied with the existence of communities of faith or juxtaposed cultures, whose members ignore each other, never meet and remain enclosed within their own universe of symbolic reference points. Nothing should be stranger, in our way of living and allowing for a mutual exchange of ideas between our communities, than a model of parallel lives which in reality masks a state of mutual ignorance.

Our responsibilities are shared. Members of the so-called traditional European societies can, at times, doubt their own identity and become frightened. When this happens, they have to refuse any imprisoning reaction by attempting, for example, to draw the boundaries of what they may consider to be an authentic European identity that is 'pure' and uninfected by some 'foreign parasite'. In any period of crisis, the temptation to fall back upon phantoms of national identity is stronger than ever, as people are carried away by fear, spilling over into the same camp as populists of the extreme right – a phenomenon which we are unfortunately witnessing all over Europe at the moment.

History, memories

We need to begin by working upon memories. From the Middle Ages, Islam has participated in the building of a European consciousness in the same way that Judaism and Christianity have. From Shakespeare to Hume, the influences of Islamic civilisation on the literary and philosophical traditions of the time are innumerable. Horizons need to be broadened through the study of these sources, which should be included in the teaching curricula at both secondary and university level.

This wider, deeper and more subtle understanding of what has moulded European identity throughout history would naturally help all people in this society to open up towards each other, including towards Muslims, and to understand that they are not so very different or strange when judged by their values and hopes. A truly multicultural society cannot exist without an education in the complexity of what shapes us and in the common dimensions that we share with others, despite our differences. The extension of this education consists in developing partnerships willing to engage together in social and political issues that affect us all, including discrimination (against women, minorities and so on), racism, unemployment and other social and urban political issues. European societies must reach this new perception of themselves collectively: with their people, all equal before the law, developing multidimensional identities that are always in motion and that are flexible enough to defend their shared values. It remains imperative to distinguish between social problems and religious challenges: Muslim and non-Muslim citizens alike need to de-Islamise social fractures, since unemployment, violence and marginalisation have nothing to do with Islam or with Islamic identity. In this way, the multicultural society of today and tomorrow should succeed in marrying the three dimensions of common citizenship, cultural diversity and a convergence of values within a constantly enriching dynamic of debates, encounters and collective engagement.

This is not an easy task, since no one opens up to another person without an effort. It is a matter of studying, re-shifting one's focus, shedding one's intellectual and cultural habits and accepting questions from fellow citizens who are not all the same but whose diversity is none the less enriching. All the laws in the world will never make us dignified and fair citizens, unless we understand that from now on our responsibilities are shared. The law can bring people together and protect them, but it cannot manage an identity crisis. This can only be achieved through education, by looking outside oneself and taking the risk to open up to other cultures, ideas and values – all of which are part of the difficult but exciting challenge of our time.

A new 'We'

If there is a contribution that Muslim Westerners can bring to their respective societies, it is surely that of reconciliation. Confident in convictions, frank and rigorous in their critical outlook, armed with a broader understanding of Western societies, of their values, their history and their aspirations, they are ideally placed to engage their fellow citizens in reconciling these societies with their own ideals. The vital issue today is not to compare social models or experiences in a fruitless debate (as we have witnessed between the United States, France and Great Britain), but more simply, and in a far stricter and more demanding way, to take the measure of each society by comparing the ideals affirmed and proclaimed by its intellectuals and politicians with the concrete practices that can be observed at the social grassroots: human rights and equality of opportunity (between men and women, people of different origins, different skin colours). We must bring constructive criticism to bear on our societies, and measure words against deeds: all citizens must adopt towards their society the same healthy self-critical attitude that Muslims must demonstrate towards their community.

Our societies are awaiting the emergence of a new 'We'. A 'We' that would bring together men and women, citizens of all religions – and those without religion – who would undertake together to resolve the contradictions of their society: the right to work, to housing, to respect, against racism and all forms of discrimination, against all offences to human dignity. Such a 'We' would thereafter represent this coming together of citizens confident in their values, defenders of pluralism in their common society and respectful of the identities of others; citizens who seek to take up the challenge in the name of their shared values at the very heart of their societies. As loyal and critical citizens, as men and women of integrity, they would join forces in a revolution of trust and confidence to stem the onrush of fear. Against shallow, emotional, even hysterical reactions, they would stand firm for rationality, for dialogue, for attentiveness, for a reasoned approach to complex social questions.

Local, national

The future of European societies is now being played out at the local level. It is a matter of the greatest urgency to set in motion national movements of local initiatives, in which women and men of different religions, cultures and sensitivities can open new horizons of mutual understanding and shared commitment: horizons of trust. These shared projects must henceforth bring us together and give birth to a new 'We' anchored in citizenship. Of course, 'intercultural' and 'interfaith' dialogues are both vital and necessary, but they cannot have the impact of the shared commitment of citizens in the priority fields: education, social fracture, insecurity, racism, discrimination and so on.

Together, they must learn to question educational programmes, and to propose more inclusive approaches to the sum of remembered experience that make up today's Western societies. These societies have changed, and the teaching of history must change with them; it must include the multiplicity of these experiences; it must even speak of the dark periods of history, those of which new citizens of the West have often been the original victims. Alongside the Enlightenment, and the progress and achievements of science and technology, something must also be said about slavery, about colonialism, about racism, genocide and more – objectively, without arrogance or a permanent sense of guilt. At the risk of touching off a competition for most-wounded-victim status, a more objective reading of the memories building the current national history must be made official. On the social level, we must commit ourselves to a far more thorough-going social mixing in both our schools and our communities. Far more courageous and creative social and urban policies are needed, of course. But, even now, citizens can foster human interchange in and through projects focused on local democratic participation. National political authorities must cooperate with, facilitate and encourage such local dynamics.

European societies will not win the battle against social insecurity, violence and drugs through a solely security-based approach. What we need in our communities are social institutions, civic education, and local job-creation and confidence-building policies. Local political authorities can do much to transform the prevailing atmosphere of suspicion – and citizens, including Muslims, must not hesitate to knock on their doors, to remind them that in a democratic society the elected representative is at the service of the voter, and not the reverse. It is imperative that we become involved in national affairs, that we do not allow ourselves to be carried away by the passions generated on the international scene. Still, it is clear that a critical discussion of how immigration is managed has yet to take place in the West: it is no longer possible to strip the Third World of its riches and in the same breath treat those who flee poverty and dictatorial regimes as criminals. Not only is such behaviour unjust and inhuman: it is intolerable. To be and to remain the voice of the voiceless of Iraq or Palestine, of Tibet or Chechnya, of abused women or of AIDS victims (particularly in Africa), is to take a stand for reconciliation in the name of the ideals of dignity, human rights and justice – ideals that are too often sacrificed on the altar of short-term political gain and geostrategic interests. In times of globalisation, both local mutual trust and global thinking pave the road towards reconciliation between civilisations.

A revolution of trust and confidence, of critical loyalty, the birth of a new 'We' driven by national movements of local initiative: such are the contours of a responsible commitment by all citizens in Western societies – for they lay claim to the benefits of a responsible, citizen-based ethic; they want to promote the richness of Western culture; they know that survival will depend, imperatively, upon a new sense of political creativity. Citizens must work in the long term, above and beyond the electoral deadlines that paralyse politicians and hinder the formulation of innovative, courageous policies. When an elected official has nowhere to turn, when he can no longer translate his ideas into reality, it falls to the voters, to the citizens, to lay full claim to their ideals and to make them a reality.

THIRTEEN

Moderate Islamist Groups in Europe: the Muslim Brothers

Sara Silvestri

Features of 'Islamism'

Islamist groups can be identified primarily by reference to four characteristics: their objectives, their narrative, their strategy and their location. Bringing about divine justice on earth is their core objective. In theory this implies respecting and implementing *shari'a* law; in practice it urges a commitment to social justice and political reform. The Islamist narrative is full of symbols and references to the exemplary, pious life led by the Prophet Muhammad and his disciples in the Muslim community of Medina. Recreating the 'golden age' of the caliphate (from the Arabic *khalifa* – 'deputy' or 'successor' of Muhammad) is both an objective and a metaphor in the narrative of political Islam. It calls for the establishment of a God-fearing polity governed by the teaching of Islam, but it also symbolises the imitation of the pious and just fathers of Islam, Muhammad and his rightly guided successors. As far as strategy is concerned, Islamist movements have always been characterised by dissent and resistance to the contemporary status quo, guided by a sense of religious revival, whether articulated in opposition to a national government deemed corrupt and areligious or to a foreign occupying force. Mosques and educational centres have been hotbeds of political Islam in countries where the state was failing to protect and care for its citizens and where political institutions were collapsing, absent or had lost the trust of the population.

Looking at membership can also be a useful way to define Islamist groups. If we consider the history of key movements like the branches of the Muslim Brotherhood in North Africa and the Middle East, the Jamaat-i-Islami in Pakistan and South Asia, and their offspring, a constant feature is that their leaders – often educated in Western establishments – and members tend to come from the middle classes. In addition, the mobilisation of university students was a major aspect not only of the spread of the Muslim Brothers, but also for the success of the Iranian Revolution.[1]

However, not all the Islamist formations that we can observe in the West, and in Europe in particular, have retained all these characteristics in terms of objectives, narrative, strategy and location. As we shall see below, once rooted and operating in Europe, Islamist groups can change their agenda and *modus operandi*. They can shift from a position of dissent against the state into one of accommodation, or at least towards forms of dialogue and compromise with political authorities. It is also important to note that Islamism has not been the mainstream ideology and method of political mobilisation adopted by Europe's Muslims.

Muslim political mobilisation in Europe

As Muslims started to settle in Europe in the second half of the twentieth century[2] – first as immigrants, then as citizens – their understanding of and approaches to political mobilisation, whether faith inspired or not, varied significantly. From the outset, the visible emergence of Islam in the European public sphere has been marked by multiple priorities (to retain, protect and assert a religious–cultural identity) and by a number of competing forces: 1) Muslims of immigrant descent creating mosques, prayer rooms and cultural centres; 2) separate initiatives led by European converts to Islam; 3) the emergence of the 'Islam of the states', i.e. activities supported by the governments of the countries of origin or by Muslim countries wielding considerable religious and political influence globally,

1. See G. Kepel, *Jihad: The Trail of Political Islam*, London: I.B. Tauris, 2006; N. Ayubi, *Political Islam: Religion and Politics in the Arab World*, London and New York: Routledge, 1991; S. A. Arjomand, *The Turban for the Crown: The Islamic Revolution in Iran*, New York and Oxford: Oxford University Press, 1988.

2. See, for example, F. Dassetto and A. Basteiner, *Europa: nuova frontiera dell'Islam*, Rome: Edizioni Lavoro, 1988; T. Gerholm and Y. G. Lithman, eds, *The New Islamic Presence in Western Europe*, London: Mansell, 1988; J. Cesari, *Être musulman en France: Associations, militants et mosques*, Paris–Aix-en-Provence: Karthala-Iremam, 1994; G. Kepel, *Allah in the West: Islamic Movements in America and Europe*, Cambridge: Polity, 1997; S. Vertovec and C. Peach, eds, *Islam in Europe: The Politics of Religion and Community*, Basingstoke: Macmillan, 1997.

like Saudi Arabia and Iran – and, to a lesser extent, Morocco and Algeria; 4) diaspora networks promoting the specific national identities and ethnic traditions of the countries of origin; 5) issue-based local groupings and associations devoted to advocacy – often against discrimination – and to service-provision for disadvantaged members of the community; 6) Islamist groups with a transnational agenda.

Domestic and international events have also contributed to shaping the issues of concern to and the type of mobilisation of Europe's Muslims. For instance, Muslim activism took on a more vocal and political nature during and following the 'Rushdie affair' and the 'veil affair' (which exploded in Great Britain and France, respectively, in 1989) and intensified exponentially throughout the 1990s in response to the first US war in Iraq and then to the invasion of Iraq in 2003. Further fuel for this process of politicisation was provided by the publication of the Danish cartoons depicting Muhammad in 2006 and, in early January 2009, by the reaction to the Israeli military response to missiles fired from Gaza.

Most Islamist movements that are present in Europe began as diaspora groups organised by exiles and political refugees concerned with reforming their home countries, or from regions of the world that are experiencing autocracy, corruption and lack of freedoms. This explains why one can find South Asian, Arab and Turkish Islamist networks in Europe that are animated by very similar ideologies and have adopted very similar strategies to one another, but in fact have operated for a long time in parallel, concerned with separate specific agendas. A useful comparison is that between the activities of the Muslim Council of Britain and the Islamic Society of Britain, whose members are of Asian descent, and those of the Muslim Association of Britain, whose constituency is primarily, though not completely, Arab.

Nevertheless, it seems that these specific agendas of Europe's Islamist groups, which were once focused on their home country or region, are becoming ever more Europeanised and engaged in a process of integration. I will examine below the emergence, characteristics and evolution of a major institution of the Muslim Brothers network in Europe – the Federation of Islamic Organisations in Europe (FIOE).

Case study: the FIOE and its offspring

The FIOE appears to be the best structured and most effective association of Muslims in Europe, although it tends to appeal primarily to Arabic-speaking individuals rather than to Muslims in general. Founded in 1989, it was chaired until May 2006 by Ahmed al-Rawi, an Iraqi-born British passport holder who immigrated to the UK in the 1970s.[3] The FIOE, which is currently headed by Chakib ben Makhlouf, a Swedish citizen of Moroccan origin, has many supporters in France, and is therefore also known by its French acronym UOIE ('Union des Organisations Islamiques en Europe').[4]

The FIOE is known among Muslim, scholarly and intelligence circles for having links with the Islamist network of the Muslim Brotherhood. This connection can be easily established by noting the past history and open involvement in the movement of several of its most prominent members, and also by noting certain Islamist themes that recur in its literature, in its members' speeches and in its current and former websites. Such themes include the primacy of Islam as an all-encompassing dimension of life (*shumuliyyat al-Islam*); the commitment to be constantly inspired by religion and to reflect one's religious values in the political realm by informing or reforming state policies; and the stress on moderation. We will return to these issues below, with some examples.

The FIOE is composed of a small but well-organised network of individuals and organisations. According to Maréchal, it is a 'secretive and informal network' that, even in some of the countries with the highest levels of activism (such as Britain, Belgium and France), reaches a total count of only 1,000 members.[5] Markfield, a British village near Leicester, used to be the headquarters under al-Rawi's leadership, but its offices are now more spread across Europe. The UK has since remained a central location for the offices dealing with finances and with *da'wa* (propagation of the faith). Until a few years ago, Geneva was also an important FIOE centre. Germany has

---

3. N. Rufford and A. Taher, 'British Muslims Say Troops Are Fair Target', *Sunday Times*, 31 October 2004, available at www.timesonline.co.uk.

4. See J. Cesari, *When Islam and Democracy Meet*, New York: Palgrave, 2004, p. 143. About half of the FIOE's member organisations are said to be in France, according to A. Boubekeur, 'Political Islam in Europe', in S. Amghar, A. Boubekeur and M. Emerson, eds, *European Islam: The Challenges for Public Policy and Society*, Brussels/Budapest: CEPS/OSI, 2007, p. 22.

5. B. Maréchal, 'Universal Aspirations: The Muslim Brotherhood in Europe', *ISIM Review*, no. 22 (Autumn 2008), p. 36.

often produced active members, and Norway, Sweden and Belgium constitute other major poles that host key FIOE departments, such as media, education and youth. Although the general secretariat is based in Brussels, one of the individuals carrying out this job is based in Austria; the current president and vice president too work mainly from their own countries – Norway and France respectively. Although a proper FIOE office devoted to EU lobbying and secretarial work was not inaugurated until 2007, the organisation had already had a strategic contact point in the Belgian capital since the second half of 2003.[6]

The FIOE has always had a far-reaching and holistic vision of its European field of action, going beyond – or occasionally anticipating – EU scenarios. Not only did the FIOE work slowly but relentlessly for at least seven years to establish its Brussels public relations headquarters, it also strengthened its eastern outreach activities, notably in the creation in Albania of an office devoted to Eastern Europeans and in the involvement in the FIOE education department of someone based in Poland. Although the FIOE network has branches in twenty-seven countries,[7] not all of these are EU member-states. Only eighteen organisations are located in the EU – the remaining ones are in Albania, Bosnia, Kosovo, Macedonia, Moldova, Russia, Switzerland, Turkey and Ukraine.

The organisation is run by a transnational group of professionals and educated individuals who are in paid positions and work full time for the FIOE. The FIOE members I have been in touch with over the past five years would not reveal in detail the organisation's sources of income, but simply referred to fees coming from the national branches. However, donations from the Muslim Brothers' networks and leading Muslim scholars and personalities (but not governments, as explained below) in countries with a majority Muslim population, and in particular in the Gulf (Kuwait more likely than Saudi Arabia), are also plausible.

The FIOE officers constantly attempt to coordinate what is done at the national level in each European country with a two-pronged international

---

6. Source: various conversations with leading FIOE figures at different times in 2003, 2007 and 2009.

7. This is the number of member-countries involved that I counted on the FIOE website, in the 'Members' section. However, the 'About Us' section of the same website mentions 'hundreds of member organisations spread across 28 European states'. See www.euro-muslim.net.

approach: they keep an eye on the wider European dimension and also on the Muslim world. It is important to note, as will be apparent from what follows, that the FIOE is not devoted to the provision of services or to the coordination of religious worship – activities that are run either by voluntary associations or by governments. The FIOE is primarily a public relations and political organisation concerned with raising the profile and enhancing the participation in the public sphere of the Muslim population of Europe. It has also been involved in activities to combat discrimination and negative stereotypes, but this type of advocacy work is not its central activity. It works primarily to raise awareness of Islam in non-Muslim environments, to urge Muslims to make all efforts to live Islamically while also abiding by European rules, to promote an institutional space for Islam in Europe and to reinforce ties with certain regions of the Muslim world.

The Federation's ties with the Muslim Brotherhood are expressed in the language used to summarise the founding principles of the FIOE – namely, an understanding of Islam through the Quran and the 'consensus of the scholars', and the adoption of an approach that combines 'authenticity' with 'revival'. These are all key terms in the Islamist tradition, especially within traditional Salafism, which is focused on the return to the example of the forefathers and to the original sources of Islam.[8]

The principle of refusing all sorts of 'interference' by the governments of its members' countries of origin are the priorities stressed by the (former) president of the FIOE.[9] Al-Rawi described the Federation as an umbrella organisation grouping together individual national associations, and divided into departments specialising on the core issues that are relevant for Muslims in Europe: 'We do not consider ourselves the only organisation: there are many organisations in Europe. We try to discuss with them the possibility of bringing them within an umbrella group, so that at least we can coordinate our activities.'[10]

Most Muslim organisations – whether local, national or international – are concerned with the propagation of the 'correct' and positive image of Islam,

---

8. For a definition of Salafism, see E. E. Shahin, 'Salafiyah', in J. L. Esposito, *The Oxford Encyclopedia of the Modern Islamic World*, 4 vols, Oxford: Oxford University Press, 1995; and S. Silvestri, 'Radical Islam: Threats and Opportunities', *Global Dialogue*, vol. 9, nos 3/4 (2007).

9. Personal interview with Ahmed al-Rawi, 14 April 2003.

10. Ibid.

an activity which is connected to *da'wa* ('preaching', but in a broader sense also 'propaganda'). However, the FIOE is much more explicit than other organisations about its aims. If, on the one hand, it provides a rather blurred definition of its purpose ('the framework [of the FIOE] aims to achieve the overall common goals of serving Muslims in European societies'), it also states very clearly that its central objective is 'to maintain the Muslim presence in Europe and to enhance and develop that presence so that Islam is properly and accurately introduced'.[11] Further on we read that the more general objectives include 'introducing Islam and its values and crystallizing an Islamic culture in accordance with the unique features of the European status quo'. Statements of this kind seem to carry considerable weight and enable people to argue anxiously that Europe is being 'colonised' by Muslims.

In the face of these programmatic declarations expressing the long-term project of the organisation, certain 'European' questions could be raised: To what extent are the members of the Federation genuinely committed to 'integration' in the EU? And when they suggest solutions for the 'general interest', are they thinking of the 'general interest' of a pluralistic, perhaps multicultural, Europe? Or are they perhaps implying that the general interest of Muslims would be that Europe becomes a 'Muslim region'?

From my interviews and informal conversations with the FIOE officers based in Markfield, there emerged a great respect and admiration for the Vatican and the institutions of the Catholic Church, as if they were exemplary models of religiously driven political coordination that should be imitated. The FIOE is definitely aware of the immense potential of Muslim mobilisation across Europe and is determined to pursue its objectives in a shrewd way. For instance, it is very careful to balance the audacious points of its programme against the bland and mellow terms that are so dear to the Western sense of fairness. It mentions the promotion of human rights, stresses the 'moderate' character of Muslim political and civic participation within the FIOE, promises to 'act transparently' towards the rest of society and pledges to 'engage in civilizational dialogue between Muslims and others in an attempt to interact positively and establish social peace and harmony'.[12] In another section of

11. 'About FIOE' section on the former FIOE website. This document is no longer available; the website www.eu-islam.com appears now to be used by a different organisation. All the quotes appearing here are in their original form. I am aware that some of them are not in very good English.

12. 'General Objectives' and 'Central Policies' sections, former FIOE website.

the former FIOE website, we could read that the Federation 'strives to play a bridging role through which continuity between Europe and the Muslim World may be enhanced in order that mutual interests, positive cooperation and world peace may be achieved'.[13]

The meaning of this 'continuity' between Europe and the Muslim world remains vague. It could refer to the 'advocacy role' of the FIOE 'on issues pertaining to the Muslim World',[14] to the preservation and promotion of Islamic culture and religious duties or to a crucial aspiration of the Federation: 'striv[ing] towards achieving recognition for Islam as an official religion throughout Europe, which would be instrumental in enhancing and promoting the European Muslim identity'.[15] This and other statements illustrating the General Objectives of the FIOE (for example, 'to activate Muslims within the framework of the European Union in a manner that serves the overall general interest' and 'to work for the representation of Muslims within European establishments and authorities') indicate very clearly the final political purpose and strategy of the organisation. Determined to guarantee a privileged place for Islam in the European public sphere, the FIOE executives seem to know perfectly well which paths to follow – namely, 'performing a civic role throughout Europe', lobbying European institutions and pursuing the channels of citizenship:

> The FIOE encourages and strives to achieve positive integration of Muslims in European societies, in a manner which collates between preserving the unique Islamic identity and enjoying and fulfilling the implications of full and complete citizenship rights and privileges, all in the manner which best achieves the common good and realizes the principles of stability and social harmony.[16]

However, when asked whether the FIOE could be defined as a 'European pressure group', al-Rawi rejected this view:

> we [do] not consider ourselves as a political lobby by any means, but really our concern [is] in political life, in European society; it is to encourage the Muslims in European society, as part of the society, to

---

13. 'Principles' section, former FIOE website.
14. Ibid.
15. 'General Objectives' section, former FIOE website.
16. 'Principles' section, former FIOE website.

participate in that political life, because this is one of the main aspects of life in Europe.[17]

He then stressed the political character of the organisation, explaining that its main concern was to 'introduce of course ourselves to the Parliament members, to the political activities; introduce our thoughts, our point of view, really, in the participation of the Muslims in all aspects of life and political life'.[18] While al-Rawi pointed proudly to the plurality of Muslim identity across Europe, he also reflected upon major difficulties that cast a shadow on the FIOE's ability to meet its objectives. Such problems include the excessive fragmentation of Muslim groups due to links with the countries of origin of their members, or to the reproduction of regional antagonisms and ethnic divisions:

> Many of these organisations are formed in line with groups' countries of origin: Bosnian, Albanian, Iranian. If we accept that for our genera-tion, we are not going to accept that for the future generation, because we consider those people all European; and for all these organisations it is better to be European than country of origin-oriented ones. [The] main difficulty [is] this one, because the people still have their traditions.[19]

On the thorny issues of alienation and extremism among Muslims, al-Rawi says:

> There are some small organisations. They are not ... I do not like to use the word extreme – [although] there are some, really, the Iranians... – but we try at least to discuss with all people to consider themselves as European Muslims, maybe for their duty, for the association, to keep [...] the security of the society, to integrate with the society ...
>
> But there are some organisations, even if they are small, they don't like to make the integration, it is not proper. Maybe they try to isolate themselves from the association; and we try, as much as we can, to involve [ourselves] in European aspects and European life.[20]

These words reiterate the pro-European stance of the FIOE. They are accom-panied by the Federation's commitment to fight the 'three main problems

---

17. Personal interview with Ahmed al-Rawi, 14 April 2003.
18. Ibid.
19. Ibid.
20. Ibid.

or differences' that cause distress to Muslims and non-Muslims alike. These problems can have 'sectarian' or 'ideological' roots, or can be associated with a country of origin. Thus, to ease any suspicion towards the FIOE, its former president affirmed: 'We try to reduce [the influence of extreme or sectarian groups] as much as we can, but it is not easy of course. It takes time. And it is there in each religion, not just in Islam'.[21]

Women and young people

As far as women are concerned, the FIOE now has a 'feminine department', and also commends the work of the European Forum of Muslim Women (EFOMW). The EFOMW is an independent organisation established in Brussels in 2006 and is run entirely by dynamic Muslim women. Its leadership is currently French, but its fourteen member organisations are based in various European countries: Belgium, France, Switzerland, Denmark, Sweden, Germany, Italy, the United Kingdom, Spain, Ireland, Greece and Bosnia. The EFOMW's core objectives include the promotion of women's participation in the socio-political and cultural construction of Europe; the representation of Muslim women in European and international bodies, in order to defend their rights and interests; and the establishment of cooperation with other female organisations to support the family and fight discrimination.[22] Without being an official FIOE member, the Forum is nevertheless at least ideologically supported by it.[23] In fact, an FIOE Newsletter (no. 12 of 2008) reported that the FIOE had recognised the importance of prioritising activities concerning, and with the collaboration of, women and young people. Moreover, the FIOE appears in the past to have supported another all-female but issue-specific transnational Muslim organisation based in Europe – the Assembly for the Protection of the Hijab (also known as ProHijab), which was launched in London in June 2004. ProHijab is a UK-based association of young Muslim women with the ambition of establishing a European-wide advocacy network to protect religious freedom and the rights of Muslim women. More specifically, it was created in response to the French law of February 2004 against religious symbols. It tends to attract and mobilise

21. Ibid.
22. European Forum of Muslim Women, 'Press Kit', January 2006 (copy privately received from a member).
23. Source: telephone interviews with FIOE officer and EFOMW officer, 13 January 2009.

British Muslim girls (of Asian origin) in their twenties who are educated to university level.

Through the conscious Europeanisation of the issue of the Islamic veil, the ProHijab assembly and its associates have achieved high visibility and secured themselves support from both their own government and the opposition. The translation of the French *affaire du voile* to the European level and back to the British milieu has had an amplifying effect: it produces the fear of the enactment of a law similar to the French one in the British context, though this possibility remains remote in light of the history and multicultural approach of the UK.

In September 2004 the ProHijab network organised a meeting at the European Parliament with the support of Caroline Lucas MEP of the UK Green Party. On the ProHijab website this activity is advertised as 'European Parliament Lobbying Seminar'.[24] The invited speakers also included other MEPs who had expressed their distress about the French law; a Catholic priest representing the Commission of the Bishops' Conference of the European Community and specialising in Christian–Islamic relations; and, as key Muslim representative, Ibrahim al-Zayyat, responsible for the Brussels Office of the FIOE. A German resident, he has been a crucial figure in Islamic activism across Europe for several years, despite his relatively young age. Before taking up this position in Brussels, he was a central figure in the Forum of European Muslim Youth and Student Organisations (FEMYSO).

Since its establishment in 1996, FEMYSO has been a dynamic Muslim presence at conferences and workshops on young people, education and anti-discrimination. According to al-Rawi, FEMYSO was created by a joint initiative of the FIOE and the World Assembly of Muslim Youth, together with several national Muslim youth organisations, between 1996 and 1997.[25] Nevertheless, the connection between the two organisations remains rather loose and ambiguous. FEMYSO tends to involve and mobilise university students and has an international committee of about ten people in their twenties or early thirties. It activities are primarily on three fronts: 1) to sensitise European society to the Muslim presence in Europe; 2) to combat faith-based discrimination and racism; and 3) to create avenues for dialogue, formal and informal, with EU institutions. The FIOE

---

24. See www.prohijab.net.
25. Sources: personal interview with al-Rawi, 14 April 2003; FEMYSO leaflet, 2003.

has occasionally featured in the background of its activities. For instance, FIOE members, including the whole al-Rawi family, attended the FEMYSO one-day conference 'Muslim Youth in Europe – Enrichment of Society?' This event, which took place on the premises of the European Parliament in Brussels in September 2003, was officially convened by FEMYSO and the European Youth Forum, with the endorsement of (mainly British) MEPs from all political trends.[26]

All of these activities demonstrate that the FIOE is building strong and visible ties across Europe to promote its own vision of coordinated Islamic political participation. The accomplishment of this objective is linked to the Federation's successful managerial approach. It consists in the ability to design and assess goals and priorities, assign tasks, set up departments and carefully and diplomatically plan and weigh every single move, bearing in mind its impact, on both national and international levels.

An 'Arab' strategy of Islamisation?

The publication (in Arabic only) of the monthly magazine *Al Europyya* ('Europe') facilitates the FIOE communication strategy within the Muslim Arab diaspora in Europe. Its editorial office is in La Courneuve (France), where the higher education department of the FIOE is also based. It is important to consider the linguistic choice of using Arabic instead of English – the lingua franca of the current era – or another European language. Incidentally, the number of Muslims of Arab origin (both EU citizens and immigrants) in the fifteen EU member-states before the enlargement of May 2004 amounted to almost 4 million – that is, about a quarter of the estimated total Muslim population of those countries.[27] With the eastward expansion of the EU, we can assume that the number of Arab Muslims has not varied much, since Islam is scarcely present in those eastern European countries, whose few Muslims are of Tartar or Turkish origin.[28] However, we should also note that the late 1990s and early 2000s witnessed a renewed interest

26. A more thorough analysis of FEMYSO's history and activities is provided in S. Silvestri, 'The Political Mobilisation of Muslims in Europe and the EU Response', PhD dissertation, University of Cambridge, 2006.

27. F. Dassetto, 'The Muslim Populations of Europe', in F. Dassetto, B. Maréchal, S. Allievi, F. Dassetto and J. Nielsen, eds, *Muslims in the Enlarged Europe: Religion and Society*, Leiden and Boston: Brill, 2003, p. xxv.

28. Ibid, pp. xxv–xxvi.

in the study of the Qur'an and of Islamic law and theology among young Muslims of South Asian descent. This has been accompanied by great interest in the study of the classical and Qur'anic Arabic language.[29] The readership of magazines and publications written in Arabic therefore has significant potential for growth, although the average young European Muslim in the street tends to speak the European language of his or her country of residence, and might speak Arabic only very poorly, if at all.

From a certain point of view, the choice of Arabic for the FIOE publication could be interpreted as a limitation, as an element of fragmentation restricting access to the FIOE's message and initiatives to Arabic speakers only. However, the FIOE website remains available in three languages – Arabic, English and French. On the other hand, the adoption of Arabic as the primary language of communication for Muslims in Europe points to a crucial transformation of long-established intellectual boundaries. For decades Muslims who have emigrated to Europe have imported literature and audio-visual material of all sorts from the Arab world. Tapes, books and leaflets – whose contents range from devotion and mysticism, through banal indoctrination to radical polemics – are sold and circulated outside European mosques and in the markets of big cities' neighbourhoods with a large immigrant population.

At the inception of the twenty-first century, however, Islamic culture is increasingly produced, and not only consumed, in Europe.[30] Europe, and more specifically the EU, becomes in turn the receptacle of an Islamo-Arabic culture, which has traditionally been regarded as 'alien' to a supposedly immutable 'European identity'.[31] Large numbers of *inhabitants* of Europe – citizens and immigrants – produce and consume *in* Europe a popular and religious (Arabic and Islamic) culture that is not traditionally regarded as belonging to Europe. The

29. Source: observation of increased number of Qur'anic-Arabic language courses offered by Muslim societies and mosques across the UK and in other European countries. In addition, I personally witnessed the presence of young practising Muslims in the 'lay' Arabic language course that I attended at Cambridge University during 2003/04.

30. M. Van Bruinessen and S. Allievi, eds, *Producing Islamic Knowledge*, London: Routledge, 2010.

31. On Islam as the 'Other' that has antagonised Europe and at the same time allowed it to develop a specific European identity, see, for example, B. Stråth, ed, *Europe and the Other and Europe as the Other*, Brussels and Oxford: P.I.E. Peter Lang, 2000.

European political culture of welcoming immigrants and protecting minorities, promoting human rights and fundamental freedoms and encouraging democratic participation, inevitably leads Europe to transform itself by incorporating the 'difference' into its own 'self'.[32] The FIOE is seriously engaged in this process of 'Islamising' European culture, though without erasing it. It has established in Sweden the Association of Muslim Schools in Europe, and has also founded a European Association of [Muslim] Media Personnel, which 'strives to enhance the participation of Muslims in European culture and media'.[33]

Indeed, one of the long-term priorities of the FIOE is that of establishing a 'Coordination Council, which along with the FIOE consists of other main Islamic organizations in an attempt to achieve a more comprehensive representation of Muslims in Europe'.[34] This plan was probably a response to an early attempt of the European Commission to establish a Muslim Council of Cooperation in Europe (MCCE), which was later dropped.[35] But the FIOE must have continued with this plan since, in Brussels in February 2008, it launched the European Assembly of Imams and Spiritual Guides. The comprehensive 'vision'[36] of the FIOE is also evident in the number of European bodies that were generated from within it throughout the 1990s. In the following pages I shall analyse the first two of these offspring, the third I have already discussed: the European Institute for Human Science (EIHS), the European Council for Fatwa and Research (ECFR) and FEMYSO.

The European Institute for Human Science (EIHS)

The European Institute for Human Science (EIHS, often known by its French name, Institut Européen des Sciences Humaines) is an educational institute

---

32. See 'Introduction' in A. Pagden, ed., *The Idea of Europe: From Antiquity to the European Union*, Cambridge: Cambridge University Press, Woodrow Wilson Center Series, 2002, pp. 1–21.

33. 'About FIOE – Central Organizations' section, former FIOE website. No mention is made on this website of the location of this European Association of Media Personnel.

34. Ibid. I am quoting the English original as it has been posted online. It may contain some grammatical errors.

35. The history of the MCCE is explained in S. Silvestri, 'Asserting Islam in the EU: Actors, Strategies, and Priorities', in F. Foret, ed., *L'Europe à l'épreuve du religieux*, Brussels: Presses de l'Université Libre de Bruxelles, 2007, pp. 159–77.

36. 'Vision' is a term that the FIOE president used frequently during our conversation (personal interview with Ahmed al-Rawi, 14 April 2003).

– compared by some to a university – that was established in the late 1990s by the FIOE in France, at Bouteloin (also known as Château Chinon). The aim of EIHS is set to educate and train Europe-based imams. It is regarded by the Federation as one of its 'most prominent successes',[37] although the link between the two organisations is not always immediately obvious to the outsider. The EIHS consists of four establishments: 1) the European College for Islamic Studies; 2) the Arabic Language Institute; 3) the Institute for the Training of Imams; and 4) the Institute for Learning the Holy Qur'an. Two branches of the EIHS were opened in 1999 and 2000 – one in the United Kingdom, near Lampeter in Wales, in November 1999, and one in Paris, France, in September 2000.[38] According to al-Rawi, the EIHS has students from all over Europe, but no numbers were provided. This is also confirmed by the personal experience of a young Egyptian man – an imam of a small mosque in Rome – who was taking an EIHS course by correspondence[39] in 2003, and by research conducted by Frank Frégosi.[40] The Strasburg-based academic has also noted that the EIHS 'operates examination centres in a number of cities worldwide (London, Frankfurt, Geneva, Copenhagen, Istanbul and Chicago)'.[41] Still drawing on Frégosi's findings, Maréchal mentions the existence of an Institute for Islamic Studies (the Institut d'Etudes Islamiques) in Paris, operating

> as an 'open university', offering a complete university curriculum open to all Muslims in the hopes of attracting persons with leadership potential that they might be educated and trained to be of value to

37. 'About FIOE – Central Organizations' – former FIOE website.
38. Personal interview with Ahmed al-Rawi, 14 April 2003; 'About FIOE – Central Organizations' section, former FIOE website. The location of the British branch is provided by Maréchal ('Modalities of Islamic Instruction', in *Muslims in the Enlarged Europe*, 2003a, pp. 61, 71), although she does not make any connection between the FIOE and the EIHS.
39. He told me that he did not have to attend courses in France, but was receiving the books, written in Arabic, through the post (personal interview, Rome, June 2003).
40. Frégosi's work, which was published in 1998, is mentioned by B. Maréchal (Dassetto, Felice, Allievi, Stefano, Maréchal, Brigitte and Nielsen, Jørgen, eds, 'Modalities of Islamic Instruction', in *Muslims in the Enlarged Europe, Religion and Society,* Leiden and Boston, Brill, 2003, p. 61).
41. Maréchal, *Muslims in the Enlarged Europe*, p. 61.

Islam, and in the hopes of giving foreign imams living in France an opportunity to receive additional training.[42]

The Belgian researcher also observes that both the Institute in Bouteloin and the Institut d'Etudes Islamiques 'are philosophically based on Arabisation and re-Islamisation' and that they 'are more centres of religious instruction than seminaries for producing imams'.[43] The combination of teaching Arabic with promoting the Islamisation of society is a characteristic of the Salafist philosophy. From an analysis of the theology taught in the two institutions, both Frégosi and Maréchal detect that one of the two has a marked connection with the ideology of the Muslim Brotherhood. However, the two scholars seem to miss the broader picture. That is, the Paris Institute is in fact one of the four main *components* of the EIHS (what the FIOE website calls the 'College for Islamic Studies'), and the EIHS as a whole is an institution of the FIOE, as specified on its website.[44]

Not much more information is available about the EIHS except for negative media portrayals and unsympathetic intelligence reports. They accuse the FIOE and the EIHS of being a hub producing extremism, and sometimes terrorists. These suspicions rely on the fact that some individuals who attended courses at the Château Chinon Institute were found to have links to al-Qaeda and other terrorist organisations.[45]

The European Council for Fatwa and Research (ECFR)

The European Council for Fatwa and Research (ECFR, where *fatwa* means 'legal opinion') is another organ of the FIOE that is composed of Muslim scholars and clerics specialising in Islamic law. It was first set up in London in March 1997, as an 'Islamic, specialised and independent academic entity' with the aim of issuing 'collective *fatwas* that respond to the needs of Muslims in Europe, which resolve their problems in conformity with the rules and

---

42. Ibid.
43. Ibid, pp. 61–2.
44. 'About FIOE – Central Organizations' section, former FIOE website.
45. I. Johnson and D. Crawford, 'A Saudi Group Spreads Extremism in "Law Seminars", Taught in Dutch. Searching for Roots of 9/11, Europeans Find 6 Plotters Took Course in Holland', *Wall Street Journal*, 15 April 2003; L. Vidino, 'Aims and Methods of Europe's Muslim Brotherhood', *Current Trends in Islamist Ideology*, vol. 4, November 2006.

the objectives of *shari'a*.[46] It currently has two branches in Europe – one in Dublin, the other in Leeds – and is presided over by a controversial figure, the Egyptian-born Islamic scholar and preacher Shaykh Yusuf al-Qaradawi, currently resident in Qatar.

The author of over fifty books, Qaradawi has become a public figure also thanks to his al-Jazeera TV programme *ash-Shari'ah wal-Hayat* ('*Shari'a* and Life') and to his website,[47] where *fatwas* and news concerning the Islamic world are regularly posted. Muslims across the world hold discordant opinions about this Islamic preacher, who is defined by his opponents as an 'extremist' and by his supporters as a 'moderate conservative'. He is considered a spiritual guide by the members of the Muslim Brotherhood and by organisations such as the Muslim Association of Britain, whereas he is accused by Western media of justifying suicide bombings and violence in Palestine and Iraq.[48] Although his speeches and *fatwas* have not explicitly done this, the *fatwas* that he issued in 2004 permitted the abduction and killing of American civilians in Iraq, in order to pressure the American army to evacuate its forces, and urged Muslims across the world to support their brothers in Palestine and to donate money to Islamist organisations involved in humanitarian work – but which allegedly also finance terrorism.[49]

Evidence of this divided attitude towards Qaradawi is the fact that, in October 2004, 2,500 Muslim intellectuals from twenty-three countries (but mostly from Saudi Arabia, the Gulf states, Iraq, Jordan and Palestine) signed a petition calling for an international treaty banning the use of religion for incitement to violence. On this occasion they condemned Qaradawi in particular and distanced themselves from his interpretation

---

46. 'Ses objectifs' – www.uoif-online.com/conseil.php. The UOIF (Union des Organisations Musulmanes de France – 'Union of Muslim Organisations in France') is the French branch of the FIOE.

47. www.islam-online.net (commonly abbreviated to IOL).

48. The media often wrongly speak of Qaradawi as the leader of the Muslim Brotherhood. However, this is in fact not the case, as the Brotherhood currently seems to be composed of different strands and of semi-autonomous national branches (for example, in Egypt, in Syria and so on).

49. AKI (ADN Kronos International),'M.O.: Fatwa di Qaradawi, Obbligo di Sostenere Gente di Rafah', *ADN Kronos International*, 25 May 2004; MEMRI (Middle East Media Research Institute), 'Reactions to Sheikh Al-Qaradhawi's Fatwa Calling for the Abduction and Killing of American Civilians in Iraq', *Special Dispatch Series*, no. 794 (2004), available at www.memri.org.

of Islam.[50] Qaradawi was also fiercely verbally abused when, in 2004 and 2005, he was invited, with the endorsement of the mayor of London, to speak at public events organised by Muslim organisations linked to the FIOE, the MAB and the ProHijab Assembly.[51]

The ECFR's Sages (scholars, wise men), of whom there are approximately thirty-five, must be resident in Europe and have a university degree in Islamic jurisprudence from an Islamic institution in the Muslim world, not Europe. Among their responsibilities are the 'publication of studies and juridical researches that solve the problems experienced by European Muslims' and playing the role of 'guides' for both Muslims wishing to live their faith in an orthodox way and for those engaged in spreading Islam.[52] In reality, many of them are from the Middle East and the Gulf, and are not even fluent in European languages.[53] This detail, together with the fact that the ECFR members and documents make heavy use of the Arabic language, is not insignificant. These factors represent a contradiction with and a limitation of the grand design of the ECFR – namely, to be a main point of reference for Muslims living in Europe.[54]

The ECFR prides itself on catering to Muslims from all Islamic schools of thought and traditions. However, it does not seem to interact with other

---

50. See 'Stop Terror Sheikhs, Muslim Academics Demand', *Arab News*, 30 October 2004, available at www.arabnews.com; Daniel Pipes, 'Anti-Islamists Petition the United Nations', 30 October 2004, available at www.danielpipes.org; and Free Muslims Against Terrorism, '"Stop Terror Sheikhs", Muslim Academics Demand', 5 November 2004, Free Muslims Against Terrorism, available at www.freemuslims.org.

51. The relationship between the FIOE and MAB is similar to that between the FIOE and the UOIF, so that MAB can be considered the 'British branch' of the FIOE. Unsurprisingly, the UOIF website has a link to and a blurb about the FIOE, and the FIOE lists both MAB and the UOIF in its 'Organizations' section, together with the League of Swiss Muslims and the Islamische Gemeinschaft in Deutschland e.V. (Islamic Community in Germany). See www.eu-islam.com. More on the MAB can be found in chapter 4 of this volume. For media coverage of Qaradawi's visit to London, see BBC News (7 July 2004).

52. 'Ses objectifs', available at www.uoif-online.com.

53. Personal interview with al-Rawi, 14 April 2003. This point is also highlighted by Alexandre Caeiro, 'The Social Construction of Sharia: Bank Interest, Home Purchase, and Islamic Norms in the West', *Die Welt Des Islams*, vol. 44, no. 3 (2004), and forthcoming publications by Caeiro, who has carried out extensive research on the ECFR.

54. Arab Muslims are about a quarter of the Muslim population of Europe, as mentioned above.

Muslim organisations across Europe that fall outside the scope of the FIOE–Muslim Brotherhood network of associations.[55] Nor does the ECFR appear to have established any independent contacts with the institutions of the EU, in Brussels or elsewhere.

The establishment of the ECFR and the growing interest in *fatwas* on the part of Muslims residing in the West is a reflection of the process of adaptation they are going through and of the increasing importance given to the practice of *ijtihad* – that is, the exercise of human reason in the interpretation of the holy sources in the light of the present circumstances. Cesari has indicated that the question 'to what extent the obligations of *shari'a* can be fulfilled in the West' is posed by increasing numbers of Muslims; as a consequence, the legal and theological reflection on the *fiqh* (juridical interpretation of the Islamic law), which used to be a peculiarity of the Muslim Brothers, is now spreading to other groups that do not belong to the network.[56]

The European Muslims' Charter

More recently, in January 2008, with a public launch in Brussels, the FIOE issued a major document called *Muslims of Europe Charter*, which allegedly had been in preparation since the year 2000. Once again, we are in the presence of a document that is aimed at correcting the bad press Muslims have had, especially since 9/11, and campaigning for Muslims' rights to practise their religion fully and freely in Europe. But this is not the only objective of the document. The *Muslims of Europe Charter*, which was allegedly signed by 400 European Muslim leaders – though they were probably all part of the same network and therefore did not represent the variety of views held by European Muslims – is also a call to unify Muslims, in light of the diversity and fragmentation of an Islam that had become a permanent fixture, not a transitory presence, in Europe. It is part of a large PR exercise in which the FIOE has engaged in order to promote a positive image of Islam (and of itself), and to unveil the Muslim contribution to Europe. In particular it shows that there are values in Islam, such as the 'common good' (*maslaha*), moderation, respect for human life, honesty, respect for the rule of law, and so on that are also Western values. The

---

55. MAB and the UOIF fall within the Muslim Brothers' network, for instance.
56. Cesari, *When Islam and Democracy Meet*, pp. 145–7.

document does not contain any critical or provocative statement against the West, and makes almost no reference to the part of the world where Muslims constitute the majority of the population. On the contrary, it calls upon Muslims to participate fully in European society and political life, and for European society to receive them fully and fairly. Politically, what is of more interest here than the content of the document is the strategy adopted by the FIOE to promote it, and the key position it is trying to carve for itself, through the symbolic significance of this initiative, with respect both to other Muslim organisations and the whole Muslim population of Europe, and to the EU institutions.

The case of the Muslim Brotherhood is particularly interesting, because the types of activity initiated by the European branch of the network in this first decade of the new millennium seem to mark a new direction for the movement's presence in Europe. In the 1970s, when most of the first generation of Muslims who belong to the MB came to Europe, they found an excellent strategic opportunity to better themselves and their children (through good education and jobs), taking advantage of the freedoms available in Europe to campaign and influence politics in their home countries. However, judging by the activities of these organisations in Europe, it seems as if the original political ideology of the movement lost its significance once it had been transplanted to an alien environment, and needed to be re-elaborated in the light of the new context of Muslims being citizens of Europe.

The transnational dimension and the commitment to the religious values that inspire political engagement of course persist, and indeed have never been hidden. Likewise, Islamist networks remain committed to charitable activities in depressed areas of the Muslim world and continue to organise campaigns in support of the brothers of the global *umma*, whether in Palestine, Afghanistan, Pakistan or Iraq. But their stress on reform and social justice is not directed uniquely to the Muslim world: it is now also directed towards European society. As the work of Tariq Ramadan shows, Islamic scholarship and spirituality are used to inject new meaning into the concept of European citizenship based on respect for diversity. This could be regarded as an ultimate sign of the integration of Islamism into mainstream European society, rather than of the emergence of an Islamic 'fifth column' inside Europe.

The European Muslim Brothers' faithfulness to the concept of *shumuli-yyat al-Islam* has been criticised as a 'totalising discourse' – in contradiction both with their efforts to promote European citizenship and integration, and with the European notion of separation between church and state.[57] My analysis of the Muslims Brothers in Europe, though, is not so alarmist. First, many policy developments and scholarly works testify that secularism is not a fixed and eternal concept,[58] and it may well be that European society will have to reconsider and appreciate anew the role of religious values, shared religious practices and the contribution of faith-based groups to policymaking. The language and the slogans driving the mobilisation of the Muslim Brothers may thus come to be regarded as not so antagonistic to European political structures. Second, there is no doubt that thirty years of the Muslim Brothers' presence in Europe have also modified the views and the objectives of the organisation. As I pointed out at the outset, most Muslim organisations were initially simply orientated towards the countries of origin of their members, but gradually became concerned with the living conditions, needs and aspirations of their own populations living in Europe. Similarly, it seems that the FIOE has gradually come to focus on activities – mainly PR initiatives – aimed at improving the visibility and voice of its members and of Muslims in general in Europe, and has almost dropped its traditional slogans and concerns. It is essentially not antagonistic to the state or to secular political institutions at all, but on the contrary seeks a partnership with them. On the one hand, this shift could be considered a typical Muslim Brotherhood attitude – in other words, one of seeking compromise and never being completely clear about final objectives. But, on the other hand, this transformation might show the degree to which the ideology has adapted to its context.

---

57. Maréchal, 'Universal Aspirations', p. 37.
58. See D. Martin, *On Secularization*, Farnham: Ashgate, 2005; S. Thomas, *The Global Resurgence of Religion and the Transformation of International Relations*, London and New York: Palgrave Macmillan, 2005.

Notes on Contributors

Abdullah Baabood is a businessman and academic from Oman with over fifteen years of international business experience. His academic interests include the GCC and its economic, political and social development, as well as GCC external relations. He has published and presented at conferences, seminars and workshops on all these subjects. Dr Baabood is a graduate in business, marketing and economics and holds an MBA in business administration, and an MA and a PhD in international relations. He is the Director of the Gulf Research Centre, affiliated to the University of Cambridge. He also holds several board memberships in a number of GCC and UK organisations as well as being a member of a range of professional and academic institutions.

Youcef Bouandel, who is currently Associate Professor at the International Affairs Program, University of Qatar, holds a licence in Politics from the University of Algiers (1986), and an MPhil (1988) and a PhD (1994) from the University of Glasgow. He has been Visiting Professor at several universities in Scotland, Bulgaria, Sweden, Latvia, Algeria and the United States of America. His research interests are comparative politics – specialising in the Middle East and North Africa – elections, human rights, terrorism and conflict resolution. He is the author of *Human Rights and Comparative Politics* (1997), chapters in edited books and over twenty research papers. His work has been published in *Journal of Algerian Studies*, *Journal of Modern African Studies*, *Journal of North African Studies*, *Third World Quarterly*, *Electoral Studies* and *Mediterranean Politics*.

Abdelwahab El-Affendi is a reader in Politics at the Centre for the Study of Democracy at the University of Westminster and co-ordinator of the Centre's Democracy and Islam Programme. He is also an ESRC/AHRC Fellow in the Global Uncertainties Programme. Educated at the universities of Khartoum, Wales and Reading, he is the author of several books including *Turabi's Revolution: Islam and Power in Sudan* (1991), *Rethinking Islam and Modernity* (2001), *For a State of Peace: Conflict and the Future of Democracy in Sudan* (2002) and *Who Needs an Islamic State?* (2008). He has also contributed to many leading journals and is the contributor or co-author of works including *Islam and Secularism in the Middle East* (2000), *Islamic Thought in the Twentieth Century* (2003) and *American Power in the 21st Century* (2004). He is co-author of the report *Contextualising Islam in Britain* (2009). Dr El-Affendi was a member of the team of authors of the *Arab Development Report* (2004) and a member of the Advisory Board and a contributor to the 2005 report. He is a member of the Advisory Board of Al-Walid bin Talal Centre for the Study of Islam in the Contemporary World at Edinburgh University, a Fellow of the RSA and a Fellow of the Salzburg Global Seminar.

Kamal Helbawy is currently the chairman of the Centre for the Study of Terrorism and an advisor to the Global Civilizations Study Center. Following his graduation from Cairo University in 1960, he worked in the field of manpower planning and training in Egypt before going on to study business administration at the American University of Cairo and subsequently specialising in strategic studies at Pakistan's Center for Asian Studies and Institute of Policy Studies. Dr Helbawy was among the founders of the World Assembly of Muslim Youth (WAMY) and served as its first Executive Director from 1973 to 1982. From 1982 to 1987 he worked as an advisor to the Arab Bureau of Education for Gulf States and from 1988 to 1994 he was in charge of Muslim Brotherhood affairs and activities in Afghanistan. After settling in the United Kingdom in 1994, Dr Helbawy became a founder member of the Muslim Council of Britain and the Muslim Association of Britain. A member of the Muslim Brotherhood from his youth, Dr Helbawy served as the official spokesman of the Muslim Brotherhood in the West from 1995 to 1997. Dr Helbawy has written widely on Islamic movements, Muslim world affairs and Afghanistan.

Khaled Hroub is the Director of the Cambridge Arab Media Project (CAMP) at the Faculty of Asian and Middle Eastern Studies of the University of Cambridge where he teaches Middle Eastern history and politics. He previously worked for the Middle East Programme of the International Institute of International Studies, London (IIIS) and from 2000 to 2006 was the host of a weekly book review programme on Al-Jazeera. He is the author of *Hamas: Political Thought and Practice* (2000) and *Hamas: A Beginner's Guide* (2006), which has appeared in several languages. In addition to his academic publications, Dr Hroub writes a weekly article that appears in six leading Arab newspapers in different countries. His most recent publication is an occasional paper on *Islamism and Secular Politics: Turkish and Arab Islamist Experiences*, which was published by the Abu Lughod Institute for International Studies of Birzeit University, Palestine (2009). He has also published a poetry collection entitled *Enchantress of Poetry* (2008) and a non-fiction literary volume, *Tattoo of Cities* (2009).

Roel Meijer is a lecturer in Middle East history at the Department of Religious Studies of Radboud University, Nijmegen in the Netherlands and is also a senior researcher of the Dutch think-tank, Clingendael. He wrote his doctorate on the subject of 'Egypt, The Quest for Modernity' and in 2002 published a book entitled *Secular Liberal and Left-wing Political Thought in Egypt, 1945–1958*. He has published widely on Islamic movements in Iraq, Egypt and Saudi Arabia and has edited several volumes, including *Cosmopolitanism, Identity and Authenticity in the Middle East* (1999), *Alienation or Integration of Arab Youth: Between Family, State and Street* (2000) and, recently, *Global Salafism: Islam's New Religious Movement* (2009). Dr Meijer is a full-time researcher with a grant from the Netherlands Organisation for Scientific Research and is currently working on a project about Salafism.

Ibrahim Moussawi is an expert on Hizbullah and Islamist political theory. He was awarded his PhD from Birmingham University and has taught at the American University in Beirut (AUB) and various universities in Europe. He is currently an associate professor in the Faculty of Media, the Faculty of Sociology and the Faculty of History at the Lebanese University. A commentator on Middle Eastern affairs, political Islam and Islamic movements, he has worked extensively in the press and TV media and was head of the foreign department (and political programmes) at Al-Manar TV, the official media outlet of Hizbullah in Lebanon. His forthcoming book, *Shi'ism and the Democratisation Process in Iran with a focus on Wilayat al-Faqih*, is to be published by Saqi Books.

Tariq Ramadan teaches at the Faculty of Theology, University of Oxford and is also a Senior Research Fellow at St Antony's College (Oxford), Doshisha University (Kyoto, Japan) and at the Lokahi Foundation (London). He is a Visiting Professor (holding the chair in Identity and Citizenship) at

Erasmus University (Netherlands). Through his writings and lectures he has contributed to the debate on the issues of Muslims in the West and Islamic revival in the Muslim world. He is active at both academic and grassroots levels, lecturing throughout the world on social justice and dialogue between civilisations. Professor Ramadan is currently president of the pan-European think-tank, European Muslim Network. His most recent publication is *Radical Reform, Islamic Ethics and Liberation* (2008).

Tilde Rosmer is a Research Fellow of the Department of Culture Studies and Oriental Languages at the University of Oslo where she is working on a project entitled 'Fault Lines of Islamism: Negotiating Progress, Participation and Patriarchy'. Since 2007 she has also been a lecturer and Fellow of the Centre for the Study of Muslim–Jewish Relations at the Woolf Institute of Abrahamic Faiths at the University of Cambridge. Dr Rosmer received her PhD in Middle Eastern Studies from the University of Oslo in 2008, the subject of her doctoral thesis being 'Mizrahiut and the Arab–Jewish Divide: Contemporary Challenges to Israel's Ethnic Boundaries'. Her publications include 'Forewarned is Forearmed ... How to Prepare for Fieldwork and Deal with Expectations' in *Cultural Studies in the Field – Methodological and Educational Experiences*, ed. Anders Gustavsson, (2005, in Norwegian); 'The Sephardi Torahnim – Shas' New Jewish Israeli' in *Israel Studies Forum*; and 'The Sephardi Torah Guardians', in the *Journal of Middle Eastern Studies*.

Murad Batal al-Shishani is a London-based analyst of Islamic groups and terrorism and also a specialist on Islamic movements in Chechnya and the Middle East. He is a regular contributor to several publications in both Arabic and English, such as the London-based *al-Hayat* and Jamestown Foundation's *Terrorism Monitor*. He is the author of *The Islamic Movement in Chechnya and the Chechen–Russian Conflict 1990–2000* (in Arabic) and *Iraqi Resistance: National Liberation Versus Terrorism: A Quantitative Study* (2005). Al-Shishani is a regular commentator on several media outlets including the BBC and Radio Free Europe Liberty.

Sara Silvestri (M.Phil., Ph.D., Cantab) is an expert on Muslim political mobilisation and Islamic institutions in contemporary Europe as well as on EU public policies concerning religion and Muslim communities. She heads the Globalising Justice programme at the Von Hügel Institute (Cambridge

University) and teaches religion in global politics at City University, London. Dr Silvestri also collaborates with the Cambridge Muslim College and has directed the 'Muslims in Europe' programme of the European Policy Centre, Brussels. She serves on the Advisory Council of the Euro-Mediterranean Foundation for Cultural Dialogue Anna Lindh, and is a 'Global Expert' with the UN Alliance of Civilisations. Her recent research and publications focus on the debate between 'radical' and 'moderate' Islam; the impact of counter-terrorism on minorities communities; and Europe's Muslim Women (book forthcoming with Hurst/Columbia University Press).

Camille Tawil is a Lebanese writer and journalist for the London-based Arabic daily *al-Hayat*. He has a BA in Media Studies from the Lebanese University in Beirut and an MA in Area Studies (Near and Middle East) from the University of London's School of Oriental and African Studies (SOAS). He has written two books on armed Islamic movements in the Arab world: *Al-Haraka al-Islamiya al-Musallaha fi al-Jazair: min al-Inqad ila al-Jamaʾa* (1998, in Arabic) and *Brothers in Arms: The Story of al-Qaʾida and the Arab Jihadists* (2010).

Bibliography

Abd al-Raziq, Ali, *Al-islam wa usul al-hukm* (Islam and the Fundamentals of Government), Cairo, 1925.

Abukhalil, As'ad, *The Battle for Saudi Arabia: Royalty, Fundamentalism, and Global Power*, New York, Seven Stories Press, 2004.

Aburaiya, I., 'The 1996 Split of the Islamic Movement in Israel: Between the Holy Text and Israeli–Palestinian Context', *International Journal of Politics, Culture and Society*, vol. 17, no. 3, Spring 2004.

Adalah, 'Special Report, October 2000 Killings', 2006, available at www.adalah. org/eng/october2000.php.

El-Affendi, Abdelwahab, *Who Needs an Islamic State?* London, Malaysia Think Tank in London, 2008.

Ahmadov, Ramin, 'The US Policy toward the Middle East in the Post-Cold War Era', *Alternatives: Turkish Journal of International Relations*, vol. 4, nos 1–2, Spring/Summer 2005.

Amara, Muhammad Hasan, 'The Nature of Islamic Fundamentalism in Israel', *Terrorism and Political Violence*, vol. 8, no. 2, Summer 1996.

Amghar, Samir, *Political Islam in Morocco*, Centre for European Policy Studies, CEPS Working Document 269, June 2007.

Al-Amin, Ibrahim, Hizbullah's 'Open Letter to the Oppressed in Lebanon and Throughout the World', 1985.

Anawati, Georges C. and Borrmans, Maurice, *Tendances et courants de l'islam arabe contemporain, vol. 1: Egypte et Afrique du Nord*, München and Mainz, Kaiser-Grunewald, 1982.

al-Ansari, Abdulhameed, '*Al-jama' at al-dinniyya wa ta'athiruha 'ala al-istiqrar al-siyasi (mantaqa al-khalij numudja)*' (Religious Groups and their Impact on Political Stability [the Gulf Region as an Example]), conference paper delivered at Religion and Society in the Arab World, Al-Itihad Annual Forum 2008, Abu Dhabi, 20–21 October 2008.

Arab Bureau of Education for Gulf States, *Nadwat itijahat al-fikr al-islami al-mu'asir* (Trends of Modern Islamic Thought), Riyadh, Arab Bureau of Education for Gulf States, 1985.

Arab News, 'Stop Terror Sheikhs, Muslim Academics Demand', 30 October 2004.

Arjomand, Said Amir, *The Turban for the Crown: The Islamic Revolution in Iran*, New York and Oxford, Oxford University Press, 1988.

Ashkenazi, Eli and Stern, Y., 'Police Close Islamic Institute Suspected of Aiding Hamas', *Ha'aretz*, 24 August 2008.

El-Awaisi, Abd al-Fattah Muhammad, *The Muslim Brothers and the Palestine Question 1928–1947*, London, Tauris Academic Studies, 1998.

Ayoob, Mohammed, *The Many Faces of Political Islam: Religion and Politics in the Muslim World*, Michigan, The University of Michigan Press, 2008.

Ayubi, Nazih, *Political Islam: Religion and Politics in the Arab World*, London and New York, Routledge, 1991.

al-Bahadli, Ali, *Al-hawza al-'ilmiyya fi al-najaf: ma'alimaha wa harakataha al-islahiyya (1920–1980)* (The Religious Seminary in Najaf: Features and Reformist Trends), Beirut, Dar Al-Zahra, 1993.

Bahry, Louay, 'The Opposition in Bahrain: A Bellwether for the Gulf', *Middle East Policy*, vol. 5, no. 2, May 1997.

Balqaziz, Abdal-Ilah, *Al-dawlah fi al-fikr al-islami al-mu'asir* (The State in Contemporary Islamic Thought), Beirut, Centre for Arab Unity Studies, 2002.

al-Banna, Abed al-Basit, *Taj al-islam wa malhamat al-imam* (The Crown of Islam and the Tragedy of the Leader), 1952.

— *Majmu'at rasail al-imam al-shahid hassan al-banna* (Collection of Messages of the Martyr Imam Hassan al-Banna), Beirut, al-Muassasa al-islamiyya li'l-tiba'a wa'l-nashr, 1974.

— *Mudhakirat al-daw'a wa dayia* (Memoirs of the Preaching and the Preacher), Cairo, Islamic House of Publishing and Distribution, 1947, 1st edition.

— *Mudhakirat al-daw'a wa dayia* (Memoirs of the Preaching and the Preacher), Beirut, Al-Maktab al-Islami, 1974, 3rd edition.

al-Banna, Hassan, *Mudhakirat al-Daw'a wa Dayia* [Memories of Hassan al-Banna about himself and Daw'a], Beirut: Al-Maktab al-Islami, 1974, Third edition.

— *Rasail Hassan al-Banna* [Messages of Hassan al-Banna], Beirut: The Islamic Foundation for Printing and Publishing, no date.

Barghouthi, Iyad, *Al-din wa al-dawleh fi filasteen* (*Religion and State in Palestine*), Ramallah, Ramallah Center for Human Rights, 2007.

al-Barghouti, Tamim, *The Umma and the Dawla: The Nation State and the Arab Middle East*, London, Pluto Press, 2008.

Batatu, Hanna, *The Old Social Classes and the Revolutionary Movement in Iraq*, Arabic translation by Afif al-Razar, vol. 1, Arab Research Foundation, 1995.

Bayat, Asef, 'Islamism and Democracy: What is the Real Question?' Amsterdam, Amsterdam University Press, 2007.

— 'The Coming of a Post-Islamist Society', *Critique: Critical Middle East Studies*, Minnesota, University of Hamline, vol. 5, no. 9, Fall 1996.

— *Making Islam Democratic: Social Movements and the Post-Islamist Turn*, Stanford, Stanford University Press, 2007.

Benard, Cheryl and Khalilzad, Zalmay, *'The Government of God': Iran's Islamic Republic*, New York, Columbia University Press, 1984.

Binder, Leonard, *Islamic Liberalism: A Critique of Development Ideologies*, Chicago, The University of Chicago Press, 1988.

Blanford, Nicholas, '50 Years On, Questions Still Surround Massacre at Houla', *Daily Star*, 31 October 2003.

Bonney, Richard, *Jihad: From Qur'an to bin Laden*, New York, Palgrave Macmillan, 2004.

Bouandel, Youcef, 'Algerian National Popular Assembly Election of December 1991', *Representation*, vol. 32, no. 117, Winter/Spring 1993/1994.

— 'Reforming the Algerian Electoral System', *Journal of Modern African Studies*, vol. 43, no. 3, 2005.

Boubekeur, Amel and Emerson, M., eds, *European Islam: The Challenges for Public Policy and Society*, Brussels/Budapest, Centre for European Policy Studies/Open Society Institute, 2007.

Brawn, Eric, ed., *Current Trends in Islamist Ideology*, vol. 1, Center on Islam, Democracy and the Future of the Muslim World, Washington, DC, Hudson Institute, 2005.

Caeiro, Alexandre, 'The Social Construction of Sharia: Bank Interest, Home Purchase, and Islamic Norms in the West', *Die Welt des Islams*, vol. 44, no. 3, 2004.

Caridi, Paola, *Hamas: from Resistance to Government*, The Palestinian Academic Society for the Study of International Affairs (PASSIA), Jerusalem, 2010.

Cesari, Jocelyne, *Être musulman en france: associations, militants et mosques*, Paris and Aix-en-Provence, Karthala-Iremam, 1994.

— *When Islam and Democracy Meet*, New York, Palgrave, 2004.

Cohen, Amnon, *Political Parties in the West Bank under the Jordanian Regime, 1949–1967*, Ithaca, Cornell University Press, 1982.

Cole, Juan, 'The Ayatollahs and Democracy in Iraq', ISIM paper no. 7, Amsterdam, ISIM/Leiden-Amsterdam University Press, 2006.

Cook, Michael, *Commanding Right and Forbidding Wrong in Islamic Thought*, Cambridge, Cambridge University Press, 2000.

Crooke, Alastair, *Resistance: The Essence of the Islamist Revolution*, London, Pluto Press, 2009.

Dakwar, Jamil, 'The Islamic Movement Inside Israel: An Interview with Shaykh Ra'id Salah', *Journal of Palestine Studies*, vol. 36, no. 2, Winter 2007.

Danawy, M. A., *Kubra al-harakat al-islamiyya fi al-'asr al-hadith* (The Largest

Islamist Movement in the Modern Era), Cairo, Jam'ia al-Islamiyya (Cairo University), 1978.

Dassetto, Felice and Basteiner, Albert, *Europa: nuova frontiera dell'Islam*, Rome, Edizioni Lavoro, 1988.

Dassetto, Felice, Allievi, Stefano, Maréchal, Brigitte and Nielsen, Jørgen, eds, *Muslims in the Enlarged Europe: Religion and Society*, Leiden and Boston, Brill, 2003.

Dawisha, Adeed, *Arab Nationalism in the Twentieth Century: From Triumph to Despair*, Princeton and Oxford, Princeton University Press, 2003.

Deeb, Mary-Jane, 'Militant Islam and the Politics of Redemption', testimony in a hearing on Islamic fundamentalism in Africa and its implications for US policy before the House Subcommittee on Africa, Committee on Foreign Affairs, House of Representatives, 102nd Congress, 2nd session, 20 May 1992.

Dekmejian, R. Hrair, 'The Rise of Islamism in Saudi Arabia', *Middle East Journal* vol. 48, vol. 4, Autumn 1994.

Diner, Dan, *Lost in the Sacred: Why the Muslim World Stood Still*, Princeton, Princeton University Press, 2009.

Einav, Hagai, 'Hundreds Gather at Akko "Peace Sukkah"', *Ynet*, 15 October 2008.

Enayat, Hamid, *Modern Islamic Political Thought: The Response of the Shi'i and Sunni Muslims to the Twentieth Century*, London, I.B. Tauris, 2005.

Ephrat, Daphne, *A Learned Society in a Period of Transition*, New York, SUNY Press, 2000.

Eriksen, Thomas Hylland, *Ethnicity and Nationalism: Anthropological Perspectives*, London, Pluto, 2002.

Esposito, John L., *The Oxford Encyclopedia of the Modern Islamic World*, 4 vols, Oxford, Oxford University Press, 1995.

Fandy, Mamoun, 'Egypt's Islamic Group: Regional Revenge?' *Middle East Journal*, vol. 48, no. 4, 1994.

— 'Al-infisam al-qatari bain ruayat al-amir wa al agendat al-jazeera', (Qatari Schizophrenia between the Amir's Vision and Aljazeera's Agenda), *Asharq Alawsat*, 4 October 2004, available in Arabic at www.aawsat.com.

Feldman, Noah, *The Fall and the Rise of the Islamic State*, NJ, Princeton University Press, 2008.

Fuller, Graham E., *Islamist Politics in Iraq after Saddam Hussein*, United States Institute of Peace, 2003, www.usip.org.

Funatsu, Ryuichi, 'Al-Kawakibi's Thesis and its Echoes in the Arab World Today', *Harvard Middle Eastern and Islamic Review*, no. 7, 2006.

Galili, Lilly, 2002, 'A Jewish Demographic State', *Journal of Palestine Studies.* vol., 32, no. 1, Autumn 2002.

Gardner, David, *Last Chance: The Middle East in the Balance*, London, I.B. Tauris, 2009.

Gerges, Fawaz, *The Far Enemy: Why Jihad Went Global*, Cambridge, Cambridge University Press, 2005.

Gerholm, Tomas and Lithman, Yngve George, eds, *The New Islamic Presence in Western Europe*, London, Mansell, 1988.

Ghabra, Shafeeq N., 'Balancing State and Society: The Islamic Movement in Kuwait', *Middle East Policy,* vol. 5, no. 2 May 1997.

Ghanem, Asad, *The Palestinian-Arab Minority in Israel, 1948–2000, A Political Study*, New York, State University of New York Press, 2001.

al-Ghannouchi, Rashid, 'Towards Inclusive Strategies for Human Rights Enforcement in the Arab World – A Response', *Encounters*, vol. 2, 1996.

Hafez, Muhammad, *Suicide Bombers in Iraq: The Strategy and Ideology of Martyrdom*, Washington DC, United States Institute for Peace, 2007.

al-Halim, Mahmud, *Al-ikhwan al-muslimun – ahdath sana'at al-tarikh* (The Muslim Brotherhood – Events that Made History), Alexandria, Dar al-Daw'a, 1978–1983, vol. 1.

Halliday, Fred, *The Middle East in International Relations: Power, Politics and Ideology*, Cambridge, Cambridge University Press, 2005.

Hasan, Noorhaidi, 'Laskar Jihad, Islam, Militancy and the Quest for Identity in Post–New Order Indonesia', Ithaca, Cornell Southeast Asian Studies Program, 2006.

Hatina, Meir, *Islam and Salvation in Palestine. The Islamic Jihad Movement*, Tel Aviv, The Moshe Dayan Center for Middle Eastern and African Studies, 2001.

Haykel, Bernard, 'On the Nature of Salafi Thought and Action', in Roel Meijer, ed., *Global Salafism: Islam's New Religious Movement*, London, Hurst, 2009.

Hegghammer, Thomas, 'Global Jihadism after the Iraq War', *Middle East Journal*, vol. 60, no. 1, Winter 2006.

— 'Islamists and Regime Stability in Saudi Arabia', *International Affairs,* vol. 84, no. 4, 2008.

— *Violent Islamism in Saudi Arabia, 1979–2006: The Power and Perils of Pan-Islamic Nationalism*, Paris, 2007 (PhD thesis), http://hegghammer.com/text.cfm?path=2006.

Hegghammer, Thomas, and Lacroix, Stéphane, 'Rejectionist Islamism in Saudi Arabia: The Story of Juhayman al-Utaybi Revisited,' *International Journal of Middle East Studies* vol. 39, no. 1, 2007.

Helbawy, Kamal, *Hassan al-banna fi milafat al-inglis* (Hassan al-Banna in the British Archives), Jeddah, Al Manhal Bookshop (limited edition), 1980–1981.

Hourani, Albert, *Arabic Thought in the Liberal Age: 1789–1939*, Cambridge, Cambridge University Press, 1989.

al-Hout, Bayan, *Al-Qiyadat wa al-Mu'assat al-Siyassiyeh fi Filasteen 1917–1948* (Political Leadership and Institutions in Palestine, 1917–1948), Beirut, Institute for Palestine Studies, 1986.

Hroub, Khaled, *Hamas. Political Thought and Practice*, Washington, Institute for Palestine Studies, 2000.

— 'A "New Hamas" through its New Documents', *Journal of Palestine Studies*, vol. 35, no. 4, Summer 2006, http://www.palestine-studies.org/journals.asp x?id=7087&jid=1&href=fulltext.

— 'Hamas in and out of Power' in A. Elshobaki, K. Hroub, D. Pioppi and N. Tocci, eds, *Domestic Change and Conflict in the Mediterranean: The Cases of Hamas and Hezbollah*, EuroMeSCo Paper no. 65, Lisbon, EuroMeSCo, January 2008, http://www.euromesco.net/images/65eng.pdf.

Hughes, James, *Chechnya: From Nationalism to Jihad*, Philadelphia: University of Pennsylvania Press, 2007.

al-Hussaini, Musa Ishaq, *Al-ikhwan al-muslimun. Kubra al-harakat al-islamiyya al-haditha* (The Muslim Brotherhood: the Largest Modern Islamic Movement), Beirut, Establishment for Printing and Publishing, no date.

International Crisis Group, 'Saudi Arabia Backgrounder: Who Are the Islamists?', *ICG Middle East Report*, no. 31, 21 September 2004, www.crisisgroup.org.

Iqbal, Muhammad, *Six Lectures on the Reconstruction of Religious Thought in Islam*, Lahore, Ashraf Publishers, 1930.

Iratni, Belkacem and Tahi, Mohand Salah, 'The Aftermath of Algeria's First Free Local Elections', *Government and Opposition*, vol. 26, no. 4 1992.

Jackson, Robert, *Hassan Al Banna — the Qur'anic Man*, translated into Arabic by Anwar al-Jundi, *Al-rajul al-qur'ani hassan al-banna*, Cairo, al-Mukhtar al-Islami, 1977.

Jerusalem Post, 'Poll: Israelis favour Arab transfer to Palestine', 31 March 2008.

Johnson, Ian and Crawford, David, 'A Saudi Group Spreads Extremism in "Law Seminars", Taught in Dutch, Searching for Roots of 9/11, Europeans Find 6 Plotters Took Course in Holland', *Wall Street Journal*, 15 April 2003.

Jones, Jeremy and Ridout, Nicholas, 'Democratic Development in Oman', *Middle East Journal*, vol. 59, no. 3, Summer 2005.

Katz, Mark, 'Assessing the Political Stability of Oman', *Middle East Review of International Affairs*, vol. 8, no. 3, September 2004, available at www.meria. idc.ac.il.

Keddie, Nikki, 'The New Religious Politics: Where, When, and Why Do "Fundamentalisms" Appear?' *Comparative Studies in Society and History*, vol. 40, no. 4, October 1998.

— *Modern Iran: Roots and Results of Revolution*, New Haven, Yale University Press, 2006.

Kepel, Gilles, *Allah in the West: Islamic Movements in America and Europe*, Cambridge, Polity, 1997.

— *Jihad: The Trail of Political Islam*, London, I.B. Tauris, 2006.

Kerr, Malcolm H., *Islamic Reform: The Political and Legal Theories of Muhammad 'Abduh and Rashid Rida*, Los Angeles, University of California Press, 1966.

Khadduri, Majid, *War and Peace in the Law of Islam*, Baltimore, Johns Hopkins Press, 1955, reprinted Clark, New Jersey, Lawbook Exchange, 2006.

Khalidi, Rashid, *Palestinian Identity: The Construction of Modern National Consciousness*, New York, Columbia University Press, 1997.

Khomeini, Ruhollah, *Al-hukuma al-islamiyya* (Islamic Government), 2nd edn, Beirut, Markaz Baqiyyat Allah Ala'zam, 1999.

Kilani, Abdul Razaq, 'Jihad: A Misunderstood Aspect of Islam', *Islamic Culture*, vol. 70, no. 3, 1996.

Kretzmer, David, *The Legal Status of the Arabs in Israel*, Boulder, Westview, 1990, pp. 36–40, cited in Yoav Peled and Gershon Shafir, *Being Israeli: The Dynamics of Multiple Citizenship*, Cambridge, Cambridge University Press, 2002.

Lewis, Bernard, *The Emergence of Modern Turkey*, Oxford, Oxford University Press, 1961.

Lia, Brynjar, *Architect of Global Jihad: The Life of Al-Qaeda Strategist Abu Mus'ab Al-Suri*, London, Hurst & Columbia University Press, 2009.

— *The Society of the Muslim Brothers in Egypt: The Rise of an Islamic Mass Movement 1928–1942*, Reading, Ithaca Press, 1998.

Lustick, Ian, *Arabs in the Jewish State: Israel's Control of a National Minority*, Austin, TX, University of Texas Press, 1980.

Lybarger, Loren D., *Identity and Religion in Palestine. The Struggle between Islamism and Secularism in the Occupied Territories*, Princeton and Oxford, Princeton University Press, 2007.

Khayyoun, Rashid, *Lahout al-siyaseh: al-ahzab wa al-harakat al-dinyyah fi al-iraq* (The Theology of Politics: Religious Parties and Movements in Iraq), Beirut, Institute for Strategic Studies, 2009.

Mandaville, Peter, *Global Political Islam*, London and New York, Routledge, 2007.

Maréchal, Brigitte, 'Universal Aspirations: The Muslim Brotherhood in Europe', *ISIM Review*, no. 22, Autumn 2008.

The Muslim Brothers in Europe: Roots and Discourse, Leiden, Brill, 2008.

Martin, David, *On Secularization: Towards a Revised General Theory*, Farnham, Ashgate, 2005.

Mawdudi, Abu Ala, *Islamic Law and Constitution*, Lahore, Islamic Publications, 1967.

— *Minhaj al-inqilab al-islami*, (The Programme of Islamic Transformation), Cairo, Dar al-Ansar, 1977.

— *Tadwin al-dustur al-islami*, (Writing down the Islamic Constitution), Cairo, Dar al-Ansar, 1991.

MEMRI (Middle East Media Research Institute), 'Reactions to Sheikh Al-Qaradhawi's Fatwa Calling for the Abduction and Killing of American Civilians in Iraq', *Special Dispatch Series*, no. 794, 2004.

Middle East Report, 'The Shiite Question in Saudi Arabia', no. 45, 19 September 2005.

Milton-Edwards, Beverly, *Islamic Politics in Palestine*, London, Tauris Academic Studies, 1996.

Ghassan Charbel, '*Khaled Mish'al: harakat hamas wa tahrir falasteen* (Khaled Misha'l: The Hamas Movement and the Liberation of Palestine), Beirut, Dar Al-Nahar, 2007.

Mishal, Shaul and Sela, Avraham, *The Palestinian Hamas. Vision, Violence, and Coexistence*, New York, Columbia University Press, 2000.

Morris, Benny, *The Birth of the Palestinian Refugee Problem, 1947–1949*, Cambridge, Cambridge University Press, 1987.

al-Mudaires, Falah Abdullah, *Al-tjamua'at al-siyasiyya al-kuwaitiyya, marhala ma ba'ad al-tahrir* (Kuwaiti Political Groups: the period after liberation), Kuwait, Al-Manar, 1996, 2nd edn.

— *Jama'at al-ikhwan al-muslimin fi al-kuwait*, (Muslim Brotherhood Groups in Kuwait), Kuwait, Qurtas Publishing, 1999.

Myre, Greg, 'Israeli Official Discusses Iran and His Controversial Agenda', *The New York Times*, 7 December 2006.

al-Najjar, Baqer, *Al-haraka al-diniyyah fi al-khalij al-'arabi* (Religious Movements in the Arabian Gulf), Saqi, London, 2007.

Nakhleh, Emile, *A Necessary Engagement: Reinventing American Relations with the Muslim World*, NJ, Princeton University Press, 2008. Nasr, Vali, 'When the Shiites Rise', *Foreign Affairs*, vol. 85, no. 4, July/August 2006.

Nasr, Seyyed Vali Reza, *Mawdudi and the Making of Islamic Revivalism*, New York, Oxford University Press, 1996.

Nevo, Joseph, 'Religion and National Identity in Saudi Arabia', *Middle Eastern Studies,* vol. 34, no. 3, July 1988.

Noreng, Ø, *Oil and Islam: Social and Economic Issues*, Chichester, John Wiley & Sons Ltd, 1997.

O'Neill, Sean, and McGrory, Daniel, *The Suicide Factory: Abu Hamza and the Finsbury Park Mosque*, London, Harper Perennial, 2006.

Østebø, Terje, 'Growth and Fragmentation: The Salafi Movement in Bale, Ethiopia', in Roel Meijer, ed., *Global Salafism: Islam's New Religious Movement*, London, Hurst, 2009.

Pagden, Anthony, ed., *The Idea of Europe: From Antiquity to the European Union*, Cambridge, Cambridge University Press, 2002.

Pappe, Ilan, 'Ingathering', *London Review of Books*, 20 April 2006.

Peled, Alisa Rubin, *Debating Islam in the Jewish State: The Development of Policy Toward Islamic Institutions in Israel*, New York, State University of New York Press, 2001.

Peled, Yoav and Shafir, Gershon, *Being Israeli: The Dynamics of Multiple Citizenship,* Cambridge, Cambridge University Press, 2002.

Peters, Rudolph, *Islam and Colonialism: The Doctrine of Jihad in Modern History*, The Hague, Mouton Publishers, 1979.

Pipes, Daniel, 'Anti-Islamists Petition the United Nations', 30 October 2004, available at www.danielpipes.org.

Poulson, Stephen, *Social Movements in Twentieth-Century Iran: Culture, Ideology, and Mobilizing Frameworks*, New York, Lexington Books, 2006.

Qassem, Naim, *Hizbullah: al-manhaj, al-tajriba, al-mustaqbal* (Hizbullah: the Approach, the Experience and the Future), Beirut, Dar Ai-Hadi, 2002.

— *Hizbullah: The Story from Within*, London, Saqi, 2005.

Qureshi, Naeem, *Pan-lslam in British Indian Politics: A Study of the Khilafat Movement 1918–1924*, Leiden, Brill, 1999.

Qutb, Sayyed, *Ma'alim fi al-tariq* (Milestones), Beirut, International Islamic Federation of Student Organizations (IIFSO), 1978.

al-Rasheed, Madawi, 'The Shia of Saudi Arabia: A Minority in Search of Cultural Authenticity', *British Journal of Middle Eastern Studies*, vol. 25, no. 1, 1998.

— *Contesting the Saudi State: Islamic Voices from a New Generation*, Cambridge, Cambridge University Press, 2007.

— ed., *Transnational Connections and the Arab Gulf*, London, Hurst, 2005.

Rashid, Ahmed, *Taliban: The Story of the Afghan Warlords*, London, I.B. Tauris, 2000.

Rida, Rashid, *al-Khilafa aw al-imama al-'uzma* (Caliphate and the Great Imamah), Cairo, Dar al-Manar, 1925.

Roberts, Hugh, 'From Radical Mission to Equivocal Ambition: The Expansion and Manipulation of the Algerian Islamism, 1979-1992', in Martin Marty and

Scott Appelby, eds, *Accounting for Fundamentalists: The Dynamic Character of Movements*, Chicago, The University of Chicago Press, 1994.

— 'Radical Islamism and the Dilemma of Algerian Nationalism: The Embattled Arians of Algiers', *Third World Quarterly*, vol. 10, no. 2, 1988.

Roy, Olivier, *The Failure of Political Islam*, Cambridge, Mass., Harvard University Press, 1994.

Rufford, Nicholas and Taher, Abul, 'British Muslims Says Troops Are Fair Target', *Sunday Times*, 31 October 2004.

Sagar, Abdulaziz, 'Political Opposition in Saudi Arabia', in Paul Aarts and Gerd Nonneman, eds, *Saudi Arabia in the Balance: Political Economy, Society, Foreign Affairs*, London, Hurst, 2005.

al-Saif, Abu Omar, 'His Life and after His Death', *Chechnya Weekly*, vol. 7, no. 3, 19 January 2006.

— 'Al-'iraq wa ghazu al-salib: durus wa ta'amulat' ('Iraq and the Invasion of the Cross: Lessons and Meditations'), 2004.

Shadi, Salah, *Safahat min al-tarikh – hasad al-'umr* (Pages from History; the Final Outcome), Kuwait, Al-Shuaae for Publishing, 1981.

Shahin, Emad Eldin, *Political Ascent: Contemporary Islamic Movements in North Africa*, Boulder, CO, Westview Press, 1997.

al-Sharif, Kamal Ismail, *Al-ikhwan al-muslimun fi harb falestin* (The Muslim Brotherhood in the War of Palestine), Cairo, no publisher, 1951.

al-Shikaki, Fathi, *Al-khumaini: al-hal al-islami wa al-badil* (Khomeini: The Islamic Solution and the Alternative), Occupied Territories, no publisher, 1979.

al-Shishani, Murad, 'Portrait of a Chechen Mujahid Leader', *Terrorism Monitor*, vol. 2, no. 8, 23 April 2004.

— 'The Iraqi Resistance between Terrorism and National Liberation: A Quantitative Study', *Iraq Studies*, no. 5, Gulf Research Centre, Dubai, November 2005.

— 'The Salafi Jihadist Movement in Iraq: Recruitment Methods and Arab Volunteers', *Terrorism Monitor*, vol. 3, no. 23, 2 December 2005.

Shuair, Muhammad Fathi, *Wasail al-'Ilam al-Matbuh fi Daw'a al-Ikhwan al-Muslimin* [Printed Media of Muslim Brotherhood Daw'a], Jeddah: Dar al-Mujtama'a for Publishing and Distribution, 1985, first edition.

Silvestri, S., 'The Political Mobilisation of Muslims in Europe and the EU Response', PhD dissertation, University of Cambridge, 2006.

— 'Asserting Islam in the EU: Actors, Strategies, and Priorities', in F. Foret, ed., *L'Europe à l'épreuve du religieux*, Brussels, Presses de l'Université Libre de Bruxelles, 2007.

— 'Radical Islam: Threats and Opportunities', *Global Dialogue*, vol. 9, nos 3 and 4, 2007.

Sivan, Emmanuel, *Radical Islam: Medieval Theology and Modern Politics*, New Haven, Yale University Press, 1985.

Steinberg, Guido, 'The Wahhabi Ulama and the Saudi State: 1745 to the Present', in Paul Aarts and Gerd Nonneman, *Saudi Arabia in the Balance,* London, Hurst, 2005.

Stråth, Bo, ed., *Europe and the Other and Europe as the Other*, Brussels and Oxford, P.I.E. Peter Lang, 2000.

Taji, Maha , 'Arab Local Authorities in Israel: Hamulas, Nationalism and Dilemmas of Social Change', PhD, University of Washington, 2008.

Tamimi, Azzam, *Hamas. A History from Within*, Northampton, Olive Branch Press, 2007.

al-Tawil, Muhammad, *Al-ikhwan fi al-parlaman*, (The Brotherhood in Parliament), Cairo, Al-Maktab al-Misri al-Hadith, May 1992, 1st edn.

Thomas, Scott, *The Global Resurgence of Religion and the Transformation of International Relations*, London and New York, Palgrave Macmillan, 2005.

al-Tilimsani, Umar, *Al-mulham al-mawhub hassan al-banna*, (The Intelligent and Gifted Imam Hassan al-Banna), Cairo, Dar al-Ansar, no date.

Van Bruinessen, Martin and Allievi, Stefano, eds, *Producing Islamic Knowledge: Transmission and Dissemination in Western Europe*, London, Routledge, 2010.

Vatin, Jean-Claude, 'Revival in the Maghreb' in Ali Desouki, ed., *Islamic Resurgence in the Arab World*, New York, Praeger, 1982.

Vertovec, Steven and Peach, Ceri, eds, *Islam in Europe: The Politics of Religion and Community*, Basingstoke, Macmillan, 1997.

Vidino, Lorenzo, 'Aims and Methods of Europe's Muslim Brotherhood', *Current Trends in Islamist Ideology*, vol. 4, November 2006.

Volpi, Frederic, *Islam and Democracy: The Failure of Dialogue in Algeria*, London, Pluto Press, 2003.

Wagemakers, Joas, 'The Transformation of a Radical Concept: al-Wala' wa'l-Bara' in the Ideology of Abu Muhammad al-Maqdisi', in Roel Meijer, ed., *Global Salafism: Islam's New Religious Movement*, London, Hurst, 2009.

Wiktorowicz, Quintan, ed., *Islamic Activism: A Social Movement Theory Approach*, Indiana, Indiana University Press, 2004.

Willis, Michael, *The Islamist Challenge in Algeria: A Political History*, Berkshire, Ithaca Press, 1996.

Zaideh, Hanna, *Sectarianism and Intercommunal Nation-Building in Lebanon,* London, Hurst & Co., 2006.

al-Zawahiri, Ayman, *Al-wala wa'l-bara': 'aqida manqula wa waqi' mafqud*, (Loyalty and Disavowal: Dictated Creed and Lost Reality), May 2006, accessed at http://www.tawhed.ws.

Zubaida, Sami, *Islam, the People and the State: Political Ideas and Movements in the Middle East*, London, I.B. Tauris, 3rd edition, 2009.

Index